DATE DUE

Ap 21 80		
May 8 89		
Ja 20 13		
GAYLORD		PRINTED IN U.S.A

THE
MUSIC CRITICISM
OF HUGO WOLF

THE
MUSIC CRITICISM
OF HUGO WOLF

Translated,
Edited, and
Annotated
by Henry Pleasants

HM

HOLMES & MEIER PUBLISHERS, INC.
NEW YORK   LONDON

Published in the United States of America 1978 by
Holmes & Meier Publishers, Inc.
30 Irving Place
New York, N.Y. 10003

Great Britain:
Holmes & Meier Publishers, Ltd.
Hillview House
1, Hallswelle Parade, Finchley Road
London NW11 ODL

LIBRARY OF CONGRESS CATALOGING IN PUBLICATION DATA

Wolf, Hugo, 1860-1903.
  The music criticism of Hugo Wolf.

    1. Music — Addresses, essays, lectures. 2. Music —
History and criticism — 19th century. I. Pleasants,
Henry. II. Title.
ML60.W74   780'.8   77-11092
ISBN 0-8419-0331-X

MANUFACTURED IN THE UNITED STATES OF AMERICA

Contents

INTRODUCTION

INTRODUCTION

Hugo Wolf's place in musical history is securely established alongside Schubert, Schumann, Brahms and Richard Strauss among the great composers in a genre familiarly known as the German Lied. Not many, even among those associated professionally with music — unless they have read the Wolf biographies by Ernest Newman (1907) and/or Frank Walker (1951) — are aware that he was also, briefly, a regularly employed music critic. Fewer still have read more than the odd excerpt or two of anything he wrote, even in his native Austria or in other German-speaking areas.

Ernest Newman, the English critic and biographer of Wagner as well as of Wolf, once wrote of Eduard Hanslick, the Viennese critic pilloried as the nit-picking, pedantic scrivener, Sixtus Beckmesser in *Die Meistersinger*, that he was remembered only for one or two mistakes he made about Wagner by thousands of people who have not the slightest idea how much good sense he talked about music. It is much the same with Wolf, who did his utmost to propagate the image of Hanslick as the reactionary pedant. Wolf is remembered as a critic, insofar as he is remembered at all, for one or two foolish things he said about Hanslick's friend, Johannes Brahms, notably his assertion, in a review of a performance of Liszt's *Tasso*, that more intelligence and sensibility were expressed in a single cymbal crash in a work of Liszt than in all of Brahms's three symphonies (the fourth was yet to come), not excluding his serenades.

My purpose in undertaking, thirty years ago, to translate a selection of Hanslick's enormous critical production — extending from 1846 to the end of the century, and far from complete in the twelve volumes of his collected works — was twofold: to make it possible for Hanslick to be judged by English-speaking readers on the basis of a reasonably broad cross-section of his work and, at the same time, to give the same readers the benefit of insights into the character and temper of musical life in Vienna and elsewhere as recorded on the spot and at the same time by a critic who was at once well-informed, perceptive, articulate and courageously engaged. My purpose in translating Hugo Wolf has been the same, although in Wolf's case there has been the added incentive of insights gained into the character, the intellectual disposition and performance, and the psychical motivation of a great composer.

The two undertakings are, indeed, complementary, for Hanslick and Wolf stood on opposite sides of the fence. Neither can be fully or even sympathetically understood without reference to the writings, attitudes, enthusiasms, aversions, convictions and allegiances of the other. It would be going too far to say that the history of western music in Europe in the nineteenth century cannot be adequately grasped without reading both Hanslick and Wolf. The tensions of the musical century, the evolutionary ferment, the confrontation of "reactionary" and "progressive" are vividly reflected in a vast body of historical, critical and biographical literature, and are more extensively documented than in any other period in the history of Western or any other music. The fascination of reading Hanslick and Wolf lies in the opportunity to experience — if only vicariously — these tensions, these enthusiasms and these aversions in the professionally and instantly recorded reactions of two intelligent and dedicated participants to the first or very early performances of works now accepted as classics or long ago discarded and forgotten. Most music lovers everywhere today can listen with pleasure to Brahms one evening and to Wagner the next. This was not the case a century ago. A Hans von Bülow, as pianist and conductor, could perceive the virtues of each, and act accordingly. But there were not many either so equipped or so disposed, and even Bülow had to bear the hostility and scorn of Wolf, among others, as the price of his courageous catholicity.

Wolf's critical output, to be sure, spans a brief period — the mere three years and three months he spent as critic of the *Wiener Salonblatt*, a fashionable Viennese Sunday journal. But they were a crucial three years. Wagner had died only eleven months before Wolf took up his duties in January 1884. The ascendancy of his star was secure, as Hanslick conceded in a notably gracious obituary. In Wagner's behalf Wolf was fighting a battle already won. Against Brahms whose third and fourth symphonies had their Vienna premieres during Wolf's stint as music critic, he was fighting a battle already lost. His advocacy of Bruckner was more timely. Bruckner's stature had been recognized in Germany earlier than in his native Austria, a fact that Wolf never tired of throwing in the faces of the Viennese. Strauss and Mahler were in the offing, and there can be no doubt as to where Wolf's sympathies and enthusiasms would have lain had he devoted the remainder of his short life to music criticism. Hanslick's career continued long enough for him to document his abhorrence of Strauss ("Don Juan" and "Tod und Verklärung") and to sustain his low opinion of Bruckner in the face of Bruckner's growing popular acceptance, at the same time conceding, it should be added, that the future might belong to them.

Appraisal of both Hanslick and Wolf as critics has been trivialized by exclusive emphasis on the way Hanslick was "wrong about Wagner" and Wolf "wrong about Brahms," and especially by the singling out of certain ill-considered utterances doubtlessly inspired by emotional ardor in the heat of battle. It was not a matter in either case of appreciating certain individuals or individual compositions. If Hanslick was "wrong about Wagner," he was also wrong about Berlioz, Liszt, Tchaikovsky, pre-*Aida* Verdi, Bruckner and Strauss. If Wolf was "wrong about Brahms," and Dvořák, too, it was because only they have survived among what Wolf would have called "the classicists" of his time. What carries us in Wolf's case beyond his being "wrong about Brahms" is his indiscriminate enthusiasm for just about everything that

Berlioz and Liszt ever wrote — and Wagner, too. When one is on the side of the angels, as Wolf certainly thought he was, one turns a blind or indulgent eye to a molting wing here and there, as Wolf did to some of Berlioz's lesser overtures, to Liszt's unlamented symphonic tone poems and Hungarian rhapsodies, and to some Wagnerian trivia that Wagnerians today prefer not to think about, much less to hear.

The issue lay deeper. It was prophetically exposed as early as 1861 when Hanslick, reviewing a performance of Beethoven's "Missa Solemnis," wrote: "In artistic richness, in intrepid greatness, in the free unleashing of an immeasurable fantasy, the Mass in D and the Ninth Symphony stand unique and alone like colossal Pillars of Hercules at the gates of modern music, saying, 'No farther!' — the one to sacred music, the other to the symphony."

Wolf was just one year old when that was written, but had he been Hanslick's age (thirty-six), given his creative and intellectual disposition, he would certainly have taken the opposite view. He would have seen in these two great works not Pillars of Hercules warning the unwary explorer of danger ahead, but beacons summoning the bold of mind and heart to a welcome, if awesome, adventure. Hanslick sensed in the later Beethoven, and found confirmed in the mature Wagner, an overburdening of the tonal structural materials and resources of Western music, a potentially disastrous abuse of those tensions implicit in modulation from one tonality to another that had been a prerequisite for the shaping of the larger-scaled masterpieces of European music from Bach to Beethoven — and Brahms. To Wolf the extravagence of Wagner's chromatic harmony, of Berlioz's instrumentation, and of Liszt's experiments in translating literature into music represented emancipation from classical discipline and schoolroom decorum. It meant new vistas, new worlds to conquer, and other worlds as yet unimagined to discover.

There was a temperamental difference, too. Hanslick was a rationalist, although sufficiently a child of the nineteenth century to savor with pleasure the relatively disciplined romanticism of Schuman, Chopin and Brahms. To him the philosophical pretentions of Wagner's music dramas were both ridiculous and offensive, Liszt's religiosity bogus, Berlioz's visions fevered and Strauss's licentious. Wolf could be rational, too. He could ridicule the plots of such operas as Nessler's *Der Trompeter von Säkkingen*, Rubinstein's *Nero* and Dvořák's *The Cunning Peasant* as acutely and as thoroughly as Hanslick could attack the dramaturgy and the German of *Der Ring des Nibelungen*, *Tristan und Isolde* and *Parsifal*. But where Wolf's enthusiasms were involved, this analytical faculty and disposition were put out to pasture, and he took all on faith. In that he was the true Wagnerite.

He was not in Hanslick's class as a writer, and in later years he would have been the first to admit it. When it was suggested to him that his criticisms be published in book form he objected, not because of anything he had said, but because of the way he had said it. (They were published by the Vienna Academic Wagner Society in 1911, eight years after his death.) Nor was deficiency of literary style attributable to his youth at the time (he was not quite twenty-four when he began). A superior sense and command of style is evident in what Hanslick wrote for publication when he was younger than Wolf was during the latter's years on the *Wiener Salonblatt* (he made his critical debut with a series of articles on *Tannhäuser* for the *Wiener Zeitung* in 1846 when he was only twenty-one). But he had enjoyed all the advantages — Wolf would probably have argued that he betrayed the disadvantages, too — of a formal education. Wolf had been, in our own contemporary terminology, the perpetual dropout. He had quit, or been expelled from, two gymnasia and the Vienna Conservatory, and had lasted only a couple of turbulent months as second Kapellmeister at the provincial theater in Salzburg. Nor was his family background and provincial origin conducive to the kind of urbanity native to the Prague-born Hanslick.

Wolf was born in Windischgraz in Lower Styria (now the Yugoslav town of Slovenjgradec) on March 13, 1860, to a family long and reasonably profitably engaged in the leather trade. His father was an accomplished self-taught musician, but never a professional, and he opposed the idea of Hugo's becoming one. Hugo never wished to be anything else, even when his professional prospects were dim. But although he was a good student when he applied himself, he resisted both formal education and discipline. The record of his conduct at the various schools he attended suggests early manifestations of the emotional instability abundantly evident in his critical writing and social behavior.

This underlying behavior pattern was almost certainly aggravated in later years by the syphilis he contracted in Vienna at the age of seventeen, which led to his insanity and early death. Newman, in his biography, described Wolf's entry upon the Viennese musical scene in the pages of the *Wiener Salonblatt* as like "the irruption of a fanatical dervish into a boudoir."

While resistant to formal education either in music or in literature, Wolf was an eager and indefatigable explorer in both domains. The consequence, so far as his writing was concerned, was an approach derived more from extensive but haphazard reading than from any studious exercise in the niceties of rhetoric and syntax. He was more concerned with what great writers had said than with how they had said it, or learned to say it. To put it in musical terms, he was writing symphonies, or at least sonatas, before mastering the craft of putting together and harmonizing an eight-measure melody.

The literary result could be absurdly pretentious, sprawling, repetitious, wordy, extravagant and heavy-handed. He was much given to sentences of unconscionable length, made even more difficult and tiresome for the reader — and translator — by substantial digression, punctuated by dashes and parentheses. He was fond of showing off his reading by reference, quotation and name dropping. He had a sense of humor, but no sense of the humorous effect of understatement (which Hanslick possessed in high degree). His jokes were ponderous and overlong. He was better at punning, but tended to go out of his way to set up the pun. With metaphor and simile, too, he lacked the light and facile hand.

He was of critical, even hypercritical disposition, but not, as Hanslick was, a critic by vocation. He was a composer. He became a critic because he could find no other remunerative employment, and needed the money. Indeed, his employment as critic was an act of charity on the part of Heinrich Köchert, a Viennese jeweller and goldsmith, who, unbeknownst to Wolf, arranged with the publisher of the *Wiener Salonblatt* to pay Wolf's salary by overpayments on the advertisements he placed with the paper.

Why his notices suddenly ceased in April of 1887 has never been established with any certainty. Again, it was probably a matter of money. Erich Werba, the most recent of Wolf's biographers (*Hugo Wolf, der zornige Romantiker*, Verlag Fritz Molden, Vienna, 1977), and a distinguished accompanist of Wolf's songs, suggests that a long term engagement as music teacher to the family of the Countess Harrach left him economically independent of what he obviously regarded as an unworthy occupation.

I should say here that in translating Wolf, especially because he was Wolf, I have been at pains to avoid stylistic cosmetics. While not altering the basic compositional structure, I have occasionally broken up the longer sentences into two or three. This I felt to be a tolerable concession to the reader's convenience. Similarly, and for the same reason, the paragraphing is largely mine, as are the headings. Wolf's own tended to be uninformative, frequently nothing more than "Court Opera" or "Concerts."

Wolf's stature as a critic was further reduced by his affinity for unbridled vituperation and his employment of a rich vocabulary of invective. Like most young critics — and I speak as one who began his own career as critic at nineteen — he was impatient of imperfection and infuriated by those who, for one reason or another, accepted imperfection as an inescapable fact of life. In his case the pen was sharpened by his identification with a "progressive" musical faction at a time when tempers were high among both the progressives and the conservatives. Brahms once described him as a "Davidsbündler," referring, of course, to the visionary — and imaginary — league invented by Schumann to do battle with the Philistines in his early articles for the *Neue Zeitschrift für Musik*. Wolf, as a Davidsbündler, was unmistakably Florestan.

His social attitudes, as reflected in these reviews, could be distressing, too. He was an intellectual snob. He was also a social snob in the compensatory manner of the small town or country boy who despises a sophisticated urban society in which he feels out of place. He was, even more conspicuously, a cultural snob of a type familiar to those who have lived some length of time in the German-language area, the kind who thinks of *Kultur* as something peculiarly Germanic. His notices abound in slighting references to Italy, France, England, America, Russia, Scandinavia, Turkey, and so on, and this from a young mar whose travel outside Austria at that time had been confined to two pilgrimages to Bayreuth.

He was, I think, rather anti-Austrian. "Austria" and "Austrian" rarely occur in his writings, and when they do there is usually a patronizing connotation. And he was anti-Semitic, although, as was also the case with the anti-Semitic Wagner, some of his closest friends were Jews. Several of them rendered him generous financial and social assistance.

But for all these shortcomings, Hugo Wolf was, or often could be, one of the finest of all music critics. He was extraordinarily acute on opera, especially Wagnerian opera. I would rate his discussions of the productions at the Court Opera, and of the work of the leading members of the company, and the occasional illustrious guest singer, as among the most perceptive I have read. Opera was obviously his first love. He had gained some professional experience in his brief tenure at Salzburg. His knowledge of the voice is astonishing in one who had never sung professionally, and his observation of singers as actors is similarly enlightened by original insight, and well informed.

Wolf as critic is, indeed, a delightful and marvelously instructive guide through the operatic world of Vienna in the 1880s. The attentive reader soon has the feeling of actually having heard and known Materna, Sucher, Lehmann, Papier, Scaria, Winkelmann, Vogl, Mayerhofer, and other surely great artists who brought such distinction to the Court Opera at that time. Certainly it is characteristic of Wolf's concern for the highest standards where music was concerned that he never treats those whom he admired with disrespect, even when deploring or disagreeing with their choice or conception of a role, or noting vocal or dramatic deficiencies on a given night.

In his dealing with other performers, too — conductors, instrumentalists, string quartets and orchestras — his critical performance is consistently first rate, and on performers, as opposed to composers, he and Hanslick usually saw eye to eye. His descriptions and assessments of such giants of the time as Richter, Bülow, Rubinstein, d'Albert, Friedheim, César Thomson and Wilhelmj add much to our knowledge of their art and their idiosyncracies. Indeed, when it comes to giving the reader an idea of how they appeared, and of what it was like to be in their presence, he is often Hanslick's superior.

What distinguishes Wolf's criticism most vividly from anyone else's is its intensity. I can think of no other critic in whose writing the individual emerges so dramatically — or explosively. He is not always likable or admirable either as man or craftsman, but there is never any doubt as to who he was and what he stood for. Nor, more importantly, is there any doubt as to his passionate dedication. Wolf loved music. He may have been excessive both in praise and abuse, but that is the kind of man he was. It is because these reviews tell us so much about the man who wrote those songs that I — a lifelong Hanslickian — have thought it worth the time and labor to translate not only his words and sense, but also, as best I could, his style. Wolf was his own man not only in what he said, but in the way he said it. To read him is to know him.

Speaking of style, a final word about my decisions as between German and English terms and terminology. I have been consistently inconsistent, opting for English or American colloquial practice in most cases, but sometimes preferring German terms — Herr and Frau, or Fräulein, for instance — simply to remind the reader of the locale and the culture. Parentheses in the text are Wolf's, brackets mine.

Finally, I wish to express my appreciation and gratitude to Hella Bronold and Walter Gürtelschmied, of the Österreichische Gesellschaft für Literatur, for their enthusiastic and invaluable assistance with the annotation, especially in the often difficult and tedious task of tracing obscure and long forgotten singers and other performers, and in identifying and explaining literary allusions and Viennese idioms. Dr. William B. Ober has offered valuable assistance in stylistic matters. I am profoundly grateful to Eric Sams, who volunteered to check my translation against the German original and who, while doing so, also provided useful suggestions and clarifications. Friendly help with literary and geographical allusions from Erich Leinsdorf, George Marek, Gerd Utescher, Dr. Howard M. Schott and Else Radant is also gratefully acknowledged.

Henry Pleasants
London, 1978

The Music Criticism of Hugo Wolf

1. Sgambati and Schubert
Rosenthal and Friedheim

January 20, 1884

The most recent Philharmonic[1] concert began with Berlioz's rollicking "Roman Carnival" Overture. The audience discerned in this a welcome salute to Fasching |the carnival season|, and it came off strongly, as always. Robert Fuchs's[2] amiable but hardly original Serenade in C for String Orchestra found less favor. Least successful was a new symphony by Giovanni Sgambati,[3] whose manifold instrumental artifices fell absolutely flat with the Philharmonic's matinee audience.

Sgambati is a pupil of Liszt, resident in Rome, who has done a great deal for the propagation of German music in the Eternal City. In his symphony he travels mostly the strangely twisting paths of his teacher, although here and there his Italian nature asserts itself clearly enough. Of self-sufficient melodic invention this Sgambati novelty can boast precious little, but at the same time intelligence, noble intention and an eager striving for new, individual effects are everywhere in evidence, and to this extent it was most interesting to make the acquaintance of this curious symphony. We know now, at least, how contemporary Italians write symphonies, how they see through their own spectacles the greatest of the art forms taken over by them from the German classicists.

A more striking contrast to Sgambati's symphony can hardly be imagined than a posthumous symphony (No. 6, in C) by our own Franz Schubert, which we heard at the third concert of the Society of the Friends of Music.[4] One could compare the Schubert and Sgambati symphonies with two receptacles, the one filled with the milk of pious reflection, the other with fermenting dragon's venom. The real Franz Schubert, as we love and esteem him, is far from evident in this most recently heard symphony. On the contrary, the great composer appears sometimes as a weak imitator of Weber, subsequently his so antipathetic rival, at other times even as a copyist of Rossini. Pure Schubertian blood pulses only in the freshly surging Scherzo, with its striking reminiscence of his own familiar "Reitermarsch,"| Opus 40, No. 3| orchestrated by Liszt. Then, too, this Schubert symphony moves from beginning to end with remorseful cheerfulness so that as we listen we finally find ourselves, like Heine's Tannhäuser[5], earnestly longing for — bitterness.

The other numbers were a very noble, very warmly felt Psalm for Soloists, Chorus and Orchestra by Hermann Götz,[6] the prematurely deceased com-

1

poser of *The Taming of the Shrew*, and Schumann's "Neujahrslied," which, as with all this composer's late works, despite some effective, even brilliant touches, leaves a frosty, unpleasant impression. The more sympathetic, then was Götz's setting of Psalm 137, performed with genuine enthusiasm by the Choral Society,[7] and in which, too, a soloist, Frau Niklas-Kempner, distinguished herself by truly dedicated singing. No other major concert work of the estimable Götz has had so decisive a success in Vienna.

Of other concerts in recent weeks we shall mention only one each by the pianists Moriz Rosenthal[8] and Arthur Friedheim,[9] who appeared before the public in contention for the palm of astonishing virtuosity. In terms of intelligence and musical sensibility, Herr Friedheim seems the superior; in terms of sheer technic, but the rather mannered Rosenthal, in Liszt's appallingly difficult *Don Giovanni* Fantasy, brought off feats of pianistic athleticism designed to make a moderately accomplished pianist's hair stand on end. The audience was quite beside itself at this labor of Hercules. We have only very rarely heard such spontaneous, earth-shaking applause in the Bösendorfersaal.[10]

1.   The Wiener Philharmoniker, founded as an independent association of members of the orchestra of the Court Opera (now State Opera) following a sporadic existence dating from a "Philharmonic Concert" under the direction of Otto Nicolai on March 18, 1842. Its concerts, since the opening of the Musikvereinsgebäude (Musical Union Building) as the new home of the Gesellschaft der Musikfreunde (Society of Friends of Music) in 1870, have been given in that building's Grosser Musikvereinssaal (Large Hall of the Musical Union).

2.   Robert Fuchs (1847-1927), a student and subsequently professor of harmony at the Vienna Conservatory. This Serenade in C is one of five constituting his Opus 53.

3.   Giovanni Sgambati (1843-1914). He was born in Rome of an Italian father and an English mother, daughter of the English sculptor Joseph Gott, long a resident of Rome. A piano prodigy, Sgambati became a pupil, devotee and protégé of Liszt during the latter's residence in Rome (1861-1869), and through him was introduced to the music of Wagner. As pianist, conductor and co-founder of the Liceo Musicale of the Accademia di S. Cecilia in Rome, he did much to encourage a taste for German music among Italian audiences. This symphony, in D, dates from 1880-1881. A second, in E flat, followed in 1883.

4.   Die Gesellschaft der Musikfreunde, founded in 1813. In return for the use of the Grosser Musikvereinssaal for its concerts, and for office and archive space in the Musikvereinsgebäude, the Philharmonic undertook to make a certain number of its members available for the Society's concerts, an arrangement encouraged by the fact that many of these were in any case professors at the Conservatory, then (but not now) owned and administered by the Society.

5.   The reference is to a three-part poem by Heine, "Der Tannhäuser, Eine Legende," dating from 1836. The first part ends with Tannhäuser announcing to Venus, after a sojourn of seven years in the Venusberg, that he has become sick of sweet wine and kisses, and longs for bitterness. The poem ends, unlike Wagner's opera, with Tannhäuser returning from his pilgrimage — his case having been pronounced hopeless by Pope Urban IV — to Venus, and rendering her an amusing account of his wanderings.

6. Hermann Götz (Goetz) (1840-1876), a German composer, pianist and organist, a student of Bülow at the Stern Conservatory in Berlin, whose principal appointment during his short life was that of organist at Winterthur in Switzerland. He is remembered now only for *The Taming of the Shrew* (*Der Widerspenstigen Zähmung*). The Psalm discussed here was his Opus 14.

7. Singverein, a constituent body of the Society of Friends of Music.

8. Moriz Rosenthal (1862-1946), a student of Rafael Joseffy and later of Liszt, who went on to become one of the greatest and longest lived of all pianists.

9. Arthur Friedheim (1859-1932) was reckoned a German pianist, although born and educated at St. Petersburg. He studied with both Rubinstein and Liszt, and achieved renown as virtuoso, conductor and teacher both in Europe and America where, as an American citizen, he died. He wrote a book of reminiscences, edited as *Life and Liszt* by Theodore L. Bullock.

10. Built by Ludwig Bösendorfer (1835-1919) of the famous family of Viennese piano builders, and opened in 1872. No longer standing, it remained for many decades the principal home of chamber music concerts and recitals.

2. *Virtuosos at the Philharmonic* *Therese Malten in* Tannhäuser

January 27, 1884

If we consider the program of last Sunday's special Philharmonic concert not in terms of its purely musical value or want of it, but rather in terms of those who played the various numbers, then it would appear that the Philharmonic's principal objective was to let virtuosos display their virtuosity.

We had five in this concert: Hector Berlioz, Ignaz Brüll,[1] Arnold Rosé,[2] Fräulein Bianchi[3] and — the Philharmonic Orchestra. This latter multi-headed virtuoso, concentrated in an incomparably harmonious unity under its highly gifted conductor, Hans Richter,[4] gave an utterly admirable account of Mendelssohn's music to *A Midsummer Night's Dream*, a performance, indeed, beyond all praise. The playing of this inspired composition is and remains one of the Philharmonic's specialties.

No less perfect was their performance of Weber's "Invitation To The Dance." Who can fail to rejoice in this wholly delightful, lovely piano piece? One cannot escape the fact, however, that the full flavor of these bittersweet dancing lessons cannot be captured at the piano in a family circle with tea and bread and butter in prospect. How different the picture revealed to our fantasy when the magic of Berlioz's orchestra engages our senses! It's as if the spirits of champagne were celebrating their mad carnival with a wonderfully sweet little princess whom they, in their excitement, have kidnapped. She, at first unhappy in captivity, expresses her childish sorrow in the touching D flat plaint of the tender oboe, then, a moment later, and like a child, delights in the merry pranks of her gay captors. In this example of orchestral virtuosity Berlioz, in his affectionate identification with the German core of Weber's nature, has given the loveliest expression to his warm admiration of the composer of *Der Freischütz.*

If we come now to the virtuosos proper, those announced as such in the program, we must, in order to continue our praise, mention Fräulein Bianchi, a tasteful singer with an uncommonly sympathetic voice, who long ago sang her way into the hearts, or rather the ears, of our opera-going public. Despite the stale, tedious aria of Mozart [presumably "Non più, tutto ascoltai," a scena con rondo with violin solo, K. 490] she was enthusiastically applauded. Herr Rosé supported her gallantly in the violin obbligato. About Herr Brüll, who appeared both as virtuoso and composer (he played his Piano Concerto No. 2), we shall waste few words. Just leave it that his playing was as uninteresting as his composition was dull, which comes to much the same thing. Hack work!

Let us turn to another virtuoso and composer: D. Popper.[5] He has a reputation, and the public respects it, especially when he plays wrong notes. He has some pretty virtuoso tricks at his disposal, but he misuses them most of the time; and if he thinks that he must always play violin on the cello, he misunderstands the nature of his instrument. He composes quite prettily, too, and his "Spinning Song," if played alternately on the violin and the cello, might be quite charming. Since, however, he prefers to play it only on the cello, it whines and croaks and groans in the highest position, and sounds like anything but a spinning song. The audience appeared to adore it, and stormily demanded a repetition. Herr Popper was gracious enough to quiet the storm with a recapitulation. At this same concert we made the acquaintance of an excellent pianist in Herr Stasny.[6] His virtues reminded us vividly of the richly gifted A. Friedheim, who has recently become so popular in Vienna. We hope to encounter Herr Stasny soon in a recital of his own.

Before turning our steps toward the opera house, we would like to mention most affectionately the charming violin virtuosa, Teresina Tua,[7] who, in her appearance with orchestra, delighted us with her engaging manner, especially telling in Sarasate's amusing "Zapateado." In her gracious appearance, music and sculpture have achieved an intimate alliance. Every movement breathed warm, blossoming life, transfigured by the sweet sounds she drew from her art. Signorina Tua conquered every heart forthwith, and was received by the audience with the utmost cordiality.

And so to the opera! The piece is only too familiar. Nor is the guest star in *Il Trovatore* any stranger. Fräulein Klein[8] rightfully enjoys the favor of our public. Her Leonora was, if not the utmost that has ever been accomplished in this role, thoroughly respectable. She has a lovely voice, and proved herself a resourceful actress. Only in the scene before the prison might we have wished for more dramatic fire. One must have experienced Patti in this scene in order to realize that it is no easy matter to do justice to Fräulein Klein's accomplishment. The other principals did not fail to do their part in achieving an orderly performance, especially Fräulein Rosa Papier,[9] whose Azucena is, in every respect, a masterpiece.

Therese Malten,[10] a visitor from Dresden, hitherto unheard here, made her debut yesterday as Elisabeth in *Tannhäuser*. She had a great success, which is saying quite a lot when one remembers that she was appearing on the same stage from which Frau Ehnn[11] addresses us with an inner conviction in tone and gesture that, from the very beginning, compel our instant belief in her Elisabeth. Neither as actress nor as singer did Fräulein Malten achieve the level of Frau Ehnn, although she has a lovely voice, and in her bearing and gestures we recognize the cultivated artist. But her action is too intelligent, too thoroughly thought out, too studied. As is so often the case with such virtues, it was all a bit too much of a good thing.

Elisabeth's words, "Verzeiht, wenn ich nicht weiss, was ich beginne"| Forgive me if I know not what I am beginning |, provide the key to her character. (She begins without, like a conductor, raising the baton, and she ends without first making certain that all is in order, and that the final chord will not expose a disaster). She loves without having sought the advice of "the counsellor for loving hearts." But she is in love, and allows herself to be guided by her emotions. In publicly declaring her love for the prodigal she troubles her pretty head not at all about the appallingly extensive significance of the term, tasteless because so sharply defined, "respectability."

Such a one is Wagner's Elisabeth, and so she is played by Frau Ehnn. She knows not what she is beginning, but something happens. In Fräulein Malten's Elisabeth something happens, too; in fact, a lot happens. But, unfortunately, she always knows exactly what she is about, and we find ourselves doubting her sincerity, with predictably disastrous consequences. Foregoing the comparison with Frau Ehnn, however, it was still a splendid accomplishment, and Fräulein Malten fully earned the enthusiastic applause that was her reward.

Herr Winkelmann[12] was in very good form as Tannhäuser. Herr Reichmann[13] delighted us especially through his noble, restrained acting. No less fine was Herr Scaria.[14] Would that this were more often the case. Why doesn't Fräulein Schläger,[15] as Venus, just wrap herself up in seven fur smocks, seven fur coats and seven fur hoods like the devil in Grabbe's comedy?[16] That would look a lot better than a flowered ball gown displaying bare arms that can bring Tannhäuser, for all his vaunted asceticism, to the point of forgetting the text. Herr Direktor Jahn[17] conducted discreetly. Still, we painfully missed our excellent Hans Richter, if only because of the tempi.

1. Ignaz Brüll (1846-1907), Moravian-born, Viennese-educated pianist, composer and educator. In addition to this concerto, he was the composer of ten operas, of which only *Das Goldene Kreuz* (*The Golden Cross*) is, if distantly, remembered.

2. Arnold Rosé (1863-1946) came from Jassy in Rumania but was educated in Vienna. He became concertmaster of the orchestra of the Court Opera (Hofoper) and of the Philharmonic in 1881, and was founder and leader of the internationally famous Rosé Quartet. He was also for many years concertmaster of the orchestra for the Bayreuth festivals.

3. Bianca Bianchi (1855-1947) made her Vienna debut as Amina in *La Sonnambula* in 1878, having already made a name for herself in London, Paris and St. Petersburg. London had, in fact, made a name for her. She was born Bertha Schwarz in Heidelberg, and studied with Pauline Viardot in Paris. When she was engaged by Frederick Gye for the Covent Garden season of 1874, he found the name unsuited to an Italian season, and changed it, without consulting her, to Valentine Bianchi. The subsequent change from Valentine to Bianca would seem to have been her own idea or, more likely, that of the impresario Bernhard Pollini (Baruch Pohl), her sponsor, teacher and, ultimately, her father-in-law. She became a resident member of the Vienna company in 1880, and remained its first coloratura soprano until 1887.

4. Hans Richter (1843-1916) was one of the first truly great conductors. Born in Raab, Hungary, he was educated in Vienna and, for some years, played horn in the orchestra of the Court Opera. He was an early Wagnerian (his mother, Josephine Csazinsky, was Vienna's first Venus in *Tannhäuser* in 1857), and, joining Wagner in Lucerne in 1866-67, he made fair copies of both *Die Meistersinger* and *Der Ring des Nibelungen*, conducting the first performance of the latter in Bayreuth in 1876. He succeeded Otto Dessoff as chief conductor of the Court Opera (and of the Philharmonic) in 1875. He established the so-called Richter concerts in London in 1879, astonishing all by conducting from memory. From 1897 to 1911 he was conductor of the Hallé Orchestra in Manchester. He retired to Bayreuth in 1912, and died there.

5. David Popper (1843-1913), born in Prague, was first cellist of the orchestra of the Court Opera (and of the Philharmonic) from 1868 to 1873, thereafter devoting the rest of his life to a career as cello virtuoso and teacher. From 1896 he taught at the National Academy in Budapest, and was a member of the Hubay Quartet. Among his compositions was a Requiem for Three Cellos.

6. Karl Richard Stasny (1855-1920) was a pupil of Brüll in Vienna and later of Clara Schumann in Frankfurt am Main. After an international career as virtuoso, he became professor of piano at the New England Conservatory in Boston.

7. Teresina (Maria Felicita) Tua (1866-1956) was born in Turin and studied violin with Joseph Massart in Paris. She had a brilliant international career as violin virtuosa.

8. Regine Klein (1856-1939) sang leading dramatic soprano roles at the Court Opera from 1885 to 1887. She was one of many Viennese sopranos who graduated to opera from operetta.

9. Rosa Papier (1858-1932) studied privately in Vienna with Mathilde Marchesi and went on to a brilliant but brief career (1881-1891) at the Court Opera. She was married to conductor-pianist Hans Paumgartner, who was her accompanist in the Lieder recitals that added importantly to her renown. They were the first, in a concert in the Bösendorfersaal on March 2, 1888, to perform Wolf songs ("Morgentau" and "Zur Ruh") in public. Their son, Bernhard Paumgartner (1887-1971), was until 1959 director of the Mozarteum in Salzburg and, until 1960, of the Salzburg Festival.

10. Therese Malten (1855-1930) was a distinguished member of the Dresden company from 1873 to 1903. In 1882 she shared the role of Kundry with Amalie Materna (who sang the premiere) and Marianne Brandt in the first performances of *Parsifal* at Bayreuth.

11. Bertha Ehnn (1845-1903), although born in Budapest, was of a Styrian family, and grew up in Vienna. She came to the Court Opera in 1868 from Stuttgart, and remained until 1885. Roles especially associated with her were Marguerite, Juliet and Mignon, but she also sang

Elisabeth, Elsa, Sieglinde and Selika (in *L'Africaine*), and was Vienna's first Eva in *Die Meistersinger*.

12. Hermann Winkelmann (1849-1912) came to Vienna from Hamburg in 1883, following his great success as the first Parsifal in Bayreuth, and was to remain until 1906 as *the* Helden-tenor of his generation. He was Vienna's first Otello.

13. Theodor Reichmann (1849-1903), born in Rostock and educated in Berlin, was one of the great German baritones of his generation, an internationally renowned Wotan, Sachs, Dutchman and Telramund. He created the role of Amfortas in *Parsifal*. He was a member of the Court Opera from 1882 to 1889, and rejoined the company in 1893 after touring England and America. He was admired for the beauty not only of his voice, but also of his person and bearing.

14. Emil Scaria (1838-1886) studied with Manuel Garcia in London, joining the Court Opera in 1872, and quickly establishing himself as one of the great basses of vocal history. Of his Gurnemanz at the Bayreuth premiere of *Parsifal*, Lilli Lehmann wrote in *Mein Weg*: "Scaria as Gurnemanz will remain unforgettable for all those who had the good fortune to see him and hear him."

15. Antonia ("Tony") Schläger (1860- ?), a Viennese dramatic soprano who, like Regine Klein, had graduated to opera from operetta.

16. Christian Dietrich Grabbe (1801-1836), German writer of historical dramas whose style and structure seem, in retrospect, to anticipate expressionism and film techniques of a century later. A contentious character, his early death was attributed to a combination of alcoholism and tuberculosis. The reference here is to his one comedy, *Scherz, Satire, Ironie und tiefere Bedeutung* (Jest, Satire, Irony and Deeper Significance)

17. Wilhelm Jahn (1835-1900) succeeded Franz Jauner as director of the Court Opera in 1881, and sustained that position until 1897, longer than any other director in the houses's history.

3. La Muette de Portici

February 2, 1884

We are most grateful to the management, ever on the alert for novelties, antiquities and other attempts at resurrection, for having brought us this time a work well worth a new mounting, not only because of the presumed centenary of Auber's birth, but also and primarily because of the exceptional affection and popularity this inspired work always enjoyed with the public.

As with all popular works, however, so it went with *La Muette de Portici*.[1] Its fate was to be played into the ground until rendered so mute by ever more crushing routine that it could bring forth only a few pitiable groans as an occasional stop gap in the repertoire. These, too, gradually diminished, and it seemed likely that there would soon be no breath at all. There it lay, dusty, unappreciated, forgotten — in the disreputable company of God knows what infamous composers — in the archives of the opera house. From there not a sound from this mute, indignant at such shameful treatment, could penetrate to the ears of a hard hearted Intendant or director. It is not, then, to be seen as providential that the keen eye of Freiherr von Hofmann[2] should have recognized the need of loosening the helpless mute's tongue?

No sooner said than done, and what he did was no less than restore her to precious life and — how noble, how generous! — have a new dress made to her measure. It is not, unfortunately, entirely becoming. To order it from Herr Tetzlaff[3] was, I think, unnecessary. The artistic sense of the late Dingelstedt[4] had already provided a most tasteful wardrobe. What her reincarnation lost by the new staging, however, was made good by her inner substance, by the truly dramatic narrative, and by the utterly characteristic music that accompanies it.

A principal role is allotted in *La Muette de Portici* to the choruses. If our choral personnel failed to realize the vitality of the populace's participation in the drama, the fault lay with the stage director. Vocally, their accomplishment was extraordinary. Fräulein Cerale[5] is certainly an excellent dancer. Had Masaniello's sister entrusted the expression of her emotions exclusively to her toes, Fräulein Cerale could be counted on to work wonders as Fenella. Since this is not, alas, the case, Fräulein Cerale pleased us only moderately. Herr Winkelmann is, of course, a Heldentenor, and so we found it perfectly understandable that the lullaby should be a failure. Fräulein Lehmann (Elvira),[6] Herr Schittenhelm[7] (Alfonso) and Herr Scaria (Pietro) gave their all to the success of the production. The opera was well prepared by Direktor Jahn.

Another meeting with Fräulein Klein, this time as Aida in the opera of that name. We could only repeat what has been said of her before, and therefore limit ourself today to confirming her thoroughly favorable reception. The achievements of others in the cast were all familiar. The performance had spirit, and the audience was numerous.

Rather as an afterthought, mention should be made of a concert given on the 20th of last month under the direction of the worthy Kapellmeister Eder. Especially outstanding in a varied program was a song by a lady (Ernestine von Bauduin), dedicated to the Kirchenverein, sung by Fräulein Fabbrini, and received with much applause. The concert given on the 22nd by the pianists Dory Petersen and Richard Burmester we can describe only as a welcome enrichment of our concert repertoire.

Finally, I must note Kammersänger[8] Walter's[9] first Lieder recital. A hall full to overflowing promised something special to the lucky ticket holders. A delighted audience was only too happy to allow itself to be melted by Walter's whispered incantation, and even the most churlish critic could not repress a friendly smile at this mutual evaporation (*smorzando*).

---

1.   The more familiar title outside France and Germany (where it is called *Die Stumme von Portici*) is *Masaniello*, the name of the revolutionary Neapolitan fisherman with whose exploits it is concerned. The role of Fenella, the hero's mute sister, is danced. The opera

dates from 1828. A performance in Brussels on August 25. 1830. is said to have sparked the uprisings that drove the Dutch from Belgium. Daniel François Auber was born in Caen on January 29. 1782.

2. Leopold Friedrich Freiherr von Hofmann (1822-1888) became General-Intendant of the Court Theaters in 1880 after a distinguished career in the civil service that had included a long term as the official theater censor. He presided as General-Intendant until 1885.

3. Karl Tetzlaff (1837- ?) was stage director (Oberregisseur) of the Court Opera from 1881 to 1889. When he staged the first Vienna production of *Tristan und Isolde* in 1883. he became the first stage director in the history of the Court Opera to have his name printed on the playbill.

4. Franz Dingelstedt (1814-1881). director of the Court Opera from 1867 to 1870. was a poet and man of the spoken drama rather than a musician. Among many aphorisms attributed to him was one to the effect that "the concert is a superfluous. the opera a necessary evil." So he left music to his conductors and concerned himself with scenery and costumes. hence Wolf's reference to his stage designs and costumes for a new production of *La Muette de Portici* fifteen years earlier. He had been brought to Vienna from the Court Theater in Munich as the successor-in-waiting to August Wolff as director of the Court Theater (Burgtheater). and his directorship at the opera was specifically provisional. It was. nevertheless. as brilliant as it was short. including such important premieres as *Romeo and Juliet. Mignon* and *Die Meistersinger*. and the removal of the company from the old Theater am Kaerntnertor to the new (and present) house on the Ringstrasse. Dingelstedt was given not only to witty aphorisms. but also to pompous prologues. two notable examples being those he wrote for the premiere of *Lohengrin* in Weimar in 1850 and for the opening of the new Vienna opera house with *Don Giovanni* on May 25. 1869.

5. Luigia Cerale (1859- ?). a Turinese. prima ballerina at the Court Opera from 1879 to 1892. was reckoned the last of the great ballerinas in the tradition of Maria Taglioni and Fanny Elssler. Leo Delibes described her as "the dancer with toes of steel."

6. Marie Lehmann (1851-1931). younger sister of the great Lilli Lehmann. was a valued member of the Vienna company from 1881 to 1902. After leaving the company she became a voice teacher in Berlin.

7. Anton Schittenhelm (1849- ?). a Silesian tenor who had joined the company in 1875. From Wolf's description of him in this and many subsequent notices. he must have been one of those fine. versatile singers of secondary roles who are more indispensable to a repertoire house than its stars.

8. Literally "chamber singer." an honorary title that. in Germany and Austria. has survived its feudal associations.

9. Gustav Walter (1834-1910). a Bohemian lyric tenor. was especially esteemed for his Mozart. But he had a wide repertoire. and created for Vienna both Romeo (Gounod) and Walter von Stolzing in *Die Meistersinger*. He joined the company in 1856. and remained until 1887. when he retired to devote the remainder of a long career to Lieder recitals. He was. indeed. the first to give Lieder recitals in public. He recorded three songs for the Gramophon & Typewriter Company in Vienna in 1905. when he was seventy-one. One of them. Schubert's "Am Meer." has been reissued on microgroove in the 12-disc EMI set titled "The Record of Singing" (RLS 724). Hanslick wrote of him at the time of his retirement: "Even in opera he was essentially a Lieder singer. a prince of song from Schubert's realm."

4. A Spate of Chamber Music

February 8,1884

On February 2 the cellist David Popper felt constrained by "popular demand" to give a matinee recital in the Bösendorfersaal and, capitulating to the urgent pressures of "popular demand," to include his "Spinning Song" in the program. Whether the ultimate cause of Herr Popper's conspicuous eagerness to oblige is to be sought in an inborn amiability or in an especially acute sense of the practical is a question to be asked of the box office. Still, the advertisement-like "'Spinning Song' by popular demand" may well have had an apologetic connotation, at the same time underlining the modesty of the composer in attributing the success of his feeble composition solely to the extraordinarily profound perception of his audiences. The perceptive audience immediately grasped the recitalist's deference. It applauded lustily and lengthily, and not a few of the listeners may have made the agreeable discovery, thanks to the recitalist's occasional lapses, that they were also deaf in both ears. Herr Popper and his audience, however, were mutually rewarded.

The violin virtuosa Teresina Tua, a day later, gave a farewell matinee — without the supplementary "by popular demand," to be sure — to a numerous audience that heard her titbits with visible pleasure. There were also piano offerings by Fräulein Paula Dürrnberger and songs sung by Fräulein Eugenia Senigaglia. Fräulein Dürrnberger's playing was smooth, clean, pure, brushed, combed and ironed. Fräulein Senigaglia would be well advised to cultivate a less mannered delivery. Her pretty voice would then be heard to better advantage.

We are truly encouraged by the zealous cultivation of chamber music and the public's enthusiastic participation in this category of the musical art. Even our contemporary composers, curiously, are producing their most tolerable music in this genre, the same composers whose piano pieces and songs, and especially their symphonies and even operas, expose the listener to tests of patience that would have driven Job right out of his mind. Why? An excellent painter once assured me that a water color is easier to do than an oil painting. Might one not compare the four-stringed instruments with the pale water color, the luxuriant coloring of the orchestra with the warm tone of oil?

From the musical point of view, the question is easily answered. It is the skillful exploitation of technic, not the compulsion to express a musical thought, that prompts our modern composers to write chamber music. That is why their adagios are so flat, so contrived, so labored — intellectual poverty with its bored grimace smirking at us over and again through piquancy, however playful. One remembers those adagios in which Beethoven's heart swelled to an immeasurable universe, embracing the hearts of all mankind, summoning each to have its share of the superhuman rapture that Beethoven's heart alone could not contain!

The modern composer is most secure in the scherzos and the finales. He need only be a proficient contrapuntist and jumble the voices together topsy-turvy to give himself the appearance of being able to accomplish something decent. Intricate inversions, schoolmasterly transitions, and always a droll fugato — or even a fugue! The public reacts to that sort of thing with awe and respect: two, three, or even four themes — if nothing else will work — piled up, burst asunder, reassembled and again urged on. It's a proper little skirmish, but without the thunder of cannon, without battle hymns and with little gunpowder; rather with plenty of Hungarian cavalry, a troop of gypsies *a la zingaresca,* a *czardas* and so on. A lovely goulash! And fun, too. Well, it's an escape from the creeping boredom of the adagios. And thus we find the chamber music of our contemporaries — always excepting the andantes and the adagios — tolerable.

To this genre belongs a trio by Raff,[1] played with brilliance and insight by Loewenburg[2] with members of the Rosé Quartet, as do Grädener's[3] Quintet in E, played by the Grün[4] Quartet and, half and half, the Quintet in G, Opus 11, of Johannes Hager[5], splendidly played by the Radnitzky[6] Quartet. Exceptions were three pieces by Volkmann,[7] of which the first, a Quartet in G minor, in the skilled hands of the Rosé Quartet, was faultlessly executed; the second, the famous Trio in B flat minor, suffered under the very erratic fingers of Herr Grün, and the third, a Quartet in E minor with a lovely adagio, played with great warmth and understanding by Radnitzky and his valiant cohorts, all of which gave us untroubled pleasure.

However amiable the intentions of our quartets in offering contemporary fare, no program should be without something by Mozart, Haydn or Beethoven. We are, accordingly, especially grateful to Herr Rosé for bringing us Beethoven's wonderful Quartet in C, Opus 59, No. 3, well played as it was.

1. Joseph Joachim Raff (1822-1882), pianist, composer and pedagogue, was from 1877 to the time of his death director of the Hoch Conservatory in Frankfurt am Main. Among his students there was the American composer, Edward MacDowell.

2. Presumably Max Julius Loewengard (1860-1915), a student of Raff's in Frankfurt am Main, who went on to a notable career as music critic in Berlin and Hamburg, and as author of several books on theory and composition.

3. Hermann Grädener (1844-1929) was the son of Karl Grädener (1812-1883), a distinguished Hamburg composer and pedagogue. Hermann was educated at the Vienna Conservatory, and spent all his life in and around Vienna as organist, violinist, conductor, composer and teacher.

4. Jakob Grün (1837-1916), a Hungarian violinist, became a concertmaster of the opera orchestra in 1868. He was professor of violin at the Vienna Conservatory from 1877 to 1909.

5.   Johannes Hager was the pseudonym under which Johann Hasslinger (1822-1898), a high-ranking official in the Imperial Foreign Office, indulged his hobby of composition.

6.   Franz Radnitzky was a violinist in the orchestra of the Court Opera, second violin in the Helmesberger Quartet from 1878 to 1884, and thereafter first violin in his own Radnitzky Quartet.

7.   Friedrich Robert Volkmann (1815-1883) was a prolific composer of Saxon birth, a protégé of Schumann. He lived in Vienna from 1854 to 1858, then settled in Budapest as professor of harmony and counterpoint at the National Academy. The Quartet in G minor was his Opus 14, the Trio in B flat minor his Opus 5, and the Quartet in E minor his Opus 35.

5. A Wagner Memorial Rubinstein's Recital

February 17, 1884

Before visiting the splendid Musikvereinssaal or our luxuriously appointed Court Opera House, let us turn our steps toward the plain Bösendorfersaal, whose grand simplicity is perfectly designed to make any audience, distracted and frivolous, aware that it is not at a fashion show or in a drawing room or even in one of those cozy sleeping compartments commonly known in the theater as loges, or boxes, but rather in a music room where custom has it that, for one's money, one is expected not only to listen, but also to keep quiet. Such a room serves at the same time to sustain the serious mood of an artistically appreciative audience (since there is no disturbance from outside) and to establish a benevolent harmony between the listener and his immediate surroundings. In this sense we should like to acknowledge the Bösendorfersaal as the most tasteful of all possible settings for the ceremony held there on February 13 in memory of Richard Wagner.

The Vienna Academic Wagner Society, the sponsor, observed February 13, the anniversary of the master's death, in the most reverent manner. The evening began with a male chorus by Wagner, "At Weber's Grave,"[1] which now, under the title of "In Memory of Richard Wagner," was subjected to some variants, both musical and poetic, that were not all to the good, least of all as far as the music was concerned. Then came a memorial address by Herr von Wolzogen,[2] whose thoughtful content bordered close on mysticism, and was therefore nicely calculated to prepare us for the true mysticism of *Parsifal* in the Grail Scene of Act I, which followed. With the consecrated strains of the grail motive, born aloft on seraph wings, the solemn ceremony came to a close. Those in attendance departed speechlessly and silently, as befits such an occasion.

Nothing is so constant, however, as change, and the sorrowing muse who, at Wagner's grave on February 13, had bedewed the imperishable laurels adorning his head with her tears, wove a crown of glory around the morose brow of Anton Rubinstein,[3] the virtuoso genius, who gave his first concert before an ecstatic audience in the Grosser Musikvereinssaal the very next day. Anton Rubinstein moves among our swarm of ivory crushers like Gulliver among the Liliputians, utterly his own man, a fixed star among the miserable shooting stars, a personality through and through. His playing of Chopin, Schubert, Tchaikovsky and even Schumann's Sonata in F sharp minor will be forgotten by none who heard it. When he lets the sound drift off into slumber, and the waves of tone sweep by as if issuing from a deep dream or from a spirit world, expiring in the tenderest, softest *pppp*, then swelling to the sensuous charm of his normal *piano*, I see in him no longer the virtuoso with his instrument, but rather a mesmerist, the instrument the pliant medium, totally subject to its master's inspired impulses. But he can unleash hurricanes, too, and when he rages through the keys like one gone berserk, then the waves of tone surge and heave until one expects them to engulf the madman, the instrument, the audience and, finally, themselves.

Yes, there is something elemental in his manner of playing, and when it comes to sheer beauty of sound no one among living pianists can touch him (Liszt, of course, always excepted). In the playing of Chopin, too, he has no rivals. As for the Beethoven sonatas, he must bow to Bülow,[4] who, three years ago, played the last six sonatas for us, and so perfectly as to persuade us immediately that Beethoven should be played in this way and in no other. The dreadfully hurried tempi, the unexampled interpretive liberties, the nonchalance with which Rubinstein treats particularly prominent passages such as the recitative phrase in the first movement of the Sonata in D minor, etc., all these were dark blemishes on the luminous glory of his heroic virtuoso deeds. Perhaps it was simply not Anton Rubinstein's night for Beethoven? We would be only too happy if, at his next recital, in the Bösendorfersaal on the 20th of this month, he could modify our opinion of his approach to Beethoven, provided, of course, that he gives us grounds for so doing.

Lortzing's[5] best and most popular work, *Zar und Zimmermann*, attracted a large audience to the Court Opera on the 15th of this month. Herr Schrödter,[6] a guest from the Landestheater in Prague, had a great success as Peter Ivanov. He unites a very sympathetic voice with expressive gestures, a charming disposition and artistic intelligence, a combination rarely encountered among tenors. All honor to Herr Schrödter! And Fräulein Pirk[7] as Marie? Well, she is the rogue Marie to the life, right down to the last detail. It was heartwarming to see two singers as gifted dramatically as Herr Schrödter and Fräulein Pirk on an opera stage, where it is usually a matter of arms swinging from right to left and from left to right for God knows what reason. Herr Reichmann sang the Tsar splendidly, especially the familiar "Einst spielt ich mit Szepter."[8] That brought the house down. Herr Wiegand[9] is a perfectly respectable singer, and this despite his unsuitability for buffo roles. The performance was good, and the audience in a receptive mood.

1. "An Webers Grabe," a chorus for male voices *a cappella*, composed by Wagner to a text of his own, and sung at the ceremony in Dresden in 1844 commemorating the return of Weber's remains from London. It was sung again at the railway station in Bayreuth on February 16, 1883, when Wagner's own body was brought home from Venice.

2. Hans Paul Freiherr von Wolzogen (1848-1938), foremost of the Wagnerites, for many years editor of the *Bayreuther Blätter* and author of an enormous number of books and articles on Wagner and his works.

3. Anton Rubinstein (1830-1894) gave five recitals on this visit to Vienna, his first in six years, on February 14, 20, 23, 24 and 27, with a different program for each. And what programs! This first included not only the Schumann Sonata in F sharp minor and Beethoven's Sonata in D minor, Opus 31, No. 2, but also the latter's Sonata in A major, Opus 101. There were seventeen other pieces, and the recital last for three hours. Hanslick, in reviewing these recitals for the *Neue Freie Presse*, noted that Rubinstein "gives his recitals absolutely alone, without an assisting artist." The solo recital as we know it today would remain a rarity until well after the turn of the century.

4. Hans Guido Freiherr von Bülow (1830-1894), pupil of Liszt, disciple of Wagner, and one of the foremost pianists and conductors of his time. He conducted the premieres in Munich of both *Tristan und Isolde* in 1865 and *Die Meistersinger* in 1868. He was married to Liszt's daughter Cosima, who left him for Wagner. Wolf's subsequent references to Bülow are less flattering, a circumstance certainly not unrelated to the fact that Bülow espoused not only Wagner, but also Brahms. Hanslick, in turn, took Rubinstein to task for his neglect of Brahms.

5. Gustav Albert Lortzing (1801-1851) was the son of an actor, and spent his entire life in the theater, including ten years as a buffo tenor in Leipzig. *Zar und Zimmermann* (*Tsar and Shipwright*), whose hero is Peter the Great, dating from 1837, was his first successful opera, and it is still a favorite in German, Austrian and Swiss opera houses. Others of his later operas, still heard in the German language area, are *Der Waffenschmied* (*The Armorer*), *Der Wildschütz* (*The Poacher*) and *Undine*.

6. Fritz Ernst Schrödter (1855- ?), born in Leipzig, and at first destined to be a painter, began his singing career as a baritone in operetta, first in Budapest, then in Vienna at the Theater an der Wien. When he joined the Court Opera in 1885 he was persuaded by Jahn to move up into tenor roles. He quickly became a Vienna favorite, admired both as actor and singer in both comic and tragic roles and especially as David in *Die Meistersinger*.

7. Sarolta Pirk (Karoline Krippel) (1863- ?), a Viennese, was a member of the company only in the season of 1884-1885, after which she moved on to Prague.

8. "I Played Once with Scepter," in which Peter nostalgically recalls the bliss of a royal childhood. The aria has been for more than a century a standby in the repertoire of every German baritone.

9. Heinrich Joseph Wiegand (1842-1899) was a member of the company only from 1882 to 1884, after which he moved to Hamburg (1884-1890) and to the Court Opera in Munich.

6. A Dog in the Manger

February 24, 1884

Light opera is not fashioned to flourish in our Court Opera House, and every attempt to establish it on those boards must be seen in advance as doomed to failure. Where festive processions are called for, or bath and battle scenes, or heaven and hell, as in so-called grand opera, a large stage lends itself to the movement of large crowds, to the ingenuity of the stage director and to the no less ingenious stage mechanic. But in light opera the thunder machine very rarely plays any role. The torrent of passions is reduced to a babbling brook wending its way cheerfully between flowering meadows, maybe once in a long while transforming itself playfully into an artificial waterfall. All this, with the dialogue and the small orchestra should go hand in hand with a proportionately smaller stage.

There is in Vienna, unfortunately, no *Opéra-Comique,*[1] and so there is no choice but to cultivate this charming genre in our opera house, which I might describe, in its relationship to light opera as a kind of Dog's Grotto[2] in reverse, to which, a few days ago, *Le Chien du Jardinier* (The Gardener's Dog) fell a victim. In a smaller theater, this little opus would certainly have delighted the public. In the opera house it passed the listener by like a shadow, leaving not a trace of its passing.

Le Chien du Jardinier, by Albert Grisar,[3] was first produced in Paris in 1855. We made the composer's acquaintance and learned to love him as a thoroughly amiable personality in his charming opera, *Bon Soir, Monsieur Pantalon.* In this opera he revealed himself as a melody squanderer, while in *Le Chien du Jardinier* he cannot compose away the appearance of a musical miser — or did the title have a fateful influence when he fell upon the gardener's dog?[4] Enough. He is stingy with his gifts, and is more thrifty with his melodies than becomes a reputable composer.

(Nowdays it's quite another matter. It is thought merely clever if one, in the role of a famous symphonist, lives off an apology for a melody — behind which the essential impudence takes cover — for an entire symphony and even as often happens, introduces the same coy melody into other compositions (of his own) and discusses it musically, so to speak — an effective weapon for achieving popularity through importunity!)

But to come back to the opera, we would like to offer the unbiased operagoer a friendly warning against entertaining the pleasant delusion that he may be witnessing a canine comedy. It is only a sly trick on the part of the librettist to use this promising title to lure an art-loving public. There is no poodle such as the four-legged acrobat, the Dog Aubry,[5] who delights the Duke of Weimar and his art-loving court with instructive and clever tricks. Nor will you encounter any four-legged genius such as the dog Braganza,[6] in the wagging of whose tail almost as much intelligence, irony, wisdom and humor are revealed as stupidities were encouraged in the book trade by the most awesome sweating of a wise Ostermann's brow since the appearance of *Adam*[7] (published by Konegen). Nothing of the kind, nothing.

To take the fable of the gardener's dog (the gardener has nothing to do with it) who neither eats nor lets his companion eat what he has left untouched, and apply it parabolically in the form of a couplet to a young coquette — that's what the story of the gardener's dog is about. The plot, for the rest, runs somewhat thus: Franz, a young peasant boy, loves Marzelline, the companion of Katharina, the rich lessee who, in turn, from jealousy and innate flirtatiousness, seeks to break up the lovers' relationship. She learns from Franz that he loves Marzelline because of her small foot. Katharina, relying on her own dainty foot, pretends an injury to it, and, sure enough, the peasant booby falls for the lure. At the sight of her little foot — and the twinkle in her eye — his heart catches fire. Suddenly Just arrives on the scene, a relative of Katharina's who has long sought her hand without getting a decisive answer. He becomes a witness to the mischief Katharina has instigated, and takes the side of the unfortunate Marzelline. But he still wants a decision. Using the fable of the gardener's dog, he gives her to understand that if she herself will not marry (eat), she ought at least not interfere with others (let them eat!). This allegory (rather blunt, but well intended) appears to have made an agreeable impression on her, although she still does not know quite how to undo the knot recklessly tied through her own flirtation. She decides to leave the resolving of all this confusion to chance, suggesting to Marzelline that they draw lots for Franz. Katharina wins, but plays the part of the generous woman, lets Marzelline have her Franz, and offers the delighted Just her hand. Now it's up to the gardener's dog to see how he can get his meal down without being laughed out of countenance.

As for the music, the first two duets are especially noteworthy. Prettily contrived and performed, they display the playful charm of French frivolity in an utterly delightful manner. The other numbers are hardly more than commonly agreeable. Frau von Naday,[8] as the coquette, was excellent, incomparably superior to Fräulein Braga[9] as the naive Marzelline. Herr Schittenhelm, as Franz, was the simple peasant boy to the life — and that is commendable progress. Herr Wiegand, as Just, impressed us as being a bit too stiff, too awkward, to bear-like, particularly in his role of matchmaker, in which one cannot emphasize sufficiently a pliant nature. The opera was carefully prepared by Kapellmeister Fuchs.[10]

The magnet that attracts all Viennese musical circles, Anton Rubinstein, gave his second recital on the 20th of this month in the Bösendorfersaal. The artist seemed on this occasion to have been in an especially inspired mood. He played Chopin again, if possible even more raptly, more irresistibly, than at his first recital. And Schumann's Fantasie in C major [Opus 17]! One must have heard it from Rubinstein in order to take it to one's heart. I had the feeling that Schumann, in the first movement of his Fantasie, had struck the fundamental tone of the romanticists' character, that sorrow-suffused plaint of nature which, sounding through all the vicissitudes of life, finally expires in a melancholy vision of harmony with nature, and in the upward surging and softly subsiding broken chords, had let it fade away — a swan song of romanticism.[11]

What is one to write about a female pianist — Signorina Luisa Cognetti — who dares to appear in a city and in a hall where, only the day before, Rubinstein's art had made our hearts tremble, and who dares, like Rubinstein, to offer only piano pieces, who dares to begin with Beethoven's Sonata in C sharp minor, and to play it in such a manner that one would gladly have had his ears cut off rather than expose a good natured and long suffering ear-drum to such indignities for any length of time. And further, your reviewer would spit fire like a dragon or cast on evil eye like a basilisk had not her playing of three Schubert songs in the Liszt transcriptions ("Du bist die Ruh," "Auf dem Wasser zu singen" and "Erlkönig") and a very beautifully contrived and highly effective etude by Anton Rubinstein stilled his wrath sufficiently to let him attest, in cold blood, to a pretty fair technic and faulty interpretation in Signorina Cognetti's playing.

1. The Ringtheater on the Schottenring, modeled on Paris's Opéra-Comique, and opened in 1874, had been destroyed by fire on December 8, 1881, just before a performance of *The Tales of Hoffman*, with the loss of some 380 lives.

2. A grotto near Naples in which a freakish distribution of gases renders it fatal to dogs and other small animals breathing close to the ground, but harmless to humans and other creatures breathing at a higher level.

3. Albert Grisar (1808-1869), a prolific Belgian composer of operettas, and sufficiently well thought of in his time to inspire a biography by Arthur Pougin.

4. "Als er auf den Hund des Gärtners kam." Wolf is making a pun or play on the German idiom, "auf den Hund kommen," roughly the equivalent of the English "to go to the dogs," but having in German rather the sense of "to fall upon hard times."

5. A trained poodle remembered in theater history as the cause of Goethe's withdrawal from the directorship of the ducal theater in Weimar. It belonged to the singer Caroline Jagemann, mistress of Archduke Karl August. She insisted on Aubry's appearance on the stage, and, against Goethe's objections, had her way.

6. Actually Berganza, canine subject of E.T.A. Hoffmann's "Nachricht von den neuesten Schicksalen des Hundes Berganza" (Latest Developments in the Career of the Dog Berganza).

7. *Mysterium Adam*, a poetic drama by Richard Kralik.

8. Katharina von Naday was a member of the Court Opera from 1884 to 1888, when she moved with her husband, Ferenc von Naday, a Hungarian actor, to Budapest.

9. Hermine Braga (1859- ?). a member of the Court Opera from 1878 to 1888.
10. Johann Nepomuk Fuchs (1841-1899). a Styrian conductor who had joined the conductorial staff of the Court Opera in 1880. He was the older brother of the composer Robert Fuchs.
11. Wolf was obviously inspired here by the motto appended to his Opus 17 by Schumann. a quotation from Friedrich Schlegel:

> Durch alle Töne tönet
> Im bunten Erdentraum
> Ein leiser Ton gezogen
> Für den, der heimlich lauschet.

> [Through every tone there sounds
> In the gay terrestrial dream
> A softer tone by far
> To which he harks unseen.]

7. The Hellmesberger Quartet

March 2, 1884

He is gone; Rubinstein is gone, and the musical gourmets who have glutted themselves on an abundance of musical delicacies in his recitals should not neglect to attend the concerts of key-slaughtering marauders, on hand as after every major battle, and to combine this attendance with a kind of musical convalescence. They should drink seltzer water on top of champagne. They should approach the concert halls with easy, measured strides as befits a patient — *andante con lentezza*. There they will be fanned by an agreeable coolness, and any thought of fire hazard will be forbidden on pain of deprivation of their peace of mind.

You will be able to stretch yourself out and be comfortable. A general sense of well-being will envelop the suffering listener, a mid-summer afternoon mood such as characterizes the transition from thoughtless rumination to total forgetfulness of the outside world, the more intensively so as piano recitals, by and large, have proven themselves the most effective means of accelerating this phenomenon. (Cello recitals are riskier, and often have a cataleptic effect upon the listener, while sustained melodies played on the harp can cause instant death. Be on your guard against harp recitals, therefore, lest you place your life in jeopardy.) It would not be long before the patients slip off gradually into a soft refreshing slumber, and since the greatest danger then is that the peaceful sleepers could be disturbed in their reverent repose by the barbaric *tutti* of hands being clapped together, it is no more than fair that we should have wished to present and commend this thoroughly agreeable and useful side of our concert life to a long-suffering, music-hungry public with these introductory words.

The Hellmesberger Quartet[1] offered us this time as its most interesting number, Schubert's Octet |Opus 166|. Horn, clarinet and bassoon blend utterly charmingly with the string quartet which, in turn, and with the winds, moves along on the fundamental tones of the double bass with the most enchanting nonchalance and amiability. One could build a Babylonian tower on this mighty bass line — but the master has no such lofty aspirations. Far be it from him to contend with the gods, or storm the heights of Olympus, or be a Titan among the Cyclops. No indeed! Smiling earth in its springtime finery, happy humans, in the simplicity of their hearts, longing passionately for pleasure and satisfaction — that is the world in which these harmonies move. Only in the introduction to the last movement did it seem to us that a storm might be brewing. One hears the rumble of thunder, shafts of lightning flash through the night. It is as if the tone poet were pulling back the curtains from the window of his elfin study to spy upon the raging elements. But today no shadow may cloud his happy spirit. He shuts out this sombre spectacle; the enraptured gaze is directed inward. Heavenly bliss invades his heart, and a world full of love and goodness is transfigured in melodies that flow out from the depths of his being.

As much as this marvelous work of Schubert's delighted us, just so outraged were we by the triviality and poverty of imagination of Goldmark's[2] Piano Quintet. Herr Zottmann,[3] who played the piano part, revealed himself as a decently accomplished pianist without any especially distinguishing characteristics. His musical bass would go with a hundred other pianists.

Brahms's Sextet in G, in our opinion the best thing he has ever written, enjoyed an indescribably beautiful performance. The ensemble was admirable throughout, and when such an artist as Hellmesberger tends sometimes to play solo within the quartet, well, one accepts it from him more readily than from anyone else, and ends by surrendering gladly!

It was high time to give some attention to *Der Freischütz*. It was presented in a new production at the Court Opera on Friday, the 29th. The sets were completely successful, especially the Wolf's Glen with the real waterfall. The eerie hunt, the diabolical goings-on and the confusion at the close made an imposing and terrifying impression. Samiel, the wild huntsman, was in rather weak voice, and made a somewhat consumptive impression — a poor devil! Frau Ehnn sang Agathe with characteristic sincerity and purity. Fräulein Pirk as Ännchen is absolutely unique, unsurpassable. The Kaspar of Herr Wiegand was admirable, both vocally and dramatically, an accomplisment fully matched by Winkelmann as Max. The small parts of the Hermit and Kilian, king of the huntsmen, were ideally realized by Herr Rokitansky[4] and Herr Felix.[5] Chorus and orchestra, under the leadership of Direktor Jahn, were splendidly prepared. The performance was well attended.

1. The Hellmesbergers were one of Vienna's most distinguished musical families. Their promi-
    nence began with Georg Hellmesberger (1800-1873), violinist, a student at the Conservatory
    and subsequently professor of violin there. Among his pupils were Joseph Joachim and
    Leopold Auer. He was also the teacher of his two sons, Georg (1830-1852) and Joseph (1828-
    1893). The latter was the founder, in 1849, of the Hellmesberger Quartet. His son, Joseph
    (1850-1907) played second violin in the quartet after 1875, and became its leader in 1887. A
    younger son, Ferdinand (1863-1940) became the quartet's cellist in 1883. All were active as
    soloists, teachers, conductors and composers in addition to their work with the quartet.
2. Carl Goldmark (1830-1915), now remembered as the composer of the "Sakuntala" Overture
    and the opera *The Queen of Sheba*. This quintet, in B flat, was his Opus 30.
3. Franz Zottmann (1858- ?), Viennese pianist and professor of piano at the Conservatory.
4. Hans Freiherr Von Rokitansky (1836-1896), a Vienna-born bass who was a member of the
    company for just short of thirty years (1861-1893). Hagen was reckoned his finest role.
5. Benedict Felix (1860-1912), a Hungarian bass, had just joined the company in 1883.

8. Wilhelm Gericke and the "Missa Solemnis"

March 9, 1884

March 4 was celebrated in the Grosser Musikvereinssaal in festive and solemn fashion with the "Missa Solemnis." To recapitulate Beethoven's colossal utterance in this work in mere words would be a vain endeavor. Exaltation, release, remorse, redemption — what do these words signify other than an attempt to provide the sensory perceptive faculty, insofar as possible, with an image appropriate to these concepts? But what can work upon our sensory perceptive faculties more tellingly than music? Whoever heard Beethoven's "Missa Solemnis," whoever felt it and understood it, was exalted, released, crushed, redeemed. It is the world religion, built upon the ritual text of Christianity and preached to redemption-hungry mortals. One whose faith in a divinity is as rock-firm as Beethoven's, as he trumpets his mighty *credo* into the world, stands exalted above all that is common, false, hypocritical in this earthly existence.

To have presented us with this gigantic work is the achievement of Hofkapellmeister Gericke.[1] and it cannot be acknowledged adequately. We have here an excellent example of how it is that outstanding accomplishment is not only a matter of talent alone, but may also be due to the circumstances that permit one to find and devote oneself to the field most propitious to his endowment and insight. One can, for example, be an excellent opera composer and yet write insignificant symphonies, *vide* L. Spohr. The symphony was simply not his field, while Beethoven, on the other hand, alongside his nine symphonies, still found himself impelled, fortunately, to compose a *Fidelio*. The fatal certainty, however, that one can, even without composing operas, also produce bad symphonies is not to be denied (however much they may delight the collective bigotry of Vienna, Berlin and Hamburg, and even if Hans von Bülow himself, in his cute harlequin outfit, stands godfather to them).[2]

For the immortal Spohr, the successes of his *Jessonda*, to the composition of which he was driven by an inner compulsion, could console him for the unhappy fate of his symphonies. But it does not fall to everyone to create a *Jessonda*, and if a symphony composer of today wished to undertake something similar, I suspect that he would fare in the dramatic field as Spohr fared in his symphonies. This is not to say, however, that Spohr's operas — no matter how old-fashioned they may sound — have so frosty an effect as our piping hot, brand new symphonies. Spohr was simply not a composer by profession. He was a Kapellmeister, and composed *Faust* and *Jessonda* on his holidays. If he had less success with the symphony than in the opera, it was because he lacked just that universality characteristic of Mozart and Beethoven, the greatest geniuses of them all. He was a dramatic composer by nature, and from this artistic soil he cultivated the most productive aspects. In accordance with the trend of the time, he was a romanticist, and if one misses in his operas the fresh, robust folk character of Weber's muse, then the fault lay in his soft nature, which commuted the fiery pulse of universal human sensibility to his musical powers of expression not directly, but diluted, as reflected in a somewhat sickly sentimentality. But all his operas carry the stamp of Spohr's physiognomy as well as that of his time.

What character can one attribute to our modern, celebrated symphonies? They are rather too sober to qualify as romantic. Classical? Yes, classical as a stilted, mannered drama by Racine. Dramatic? Now, that would be utter nonsense. What then? I believe firmly that they are as wanting in character as everything else in our modern times. One tries this, tries that, and tries the other thing, and despite the astonishing progress of electric technology, there is no ignition of the cerebral spark capable of penetrating the Egyptian darkness of our artistic and social malaise . . . .

But to return to our conductor of the "Missa Solemnis," Herr Gericke and we alike must acknowledge a providential dispensation in the fact that the direction of the concerts of the Society of Friends of Music was placed in his hands. His achievements in the opera[3] had suggested nothing better than a routined Kapellmeister, capable of commanding his orchestra with a barren baton, much as a corporal commands respect with his dreaded stick. But as soon as he exchanged the opera for the concert hall, this baton began to sprout. The corporal's stick transformed itself in his hands into a field marshal's baton (the symbol of intellectual superiority) through which he was now able to bring life and verve to the ranks of chorus and orchestra. It was not the smooth, skilled Kapellmeister that we saw on the podium this time. It was the earnest, glowing, sensitive, understanding musician with the assured eye and the loving dedication to a superhumanly exalted work whose horrendous difficulties he overcame in a manner that prompted an ecstatic audience to express its appreciation in stormy ovations.

And we let such a man leave Vienna when certainly only minor concessions would have sufficed to keep him here. But is it any different with Frau Papier-Paumgartner? This artist, who among the participants garnered the lion's share through her truly classical interpretation, the sweetness of her voice,the warmth of expression, the uncommon sense of rhythm, the thoroughly immaculate phrasing, in short, through everything that stamps her as a singer of the first rank — is she not also being allowed to leave[4] as if such artists were as easy to come by as Borsdorfer apples.[5] Well, it's an old story. When we possess a treasure we give it no notice. Only after its loss do we begin to appreciate what we had, and then, as a rule, it is too late.

After Frau Papier, all honor to Frau Wilt.[6] The voice, to be sure, with its unusually warm coloring, has remained the same, but she seldom manages to attack the upper notes securely, and this tremulous vibrato is distressing to the listener. Herr Rokitansky, on the other hand, attacks very resolutely, and as the Lamb of God, too, he bawled as if he were a hungry polar bear about to devour a team of arctic explorers, certainly eager to grant them eternal peace, but without having shown them any pity. What do I care for his beautiful voice? Beautiful voices are cold beauties, resplendent marble. If the latter will change to flesh and blood, if it will betray some heart and soul, we would gladly accept a sacrifice of a third of its cold beauty. With Herr Walter, to be sure, neither the one nor the other applies.

We have almost forgotten concertmaster Grün, who played the wonderful violin solo in the Benedictus so graphically that we began to see green.[7] We felt a sensation as if after every stroke of the bow we should bite into green apples or taste green verdigris. Green lizards danced around us, and suddenly one saw oneself as a poor shipwrecked mariner in the endless green of the sea, with long-tailed sea monsters, all wearing green livery and fiddling away like mad, until hope (for eventual rescue) took us in her arms. Hope, however, ashamed that one identified with her color should have played the concert, and from grief that he should have disfigured this particular Benedictus, had donned mourning, so finally we saw black, and regarded it as a tremendous act of charity. The excellent achievement of chorus and orchestra is to the credit of the conductor, to whom we cannot be sufficiently grateful for bringing us, after a lapse of ten years, a work which Beethoven himself declared to be his best.[8]

1.   Wilhelm Gericke (1845-1925), Styrian conductor who, in 1880, had succeeded Brahms as conductor of the concerts of the Society of Friends of Music. He was conductor of the Boston Symphony from 1884 to 1889, succeeding Sir George Henschel (hence Wolf's subsequent reference to his leaving Vienna), and again from 1898 to 1906.

2.   The reference is to Brahms.

3. He was second Kapellmeister 1874-1884.

4. She did not leave.

5. Borsdorfer apples. A type of apple with a sweetish winish flavor.

6. Marie Wilt (1833-1891), a Viennese soprano as famous for the opulence of her person as of her voice. She was the Donna Elvira of the performance of *Don Giovanni* that opened the new opera house in 1869, and she created the role of Sulamith in Goldmark's *The Queen of Sheba*. She committed suicide by jumping from a fourth-story window.

7. *Grün* is German for green.

8. Wolf offers no authority for this statement, but Beethoven did, in a letter to the publisher Simrock dated September 13, 1822, describe the "Missa Solemnis" as "possibly the greatest |work | I have written."

9. Stanford's Serenade Brahms's "Tragic" Overture

March 16, 1884

The Philharmonic concert on the 9th of this month brought among other things, unfortunately, a novelty by C. V. Stanford, a Serenade in Five Sections for Large Orchestra.[1] All that was missing to put the audience in a proper evening serenade mood, aside from some Turkish music,[2] was the four Wagner tubas and maybe four bells. It is truly astonishing to what extent, and without rhyme or reason, our modern composers defy the boundaries of musical resource and form. The usual rationalization is that such are the consequences of Wagnerian music. It has turned the youngsters' heads. No one can function any longer without a big orchestra, and so on.

(To all those who utter such nonsense we urge them to open Volume X of Richard Wagner's collected writings | *Gesammelte Schriften und Dichtungen* | and have a long, hard look at the essay, "Über das Dichten und Komponieren" (On Poetry and Composition), and since nothing is gained by half measures, to give commensurate attention to the next chapter, "About Operatic Poetry and Composition in Particular." Above all, however, let all composers now living and writing (Liszt is the only exception), before tearing their hair and gazing vacantly into space, lost in thought, recall these two essays or, if they have not already read them, make their acquaintance immediately, lest there be another disaster. Herr Stanford, had he followed this admonition, would have behaved like a gentleman, and dropped the idea of composing a serenade, just as many a symphony would never have merged from the dark womb of oblivion into the sunlight, always assuming that we are dealing with honorable musicians who had been thus persuaded to honor truth and not deception and pretence.)

No one is compelled to confess his weaknesses in public for all the world to hear. If one cannot compose, let him make his own adjustment to that fact. He can even claim to be a composer for all I care, but as an artful politician he dare not let the claim be put to the test. As Susanna puts it in *The Marriage of Figaro*, "To prove that I were right would be to concede that I could be wrong."[3] But what else do our modern composers tell us in their works than that they cannot compose? It must be either an especially agreeable sensation or a horrible delusion that prompts our modern composers to expose themselves to the public in all their odious nakedness. The miserable shred of an operetta tune would at least give them some cover, but they prefer to present themselves naked like the flayed Marsyas.[4] Truly, they arouse our compassion, and, as incurable invalids possessed of an *idée fixe* that they can compose, we shall detain them under the scalpel no longer.

In order to rectify such twisted notions, just recall, for example, the "Siegfried Idyll." That's a very serious piece, certainly not composed just for the fun of it. Look at the orchestra: one flute, one oboe, one clarinet, one bassoon, one horn, one trumpet and the string quartet. Does it not sound lovely even without any doubling of the winds? Without the other four horns and two trumpets? Without tympani? What a concise, homogeneous form, to say nothing of the substance! Could this piece have been called anything but an idyll? And wherein lies this striking characteristic? In the fact that Wagner, at the time, had no intention of writing a symphony and, in case of failure, of promptly baptizing the result an idyll. He simply wanted to write an idyll and nothing else. He conjured up the vision of an idyll, and to the extent that he saw this vision clearly, so it works on the listener's sensibilities. The listener would not even need the designation, "idyll," to recognize inescapably a mood of that character.

Who, however, would divine a serenade in the Stanford novelty, even when it is so designated in the program? The woodwinds moan, the timpani boom, the brass shriek, the hairs fly from the fiddle bows like spirit apparitions in the air, and it requires truly little imagination to read out of it, if not the turmoil of the migration of nations, at least certain amiable episodes from it, such as the sack of Rome by the Vandals or something of that kind, vividly illustrated. What does all this silly uproar have to do with a serenade? We greatly fear that this serenade owes its crippled existence to a symphony gone wrong. To call so formless and empty a monstrosity a serenade simply because one permits oneself on this (shall I say?) cosmopolitan ground (where, these days, every dabbler sees in the serenade the most congenial and comfortable form in which to say nothing) to indulge to his heart's content in swollen phrases and banalities is an unholy, shameful misdemeanor, and one which revenges itself, moreover, on the composing miscreant. For whoever offers the public something unintelligible and absurd has no right to complain if he remains ununderstood and is rejected. This is what happened to the composer Stanford and his serenade, and it served him absolutely right.[5.]

Brahms's "Tragic" Overture reminds us vividly of the ghostly apparitions in Shakespeare's dramas who horrify the murderer by their presence while remaining invisible to everyone else. We know not what hero Brahms murdered in this overture, but let us assume that Brahms is Macbeth and the overture the embodiment of murder in the spirit of Banquo, whom, with the first down-bows falling like the blows of an axe, he is just murdering. In the course of the composition the ghost of his victim appears again and again, the blows of the axe reintroduce the motive of the murder as at the opening of the overture, reminding him pointedly of these events. Horrified, he turns away and seeks in feigned repose to pull himself together. Brahms-Macbeth expresses this excellently in a very stilted, artificial middle theme. This spectacle repeats itself until the end of the overture.

Now let us move from the ceremonial chamber of the royal palace to the concert hall of the Society of Friends of Music. The audience knows as little of the content of the "Tragic" Overture as Macbeth's retinue knows of his murderous deed. The overture begins. Axe blows or down-bows! Motive of the murder! Pangs of conscience! Banquo's ghost appears. Brahms-Macbeth groans and moans in the woodwinds. Why all the moaning and groaning, the audience asks? The ghost vanishes, and one hears the stilted middle theme. Brahms-Macbeth feigns composure and repose. Suddenly the ghost reappears, but the audience cannot grasp Macbeth's stammering and yammering, since it knows nothing of the murderous deed, and consequently does not see the ghost. Utterly in the dark about such embarrassing scenes, it would gladly withdraw. But Lady Macbeth enters in a guise of amiability, and addresses the audience as in Shakespeare: "Sit, worthy friends; my lord is often thus, and hath been from his youth; pray you, keep seat; the fit is momentary; upon a thought he will be well again: if much you note him, you shall offend him and extend his passion." The last sentence strikes us as containing much food for thought.

Aside from these two pieces, Beethoven's Violin Concerto was played by Herr Arnold Rosé with his characteristic purity and polish. The concert ended with Volkmann's fresh effervescent Symphony in B flat, an engaging, spontaneous composition without pretensions and without any special orchestral extravagance.

What keeps the piano virtuoso Busoni,[6] who commands a very find technic, from being a proper virtuoso, the pianist Vladimir de Pachmann[7] possesses in abundance. His touch is enchantingly beautiful. His playing is sometimes mannered, but it is always eminently rhythmical, as shown by his splendid reading of Schumann's Sonata in G minor. His true metier, however, is Chopin, whom he understands as none other after Rubinstein. Since the latter departed Vienna, de Pachmann has been the first pianist whose distinguished accomplishments could hold a spoiled audience continuously enthralled.

1. Sir Charles Villiers Stanford (1852-1924), Irish organist, composer, conductor and peda-

gogue, whose name is especially associated with the University of Cambridge, where he was professor of music from 1887 until his death, and with the Royal College of Music, where he was professor of composition from the time of its founding in 1883. He was knighted in 1901.

2. The term "Turkish music" was given to an early form of military band music inspired by Turkish janissaries, and featuring kettledrums, bass drums, tenor drums, cymbals, triangles, etc.

3. No such words are put into Susanna's mouth in Da Ponte's Italian original.

4. The mythical flutist who challenged Apollo to a musical contest, Apollo playing the lyre. Marsyas lost, and paid for his impudence by being tied to a pine tree and flayed.

5. Wolf was doubtless not unmindful of the fact that Brahms, composer of two serenades, one of them "for full orchestra," had received an honorary doctorate at a concert at Cambridge directed by Stanford as director of the Cambridge University Musical Society in 1877.

6. Ferruccio Busoni (1866-1924), who had attracted Hanslick's attention when he appeared as a child prodigy in Vienna at the age of nine.

7. Vladimir de Pachmann (1848-1933), Russian pianist, then (1884) reaching the peak of a notable career. His affinity for Chopin, noted by Wolf, and certain amiable eccentricities, led to his becoming known as the "Chopinzee."

10. Il Matrimonio Segreto
Brahms's Quintet in F

March 23, 1884

Cimarosa's *Il Matrimonio Segreto,* recently revived at the Court Opera, is no more viable than Piccini's *Dido* or Paisiello's *Cosa rara,*[1] two contemporaries of Cimarosa. The memory of all of them is obscured by the sun of Mozart's genius.

Mozart is, in a certain sense, related to them artistically, although not to be numbered exclusively among the Italians. He shares with Cimarosa and his countrymen the Italian vivacity, the unaffected charm and the light flow of musical declamation, but the Italians could never have written a *Die Zauber-flöte,* which could only proceed from the spiritual depths of the Germans. That Mozart could make the best aspects of Italian operatic procedure his own was in no way an infringement of his German nature. Cimarosa, on the other hand, seems to have concerned himself with Mozart, with consequences both agreeable and disagreeable — disagreeable for the composer, to whom many a pretty inspiration from *The Marriage of Figaro* occured while composing *Il Matrimonio Segreto* (for *The Marriage of Figaro* was written seven years before *Il Matrimonio Segreto*), agreeable for the public, who would rather hear a wealth of Mozartean reminiscences than the boundless accumulations of old-fashioned phrases by Cimarosa.

We find the composer of *Il Matrimonio Segreto* far more interesting as a forerunner of Rossini, especially in the comedy scenes, in the first finale, in the duet between Geronimo and the Count, etc. There he is thoroughly original, witty and astonishingly skillful. In those pieces we catch a breath of that intoxicating fragrance we inhale with so much pleasure in *The Barber of Seville*. It's curious. Only where Cimarosa reminds us of Mozart and Rossini does he excite our interest; only then does he reveal himself as an inventive mind, although this only questionably so with regard to Mozart.

Herr Hofkapellmeister Fuchs would have been better advised to let the *secco* recitatives be offered as spoken dialogue rather than add an orchestral accompaniment to the tasteless singsong. The individual musical numbers would then figure more prominently and, in any case, work more refreshingly than is now the case. Among the performers Herr Mayerhofer,[2] especially, won plaudits for his delightful characterization of the deaf Geronimo. Herr Horwitz,[3] as the Count, discharged his assignment with much skill. Fräulein Braga (Lisette) and Fräulein Meisslinger[4] (Aunt) carried their parts off well. Fräulein Lehman could do with a bit more flexibility as Carolina. Herr Walter (Paolino) could as well have been playing a nutcracker as a tender lover. One does not master a role with grimaces and hoarseness.

The admirable Rosé Quartet brought its season to an uncommonly satisfactory close with an interesting program. After Robert Schumann's wonderful Quartet in F, Opus 41, one of the choicest pearls in the post-Beethoven literature of chamber music, came the Violin Sonata, Opus 19, of Rubinstein, played by Benno Schönberger[5] and Arnold Rosé. It is a piece like so many others from the pen of this composer, that promises well in the beginning and finally produces nothing of any account. The musical current that surges passionately through the first movement winds considerably more placidly in the dull open spaces of a rather parched fantasy in the Scherzo until, in the Adagio, it totally loses itself in the sand. Then, in the Finale, with spurs and whip, the composer goads his fantasy, without, however, expressing anything more than a confused puffing and blowing in a strenuous battle between piano and violin. Herr Schönberger is thoroughly at home as the interpreter of wanton and wasted effort. A soft, pliable touch is not to be numbered among his attributes. His specialty, certainly, is muscular display, which, bereft of all charm and malleability, is not designed to make a particularly favorable impression. This youthful pianist, with his musical temperament, may, in time, ripen into a sound master if, instead of losing himself in externals, he would delve into the nature of the musical art.

From the tangle of wild disorder into which the Rubinstein sonata had charmed us, we arrived, with the opening measures of Brahm's Quintet in F, Opus 88, in a delightful, open, sunny meadow where, guided by the knowledgeable composer, all went very well indeed. What we have heard of Brahm's recent works has left us rather cold. Some of it has been absolutely repulsive, especially the symphonies, which have been canonized by certain critics in such a manner that one could only regret their bad taste, their blindness, if one did not know that "personality" constitutes the spectacles through which a work of art is viewed, and according to which it is assessed. It is well to distinguish whether the works of a living composer are regarded by a benevolent or a hostile eye. The critic is, after all, only human, and subject to personal influences. But in the end he is still a critic, and as such he has no business expressing his friendship for the author by immoderate praise of his tortured products while inversely, and from contrary motives, smearing inspired composition with odious slander. One gets at the truth by roundabout ways, but one must get to it eventually, unless, of course, one prefers to deceive the public, as big a crime as, for example, the hoodwinking of a wise and worthy police.

Returning from these digressive general observations to the Brahms Quintet, the first movement impresses us as the most beautiful. The composer's fantasy revels only in picturesque images. The chilly November fog that usually hangs over his compositions, stifling every warm utterance before it has a chance to be heard — of this not a trace here. Everything is sunny, now brighter, now more shaded. An enchanting emerald green envelops this fairyland spring vision. Everything is verdant and budding. One actually hears the grass growing — all of nature so mysteriously still, so blissfully radiant. It was only by forcing himself in a moment of quick decision that the composer was able to free himself of this enchantment, so firmly did the muse hold him in her spell. In the second movement the shadows lengthen. Evening and, gradually, night veil the fantastic vision of the wondrous life revealed in the first movement. Deep meditation and silence. A lively, delightful picture pervades the profound solitude. It is as if glowworms were dancing their rounds, so glowing and sparkling is the rushing instrumental figuration. But the picture vanishes. The previous stillness returns, only to be interrupted by a similar motif. The mysterious tone picture evaporates in eerie harmonies, modulating between dreaming and waking. But now the composer, who, for two movements, has yielded to the intoxications of floral fragrance, seems suddenly to have become ill at ease in the magic garden of romanticism, for with a sudden lurch he seats himself at the school bench in Altona, joyfully reminding himself in the Finale of his contrapuntal studies with Marxsen.[6] We have no wish to follow him thither. This quintet strikes us as a splendid companion piece to the lovely Sextet in G, and we are grateful to Herr Rosé for offering it to us in a finely understood performance.

The Hellmesberger Quartet would have done well to let the blessed Herbeck[7] rest in peace. Herbeck did great things for the musical life of Vienna. That is all true and most commendable. But to think of honoring his memory with a performance of his String Quartet in F is no favor to the late Herbeck, nor will it persuade the public to treasure him more greatly or love him more fervently. Herbeck was an accomplished musician, but not even a mediocre composer. For composition he lacked the most rudimentary craftsmanship, not to speak of any special talent. Dvořák's new Piano Trio in F minor is not without some interesting moments. The second movement especially, given a Bohemian physiognomy by a folk tune, stands above the others. The last movement, because of its rhythmic monotony, has a sheerly soporific effect. Only with the opening measures of the Beethoven String Quartet did music-sated spirits awake, especially when Hellmesberger played the Adagio with his characteristic sweetness and warmth, excellently supported by his colleagues. That Herr Hellmesberger, however, has moved his quartet into the Grosser Musikvereinssaal remains an inexcusable absurdity, however large the audience.

1. The composer of *Una Cosa Rara* was not Paisiello, but Vicente Martin y Soler (1756-1806). It was produced in Vienna in 1786, and Mozart quotes an air from it in the supper music in *Don Giovanni*. The *Dido* of Nicola Piccini (1728-1800), a composer better remembered for his rivalry with Gluck in Paris, was produced in Vienna in 1783.

2. Karl Mayerhofer (1828-1913), a Viennese, the company's leading basso buffo over a span of forty years (1854-1895). At the time of his retirement he was reckoned to have taken part in some 4,000 performances.

3. Willibald Horwitz (1843-1903), a Bohemian baritone who sang leading roles at the Court Opera from 1879 to 1900. He was also active as composer, conductor and pedagogue.

4. Louise Meisslinger (1861 ?), a Viennese, only briefly (1883-1886) with the company.

5. Benno Schönberger (1863-1930), a Viennese virtuoso who settled in London in 1887, where he taught at the Royal Academy of Music while continuing as a public performer.

6. Eduard Marxsen (1806-1887), with whom Brahms studied in the Hamburg suburb of Altona.

7. Johann Herbeck (1831-1877), a Viennese, conductor of the concerts of the Society of Friends of Music (1859-1870 and 1875-1877) and Director of the Court Opera (1870-1875).

11. *Berlioz's* King Lear
A Stagione

March 30, 1884

At last, at last, we have had a performance of Hector Berlioz's Overture to *King Lear*,[1] announced year in, year out, but hitherto always postponed. Now, for the first time, we saw this monster of musical ingenuity unfold its gigantic frame, which already had fairly scared us out of our wits in the piano score. With its awesome demonic eyes, the one cocked at Germany, the other at France, it fascinates the listener as the rattlesnake fascinates the rabbit. Berlioz draws truly magic circles around the listener, holding him with uncanny power in the spell of the musical structure until the last tone has died away. Restored to human awareness, the listener may feel as if he were awakening from a deep wild dream that had borne him over black abysses, over deserts and primevil forests, over volcanos and icebergs, even fleetingly over luxurient flower gardens — but exhausted and drained, and with no desire to hear any more music.

Haydn's Symphony in D, which came next, had a disturbing rather than refreshing effect upon the audience's receptivity. Two muses so blatantly contrasted as those of Haydn and Berlioz do not go well together. The listener is still too intoxicated from the exotic fragrance of Berlioz's music to relish immediately and consciously the fresh, clear air wafted toward us from Haydn's works.

Although Berlioz's *King Lear* Overture contains wonderful moments, we do not find in it a psychological portrait in the manner of Beethoven's *Coriolanus* Overture or Wagner's *Faust* Overture or the Overture to Schumann's *Manfred*. Granted, the exalted figure of King Lear is much more difficult to grasp psychologically than a Coriolanus, whose essential nature is rigid, intractable independence, an iron will and stubborn pride. It is more difficult than the figure of Faust in that sombre, brooding mood described in Goethe's verses, and which Wagner took as the nucleus of his musical conception. And it is more difficult than the figure of Manfred, who, consumed by the tortures of an awful guilt, sets forgiveness by Astarte and release from life as his only objectives.

These are all sharply profiled characters, formed out of their innermost nature — defiant, reflective, misanthropic — not as a result of circumstances, but because nature fashioned them thus. In the inevitable contact with the world, however, there entered into their lives from outside a factor that, through the utmost conceivable contrast, worked on them with such appalling force that, in the struggle between the two, the tragic conflict, and, from that conflict, the tragic end were foreordained. Thus, for Coriolanus, the pleading woman was fateful when he uncharacteristically yielded to the pitiable entreaties of mother and wife. Similarly fateful for Faust was the suddenly wakened sensual impulse suggesting to him that in the intoxication of pleasureable indulgence he might find the truest insight. He summoned the devil until, finally, the devil appeared twenty-four years later (reckoning the year at 365 days), as the *Faust* puppet play has it, to take Faust home as a tasty roast soul.

Now, what Manfred suffered for his sister, Astarte, who shattered his whole being to its very foundations, is hardly to be encompassed in an overture. And still, Schumann's overture tells us just as much as Byron's three-act poem. Yes! And even had the poem been extended to ten or twenty acts, Schumann's music, in the overture as it is composed, would still have completely exhausted the lyrical substance musically. In the simplest strokes Schumann had expressed plastically the core, the focal point of the drama.

In *King Lear*, on the other hand, what a range of emotions — from the mighty ruler still in possession of all his faculties to the demented beggar who, even in this lamentable condition, reckons himself every inch a king. To find here, and sustain, the fundamental tone would be an unprecedented masterstroke of musical invention and structural genius. Only a Beethoven or a Wagner, probably, might have managed to master a subject so coyly elusive of purely musical treatment. Of one thing I am certain: Berlioz was not the man for the job. The *King Lear* Overture is vastly imaginative in its conception, delightfully melodious, especially in the two middle themes of the introduction and the following Allegro, and brilliantly orchestrated. The development is sometimes distorted, confused, but always bold, always interesting, always gripping, exciting, astonishing, often even irresistible — "But, but, but, and here comes the joker," says Busch,[2] and the joker here is the negative fact that this piece, just described, is not by any manner or means an overture to *King Lear*, if only because with Shakespeare anything goes better than an effort to be artistic, fanciful, bizarre, formless and interesting. If the Overture to *King Lear* does not measure up to the ultimate requirements of art, however, it is still exactly as we have described it, and in our time especially, when good old mediocrity is more widespread than ever, a so madly ingenious piece as this of Berlioz is a purifying shaft of lightning beneath the leaden, sultry cloud masses bursting in our concert halls in the form of new overtures and symphonies.

About the Overture to *The Wedding of Camacho*[3] there is less to be said than of the Overture to *King Lear*. Mendelssohn, in this overture, written in his sixteenth year, gave evidence of a precocious talent. The composition is fresh, amiable, pleasing, and just as clear and transparent as his later masterpieces written in his twenties. Finally, there remains to mention Fräulein Clotilde Kleeberg,[4] who played Schumann's Piano Concerto in A minor very delicately. She was cordially received.

> Italien! Italien!
> Was hast du für Kanaillen?
> Da werd' ein anderer froh.
>
> | Italy! Italy!
> What a rabble you have!
> Let others delight in you! |

Since this enthusiastic characterization of Italy (in a poem by Robert Reinick)[5] does not, fortunately, apply to the *stagione*, nor refer to the police or any other juridical body or political authority of the Italian Kingdom, but rather to a citizenry, principally in the south, which is more odious to the most innocent people than a German to the Frenchman, and whose generic designation conspicuously rhymes with the adjective *froh* | glad |[6] — since, with all that, we are adequately absolved of any infamous suspicion, so let the Italian *stagione* begin, with *William Tell* in the lead. A large audience attended this performance, sometimes singing along with it, sometimes applauding.

In Italy, where only Italian music is performed, one may be charmed by the grotesque operatic vocalism and the extravagent gesticulation of Italian singers. It is more important there to sing effectively than to sing beautifully, and gestures support the sound rather than the text. Thus an Italian singer will relate the most shattering occurrence with unexampled composure if there is no high B or C in prospect. But let the composer provide suitable opportunity for laryngeal exercise, and the most commonplace situation will excite the same singer to demonstrations of concern and agitation more or less farcical depending upon the vocal display involved.

To the Italian *rabbia*, the most insidious villain singing the most sinister vengeance aria, and the most sentimental lover uttering the tenderest lyrical effusions, are all one. The high notes are decisive. The plot is of no concern to the Italian singer *eo ipso,* and even the individual recitatives, arias and concerted pieces interest him only insofar as they provide adequately for the requisite vocal display. The singer wants to bellow or whisper, and the audience will be bellowed at or whispered to. There is mutual understanding, and no one should be astonished by an intimacy, however coarse, between one side of the footlights and the other that permits, for example, a singer just slain in combat on the stage to be revived by the wonder drug of applause, take his mortal enemy's arm in his own, advance to the footlights, join him in humble acknowledgment of the audience's gracious expressions of esteem, and then, once quiet has been restored, fall furiously upon his newly found friend and, fortunately, do him in, whereupon the mutual endearments of singer and audience begin all over again, and continue as long as both sides enjoy it.

We take these grotesque procedures for granted, as we have said, on an Italian stage before an Italian audience, touching in its naiveté. The German, assuming that he is not stupid, thinks it all amusing and not ill-suited to good, clean fun. (Let's be clear about it: we are talking not about Italian music, for which we have due respect, and especially for a *William Tell,* but only about the Italian singer as such, and insofar as he is also an actor. But that one can sit there with an expression on his face as if he were experiencing a holy of holies! That shows us with what feelings this public attends a German performance: just as prim and respectful — and just as inattentive and indifferent. Our German singers may be anything but actors (there are some exceptions), but they still harbor, thanks to Richard Wagner's healing influence, a spark of artistic intelligence, sobriety and emotion.

Now, back to the Italians. The tenor Mierzwinski,[7] a native Pole schooled in the Italian manner, is the center of attention. Fame has told such wondrous tales of his achievements that it was not surprising if our expectations were somewhat disappointed. He has a light, appealing top, of agreeable timbre, but without any special brilliance. He is less successful in *cantilena* than in the heroic and the emphatic, especially in the recitatives. In the second and third acts he had truly imposing moments, and they aroused a storm of applause.

Signor Aldighieri[8] (William Tell) is familiar to us as an admirable bass-baritone. We had had an opportunity three years ago to make his acquaintance as a capable singer. Signor Gasperini did not look at all a Walter Fürst as we usually picture him, but with his villain-bass he came out of the affair honorably. Thoroughly unsatisfactory, however, was Signora Malvezzi in the role of Mathilde. She is unlikely to enjoy any particular success in any other role, and for the simple reason that she has no voice. The other participants, recruited from soloists of our Court Opera, managed with the Italian text quite well. Signor Bimboni,[9] the distinguished conductor, directed the opera with the utmost spirit, and was enthusiastically applauded following a fiery performance of the overture.

Less rewarding was the following evening, when two novelties, were introduced. Herr Bachrich,[10] who for about a year now has been "taking" composition, or "prescribing" it |he had once been an apothecary|, and in his new opera, *Der Heini von Steier* | Heini from Styria| has set off in the new direction which brings one to one's destination only via the most tortuous detours of odd modulations, enjoyed an uncommonly cordial reception from the connoisseurs and a segment of the rest of the audience. We would, however, advise the new-directed (as Wagner so trenchantly labelled this type of composer) not to develop so much "direction" in such trifles, involving no more than the duration and the substance of one act. Disconcerting harmonies, muted and divided violins with harp and glockenspiel, etc., etc. should be reserved for more appropriate occasions, such as, for example, if Richard Kralik[11] were to write a Bühnenweihfestspiel | Consecrational Festival Drama, the designation given by Wagner to *Parsifal* | and assign the composition of the music to Herr Bachrich (although the musically active poet might absolve this task himself, since he has already grasped the prohibition of open fifths and octaves). The incredibly banal text by Herr Wittmann,[12] which may soon pose a threat to the poems of Richard Kralik, extends to its musical confederate a sisterly hand. Music and poetry most intimately related and united — what a consoling glimpse of the music of the future! O, Wagner!

1. Opus 4 (1831).
2. Wilhelm Busch (1831-1908), poet, philosopher and caricaturist, creator (1858) of the now proverbial (in the German-speaking world) Max and Moritz.
3. A two-act opera to a libretto by August Klingemann (1777-1831) on an episode in *Don Quixote*, produced in Berlin on April 29, 1827. There was only one performance.
4. Clotilde Kleeberg (1866-1909), a French pianist, highly regarded in her time.
5. Robert Reinick (1805-1852), a poet-painter of the Biedermeier period.
6. i.e., *Floh* (flea). The poem, "Das Herrlein in Italien" (The Little Gentleman in Italy), one of Reinick's *Romanzen und Balladen*, tells us how this German traveler, journeying from city to city, and finding little good to say about the Italians or anything Italian, is confronted everywhere by a voracious flea. Upon his return to Germany, he tells of nothing but the sound of mandolins, orange groves, folk music, Torlonia and the Vatican. His listeners are enthralled — and there is no flea to bite him!
7. Wladislaw Mierzwinski (1850-1909) had a considerable international career. The English

critic, Hermann Klein, said of him that had his art been as good as his voice "he would have escaped declining favor and a regrettable fate in after-years." He became a hotel porter in Nice.

8.   Gottardo Aldighieri (1824-1906) created the role of Barnaba in *La Gioconda* in 1876. The words of Luigi Arditi's "Il bacio" are dedicated to him.

9.   Oreste Bimboni (1846-1905) was one of the ranking Italian conductors of the time. He was one of Colonel Mapleson's conductors in London and on his American tours.

10. Siegmund Bachrich (1841-1913) was first violist of the orchestra of the Court Opera and of the Philharmonic. He was also violist, first of the Hellmesberger, and later of the Rosé Quartet.

11. Richard Kralik (1852-1934), philosopher, historian and poet, dreamed of reviving medieval mystery plays. He did, in 1893, produce a Weihnachtsfestspiel (Christmas festival).

12. Hugo Wittmann (1839-1923), a German journalist and musician, had come to Vienna via Paris in 1872. In Paris he had been correspondent for the *Neue Freie Presse*, whose editor he became after settling in Vienna. He was the author of many comedies, operetta libretti and short stories.

12. Mierzwinski — and Others — Sing Il Trovatore Ladies in the Moonlight Friedheim Plays Liszt

April 6, 1884

Il Trovatore will be repeated, primarily in order that we may hear again, as at the last performance, a succession of those high notes with which Signor Mierzwinski favors the *stagione* audiences so generously. "Bon appetit," one feels like calling to the parterre, to whom every B and C from Mierzwinski's throat seems at least as savory as a fresh, succulent oyster.

Just watch them in that sublime moment when the tenor gazes down ecstatically from the beatific heights of his C or C sharp. They click their tongues in delight, pat their bellies contentedly. They become real frog's legs under the influence of Herr Mierzwinski's galvanic column of Memnon.¹ The ambitious among them attempt to imitate him, singing in the same register; the more modest opt for the safer terrain of the octave below; the true enthusiast, however, sings along pantomimically (a sign of great emotion), separating the upper and lower jaws according to the height and duration of the attacked tones — a silly business, but one that may well afford more pleasure than Verdi's *Il Trovatore* — or even Mierzwinski's.

Things have a more earnest appearance in the concert halls. Fräulein Soldat,[2] most admirably supported by Fräulein Baumaier[3] with incidental piano offerings, revealed herself in Spohr's Violin Concerto in the Form of a Scene and Aria[4] an outstanding artist on her instrument. A full, warm tone combined with a thoroughly schooled dexterity and, beyond that, a fine musical sensibility — that is more than we have been provided heretofore by violin-playing ladies. We salute in her a true artist, and look forward to hearing her soon again.

Now really, the C sharp minor sonata again! Is it no longer possible for a pianist to get by without moonlight? The "Moonlight" Sonata, played by Fräulein Clotilde Kleeberg! By her, of all people? Yes, of course, certainly by her, on whom so much applause was expended for her playing of Schumann's Concerto in A minor at the recent Philharmonic concert. Why? She did not play it badly, and would have been awarded the first prize at the Conservatory for it. So, and what more? Not bad, that's all. But one can play the A minor concerto beautifully, indeed, very beautifully, and still play the C sharp minor sonata very badly. If in this marvelous sonata the moon must shine, I recognized in Fräulein Kleeberg's performance only the dark spots and the silly grimace they form. Signora Cognetti has recently committed the ghastly deed of playing the C sharp minor sonata, and now Mademoiselle Kleeberg follows her with similar lack of success. One must be both musician and poet to avoid disturbing the moonlit dream of the first movement. Fräulein Kleeberg is neither the one nor the other, as one noted, too, in her dry playing of two uncommonly poetic pieces by Schumann, "Des Abends" and "Traumeswirren," which she muffed completely. She played quite nicely some smaller pieces by Mendelssohn, Schubert, Henselt and Chopin.

In this same recital Frau Nicklass-Kempner sang some Lieder as well as the recitative and aria of Susanna from *The Marriage of Figaro*. This singer, whom we have had the opportunity of hearing on several occasions, knows how to achieve great effects with modest means. She sings extremely tastefully, her tones go to the heart, she feels what she sings, and her voice, not notably lovely in itself, sounds soft and round as soon as she gives it a particular expression. Such are the true singers, not the shouters or the whisperers, the one as revolting as the other.

If we think of Liszt as the lion of the piano, and of Rubinstein as the tiger, then the young virtuoso Arthur Friedheim is the panther. As such he is inwardly closer to Rubinstein than to Liszt, although more drawn to the latter, as a glance at the program will show.

Like Rubinstein, he never for an instant allows the piano out of his gaze, but eyes it greedily. That is how tigers and panthers are with their prey. Liszt and his imitator de Pachmann, on the other hand, seem rather to go strolling during a performance, letting their gaze wander where it will, anywhere but up and down the keyboard. That is how lions toy with their victims. Rubinstein and Friedheim seize theirs by the throat. And they have the same cat-like nimbleness. The tiger, however, has the softer paws, much softer than the panther, and these would stand Friedheim in good stead.

It was a happy thought of his to play only Liszt. It would do the Philharmonic no harm to play an all-Liszt program just once, or all-Berlioz, instead of serving up the same old fare over and over again, varying only the sequence. That it is possible to listen to a whole evening of Liszt's compositions without a sense of fatigue can be attested by everyone who heard Friedheim's last recital. Any nagging doubt would have been dispelled had he seen fit to reduce by half the six Consolations, which are all of the same character, often in the same key and in deliberate tempi, and which simply cannot be numbered among the master's best works.

How deeply Friedheim has penetrated to the heart of Liszt's piano music was so wonderfully demonstrated in the inspired eccentricities of the Sonata in B minor, in the Rhapsodies Nos. 9 and 13, in the Consolations, the two transcriptions and so on that to describe his astonishing accomplishment could only be to degrade it.

The most appalling difficulties are child's play to him. Never, except with Liszt and Rubinstein, have we witnessed a fabulously cultivated wrist execute such *tours de force*. One had scarcely recovered from one astonishment when one was astonished anew. He is the Liszt interpreter *par excellence*. If he could just come to terms with himself and penetrate into the spirit of Beethoven, that mastery would be within his grasp to which his restless ambition will open the way, and the genius that is his endowment would lift him to the summit.[5]

1. In the Nile. It was said to produce a sound similar to the snapping of a harp string when struck by the first rays of the rising sun. Memnon was the son of Aurora. The frogs' legs metaphor and the adjectival "galvanic" derive from Luigi Galvani (1737-1798), of Bologna, who experimented on frogs in investigating muscular reaction to electrical stimulus.

2. Marie Soldat (1863-1955), a Styrian violinist, pupil of Joachim in Berlin. She formed a female string quartet in Berlin in 1887, and another in Vienna in 1889. She was especially noted for her playing of Brahms.

3. Marie Baumeier, or Baumayer (1851- ?), a Styrian pianist, pupil of Clara Schumann, a close friend of Brahms, and the first, after Brahms himself, to play the Concerto in B flat in public (in Graz).

4. The Violin Concerto No. 8, in A, Opus 47, more familiarly known to violinists simply as "Gesangsszene" from the fact that it was composed in the form of a *scena ed aria* for Spohr's tour of Italy in 1816.

5. Hanslick, reviewing a performance by Friedheim of Beethoven's Concerto in C minor in the previous season, has left us an amusing description of the young virtuoso: "(He) is truly Arthurian in appearance, is slender, pale, interesting, affects a stonily indifferent countenance and very long hair that falls over his face like a thick veil when he bows — a spectacle in which the audience found much affectionate amusement. During the orchestral introduction the virtuoso reclines, deeply imbedded in the easy chair as if he were already exhausted before having begun, and touching his forehead from time to time as if trying to recall what it is that he has to play, or to determine if he is still of this world. But with the first solo entrance he swoops down upon the keys like a vulture from above, ascending again after each mighty chord . . . ." Hanslick, too, had reservations about his playing of Beethoven.

13. Schubert and Beethoven — and Brahms Berlioz's "Grande Messe Des Morts"

April 13, 1884

With the last concerts of the Philharmonic Orchestra and the Society of Friends of Music the musical season dies a natural death. Such concerts as yet lie in store lead an illusory existence, there being no further good reason to make music or listen to it. Reawakening nature now summons the enthusiast to her realm with an enchantment more compelling than that of the loveliest music in the musty concert hall. The song of the birds, the buzzing of beetles, the cheerful murmur of the brook, the soft song of balmy spring breezes, all the mysterious stirring and heaving of the newly decked earth — what heavenly music! One need not be a subscriber or a Founder to hear such music, nor be at any certain place at any certain time. And one is spared the distracted, gaping, captious, insensitive neighbor. One simply goes off one day with Eichendorff:

> ⌊So jubelnd recht in die hellen,
> In die singenden, klingenden Wellen
> Des vollen Frühlings hinaus!

> So, joyously off into the bright,
> Singing, sounding waves of
> High spring!¹⌋

The attentive ear will be greeted by symphonies, hymns, songs and choruses such as no man has ever contrived. And so music, the heavenly queen, remains through summer and winter alike a cherished, faithful companion!

But once again to the Grosser Musikvereinssaal. It was more or less familiar matter that the Philharmonic offered in their last concert. We welcomed such pieces the more affectionately as the charm of eternal youth and beauty makes them appear ever fresh and new. Schubert's Symphony in B minor, a faithful mirror of its creator's artistic individuality, is, alas, but a fragment! Thus its form resembles the composer's own mortal life, cut off by death in the bloom of his life, at the summit of his creative power. Schubert lived only half a mortal span, both as man and as artist. His lifetime endured just long enough to complete two symphonic movements, perfect in form and substance. We possess in the Symphony in C major, to be sure, a precious testament; but all the flowering richness of its invention, all its luxuriant melodic charm, cannot blind us to the looseness of its symphonic structure. The Symphony in B minor is not only more concise, more uniform in structure, than the Symphony in C major; in its themes the dramatic Schubert speaks to us just as persuasively as the elegiac dreamer. In it he presents himself as completely as in the songs, in which, to be sure, he achieved the utmost. But the B minor Symphony has remained a fragment, and spiteful death put an end to Schubert's ambition to follow in the Titan Beethoven's footsteps with that success which signals from a tempting distance the achievement of the noble objective.[2]

As if by agreement between muses and fates, the fruitful isle of song was Schubert's birthright from the former, to be transformed by the bubbling spring of his melodies, in the short span of his mortal existence, into a fabulous magic garden whose freshness and fragrance will never, never fade. From this enchanted island he now beheld the giant Beethoven crossing the ocean in the storm, defying the elements in his furious passage. Then was the islander's heart seized by a mighty urge. To follow Beethoven in his desolate and dangerous course was now Schubert's only thought. But that was hard, for the Titan loved to sail among rocks, sandbanks, reefs and whirlpools and surf. And if he made for the open sea, he surged ahead on the wings of the storm, calling down thunder and lightning, a god annihilating with a mere glance whomever he encountered.

In quieter moments, when the death-defying voyager surrendered himself to the billowing play of the soft swell and took his ease, there appeared in the distance a flower-decked craft, and in it the amiable islander, observing with awe and astonishment the strange deportment of this sea monster. The latter, sensing an intruder, sailed off, ill-humored and morose. Such repeated attempts to approach the other had a profound effect upon the cheerful islander. He tended his garden industriously; but he also grew more accustomed to the ocean, surviving many a storm in his little boat, managing many a tricky passage through the cliffs and reefs. He aspired to become a true sailor, and he would have succeeded, but — he died —.

How far Schubert fell short of his idol was evident in the concluding number of this concert, Beethoven's Fifth Symphony. What Schubert lacked was the ripeness of maturity. We know that Beethoven wrote his first symphony after attaining his thirtieth year, just as we know, too, that Schubert died at the age of 31. Our famous symphonist, on the other hand, is half a century old. From this we may assume that it was high time to title his third symphony, in F, *Eroica*, while Volkmann's Symphony in D minor is still ticketed as "characterless." How much difference a title makes! I am glad that Volkmann did not straight away call his Overture to *Richard III* a "Tragic Overture" and thus avenge himself for what was denied him in the symphony.

The Overture to *Richard III* reveals an endowment so touched with genius that only the most hopeless delusion can put a "Tragic Overture" by its side. In this one overture Volkmann shows his superiority over all the orchestral works of our famous symphonist, not to mention his Symphony in D minor, a masterpiece of the first rank, and of which one takes as good as no notice whatsoever, or writes it off, derisively, as run-of-the-mill. Where, now, is criticism? There remains to mention the attractive Overture to Spohr's *Jessonda*, played, as was everything, else, with the expected precision and delicacy, and we have done, for the time being, with the Philharmonic.

At the concert of the Society of Friends of Music on Tuesday of Holy Week, Berlioz's "Grande Messe des Morts" was performed with the same perfection as last year. Our most heartfelt thanks to the conductor, Herr Gericke, for the reprise of this immense work. It is the last time we shall encounter him in the concert hall.[3] We lose more in him than he in us. It was a feat ·to have performed the Berlioz Requiem. It was under his distinguished leadership that this happened, last year, for the first time. What other fascinating and marvelous works of Berlioz might we not have heard had Gericke been so honored according to his deserts that he would not have felt compelled to leave? But to the Viennese a Strauss waltz is preferable to, for example, *The Damnation of Faust*, and so in us he loses nothing. And yet, if the Requiem, because of its four orchestras, was regarded as only a curiosity, and if the audience, accordingly, allowed its ears to be blown at, well, that was that, for everything else, in the eyes of the majority, was only dull stuff. We heartily wish Herr Gericke good fortune in his long journey to the land where no nightingales sing.

At the big concert for the benefit of the German Charitable Association we heard Signor Mierzwinski sing a song by Tosti and the "Sicilienne" from *Robert le Diable*, which he had to repeat. Frau Lucca[4] sang an aria from Ponchielli's *La Gioconda*, which also was encored (as dull and tedious as it is), along with a song by the opera singer Horwitz (an infinitely amiable composition addressed to the Christian forbearance of the listeners), sung to thunderous applause. Herr Burmester played Liszt's Hungarian Rhapsody No. 13, feebly and unimpressively, and Schubert's "Wanderer" Fantasy with orchestra accompaniment not much better. Four pupils of Herr Hellmesberger, Jr., played very nicely a disarming composition of their excellent teacher, who accompanied the violin quartet at the piano. His charges acquitted themselves well. Composer, accompanist and teacher in one person, and the youthful quartet, were enthusiastically applauded. The concert delighted the audience, and why not? Mierzwinski is now the watchword!

1.   From "Frühlingsfahrt" | Spring Journey |, by Eichendorff, set by Schumann as his Opus 45, No. 2. Wolf here quotes Schumann rather than Eichendorff, who does not say "in *die*."

2.   The German syntax of this sentence is troublesome: "Aber die H-moll-Symphonie ist ein

Bruchstück geblieben, und dem Streben Schuberts, den Spuren des titanischen Beethoven mit jenem Erfolge nachzugehen, dem die Erreichung des hohen Zieles aus lockender Ferne winkt, hat der tückische Tod ein Ende gesetzt."

3.   A premature farewell, as Wolf acknowledges in a subsequent review.

4.   Pauline Lucca (1841-1908), born in Vienna of Italian parents, one of the greatest sopranos of her generation. An illustrious international career took her to all the great capitals of Europe and America in an astonishing variety of lyric and dramatic roles. She was as admired for her dramatic as for her vocal accomplishments.

14. A Dubious Stagione

April 20, 1884

The performance of *Gli Ugonotti | Les Huguenots |* had not at all the character of the *stagione*. Aside from Herr Mierzwinski and Fräulein Malvezzi, the participants were all local: German singers[1] singing in Italian. If you want to call that an Italian performance, you can accept, too, for better or worse, a Nevers sung in German by Herr Sommer.[2] Do Mierzwinski and Fräulein Malvezzi constitute a *stagione,* and with a Fräulein Malvezzi, moreover, who, with her threadbare, shrill voice suggests an Italian singer only in her misdemeanors? What a *stagione!*

Frau Lucca, a German dramatic soprano, numbers Valentine among her most celebrated roles. Whoever has heard Lucca knows what that means. Alongside her vibrant Valentine, Herr Mierzwinski's dry Raoul cut an almost miserable figure. Raoul, as is more or less true of any role, needs not only to be sung, but also to be acted, a fact utterly lost on Herr Mierzwinski. I would gladly have made him a present of every B flat, C and D flat for just one elegant, characteristic gesture. Mad generosity! What would a respectable audience have said about that, doing barter trade with others' ears! No, that would have been too monstrous even for a Tartar Khan, and still worse for a Christian music critic.

We found Fräulein Bianchi's dignified, tasteful singing uncommonly sympathetic. Herr Rokitansky sang Marcel gloriously. To Herr Sommer we recommend a good Italian diction teacher. He could take Herr Wiegand as a model, who sings pure Tuscan. Orchestra and chorus did their damnedest to throw each other off the beat. It was a long, bitter struggle, raging forward and backward inconclusively until the end. One was left in doubt whether the Huguenots were following the conductor or the conductor the Huguenots. One thing was clear. The Huguenots were not following the notes, and that was precarious.

Matters took a more Italianate course in *Lucia di Lammermoor* than in *Les Huguenots*, even without the indisposed Mierzwinski, for whom Signor Bertini[3] substituted in the role of Edgar. The latter is most favorably remembered from his visit to the Carl Theater last season. Fräulein Bianchi, too, was unwell, and it was a bit of luck that led the management to find a coloratura substitute in Fräulein Alt[4] from the German Theater in Prague. She has a most appealing voice and a flexible throat, and she knows a thing or two about acting. When one considers that she learned her part in Italian in only a few days, and that she undertook the role of Lucia only as a stopgap, her achievement was doubly deserving of the favorable opinion it earned simply on its own merits. Signor Salvati (Lord Arthur) is a rather provincial singer with no outstanding characteristics. Herr Schittenhelm and Herr Wiegand valiantly held their own with the guests.

The last quartet concert by the Hellmesbergers brought us among other items a novelty by Prince Heinrich XXIV Reuss.[5] The prince may well have intended to write a good quartet. If he failed, his fate was the reverse of Mephistopheles', "who always intends to do evil and ends by doing good." But such is the way of the world, and the prince may console himself in the knowledge that many, many others have fared no differently. Only the genius, the higher spiritual power, constitutes an exception to this rule, and that because nature and not circumstances takes a hand. The prince's string quartet moves not so much in a bourgeois as in a downright petit-bourgeois sphere. How insipid, how dreary this spurious first movement! The Scherzo is rhythmically brighter, if also weak in invention. But how desolate the Adagio, and thin the last movement! Let us say no more about it. Nothing is to be gained by detailed criticism. Frau Basch-Mahler[6] played the piano in Schumann's Quintet in E flat in such a way that she never got stuck or lost the beat. She made no mistakes and broke no strings. Everything went smoothly and vigorously, with military precision. Beethoven's Quartet in F minor brought the evening to a close. Every music lover knows how Hellmesberger plays Beethoven, but everyone knows, too, how badly every kind of chamber music comes off in the Grosser Musikvereinssaal. Herr Hellmesberger is his own worst enemy so long as he occupies the cursed hall with his puny forces. It is incredible that such a musician can behave so unmusically as to play quartets in the Grosser Musikvereinssaal. Maybe he will transfer his quartet evenings to the Freudenau |a race track|. There would be more room there. And in time, perhaps, he might even move on to the Puszta |the Hungarian plain |and end, finally, in the Sahara.

---

1. German, that is, in a cultural sense, as opposed to Italian. Karl Sommer was a Carinthian (see below) and Pauline Lucca Viennese.

2. Karl Marcel Sommer (1855-1900), a Carinthian baritone, was a member of the Court Opera from 1881 to 1893.

3. Tobia Bertini (1856-1936) had sung just six months earlier in New York for Colonel Mapleson who, at the Academy of Music, was doing operatic battle with the newly opened Metropolitan. Bertini sang only one performance, as the Duke in *Rigoletto* on October 24, 1883, when, as recorded in *The Mapleson Memoirs*, "in 'La donna è mobile,' he cracked on each of his high notes, whilst in the 'Bella figlia' quartet his voice broke in a most distressing manner while ascending to the B flat, causing loud laughter among the audience." Mapleson promptly sacked him, and demanded that Bertini return an advance of $1,000. Bertini not only refused, but sued Mapleson for $50,000 for breach of contract. Mapleson is silent as to the outcome.

4. Jenny Alt (1865- ?), a coloratura soprano from Pressburg. She subsequently sang in Wiesbaden, Weimar and Berlin.

5. Prince of Reuss-Köstritz (1855-1910) wrote a considerable quantity of chamber music and six symphonies.

6. Fanny Basch-Mahler (1857- ?) had been a pupil of Julius Epstein at the Vienna Conservatory and of Jean François Marmontel in Paris. She was highly regarded as pianist and pedagogue.

15. Farewell to Gericke Liszt's Symphonic Poems

April 27, 1884

In the next to last number of our paper we bade a premature farewell to Herr Hofkapellmeister Gericke. That was a mistake. Since, however, in all levels of society, only the Pope can assume the prerogative of infallibility, while error only too often constitutes the dark side of a critic's judgment or opinion, we can live with the burden of error the more easily in the knowledge that to err is human. Besides, if singers, jugglers, rope dancers, actors, etc., are allowed three or four farewell appearances, why should a music critic not grant a Hofkapellmeister a double farewell? Indeed, we could wish that Hofkapellmeister Gericke might give seven farewell concerts in the next winter season, thus granting both to conductor and public their just deserts. How unwillingly we see him go will have been made plain to Herr Gericke, we hope, by the consistently lively public response to the Society of the Friends of Music concerts under his direction. In fact, it has been due solely and exclusively to this conductor's aspiring industry and rare dedication that the concerts of the Society have put those of the Philharmonic deeply in the shade. He shrank before no difficulty, nor found anything unattainable in the domain of musical notes. The relentless monotony in the choice of older compositions, and the almost invariably unhappy choice of novelties, in the programs of the Philharmonic could not hold the balance against Gericke's flair for both older and newer works, either in their placement in the programs or in the intensive study that went into their performance, despite Richter's conductorial genius and a better (because more unified) orchestra.

As always, so too in the last Society concert, Herr Gericke managed to offer us an interesting program. The concert began with Bach's wonderful cantata, "Es ist dir gesagt, Mensch, was gut ist" | You Have Been Told, Man, What Is Good |. (Bach expresses these words so categorically in an energetically elaborated polyphonic movement that even had he not repeated this admonition so often, one would still have got the gist the first time.) Thunderous applause resounded through the hall after the imposing, unutterably reverent final chorale. A laurel wreath, presented to the departing conductor after this number, diverted the applause, ignited by the cantata, to him who had brought this masterpiece to life. Kapellmeister Gericke was now the object of stormy ovations. Next to him on the honors list, as was only to be expected, was Frau Paumgartner-Papier, who sang the alto aria, and, above all, the recitative, so irresistibly beautifully that the applause went on and on. We shall not much longer enjoy the rare pleasure of hearing Frau Papier sing. It has been seen fit to let her go. Some ballet dancers will probably be engaged to replace her. Well, that, too, is a point of view![1]

A not especially happy choice was the Uhland ballad,[2] "Des Sängers Fluch" (The Singer's Curse), extracted by Richard Pohl[3] and composed by Robert Schumann. This composition bears the opus number 139, thus falling in the last period of the master's mentally disturbed creation. With the exception of the first and last strophes, in which the bardic tone is struck with a master's hand, and with the exception, especially, of the Provençal song, which refreshes the listener, half maddened by the desolate barrenness of all else, like an oasis in the desert, one could only despair, and curse the old bard, the king, the castle, Pohl's patchwork and the composition. As beautifully composed as this Provençal song is, a performance of the complete work is too high a price to pay. It was Frau Papier, again, who through her consistently eloquent singing as the narrator, gave meaning and significance to it all. Herr Wiegand's rough voice was well suited to the role of the bloodthirsty villain of a king. Herr Sommer, as the bard, seemed not to have taken the death of the youth much to heart; he was obviously bored by the whole business, and cursed as gently as possible, not at all in a manner becoming a proper heathen. We almost forgot Herr Walter, and yet it was he who sang the best piece, the Provençal song. A beautiful song, so beautiful, indeed, that one forgets the singer. I love this Provençal song.[4]

Last came Franz Liszt's "Tasso (Lamento e Trionfo)," a symphonic poem. How it warms my heart to see a Liszt symphonic poem staring up at me from the program in this day and age when symphonies, suites, serenades and stuff of that kind sprout like weeds from the barren soil of absolute music! Liszt and symphonic poetry! That, for the pedants and the members of the establishment is: *Hannibal ante portas.* Dear people, what frightens you so when you see a symphonic poem and its creator on a program? Certainly not the cymbal crashes, which have not killed anybody yet, and which, at worst, excite your laughter, while listening to the newest symphonies or violin concertos drives you from sheer boredom to working out arithmetical problems on your coat buttons, and leaves you for a week incapable of laughter. (They have, as a rule, no cymbal crashes, despite Beethoven, who even added the big drum to the snare drum already at hand — my God! and in the Ninth Symphony at that! How impure, how unclassical that is — yes? or no?) But it cannot be the cymbal crashes that take you aback. The mere mention of the term "symphonic poem" brings the sweat to your foreheads. Even before entering the concert hall you smirk at, or tremble before, this monster, "symphonic poem." Why? Is your scorn or your abhorrence directed at the term, "symphonic poem," or at its creator, Franz Liszt?

If the first, you must concede that the form, at least, is original and, as such, a step forward. If you want symphonies today as Beethoven wrote them, then turn the clock back a century, wake the master from the dead, but don't place beside him our epigones, these impotent contemporary symphonists decked out in classical garb and flirting with the classical spirit. You complain that Liszt's music is too concerned with externals. What good eyes you have, what good ears! How clever you are! Now suppose that Liszt were to provide no program, nor come to the assistance of your keen wits with a poetically fashioned Preface, would you then,too, you hairsplitters, tell us how, thanks to Liszt's thoroughly descriptive music in "Mazeppa," you learned just how many hairs there were on the tail of the horse to which Mazeppa was bound?

I have just referred to a poetically fashioned Preface. I lay special emphasis on the appendicular "poetic," for had you understood the poetry of the Preface (to "Tasso") you would have grasped, too, the poetry, the poetic composition of the symphony, the symphonic poem. A poetic picture, a soul-stirring representation of a state of mind encased in a splendid, glowing frame of characteristic decoration, and flooded with the most efflorescent magic of a masterly instrumentation — should this wondrous work of art strike you with horror, or even elicit a smile? Do you not imagine in the "Eroica" (I mean the real "Eroica" of Beethoven)[5] the black hussars arrayed against a troop of cuirassiers, or uhlans and infantry having at one another, Napoleon Bonaparte blowing his nose, scratching, or coughing, commanding, riding, blinking and similar absurdities? Do you not hear in the Seventh Symphony a country wedding and all the trimmings extended over four movements? And all this without a program!!! It is a great pity that Beethoven was not so amiably disposed toward the public as Franz Liszt. One must put his own brain to work to conjure up a pretty tale for such a Beethoven symphony. But the fatal catch is that each regards his own interpretation as the correct one, leading to much strife and disagreement, and proving nothing. From all this one concludes that we should be grateful to Liszt for the proffered program. As for Liszt's music, it is more intelligent than deeply felt, but vividly and warmly fanciful, and always plastic. Are the themes in our celebrated new symphonies plastic? As a rule, not. And when they are, then they are so

Arthur Friedheim as a young man

Hermann Winkelmann as Parsifal
*(All photos except p. 12 courtesy Bildarchiv der
Oesterreichischen Nationalbibliothek)*

Amalie Materna as
the Brünnhilde of *Die Walküre*

Rosa Papier as Orpheus

Rosa Sucher as Isolde (1886)

Lilli Lehmann as
Leonore in *Fidelio*

Gustav Walter

Eduard Hanslick at the age of 50

Augenblicklicher Zustand des Hofkapellmeisters Hans Richter nach den ermüdenden Proben und Aufführungen von „Tristan und Isolde".

Hans Richter as caricaturist Hans Schliessmann imagined him following the rehearsals and first Vienna performances of *Tristan und Isolde*

Alfred Grünfeld

Hugo Wolf (1895)

Ludwig Speidel

Hans Rokitansky as
Bertram in *Robert le Diable*

Arnold Rosé

Max Kalbeck

Heinrich Vogel as Tristan

**Bertha Ehnn as Mignon
(lithograph by Ignaz Eigner)**

**Franz von Rei-
chenberg as Merlin**

Zög' dieser Russe dereinst einem Heer voran —
Er nähm' uns gefangen Mann für Mann.

**Anton Rubenstein ("If this Russian were to arrive at the head of an army,"
says the caption, "he would take us prisoner one and all.")**

Karl Mayerhofer as Papageno

Theodor Reichmann

The Bösendorfersaal (painting by Leo Delitz)

The Court Opera (Hofoper, now Staatsoper) as it appeared in Wolf's time and much as it appears today

Hans von Bülow in action as caricatured by Hans Schliessmann

The Grosser Musikvereinssaal as it appeared in Wolf's time and as it still appears today

Wiener Salonblatt

Erscheint wöchentlich.

Eigenthümer und Herausgeber: M. Engel.   Redaction und Administration: I., Nibelungengasse

Hofoper.

Seit dem Abgange der Frau Kupfer ist ein Rollenkreis im Repertoire vakant geblieben, dem sich unsere hiesigen „Kräfte" so sehr gewachsen zeigen, daß eine Zugoper, wie z. B. „Lohengrin" im Archive vermodern müßte, wenn die schöne Sitte der Gastspiele, die ja fremden wie einheimischen Künstlern Ehrenbürger- oder doch Ehrenmitglieder-Rechte an unserer Hofbühne erwirbt, solche — Caffagefahr nicht glücklicherweise verhinderte. Anstatt auf einheitliches Zusammenwirken, verständnißvolles Durchdringen des Ganzen hinzuarbeiten, um solchergestalt selbst der minder gelungenen Leistung des Einzelnen den Schein der Totalität zu retten und eine nach Kräften ideale Auffassung zu erzielen, geschieht just das Gegentheil von alledem. Mit einer Ausdauer und Hingebung, würdig, im Dienste der besten Sache zu stehen, bemüht man sich nicht nur um das Engagement mittelmäßiger Kräfte oder um die Erhaltung solcher, man nimmt auch sorgfältig Bedacht, dieses geringe Kapital von Leistungsfähigkeit, das, zusammengehalten immerhin eine stattliche Summe ergäbe, zu zersplittern, dem Egoismus das Wort zu reden, den Geist der Gemeinsamkeit zu ersticken. Die Würde und das künstlerische Ansehen des Institutes zu heben, werden energische Reformen nothwendig sein, soll die Bühne desselben schließlich nicht einem Zigeunerlager gleichen, darin jeder nach Belieben seine Wege geht, — soll die Kunst ihren Dienern mehr sein, als nur der brodelnde Suppenkessel, gemeine Bedürfnisse zu befriedigen. Man spricht wohl rühmlich von den Koryphäen unseres Operntheaters und wie sie diesem Institute zur Zierde gereichen. Mich dünkt, in diesem Lobe liegt aber wenig Schmeichelhaftes für das Institut selber, wenn man müßte denn zu stimmen, daß solches Lob auf Gegenseitigkeit beruht, was aber keineswegs der Fall ist. Frau Materna, um ein Beispiel anzuführen, schmückt allerdings als ein kostbares Juwel unser Operntheater, aber inwiefern ziert das Operntheater Frau Materna?

Vielleicht durch einstige Expectanz auf die Ehrenmitgliederso Dies jedoch zugegeben, bleibt das Verhältniß, so gewichtig folgenschwer eine derartige Auszeichnung für den Künstler sein immer ein einseitiges, weil rein äußerliches. Es kann Frau Ma wenig bekümmern, welcher Bühne ihre Kräfte ihre Gute kom Sie wird sich auf jeder Bühne fremd oder heimisch fühle nach der Beschaffenheit ihrer Umgebung, ob sie nun in New oder Wien die Bretter betritt. Ob aber unsere Burgschau auf jeder beliebigen Bühne sich zurecht finden, oder ob sie vielmehr einzig und allein in einer Atmosphäre gedeihen dü die, von dem Culturregen heiligen Nothschweißes vieler wo Künstler seit einer langen Reihe von Jahren geschwängert auf den heutigen Tag sich fruchtbringend erwies, — das ist andere Frage. Einstweilen weiß ich nur so viel, daß Herbert-Förster als Elsa in „Lohengrin" auf unserer B kaum Wurzel fassen wird, wie sehr auch eine Notiz der „ Freien Presse" der entgegengesetzten Anschauung Ausdruck liehen. Frau Herbert-Förster vom deutschen Theater in New ist eine stattliche Dame, leider nur zu stattlich, um eine Lichtgestalt wie Elsa innerhalb der Grenzlinien des Schön halten. Die Darstellung betreffend, behilft sich die Sängerin den bewährten Mitteln der Routine, die den Begriff des ventionellen schon mit einschließt. Stimme — mäßig. Vortro ziemlich correct, aber nicht erwärmend. Besondere Kennzeiche keine. Herr Winkelmann gilt als ein vorzüglicher Loher Wir wollen diesmal mit ihm nicht darüber rechten, wollen nur nahe legen, daß seine hohen Töne die Claque übe Gebühr enthusiasmiren und daß ihre lärmenden Demonstrat bei offer Scene seinem Ohre unmöglich so angenehm se können, als mißtönig dem unsern. — Ausnehmend schön und sang und spielte Herr Reichmann den Telramund; wir m diese erfreuliche Wahrnehmung umso kräftiger, als uns nur d die traurige Nothwendigkeit auferlegt wird, die Schwächen verdienstvollen Sängers schonungslos aufzudecken. Was abe man über den König des Herrn Rokitansky sagen? Das R auszusprechen wäre fast unschicklich; aber denken kann man

— Hugo Wo

Wolf's last notice in the *Weiner Salonblatt* (24 April 1887)

because they always were, before our famous symphonist "invented" them. We have just said that Liszt's music is more intelligent than deeply felt. That is not to be taken too literally. In truth, Liszt strikes us as being by nature no more the absolute musician than Berlioz. What Liszt has over Berlioz is that with the utmost security he has created a new form in the sense that he wittingly gave priority to the poetic idea, then, in order to develop the idea artistically, had to depart, inevitably, from the traditional symphonic form. His inspiration, drawing upon a certain poetic theme, simply could not arbitrarily be elaborated within the confines of a stereotyped form. He had to let the musical form be determined by the substance of the poetic outline. The latter, accordingly, was not, as with Berlioz, of decisive influence upon the musical content alone, but, as with Liszt, also upon the form.

In this sense, the "symphonic poem" is for modern music what Haydn's symphonies were for that master's contemporaries and successors. Beethoven, as an absolute musician, spoke the last word in the symphony, just as Liszt, as poetic musician, has spoken the first word (perhaps also the last) for the symphonic poem. How much might not be said about the choice of poetic themes in which Liszt's entire artistic greatness is revealed!

As we are now reaching the end of our space, we hope for a subsequent opportunity to pursue the subject. Such original, bold and inspired creations as Liszt's are dismissed by our critics with sovereign disdain, or with mocking commiseration, while these glue pots, these obscenely stale symphonies of Brahms, false and perverted to the bottom of their very soul, are hailed as wonders of the world. Who can remain still? There is more intelligence and sensitivity in a single cymbal crash in a work of Liszt's than in all three of Brahms's symphonies,[6] with the serenades thrown in for good measure. The very idea of comparing Liszt with Brahms! Genius with the epigone of an epigone, the eagle with the wren! Enough!

Two highly successful *stagione* presentations drew large audiences to the Court Opera House: *Il Trovatore* and *Lucrezia Borgia*. Signor Bertini, who sings as few others can, sang the Manrico in *Il Trovatore* and the Gennaro in *Lucrezia Borgia* to stormy applause. If only Signor Bertini were not so wooden and hapless in his movements upon the stage, we could not wish for a better singer. His voice is not so bright as Mierzwinski's, but it is more malleable, more flexible. Cantilena suits him beautifully, which was not the case with Mierzwinski. Signor Bertini is a splendid substitute for the Polish Italian.

We also had occasion to admire Signora Turolla as Leonora and Lucrezia. At the close of the second act of *Lucrezia Borgia* particularly, her highly dramatic performance, involving both facial expression and gesture, succeeded in igniting the audience. Her voice is not especially beautiful. Insecure attacks and frequent register changes are initially disturbing. But this singer has so many cherishable attributes that we end by almost losing sight of her shortcomings.

New to us was Signor Pinto. In the role of the Duke of Ferrara he unleashed a sturdy bass, at its most comfortable in the lowest regions. Things did not go so well toward the top. A special word of praise for his animated acting. Frau Kaulich.[7] filling in for the indisposed Frau Papier, undertook the role of Maffio Orsini, and carried it off well. His Majesty the Kaiser graced the performance of *Lucrezia Borgia* with his exalted presence. Signori Bertini and Pinto and Signora Turolla excited a veritable hurricane of applause after the second act of *Lucrezia Borgia* from an audience highly stimulated by an eminently successful performance.

1. As noted previously, she did not leave.
2. Ludwig Uhland (1787-1862), Swabian poet and philologist, especially noted for his historical ballads.
3. Richard Pohl (1826-1896), German music critic in Dresden, Weimar and Baden-Baden (where he was born and where he died), noted as an early champion of Wagner, Liszt and Berlioz.
4. Published as a solo song in Vol. III of the Peters edition of Schumann's Lieder.
5. Hans Richter had described Brahms's Symphony No. 3 as his "Eroica."
6. The appearance of Brahms's Symphony No. 4 was still a year and a half off.
7. Louise Kaulich (1855- ?), Viennese mezzo-soprano who had joined the Court Opera in 1878 and was to remain with it for twenty years. She came of a theater family, and was highly valued for an enormous and astonishingly varied repertoire, the speed and accuracy with which she could learn new parts, and her ability and readiness to step in at short notice for indisposed colleagues.

16. La Gioconda

May 4, 1884

An uncommonly feeble product that, one hopes, will very soon, and forever, vanish from the repertoire. The author of the absurd libretto, brewed from leftovers of the cheapest, most banal, most brutal fustian, is assumed to be the infamous Arrigo Boito, hiding behind the anagram, Tobia Gorrio. And from whom else could this book of horrors come but the author of *Mefistofele*? But why the mask? If Boito had the nerve, the gall, to write *Mefistofele*, and the cheek to present himself as the author of that absurd work, what had this dull lunatic, of all people, to lose by setting his name to the libretto of *La Gioconda*? Indeed, we can even tell this perverted Tobia Gorrio confidently that his text for *La Gioconda*, trivial, dirty, cannibalistic as it may be in invention and execution, does not touch the monstrous, idiotic bombast of his *Mefistofele*.

(Richard Kralik, an enthusiastic admirer of Boito's muse, and himself active in that direction, would, of course, see in what I have just said only a lamentable circumstance. In fact, we prefer gay lunatics to gloomy ones, which is why "Adam" or "Die Offenbarung" (The Revelation) has given us more pleasure than "Roman" (Novel) or "Die Türken vor Wien" (The Turkish Siege of Vienna) -| all poems by Richard Kralik |. Earnestness simply does not become Herr Kralik. As an unwitting competitor of the amiable humorist Busch, however, he can always draw a friendly smile, sometimes even set us off in a gale of laughter. Unfortunately, we have, so far, had no drawings to go with his tales. We hope that in this respect, too, Herr Kralik will not lag behind his model Busch.)

The musical part of this opera, moreover, is not much better than the textual (I decline to use the term "poetical"). Above all else, Ponchielli lacks originality. He has a commonplace physiognomy, and his fantasy the pace of a stubborn donkey that, after every second step, keeps mulling over the first. His melodies, banal and flat, are really only patched together from the sediment of opera phrases by Gounod, Verdi and Meyerbeer, and thus not even modeled on the true melodies of these opera composers. All the would-be melodic numbers in *La Gioconda* seem to be edging toward a final fermata, assuring the singer, at least, of an effective exit, but utterly incapable of disguising the want of genuinely felt melody, no matter how openly this final fermata is bawled out. *La Gioconda* is composed solely for the singer, and not for the public. Therein lies the severest criticism.

Signora Pantaleoni,[1] too, seemed to be fully of this view. She overdid matters in a way that often bordered on the farcical. There were times when what she uttered had nothing to do with singing, but rather with gargling and strangulation. It is a pity that Signora Pantaleoni, unquestionably a gifted singer, should allow herself to be tempted to such excesses. Laura was well attended to by Signora Giuli-Borsi. Fräulein Meisslinger sang the grateful part of La Cieca beautifully. Among all the participants, Signor Dufriche[2] made the most agreeable impression. As the villainous Barnaba he was equal to every requirement, both dramatic and vocal. The boyish voice and comical appearance of Signor Valero[3] (Enzo Grimaldi), on the other hand, I found inordinately comical, quite in contrast to the audience, which took this singer absolutely seriously, and applauded him enthusiastically. For my part, he was heartily welcome to the applause. Signor Pinto (Alvise) always fills his place, no matter where you put him. The opera was very attractively staged, and well prepared. The audience was attentive, and the opera appeared to have had a success. Whether this success will endure, further performances will show. We doubt it.

Next day came *L'Africaine,* in Italian as *L'Africana.* The appearance of Signora Turolla in the role of Selika was awaited with great expectations, which she satified in every respect. Bertini (Vasco de Gama) insinuates himself ever more into our hearts with his exceptionally mellow voice. The Nelusko of Signor Salvati was an admirable accomplishment. Of Signor Pinto one could say once and for all: "always in the right place at the right time.[4] Signora Malvezzi, too, managed the thankless part of Inez expertly.

There remains to mention a young singer who sang Princess Isabella in *Robert le Diable*. She is Fräulein Baier[5] from the Landestheater in Graz. Her singing betrays good schooling, but every tone also tells us that she is still a student. Her movements are immature, awkward and hesitant. Time will take care of that. She was cordially received, and had a nice success with the "Mercy" aria. Fräulein Baier will fit well into smaller roles, and as she is already engaged at the Court Opera, we will have occasion to renew her acquaintance in more suitable roles.

1.   Romilda Pantaleoni (1847-1917) created the role of Desdemona in Verdi's *Otello*. She was also much admired for her Gioconda and for her Margherita in *Mefistofele*.

2.   Eugène Dufriche, a distinguished French baritone who was to have many seasons at Covent Garden and two at the Metropolitan.

3.   Presumably Fernando Valero (1854-1914), a Spanish tenor, pupil of Tamberlik, who sang at the Metropolitan during the season of 1891-92. He was La Scala's first Turridu in *Cavalleria Rusticana*. Four sides he recorded in London in 1902-03 are collector's items.

4.   I.e., like Walther von Stolzing in *Die Meistersinger* (Act I, scenes 1 and 3).

5.   Anna Baier (1860- ?), a Viennese contralto who was to remain for many years a resident member of the Court Opera.

17. Mefistofele

May 11, 1884

Characteristic of the corruption into which our theater public has fallen are the continuing performances of *Mefistofele*, a work so infamous that no invective can do justice to the subject. That Vienna is not a German city, or that it has, at least, no German theater public, has been demonstrated with lamentable certainty, unfortunately, by the applause accorded this miserable caricature of Goethe's *Faust*.

The German, patient and long-suffering as he may be, would never consent to see his nation's pride, Goethe's *Faust*, violated before his very own eyes. Nor would he accept the indignity of beholding himself in the grimace to which Boito has degraded the Goethean Faust, that stirring image of the German species. Fortunately, the German people have preserved their innocence, the integrity | *Faust* | of their way of thinking, the purity of their sensibility in artistic matters, as shown by the fact that Boito's monstrous *Mefistofele* finds no public in Germany, and probably would not find one if it tried.[1] Only the Viennese public has a proper understanding for Boito's vile deviltry. And this Vienna prides itself on being the first musical city of the world, as if a city's musical qualifications could be determined solely by the excellence of its orchestra, its singers and its conductors!

Vienna possesses a precious vessel in its distinguished orchestra, to be sure, but the vessel is filled with sulphate, lye, vinegar, nitric acid, sulphuric acid and cyanide of potassium, which is odd, if not unnatural. But utterly incomprehensible and perverse, it seems to me, is the relish and the delight with which our public recklessly drinks these love potions down, and without injuring itself in the slightest, not to speak of dying. Which just goes to show that not only the church, but also the theater public rejoices in a good stomach.

In recent times, however, Vienna has had to renounce, for better or for worse, any proud claim to being the world's first musical city. Neither in the opera nor in the concert hall does one any longer encounter the hearty, healthy type of the amiable Vienna of old. A sinisterly officious element has made itself at home in our city, greeting everything with derision and scorn. Like an evil, creeping poison, it gradually undermines, dissolves and cripples the sound core of a strongly developed artistic sensibility, of a healthy manner of outlook and perception still characteristic of those yet unspoiled residents of Vienna. Under the influence of this subversive element, the truly engaging amiability of the old Viennese has been passed on to his sons and grandsons only in the form of that morbid affability typical of our theater community -- an affability vacillating between utter want of character and bottomless indolence.

The essential charcteristic of this subversive element is frivolity. One is hard put to tell whether the fatal affability of the true Viennese, or the frivolity of that other part of society (by far the larger part of our theater public, and unquestionably more devoted to commerce than to conversion) is the more ominous for our artistic life. Both elements, in any case, are gnawing at the roots of any healthy evolution, and from year to year we see the cultivation of those institutions responsible for a people's cultural nourishment being subjected to brokers and speculators, paying homage to the bestial taste of the theater-going rabble, and instead of dictating laws, accepting laws dictated to them in return for vile coin.

In view of all this, a public content merely to wallow in the lowest depths of the sewer (as in our modern operetta) should find the deadly fumes of Boito's hellish brew enchanting. The perfumed wit of Offenbach's operettas was not coarse enough for noses attuned to the fragrance of putrefaction, for their indolent spirits too fine. In Offenbach there was, at least, something to discern, to smell, even to feel, and, above all, something to laugh at. Nowadays no one wants to laugh, or to cry, or to be moved, or even to sleep. Boredom is the thing. Boredom is the driving, the single animating force of our theater community!

Composers! You who wear out your feet and your heads in the exhausting search for effective opera subjects, stop, stop! Leave the West Goths and the East Goths and the Saxons and the Friesians, the Irish and the Icelanders in peace. We have seen more of them already than we can stomach. If you want to be truly interesting and original, write a piece for five or six evenings (that should be enough, Wagner having been content with four), and take as your heroine Boredom!

Boredom as an allegory! How charming! You could fail only if, by chance, you were to have an idea. In order to avert such a catastrophe, I would suggest that, above all, you banish every Wagner score and piano reduction from your memory (and without cuts!). Then you could be certain that not the slightest accident of an idea could ever disturb the enraptured public's edifying repose. O, what marvelous, delightful, heavenly prospects for the music of the future!

A pity, only, that the old masters come off so badly. One's heart bleeds to see how *Fidelio, Die Zauberflöte, Der Freischütz, The Marriage of Figaro* and so on fail to fill the house at half prices while the filth of a *Mefistofele*, a monstrosity conceived in the fever of delusions of grandeur, draws the public again and again at prices twice raised. --

A remarkable feature of all this is the refinement with which the public surrenders itself to boredom. It carefully avoids the classical operas just enumerated. These, in the public's view, do not attain the higher forms of boredom. The boredom the public experiences in them is boring. But that is not always the case. The more absurd the plot, the sillier the music, the more stupid the stage direction, the more vulgar the whole business, the more pleasureable the boredom!

In this pleasure, however, lies the whole wretchedness and depravity of it all, since the normal person may well be bored, but is utterly unable to find the slightest pleasure in boredom, let alone the highest. But that's how it is with our public. As long as such people occupy our theaters, and especially our opera house, just so long will the idiocy, the filth, the vulgarity, the mendacity of our public artistic life triumph over every true work of art, and just so long will this disgusting vermin of the Boitos and the hypocritical pack of our symphony composers prevail over the nobility of Gluck's virtually forgotten operas and the inspired revelations of an insolently scorned but nevertheless great and immortal Franz Liszt.

So wallow in the bottomless pit of a *Mefistofele*! Let the good Lord speak with the devil as man to man! But don't count too heavily on this kind of humanity. God will not always show up in the last act to haul from the mud him who has sold his soul to the devil as he does for that noble long-suffering wrestler Faust! Have a care!

Our assessment of the last performance of *Mefistofele* can be brief. Signora Turolla, as Gretchen, Signor Valero as Faust, and Signor Castelmary[2] as Mephistopheles sang and acted their parts with extraordinary dramatic vividness. Since Boito's Marguerite is related only by name to Goethe's Gretchen, and otherwise has not a trace of anything in common with her, Signora Turolla was true to the role in the best sense in making of her a demented tramp, just as the composer sketches her. Since, further, the Boito Mephistopheles resembles a drunken journeyman tailor, who in his stupor imagines himself to be the devil, so Signor Castelmary excellently realized this figure, so blatantly tossed off by the composer-poet, with the appropriate bleat. Signor Valero sang Faust comically enough. Just imagine a gray-bearded, bent-over old man lost in dour meditation, and, on top of that, the mutating voice of a fourteen year-old boy and the forever bewildered countenance of Signor Valero as Faust, the widely learned, widely travelled Faust! Very funny! And, in fact, very characteristic. What kind of two poor souls Boito conjured up from purgatory to fashion Faust is hard to determine. Presumably those of a diver and a balloonist. No one will be able to figure out what this brother's heart contains.[3]

1. Wolf seems not to have been aware of the fact that *Mefistofele* had been produced (in German) in both Cologne and Hamburg in February of 1881.

2. Armand Castelmary (1834-1897), French bass-baritone, whose long career, embracing Paris, London and New York, ended tragically and memorably when he died on the stage of the Metropolitan Opera House in the arms of Jean de Reszke during a performance of *Martha* on the night of February 10, 1897.

3. A play on Faust's exclamation in Goethe's *Faust*: "Das also war des Pudels Kern" -- literally, "so that was the poodle's nucleus" -- when Mephistopheles, having entered his study disguised as a poodle, suddenly assumes human form.

18. An *Italianate* Aida

May 18,1884

With the performance of Verdi's *Aida*, this year's *stagione* came to an end. The departure of the Italians, as far as we are concerned, is a matter of utter indifference. Quite aside from their hardly notable individual achievements, seldom surpassing the level of mediocrity, we could not accept the grotesquely ludicrous overall impression of the Italian productions, adequately prepared as we were by analogous proceedings in our own German performances. There is no cause for surprise, however, in the manner in which the *stagione* was welcomed by our opera public, nor in the fact that even bad Italian performances were found preferable to good German performances (and there are such from time to time).

We are, in any case, pretty clear about the character of this public. As we pointed out in our last issue, it is made up for the most part, of the so-called modern Young Germany, i.e., German-Humanitarian-Liberals and Christianity-professing foreigners or intruders (call them what you will). What other business such people have with the intellectual productions of our German masters is hard to imagine. A certain sheer admiration, perhaps, or the prospect of tangible benefits in the form of a tolerable occupation such as a teaching position or something of that sort. The German masters have sprung from the heart of their nation, were weaned on it, and in the benevolent sunshine of the German spirit achieved that full flowering of power and glory that can properly be comprehended in all its characteristic individuality only within the spirit of German intellectual life.

Nevertheless, we are being enlightened most generously these days about what is German, humane, Christian and liberal. And by whom? By Germans? By Christians? By activist freedom fighters? By practicing apostles of humanity? Indeed! There is something at once touching and comical about all this Young German propagandistic activity. But there is a good side, too. It is unlikely to produce another crusade to the promised land. With all the thousands of modern Christs turning up in every part of the world, each country will soon have its own Jerusalem and its own Holy Sepulchre. May these sepulchres blossom and flourish!

This performance of *Aida* was unquestionably the Italian company's best. Signora Turolla, particularly, in the title role, was able to sustain our interest from beginning to end. In no other role had she so succeeded in blending the arts of the singer and the actress as in the uncommonly grateful role of Aida. Italian singers tend to be so carried away by the plaudits of the *rabbia* as to utterly lose sight of the distinction between "projecting passions" and "being passionate." But on this occasion it seemed to me that artistic understanding had the upper hand in Signora Turolla's conception and projection of the part, so far preserving her from coarse exaggerations as to make us quite willing to overlook certain crudities that occurred here and there, and which are so habitual with her as to have become second nature.

Signor Bertini was the Radames. From his voice we can expect everything, from his acting nothing. He suggests to me a good instrument in a handsome case. The instrument as such is excellent, and he who uses it knows how to make it yield beautiful sounds. But the body containing the instrument is something totally apart, lifeless, as meaningless to the instrument as a fiddle or flute case to the fiddle or the flute. An opera singer, however, should never prompt such a comparison, for he has, after all, two arms, two feet and two eyes, and he can, at the right moment, put them to work.

But there is something uncommonly touching about Signor Bertini's detachment. He smiles whether it is a dagger or his beloved's head that is pressed to his heart, ever pleased with himself. Not for a single instant does it occur to him to believe in what is happening on the stage. He knows perfectly well that he is not about to be struck down, however furious the action. Nor is it possible to determine from that ever happy smile whether he believes his partner's protestations of love or not.

O happy Bertini; from whom joy and sorrow, hope and despair, love and hate, happiness or misfortune -- it makes no difference which -- can draw only a smile! A paragon of stoicism! He can summon happiness with a song, and sing away his pain.

Happy Bertini!

19. La Juive

May 25, 1884

We are accustomed to being taken unawares by a performance of *La Juive*, since such a performance is usually announced by the red playbill. If the red pirate flag is hoisted at the Court Opera, instead of the usual white flag of truce, it means a raid on the repertoire. *La Juive, Faust* and *Der Freischütz* customarily take turns in sharing the honor of venturing forth under the red flag from the harbor of the archives into the hazardous sea of the stage, where their task is to prove their viability as stópgaps as best they can. They fail often enough, and then they have a bad time of it. In such a ticklish situation, of course, one cries out: "Help, Samiel!" But Samiel [the wild huntsman of *Der Freischütz*] is a knavish fellow. He smirks, and thinks to himself: "God helps those who help themselves." This might well be taken to heart by the Jewess, who in her hour of need appeals directly to her divinity, the cruel god of the Jews, and reckons it both seemly and opportune to have the bloodthirsty Jehovah and her sincere faith on the tip of her tongue, expecting miracles of both. Gounod's Faust makes a shrewd calculation: "If heaven abandons me, then hell is not to be despised." Mephistopheles and Samiel, however, are brothers under the skin, and similarly given to cynical quotation. Mephistopheles recites, perhaps unctuously, "Who places his trust in God has built on a firm foundation," makes a merry face, and thinks to himself: "The devil will get you yet."

You see, neither heaven nor hell, nor god nor devil, nor magic bullet nor any faith, however sincere, is of any use to these poor condemned wretches. A well prepared orchestra, a good cast, intelligent staging -- these constitute the Solomonic key that could bar the hellish brood of trivial routine and thoroughly inartistic procedure. (The régisseur of a court theater threw a tantrum during a rehearsal of *Mefistofele* because the key in question, which he seems to have envisioned as having a huge bit and handle, and which he intended to have swung in such a manner as to impress some concierge in the fourth gallery, was not immediately at hand.) But now to the business of the day.

Signora Turolla, the extension of whose guest engagement leaves her as the sole surviving and also the most agreeable holdover from the *stagione*, sang Rachel in *La Juive* with much warmth, sensitive insight and dedication. Especially beautiful was the Romanza of the second act, in which the mood is extraordinarily well sustained by the composer. It is no easy matter to sing this scene in such a way as to bring home to the listener the conflict raging within this girl, animated both by fear and by love, who longs for her lover and yet recoils before his appearance, which may bring with it the disclosure of a secret she has been suspecting with ever increasing apprehension. Signora Turolla managed to make of this Romanza, with the implications just noted, an interesting and convincing achievement. Despite all that, we cannot reward her with unqualified praise. Signora Turolla can be as offensive as she is also attractive. If she sang the Romanza like an artist, in the duet with Eudora (Act IV) she was, thanks to wretched excesses, both vocal and dramatic, a perfectly ordinary ham actress. The fatal forced chest tones, particularly, are often the Moloch of her passionate outbursts, to whom the loveliest blossoms of her talent are sacrificed. As long as she serves this idol, she will, indeed, arouse our interest, but never excite the inner exaltation and rapture that come only with the compelling truth of a perfectly artistic accomplishment.

Next to Signora Turolla the dominant figure was Herr Rokitansky with his bottomless bass in the role of the Cardinal. Herr Wiegand was a splendid protagonist of the redoubtable Lord Mayor Ruggiero, an eager anti-Semite who would have little truck with Jews. The figure of Ruggiero is the most sympathetically touching in this opera. How dull, how insipid, how miserable, by contrast, is Prince Leopold, especially as sung by Herr Schittenhelm. The Jew Eléazar, too, is hardly an amiable character. Herr Broulik[1] seemed ill at ease in the Jewish kaftan. I don't blame him. Fräulein Lehmann was more than the noble Princess. She "chilled right to the heart." In her singing as well as in her facial expressions she suggested not the slightest leaning toward the weakling Leopold. Fräulein Lehmann herself may be quite right about this, but a Princess Eudora should summon more warmth and passion. The librettist and the composer demand it. There was a large audience, and no want of applause.

1.   Franz Broulik (1853- ?), who had joined the company in 1882 and would leave at the end of the 1883-1885 season to continue his career in Budapest.

20. Hapless Guests

June 1, 1884

How is it that our opera house so readily opens its doors to every singer who entertains the notion of making a debut there? Be the singer serviceable or not, a somebody or a nobody, whether he be from a theater of the first rank or the second, whether he be of good repute or bad, he is taken on for a guest engagement, and that's that, period. The management may reckon the matter as settled with that period, but it is the public and the critics who apply the blotter, or put a question mark above it according to their favorable or unfavorable verdict. Public and critics may not, of course, agree. It is self-evident that an unsophisticated public cannot be of one mind with knowledgeable critics, and vice versa. In the present case, with such a minor matter as the appearance of Frau Plankensteiner-Wilt and Herr Udvardy, the respective opinions were unanimous. But it means nothing. It throws no special light on the judgment either of the public or of the critics that they happily noted the inadequacy of both guests "with little wit and much jollity".[1] It would be more to the point to reflect for a moment upon the question of why, summer and winter, on the stage of our opera house, guests come and go when we have a resident company.

The continual engagement of visiting singers suggests that our theater could not subsist without importing alien throats, and in this suggestion there lies, to be sure, a tiny grain of truth. Just take a look at the Court Theater by way of comparison, and you will agree. A good theater cannot be a refuge for itinerant singers or actors, as can be demonstrated in the example of the aforementioned Court Theater. The management of this institution regards itself as in no way called upon to follow the example of the management of our opera house. The public is fully in agreement with the policies prevailing at the Court Theater, and this not only because the Court Theater possesses first-rate actors, but also because these actors succeed in complementing one another, in playing, so to speak, into each other's hands. Thus, light and shade are properly distributed, and any monotony which, through the predominance of the individual at the expense of others, might detract from the whole is avoided by the effective participation of all. The Court Theater, in short, is guided by an artistic spirit that, as is the nature of the case, can embrace only productive elements, while the inartistic management of the Court Opera reveals only a destructive tendency.

It is not a pleasant task to illuminate the inadequacies of our opera house, nor would one quickly exhaust the subject. But as far as the mania for bringing in guests is concerned, now become an *idée fixe*, this would make sense only insofar as one were to summon as guests better artists than we have at our own disposal, since the opera house, in respect of its roster of singers, cannot survive comparison with the company at the Court Theater, and an ideal performance can be achieved only by calling upon singers from the outside. But to achieve an ultimately bad performance by outsiders is as ludicrous as it is stupid.

Herr Udvardy, who as a small boy did badly in walking school, since he waddles on the stage like a duck, made his debut as Raoul in *Les Huguenots*. He might possibly have managed the part of a sleepy night watchman, but let us hope that it never again occurs to him to play a fine cavalier whose bearing and courtly manner capture every heart at his mere appearance. A splendid Raoul is he who trips over his own feet! And then the voice, as agonizing for the listener as is a dull razor for a shaver. This is a voice to "drive men mad," not to "soften stone."[2] The aforesaid goes for his performance as Faust in

Gounod's opera, too. He had, on this occasion, a worthy partner in Frau Plankensteiner-Wilt as Marguerite. She chirped in the love scene like a languishing grasshopper, and was, in fact, more amusing to hear than one had expected. Herr Udvardy may be a star in Königsberg, and Frau Planken-steiner-Wilt³well placed in Olmütz, but the boards of our opera house are too hot for those who have not survived a baptism of fire in another major theater. This is something the two guests might well have considered. More to the point, the management, in view of their utter inadequacy, should never have agreed to their appearance. Fortunately, Frau Paumgartner-Papier, the darling of our public, was the Siebel, and the golden tones of her sumptuous voice threw a transfiguring lustre upon poor Faust and poor Marguerite, rendered the more pitiable by the ghastly self-deception of the two guests.

1.   "mit wenig Witz und viel Behagen," Mephistopheles's wry comment to Faust on the inebriate revelry in Auerbach's cellar.

2.   "So ein Lied, das Stein erweichen und Menschen rasend machen kann," from "Die Katzen und der Hausherr," one of *Vier Äsopische Fabeln* by Gottfried Lichtwer (1719-1783).

3.   Frau Plankensteiner-Wilt may have retreated to Olmütz, but Anton Udvardy went on to New York for the first German season at the Metropolitan (1884-1885), where, in very distinguished company, he sang Max, Florestan, Don Ottavio, the Duke in *Rigoletto*, Raoul, Arnold and Eléazar.

21.   Lohengrin *and* Tristan und Isolde *with* Sucher *and* Vogl

June 8, 1884

Frau Sucher¹ from Hamburg and Herr Vogl² from Munich as guests in our opera house -- that's something to hear! Vogl | bird | is well known by his song, and in Frau Sucher |searcher| we have long acknowledged a rich find. Elsa and Lohengrin were the debut roles of their engagement.

How lovely Elsa looked as she made her entrance! "Wie erschien sie so licht und rein!"³ She was the embodiment of innocence personified. How noble and natural her movements, how chaste her bearing, how softly transfigured her features! Gone every trace of Frau Sucher, and in her stead -- Elsa!

The illusion, unfortunately, was not always sustained. The "Dream" was initially rapt and tender, despite a voice neither very mellow nor very pliant.

But in the continuation she was tempted to vehement accents unbecoming an Elsa. "Will er Gemahl mich heissen, geb' ich ihm was ich bin"[4] can, without sacrificing decisiveness, still be sung with that devotion and humility implicit in Elsa's total surrender to a higher power, and therefore characteristic of her every act and impulse.

Another bad habit of our infinitely estimable visitor disturbed us in some degree. Frau Sucher likes to stress the last tones of a musical phrase, thereby violating not only the composer's directions, but also the natural flow of declamation. In the verse, "vor Gott sein Eh'gemahl zu sein,"[5] for instance, she gives special weight to that auxiliary "sein." She eases up on the word "Eh'gemahl," and then hits "sein" with such explosive force that one expects her to box Ortrud's ears to drive the point home. Similarly, in the passage, "für dich wollt ich zum Tode gehn,"[6] she stressed the "gehn." Now Lohengrin would not have doubted the intensity of her love had she chosen to ride to her death in a comfortable Pullman car.

In sum, the outstanding virtue of Frau Sucher's Elsa is the thoroughly intelligent, noble conception of the role, both in action and in song. She was at pains to subdue her own lively, vigorous and intrepid nature. If she was not invariably successful -- well, it's easier to be at once God and Satan than to be both a good Elsa and a proper Isolde. Frau Sucher is the latter in the highest degree. But more about that in due course.

Herr Vogl (Lohengrin) vindicated fully the reputation that had preceded him from Munich and Bayreuth. He is both an excellent singer and a resourceful actor. To the first pronouncement of the injunction against questioning, however, he gave too little significance, probably hoping to augment the effect of its subsequent reiteration. But the contrasts were wrong. With but a few strokes (to borrow from the painter's vocabulary) a great actor can prepare a significant climax. The purpose of the reiteration is not to frighten Elsa. The injunction, which echoes initially only in her ear, is supposed, like her savior's courtship, to penetrate to her heart. Herr Vogl's tone in the reiteration of the injunction should have been more solemn, but not stern.

But he sang the last verses, "Woher ich kam der Fahrt,"[7] etc., on the other hand, with a muted voice and with such an expression of solemnity and mystery in his countenance that none of his companions on the stage, certainly, can have doubted his divine mission, and even the unimpressionable parterre may have found itself half believing. This was an extraordinarily ingenious and intelligent nuance on Herr Vogl's part. His enunciation, unfortunately, reminds us so forcefully of Gustav Walter's that we cannot adequately condemn this regrettable circumstance. His habit, too, of swelling a tone out, and then suddenly breaking it off in a disruptive manner, is likewise reminiscent of Herr Walter. One's pleasure in our visitor's certainly admirable accomplishments was sensibly diminished by these cursed reminders of Herr Walter.

Herr Rokitansky wore the king's habiliments, and what he sang bore some resemblance to what King Henry is actually supposed to sing. But this excellent bass is so in love with himself and his baronial dignity that he declines to exchange his certificate of nobility even for the mantle of a king. He presents only himself, and very specifically himself, as a baron. But what does his profession require of him? The complete denial of his own identity. If Herr Rokitansky finds it impossible to reconcile the baron with the opera singer, he should make a choice one way or the other. And if he cannot forego the material advantages of his engagement at the Court Opera -- and one can need money without compromising one's baronial status -- then he ought to do his job. The least that can be asked of him is that he take it seriously.

None of all this does Herr Rokitansky appear to grasp. Not even a galley slave can have done his distasteful work more peevishly, more unwillingly, more indifferently, more apathetically, more resentfully than Herr Rokitansky sings and acts his parts. How was his King Henry? It was a visual and aural horror. The ratchety voice of the most loutish police inspector interrogating a confirmed criminal is the song of the nightingale compared with Herr Rokitansky's bark as he receives and interrogates the touching figure of Elsa, a vision of innocence as she approaches. Elsa should place her trust in such a monster? An encounter such as this should properly have left Elsa speechless, and the words, "mein armer Bruder"[8] unsaid.

Moreover, with what disregard for the rhythm, with what total want of expression, with what disdainful bearing did Herr Rokitansky offer the verses, "Was deutsches Land heisst"[9] and "Für deutsches Land das deutsche Schwert!"[10] As played by Herr Rokitansky this King Henry must be branded a traitor, secretly conspiring with the Hungarians under the table, and making a bad job of feigning enthusiasm for German splendor. Herr Rokitansky may think as he likes of and about the German Empire; he may find King Henry a simpleton and all Germans clowns; he may attribute more significance to a well-focused chest tone, in which one might well hibernate, than to *Lohengrin* and Wagner's other works -- that is all his business, which has nothing in common with ours. But when we are involved with others in a common endeavor, then the poet or the composer, or the poet-composer is sovereign, the singer only the composer's executant, and the sophisticated element among the audience can judge of each. When Herr Rokitansky presumes to impose his opinions on us, if they are not compatible with the author's, we reject them, as we have just now done, and as we shall always do!

The Telramund was Herr Sommer. This singer could, with the help of his excellent voice, conjure up at least a pale shadow of Telramund, if only he did not sing so tearfully. Telramund is no whiner, no infatuated puppet, no moonstruck booby. He is a hero through and through, and so he should be played. Herr Sommer would be well advised to put more vigor, more decision, more bite into his phrasing, and more strength and ferocity into his acting.

Herr Wiegand (Herald) should rid himself of the notion that sumptuous tone is the opera singer's ultimate responsibility. When one is summoning a champion for Elsa he should address himself to the background and not to the parterre, which is unlikely to yield a swan-drawn hero. Herr Wiegand should be on his guard against such absurdities. We have often noted similar incongruities in his work.

Fräulein Schläger (Ortrud) managed the invocation of the heathen gods effectively, thanks to her colossal voice. For the rest, there is not much to be said for her projection of this role. Herr Direktor Jahn, who conducted the performance, did not invariably find the right tempo. He might, too, have given more attention to the *p* and *pp* of the choruses. And what kind of stage direction was that in the fourth scene of the second act? What negligence! The music is supposed to accompany the solemn procession of Elsa and her retinue, but neither Elsa nor her retinue is on hand. They arrive thirty measures late, and then have to scurry along to make up for lost time. This kind of thing is all very disturbing. Everything possible should be done to see to it that it does not happen again!

As Isolde, Frau Sucher was now truly in her element. Her projection was almost entirely successful: a profoundly mortified woman, fretting and fuming, swearing vengeance and death, disdainful, embittered, angry, impatient, impetuous, at once furious and tender, at once gentle and forceful, a chaos of conflicting sentiments concentrated at one focal point in which her entire nature is gathered in a colossal psychological portrait and then resolved in her love for Tristan -- a woman racing through all the major, minor and chromatic tonalities of love.

In no other dramatic soprano of our acquaintance have we encountered such a lively and characteristic play of features, combined with attitudes and gestures at once so eloquent and so lovely. Her voice, if not notably ample, held up perfectly right through to the end. But much as Frau Sucher delighted us in the first two acts, it seemed as if she had been forsaken by her own guardian spirits in the third. The "Liebestod" could have been more transfigured, more removed from the workaday world. Well, so in this she was not successful, but we shall not quarrel with her on that account. One who negotiates securely the dizzy paths of the first act may well stumble in the less hazardous paths of the third.

Herr Vogl (Tristan), too, came to grief in the third act. But for a Tristan the third act is the test of his talent, just as the first act tests an Isolde. I would like to see the tenor who can survive the cliffs of that third act as happily as Isolde's ship survives the surf. Herr Vogl had some fine moments, and the uncommonly picturesque attitudes on the sick bed were surprisingly effective. But he seemed to work himself into a state of exaltation from which he could not escape, and consequently there was something contrived and cold about his most terrible agitation. Another thing: Tristan should not collapse before Isolde has taken him in her arms.

If Herr Vogl shared every other Tristan's fate in succumbing to the inhuman demands of the third act, he surpassed every other in the first. As he portrays Tristan, there can hardly have been a listener who was not brought closer to Tristan's heart and soul, or to whom the motivation of his behavior vis-a-vis Isolde and King Marke was not made utterly intelligible. This Tristan cannot have remained a hieroglyph to anyone in the theater. And if there was an exception, then this must have been someone who had never observed the magic realm of nighttime, or lovingly glimpsed the ideal world in which Tristan and Isolde live and breathe.

From Frau Papier we have grown accustomed to expect an excellent Brangaene ever since the first performance of *Tristan und Isolde* [the first Vienna performance, on October 4, 1883.] Herr Rokitansky (Marke), contrary to all expectations, was better than we had feared. He tried, at least, to impersonate King Marke, and that is saying a good deal. Herr Sommer (Kurwenal) was quite good, but it was comical to hear the hospital attendant whimpering in emulation of the fatally ill Tristan. Herr Sommer should make his Kurwenal more robust, and, above all, he should accommodate himself to the composer's directions. "Sein Haupt doch hängt in Irenland, als Zins gezahlt von Engeland"[11] he consistently sings incorrectly. Why does he slur the notes G and A on the preposition *im* and *von* on to the D and E flat, of the two following measures? That is not the way it stands in the vocal score, and the Kapellmeister should see to it that the singers commit no mischief. But the Kapellmeister! One could intone a pretty jeremiad on that subject. Herr Fuchs conducted the performance with such zeal that he utterly overlooked every tempo change. Herr Fuchs is an industrious fellow, and always in a hurry. One noted it especially in the gay tempo with which he flogged the Prelude along.

1.   Rosa Sucher (1849-1927), one of the great Wagnerian sopranos of her generation. At the time of this visit to Vienna, she was the prima donna and her husband, Josef Sucher (she was born Rosa Hasselbeck, or Halsbeck) the conductor at the opera in Hamburg. They later settled in Berlin. She was highly valued at Bayreuth, where she sang at every festival from 1886 to 1899.

2.   Heinrich Vogl (1845-1900), a great Wagnerian tenor, associated throughout his career with the opera in Munich, along with his wife, Therese (Thoma) Vogl, the first Sieglinde (in Munich in 1870) and a greatly admired Isolde. Vogl had been the Loge of the first productions of *Das Rheingold* in Munich (1869) and Bayreuth (1876), and the Siegmund of the first production of *Die Walküre* in Munich in 1870. He was also the first Tristan after Schnorr von Carolsfeld, who had created the role in Munich in 1865.

3.   "So radiant she appeared, and pure," sung by the knights at Elsa's entrance in Act I.

4.   "If he will call me wife, so shall I give him what I am," Act. I, Scene 2.

5.   "To be his bride before God," to Ortrud in Act II, Scene 2.

6.   "For you I would go to my death," from the love duet in Act III, Scene 2, when Elsa promises silence if Lohengrin were to confide the secret of his identity.

7.   "Whence the journey brought me," the question that Elsa must never ask, Act I, Scene 3.

8.   "My poor brother," Elsa's first words, Act I, Scene 2.

9.   "Whatever one knows as Germany," Act I, Scene 1.

10. "For German soil, the German sword," Act III, Scene 3.

11. "His head now hangs in Ireland, as tribute paid by England," Act I, Scene 2.

22. Sucher as Leonore, Vogl as Tannhäuser Opera Etiquette

June 15, 1884

Fidelio -- with Frau Sucher and Herr Vogl as guest artists. Two loquacious neighbors ruined the overture for me by their inconsiderate behavior. They were of that infamous category of public nuisance (Kapellmeister Kreisler[1] called them people with the souls of servants) that chatter during the performance, rattle their fans, let their gaze wander absently, greet their friends, wave to acquaintances, noisily lift and lower their folding seats, snap their opera glass cases open and shut, beat time with their feet, drum with their fingers, and commit more similar mischief. One of these creatures, during the playing of the great *Leonore* Overture, uttered to her companion (how characteristic of such miserable people!) the following remarkable words: "Look at this audience! So quiet and attentive. You'd think they were in a concert hall!"

I was dumbfounded by this shameless naiveté. There we have it! The perfectly natural and obviously appropriate deportment of a civilized audience -- a situation where not even a cannibal would be other than attentive and still as a mouse the minute the first strains of the overture resound through the hall -- regarded as curious and abnormal! Is what we hear in an opera house any less music than what is played in a concert hall? Does the quality of music depend upon the nature of the place in which it is listened to? Has anyone ever heard such hair-raising nonsense? Is the music of Mozart, Wagner, Gluck not music at all because it is produced in a theater? Are the absolute musical compositions of these masters there only to transport the bored, dirty, heedless creatures, fluttering from loge to parterre and from parterre to loge, on the golden surface of blossoming tone? An ignominious office even for the prudish muse of our symphony composers, riding the pack donkey or the camel. But to see the true, pure and unique muse of our dramatic composers, Gluck, Mozart, Weber, Marschner and Wagner, sacrificed to the cold scorn and the contemptuous stupidity of those people who betray themselves as inferiors in the theater and concert hall could turn a dove into a tiger from anger and pain. What is one to make of my estimable neighbor's clever words? That one goes to the theater to hear music? Good heavens, no. Anything but that! The best, the most sensitive, the most intelligent among these wretches go to the opera house to revel in an effective stage set, the pretty voice of a singer, the voluptuous hips of a ballerina. They have an eye for everything immaterial that takes place upon the stage. Only toward the music do they adopt a threatening attitude.

To a second category belong all those operagoers who attend the opera only in order to inspect continuously, both during the overture and even when the curtain is up, the boxholders, the newest fashions, the ladies' dresses, etc. These people preserve the most impervious indifference to the most obvious, the most effective happenings on the stage. For them the main thing is not the singer, male or female, but the virtuoso manipulation of the opera glass. The superlative category of such creatures, however, is composed of those who come for no other reason than to be seen. They always arrive after the overture, conduct themselves noisily, like ill-bred youngsters, as they enter. They happily make a racket with their seats and with the inevitable opera glass case, and then begin -- a conversation! This is conducted in a lively manner, and, despite its gaiety, one can detect the basic subject -- business. The bull and bear | markets | alternate in their conversation no less than *forte* and *piano* in the orchestra. Figures occur frequently. If ladies are involved, there will be amiable discussion of familial matters. How the cook knows how to prepare roast goose in a special way, how clever, how talented, how promising (!) their delightful children are, how little Elsa, despite the fact that she is just five, plays all of Mendelssohn's "Songs Without Words" from memory, how little Siegmund, or even Siegfried, is writing poems, and what a joy it is to experience such things. Etc. Etc. Too much, too much, I say with Tannhäuser.[2]

Let's change the subject.

Frau Sucher was all Fidelio to her colleagues on the stage, all Leonore to the audience. I feel that with these words I have given her the most extensive praise. She sang this wonderful music beautifully and with a warmth that mounted to consuming passion and resolution in the recitative and the allegro of the great aria. This artist has recently demonstrated that it is possible to achieve -- even without the *salto mortale* from the high to the low B -- an effect beyond the capacity of mere voice alone, be it ever so wide-ranged and sumptuous.

Herr Vogl, as Florestan, appealed more to the intelligence than to the heart. More conspicuous than usual was his distressing habit of attacking a note softly, swelling it out suddenly, and then just as suddenly breaking it off. I must confess that this peculiar way of singing affected me painfully. It is confined to his upper notes, and since Florestan moves in and around regions as high as the dungeon where he sits is deep, this | contrast |, perhaps beautifully conceived by the composer, was certainly not beautifully realized by Herr Vogl. That our distinguished visitor's performance was not lacking in stimulating dramatic insights was, in an artist of his intelligence, to be expected. The Rocco was Herr Baumann,[3] from Frankfurt am Main. He surprised us most agreeably with the naturalness of his acting, with his enunciation and with his exemplary vocalism. Herr Beck's[4] achievement as Pizarro is familiar. His voice is still strong, his movements still fresh. Age seems not to have affected him. Let us hope that he remains with the company for years to come.

As Tannhäuser, Herr Vogl was examplary in the first two acts. In the third, as in the third act of *Tristan und Isolde*, he could no longer sustain his flight on the wings given him by nature, and when he took to the flying machine, flapping around in anxious confusion, he bumped into every nook and cranny within the bounds of the artistically beautiful without finding the direct flight into the free air of immediacy. Herr Vogl is a splendid, abundantly endowed but always reflective artist. The thought-out, contrived, calculated, even highly imaginative character of his impersonations is no less damaging for all the excellent effects he so often achieves. It is all very well to make up through art what nature has failed to provide. But the paths of art should not deviate from those of nature, lest art be lost in artifice. Herr Vogl's acting sometimes borders on artifice. But while he does not have the elemental forcefulness, the immediacy of feeling that distinguish a natural-born Wagner interpreter such as Niemann,[5] he still has treasurable assets in sufficient abundance to outclass all our tenor-singing Wagner interpreters by far.

I was especially impressed by his costuming. This is something consistently overlooked in opera, and it is something to which it is impossible to pay too much attention. The noble, simple robe of Herr Vogl's Tristan, for example, bespoke the intelligent sensitive artist. He wore the same costume through all three acts, too. And why not? Women may deck themselves out in a variety of dresses. That is their domain, and therein lies half their worth. But there is no reason why Tristan should present himself as a parlor hero seeking to impress his lady love through the art of his tailor. Herr Winkelmann, as Tristan, saw fit to change costumes thrice, appearing in the first act in inappropriate pompous armor, in the second act in an informal dressing gown, and in the last in the habiliment of a Capuchin. He even played each of the three acts in conformity with the costume. Had he added to the cozy dressing gown of the second act a long pipe and pretty flowered slippers, it would at least have been something to laugh at. As it was, one could only be angry.

Herr Vogl, as Tannhäuser, wore a fiery red mantle over his shoulders at his first appearance in the Wartburg. The color was most becoming to the impetuous, sensual nature of Tannhäuser, the minstrel of love. From this one noted immediately that Herr Vogl comes from a city |Munich| inhabited almost exclusively by performing artists, whose benevolent influence on the theater can be recognized in such significant decorative details.

Frau Sucher is too heroic in her impersonation of Elisabeth. The childlike, the pure, and the naive are irreconcilable with her own personality (and women are, to be sure, always subjective). Her talent shone forth in those few moments when Elisabeth is propelled out of her true nature by an awful catastrophe. If she left much to be desired in the first half of the second act, she was magnificent in the second half, and her bearing while she pleaded for Tannhäuser's life was exemplary.

Herr Sommer has no inkling of the noble nature of Wolfram von Eschenbach, and on this occasion he was vocally unsatisfactory, too. Everything about him was rough and uncouth. Nor does Herr Schittenhelm have what is required for a worthy portrayal of Walter von der Vogelweide. *A propos*! Why do the singers and the Landgrave shun Elisabeth's funeral procession? Are they not closer to the departed Elisabeth than the common folk who surround the coffin? But the soloists are always in a hurry to be hasty. What does the stage director have to say about it?

Herr von Reichenberg,[6] from Hanover, as the Landgrave, cut an unintentionally comical figure. What a pompous, mawkish ass! What a to-do for a mere harlequin pirouette! What huffing and puffing for a couple of hollow tones! Herr Reichenberg cannot even enunciate correctly. Is it to be expected, then, that he can sing correctly? He makes an *o* out of an *u* in order, of course, to get from the *o* the additional tone that *u* will not yield. But why he also pronounces *oe* as *ui* is as incomprehensible to me as the childish good spirits that his Landgrave displayed in the second act with so much delight and self-satisfaction. This conception is original, to be sure, but only in the sense that it has a comical rather than the expected sober effect, just as this same Herr Reichenberg, in comical parts, can probably put the audience into the deepest mourning.

Another thing that displeased me about Herr Reichenberg was his arbitrary way with Wagner's verse. If these wilful variants were attributable to a treacherous memory, and he was merely making emergency calls on his own poetic vocabulary, well and good! In that case I shall only commend his ingenuity. But if it happened because he found his own text more suited than the composer's to a flattering flow of vocal sound, then may Herr Reichenberg make his next guest appearance among cannibals and fire-worshippers. A barbarian belongs among barbarians. A cultivated public -- as ironical as it may seem to speak of a cultivated opera public -- should be spared such outrages.

What I do not understand is why the conductor stands for such mischief. Where will we all end if he lowers himself to the status of the singers' obedient servant? Is the conductor to be a mere timebeater in the orchestra pit? Or should he maintain continuous liaison with the singers and with the stage? Should he not have a decisive word in a work of art that, like the dead creatures of Prometheus, stands before us in human form but can receive the divine spark only through the all-animating, all-permeating spirit of music?

It is all very well for the stage director to lubricate the stiff joints of his singers with the oil of professional craft. This is essential as a preparation for that further artistic development that is the responsibility of the conductor, assisted by the stage director. Will anyone deny that music speaks more eloquently than gesture? And if gestures are to reflect or grow out of the musical communication, how can this be made clear to the actor by an unmusical stage director?

Unless the singer is, himself, outstandingly gifted both musically and dramatically, able to comprehend the impetuous language of music in its innermost marrow, and translate it into visible movement and gesture, then only the conductor can determine whether his bearing and facial expression are appropriate, either approximately or entirely, to the phrase that has called them into play. All this assumes, of course, that the conductor himself is not blind to plastic art. How difficult it is to find such a conductor! If he were to be found, his activity would be confined to the orchestra. If he were not so confined, no one would follow his directions anyway. And so, having arrived at the *ultimo ratio*, we close this chapter.

Siegfried, musical drama in three acts by Richard Wagner. Confronted with such an accomplishment as Herr Vogl's Siegfried, even the most exacting criticism must be silent. Herr Vogl showed us, from his first entrance to the fall of the final curtain, the ideal Siegfried. Never, probably, has he sung more beautifully. How truthfully, how convincingly and how naturally he acted this most splendid of all figures of the theater, the young hero, Siegfried! It is impossible to do justice to his masterly, almost miraculous achievement. So we shall say no more.

Frau Sucher, as Brünnhilde, was a worthy partner. One could have shouted with rapture along with the glorious couple in the third act. It was truly Siegfried and Brünnhilde, no longer Vogl and Sucher. This day will remain indelibly impressed upon our memories. We cannot be sufficiently grateful to Intendant, Herr Baron Hofmann for having secured this artistic Castor and Pollux for our theater, if only for a short space of time. Herr Baumann (Wanderer) handled himself well, although not in a manner to challenge comparison with Herr Scaria. But he did his best within his capacities. The other participants discharged their difficult tasks industriously. Even the orchestra, under the direction of Kapellmeister Fuchs, played with zest, and mostly in the right tempi.

May the sympathetic reader of our periodical permit me a few words of seasonal farewell. First of all, may he kindly excuse the many typographical errors that have crept into almost every one of my articles. I gladly confess that the fault was mostly mine. If my strictures have seemed to him to be unduly severe, let him remember that everyone who stands up for truth and justice, and who takes the field against deceit, will, from time to time, become a bit hot under the collar. At such times one is not very choosy with words. Truth is not the language of decorum, which is the language of diplomats. As Goethe has said: "In German, when one is polite, one lies." And anyway, elegant writing was not my concern. He who pays too great heed to form tends only too often to lose sight of substance. It is best, of course, when form and substance are all one. To achieve this union shall be my constant endeavor if, in the next season, I shall be reminding the sympathetic reader of my existence.

1.   The Kapellmeister in E.T.A. Hoffmann's "Fantasiestücke in Callots Manier," which inspired Schumann's "Kreisleriana."

2.   "Zu viel, zu viel!" — Tannhäuser's very first words in Wagner's opera, uttered in response to Venus's query, "Geliebter, sag', wo weilt dein Sinn?" (Tell me, beloved, where does your mind wander?)

3.   Carl Baumann, a German baritone who sang at the Metropolitan in the first German season of 1884-85.

4.   Johann Nepomuk Beck (1827-1904) was principal baritone at the Court Opera from 1853 to 1888. He had been Wagner's first choice for Hans Sachs. He did not sing the Munich premiere, but he was the Sachs of the first Vienna *Die Meistersinger* in 1870.

5.   Albert Niemann (1831-1917), one of the earliest and greatest of Wagnerian tenors. He was the Tannhäuser of the ill-fated Paris production of 1861 and the Siegmund of the first Bayreuth *Ring*.

6.   Franz von Reichenberg (1853-?), a Styrian bass-baritone who had joined the company in 1884. He was the Fafner of the first Bayreuth *Ring*.

23. Der Vampyr, *Romantic Opera by Heinrich Marschner*

October 19, 1884

Fifty-six years have passed since *Der Vampyr*[1] was first produced in Leipzig in 1828 and established its composer's reputation. He died long ago [in 1861]. The one-sided romantic movement has had its day. A new transition period emerged in the French grand opera. However rotten it was at its core, however superficial and vulgarly painted its shell, however useless its allegedly dramatic trapping, it still advanced the limited horizon of the sickly, introspective romanticists. This was primarily on the basis of the historical opera as conceived by Scribe, which in contrast to the mystical haze of the romanticists advanced their modest world of illusion so close to reality that the emphasis was no longer on the mere expression of feeling but was transferred essentially to the dramatic situation, a process in which more resin was wasted than true music was made. This will-of-the-wisp, too, had to fade before the sunlight of the Wagnerian artistic ideal. A new world of the spirit had opened up before us, from which alone we draw our spiritual and emotional nourishment: the Wagnerian music drama.

One may well ask in astonishment what this introduction has to do with a review of *Der Vampyr*. Well, if this opera had been indifferently received, it could have been an apology for the author of the bad libretto. Since, however, despite its silly subject, and despite its fifty-six years, it delighted the audience, one can discern therein a proof of the great genius, the eminent dramatic endowment of the composer, who only in Vienna, unfortunately, is unjustly neglected. Just observe the empty spaces in the parterre and even in the gallery at a performance of his masterpiece, *Hans Heiling*. These are sad omens. And now to the subject in hand.

About the reason for which Lord Ruthwen is condemned to wander around as a vampire, the libretto, curiously, tells us nothing. In general, legend has it that criminals, dying under a church ban, cannot decay after death, but must wander as vampires, gnawing on their own corpses, tortured by pangs of conscience lingering from the curse associated with their crimes, sucking the blood of their friends and relatives. This belief was, and to some extent still is, common in the countries of the southern Balkan peninsula. The ancient Greeks, too, suffered under similar delusions. Their demons were beautiful, ghostly women who, through various magic arts, lured youths in order to relish their fresh blood. It was the same with the lemurs of the Romans. One sees from all this that the legend of the vampires is no product of modern times, although the belief in these bloodthirsty monsters is no longer so prevalent among the people as in olden times.

I shall now relate in its bare outlines the course of the narrative, combining the synopsis with an assessment of the music.

At the rise of the curtain we behold a wild, romantic, rocky terrain, the vampires' cave, as it is popularly known. Weird shapes and forms, witches, spooks, will-of-the-wisps and more of the same swirl about in mad confusion. It is a fantastic picture, animated by wonderfully descriptive music that transports us, as if by the stroke of a magic wand, into the spirit world. Here, already, the tone poet reveals himself in all his individuality. Invention and the most striking graphic gift lend this scene a special distinction. Indeed, throughout this work Marschner is bold and original whenever the demonic-fantastic element is dominant, whereas he is too heavily influenced by Weber's magic in the treatment of purer realms. But more of that at the proper time.

Attended by thunder and lightning, the Master enters, leading Lord Ruthwen by the hand. In a short, impressive melodrama, the Master advises his hellish subjects that he wishes to grant the vampire's request to spend a year among humans, but only on condition that he contract, before the coming midnight, to deliver to hell (in other words to suck their blood) "three brides, tender and pure." (A spoiled devil, this. Samiel, in *Der Freischütz*, contents himself with the poor soul of a devout young hunter, and throws a full year's grace into the bargain.) Lord Ruthwen swears to this tidy contract (he would hardly have become a vampire because of perjury, since we cannot assume that the devil would be stupid enough to accept the oath of a perjurer), and, anticipating the approach of one of the victims, he motions his blood-sucking colleague to leave the stage. This takes place to a charming chorus, a splendid companion piece to the first. On the stroke of one the hellish brood has vanished. The vampire remains behind, alone.

Now comes the great recitative and aria. This piece, in my opinion, constitutes the musical high point of the opera. The night-shrouded spookiness of the preceding scene rises to a peak of demonically glowing passion, to outbursts of cruelly lustful outcries, to a riot of convulsively drunken rage, ungovernable craving and sensual frenzy unprecedented and unexampled in the entire literature of music:

Und wenn der brennende Durst sich stillt,
Wenn das Blut dem Herzen entquillt,
Wenn sie stöhnen voll Entsetzen --
Welch Ergötzen, welche Lust!

[And when the burning thirst is sated,
The heart's blood's flow is unabated,
When they groan, by horror struck,
What joyous rapture, what rare delight!]

In the rising and falling chromatic figures for the violins that accompany these words, one can fairly see the victim's blood trickling. One sees the sharp white teeth boring greedily into the victim, one hears the death rattle of the deceived, punctuated by shrill hellish shouting and the insane laughter of the vampire. An unspeakable lament moans through the racket of the piled-up masses of sound from time to time, and then with a cry of the most desperate horror this grandiose-ghastly tone picture buries itself in the broad chords of D minor, spreading like the jaws of hell -- destroyed --.

The awaited bride appears. We know immediately that it is she, for in her flight from her parents' home she still wears her wedding dress. That is childish, and extremely inconvenient, too. One does not wander around in rocky chasms done up in a bridal veil. Nor did we see any priests, witnesses, bridesmaids, etc., on the stage. Such absurdities should be avoided. The vampire plays the tender swain, and in a pretty duet they assure one another of their mutual love, devotion and more of the same just as any ordinary loving couple would do. Hardly has the vampire secured his beauty when the disconsolate father and his following arrive in hot pursuit. The area is thoroughly searched, and the conclusion reached that this is an accursed place, the vampires' cave. Horror-stricken at such intelligence, everyone hastens to leave this eerie locale when the bride's calls for help are heard, answered by the vampire's satanic laughter. The crowd dashes into the cave, hauls the vampire on stage, and he, fatally stabbed by the maddened father's dagger, falls to the ground. The unhappy father is then told that his daughter has fallen victim to the vampire.

Now everyone takes to his heels in earnest, and only the wounded Ruthwen breathes his agony into the desolate ravines, echoing scornful laughter from hell. He is doomed unless some mortal take pity on him, and lead him to the summit, in order that the moon may shine in his face. Only the absorption of its beams, and nothing else, can cure him from head to foot. And, indeed, the savior nears. Aubry, a Scottish nobleman, chances by, and recognizes in Lord Ruthwen an old acquaintance who had once saved his life. He promptly undertakes the role of good Samaritan. But first Aubry, who sees his suspicions confirmed that Lord Ruthwen had become a vampire -- as he had heard told in London -- must swear to keep this awful secret to himself for twenty-four hours. Out of gratitude he accepts this condition -- soon to become fateful for him -- and swears his oath. This oath is now the dramatically tied knot about which the entire interest of the narrative winds like a bookworm, and which, through a mighty stroke in the last act (when the clock strikes one) is happily unravelled.

But to get back to our story, we follow Aubry and the vampire as they ascend the heights, and we do it from the orchestra. An uncommonly evocative melodrama describes the severely wounded vampire's tortuous progress up the rocky peak. The twilight, the ominous stillness, the portentous silence of a transfixed nature, the tenderness of shining moonbeams and the gradually increasing intensity of the pale light -- they find here their most eloquent expression. It is a masterpiece of atmospheric tone painting, in which Marschner achieves the surprising, the astonishing, with the simplest means. Now comes a moment that makes the heart quake. The vampire, drawn by the moonbeams, lifts himself, first slowly, slowly, like a puppet, without the slightest movement, on high. The deathly pale countenance, appearing even more spooky in the moonlight, comes alive, the breast begins to breathe, the limbs to move, and suddenly, with a mighty chord in the orchestra, the vampire stands, hale and hearty, before our spellbound gaze, which, even after the fall of the curtain, remains fixed in the direction from which that grisly vision appeared.

We shall cover the ensuing two acts more briefly, as they do not, on the whole, achieve the significance of the first. But there are exceptions.

We pass over lightly the opening scene and aria of Malvina, a lovely spring-like strain without any special individuality, and sometimes vividly reminiscent of Weber in its melodic flow. The character sketched by the librettist must command our attention more than the soprano, rather grudgingly treated by the composer, if only because she is the only one of the three brides who does not episodically come and go. Malvina loves Aubry. She herself tells us as much in the opening aria. Aubry loves Malvina, as we are informed at some length in a charming love duet. But now her father, Davenaut, enters, and tells his daughter that he has found for her in the person of Lord Ruthwen a tender bridegroom and for himself a son-in-law who will bring honor to the family. That, of course, throws everything into confusion. Plaintive weeping and wailing from the daughter. Silent despair on the part of the unhappy Aubry. Rage and angry outbursts from the father -- an old story, as it has happened so often before, and will happen again.

Lord Ruthwen appears, and is introduced to the prospective bride who, naturally, feels nothing for him but revulsion. The wedding is to take place that very same day. Vain remonstrances. The father is adamant. Now Aubry recognizes Lord Ruthwen as the vampire whose life he has just saved. He thinks to make an end of the confused affair at one stroke, and betray the vampire's secret. But the wretched oath, of which Ruthwen reminds him most urgently, ties his tongue, and it looks as if Malvina will be torn from Aubry for ever. At the end of the act, at least, we are left in uncertainty. The finale of this act begins with an utterly delightful chorus which subsequently yields to a new strain that pleases me less. The conclusion is rather effective.

What life there is, however, at the beginning of the third act! What freshness, what dithyrambic high spirits in the folk scenes, or rather drinking scenes. I wish to mention here the masterfully composed quintet and the ensuing chorus. Never has drunkenness been set to music so delightfully, so merrily, as in this quintet, and it was especially well served by the inexhaustible high spirits of Herr Mayerhofer and Herr Lay.[2] In this act we make the acquaintance of the third bride, Emmy. She is engaged to George, a tenant farmer on Ruthwen's estate. Predictably, this beauty, too, could not withstand the flattering words and irresistibly charming appearance of the vampire. In a duet — probably the best number after the great aria of the vampire — wonderfully fashioned, compellingly expressive, intensely dramatic and melodically most blossoming, she gives herself to the monster, to experience personally the fate of which she has just warned her wedding guests in a Romanza — that of becoming the vampire's victim. This Romanza may well have echoed in Richard Wagner's ears when he composed the Ballade in *The Flying Dutchman*. The form is exactly the same. Here, as there, the tale of the pale man. For the horrid fate of the vampire, too, one hears the voice of sympathy, and the chorus, as well, deeply moved, joins in the refrain. That the Ballade in *The Flying Dutchman* is more gripping, much more, is so obvious that supporting argumentation would be superfluous. There is a tremendous difference between the one and only Dutchman and the many vampires wandering around the world. Even the sudden appearance of the vampire at the conclusion of the Romanza, and the attendant horror of the wedding guests, provide only a superficial counterpart to the similar situation in *The Flying Dutchman*. Wagner, certainly, had absorbed all the elements of romanticism, but what with the romanticists was superficial and empty is sublimated by Wagner to symbolic profundity, to plastic images founded on exceptional human interest.

But now the vampire must quickly be packed off to the devil, for otherwise he will end by sucking the blood of poor Malvina. Let's get on with it. The scene changes. The time for the wedding ceremony approaches. Bridal chorus as at the begining of Act III. As the pair approaches the altar, Aubry rushes to intercept them, hurling sarcastic references to Lord Ruthwen's blood-sucking propensities. Excitement and confusion among the wedding guests. Aubry is thrown out. Malvina now resolutely declines to give Ruthwen her hand. Davenaut, beside himself with rage, curses his daughter. Great horror among the bystanders. Ruthwen demands an instant decision. His fate hangs upon seconds, as midnight will soon be passed. The altar is approached again, and again Aubry intervenes, pleading with Davenaut and on the point of uttering the decisive word: that Ruthwen is a vampire. Suddenly, there is a mighty detonation. The earth opens up, spewing fire, and the devil, with grisly gestures, seizes the vampire. As the latter is sucked beneath the surface, Aubry tells the bystanders just who Lord Ruthwen had been. Thus Aubry has revealed his secret just seconds before midnight and one may hope that he will be spared all the horrors threatened by the vampire in his big scene. Joy, emotion, jubilation! Aubry leads Malvina to the altar, and with a theme all but identical with the middle episode of the Overture to *Euryanthe* the opera ends to the great satisfaction of all men of good will!

The production was brilliant. Herr Reichmann, as the vampire, surpassed himself, and he is always an artist who hits the nail on the head. He got a tremendous ovation after his big scene and at the close of each act. After him we would mention especially, and ahead of all others, the splendid achievement of Herr Winkelmann as Aubry. The three unfortunate brides, Frau Kupfer[3] (Malvina), Fräulein Pirk (Janthe) and Frau Naday (Emmy) gave of their best. Herr Reichenberg (Davenaut) speaks beautifully; if he could only sing beautifully, too. All praise to Herr Direktor Jahn, who was responsible for rescuing the opera from the dust of the archives. If the choristers had sung the *pp* passages of the first act more softly, they would have been still better. The house was sold out. The audience was enthusiastic. The opera will have, one hopes, a long run. Good luck, blood-sucker!

1. Derived from *The Vampyre* by Dr. John William Polidori (1795-1821).
2. Theodor Lay (1825-1893), baritone, a member of the Court Opera from 1856 to 1891.
3. Mila Kupfer, née Ludmilla Berger (1850-1905), a Viennese soprano who sang at the Court Opera from 1875 to 1885. She subsequently switched to Italian opera and continued her career in Italy, Spain and South America. She ended it as a singing teacher in Vienna.

24. Le Postillon de Longjumeau[1]

October 26, 1884

A crazy notion, to balance on a rope when drunk to keep from falling over; or to tell a second person a secret in such a secretive manner as to imagine that you have given nothing away or, more to the point, to a third person — since secrets shared by two are often kept — or, in a state of pitiable decrepitude, and with a cold, hoarse voice, to solicit the applause of the Viennese public, that Viennese opera public that quietly accepts the most incredible absurdities in matters affecting its intelligence, its artistic sensibilities, but bares its teeth when a hoarse dissonance interrupts its eternal lullaby, as Herr Theodor Wachtel,[2] Royal Prussian Kammersänger, did recently.

What in heaven's name can have prompted Herr Wachtel, now in his declining years as an itinerant singer [he was sixty-one], to torture people? Has he, then, no friends to restrain him in his grisly undertaking? Or is the demon of vanity in him more powerful than any reasonable representations? Herr Wachtel resembles precisely in that respect those old spinsters who, decrepit as they may be, cannot leave off coquetry and flirtation, a spectacle that tickles the risibilities.

How does Herr Wachtel sing? It's hard to say anything about it because, in fact, his singing hardly differs from the yowls of a tomcat of modest vocal endowment whose tail has just been stepped on. He can, on the other hand, click his tongue with a skill no coachman will match. One notes immediately that he has had much practice,[3] and the postilion of Longjumeau becomes a credible Herr von St. Phar.[4] What all did Wachtel not attempt in trying to produce one half-way decent tone? In vain. But what remained denied to the singer stood the postilion, at least, in good stead, and if Herr Wachtel will make no effect with what is left of his voice, the whip-cracking effects in *Le Postillon de Longjumeau* are still securely his. They earned the most applause.

Herr Stoll,[5] as the Marquis vividly projected the pompous demeanor, the silliness, the comical precision of the mawkish fop. We are happy to encounter a fine actor in our opera house again. About the voice I can offer no judgment, as the Marquis' music is mostly *parlando*. Our admirable buffo, Herr Mayerhofer, helped the very antiquated subject along with some novel business. Predictably, Herr Mayerhofer, in the second act, had to let the upstart tenor sing like a quail [*Wachtel*], while comparing his voice with the fluting of a nightingale.

But how would it be if the guest's name were Hahn [rooster] or Hahn-hahn? Would he not have had to crow like two roosters? And did Herr Wachtel not indeed crow like two roosters? But how can a quail crow like two roosters? We leave it to Herr Mayerhofer's amiable humor to solve this scientifically ticklish problem.

1.   Comic opera by Charles Adolphe Adam (1803-1856), first produced in 1836.

2.   A German tenor (1823-1893), whose long career had taken him not only to most of the German opera houses, but also to London, Paris and North America, where he ranged as far west as California. Especially noted in his prime for a high C from the chest, he retired in 1887.

3.   His father had owned a stable in Frankfurt am Main, and on the latter's death young Theodor continued the business before taking up singing.

4.   The plot has to do with a postilion whose singing is overheard by the Marquis de Corcy, a talent scout for the Opéra. He is engaged, and takes the stage name of St. Phar.

5.   August Stoll (1853 ?), a former operetta tenor who had just joined the company. His theatrical flair, noted by Wolf, is reflected in the fact that in the following year he became a stage director, continuing as singer in character parts. Such was his routine and versatility that on one occasion he, a tenor, saved a performance of *Aida* by singing the king.

25. A Monologue Recalled by Hugo Wolf

November 1, 1884

One thoroughly unpleasant night, not long ago, I spied a stranger standing before a kiosk, trying earnestly by the gaslight to decipher the Philharmonic prospectus. I step a little closer, and hear a monologue, now quiet, now agitated, which seemed to contain so much truth that, upon returning to my lodging, I wrote it all down, determined, on some suitable occasion, to publish it. I do so herewith:

"Philharmonic concerts", — so he began — "probably the same old hackneyed stuff. Let's see, Bach, Mozart, Beethoven, Haydn — good, good. — The public loves classical music. It is very cultivated, very serious, very upright, very severe! Beethoven, Mozart, Haydn are actually already too familiar, too melodious, too intelligible. But Bach! Only a violin concerto this time, to be sure, but even if there are no double fugues, no twelve-voiced canons, one can still be sure of some masterly counterpoint" — here he mimicked derisively the public's rapture. "Ah, Bach! Yes, of course. That's music! Everything granite, bronze, everywhere deep, elemental, great, exalted, genius!" Then in his natural voice: "Goodness me! I do believe that the Philharmonic audience would rather flounder in the Pontine marshes than hear compositions of this esteemed master if they did not adorn the programs of the Philharmonic. But what does one not suffer for fashion? Bach has become fashionable with the Philharmonic audience, and it is thought good form to tick off all the Bach cantatas with one's fingers and, in the middle of a Mendelssohn Song Without Words, to exclaim: 'Very nice, charming, but why don't you play the St. Matthew Passion, or the St. John, or the Christmas Oratorio, or the Well-Tempered Clavier?'

" 'I'll play you the Italian Concerto.'

" 'That's nothing. Play the B minor Mass from memory, or at least from the score.'

" 'Good heavens, the man is cultivated!' —

"Innocent soul! — Don't believe a word of it. Play your 'Songs Without Words,' for your Bach enthusiast is already scared stiff that you may inadvertently lay out a dozen Bach cantatas on the music rack. He would as soon swallow vitriol as listen to a cantata from beginning to end.

"How many make the detour via Bach's complete works, which they 'would like to hear,'" in order to pull up at last at |Johann Strauss's | *Der lustige Krieg*, or, if all goes well, at Chopin's Waltz in D flat. Yes, what all of Bach's profundity cannot achieve, fashion brings to pass. It is the intermediary between this composer and our public. And, since Bach's authority, fortunately, comes to the latter's assistance, one may safely assume that its applause is sincere, i.e., that it originates in a firm belief in Bach's enormous classicism!

"Brahms? Goodness! He gives old Bach a run for his money when it comes to classicism. Herr von Bülow, to be sure, modestly terms our shrewd symphonist merely Ludwig II, thus denying him the ultimate classicism, since he presumes to acknowledge in Herr Brahms a perpetuator of Beethoven when Ludwig I, in his last period, cannot be called a classicist in any strict sense of the term. Can it be, perhaps, that Herr von Bülow errs? Was it, perhaps, not at all his intention to injure his friend Brahms by so thoughtless a word, and thus to have underestimated his classicism?

"What else do we have here ? Schumann, Schubert, Mendelssohn - Dvořák? But not a symphony, for God's sake? No! Slavonic Rhapsody — in God's name!" — Let the amiable reader not be surprised at the double invocation. One grows pious in adversity, and to hear a piece by Dvořák seems to my stranger to represent a misfortune. — "Robert Fuchs? Aha, another serenade? No, a symphony. Robert Volkmann — probably a symphony? No, a serenade. Next year it will be the other way around: symphony by Volkmann, serenade by Fuchs. Oh, well, we must have variety, and the Philharmonic know all about that! 'Penthesilea' by Goldmark — a splendid subject for musical development; but the composer's talent is not commensurate with the greatness of the material. Only a Makart¹ could have caught Penthesilea in colors, only a Liszt or a Berlioz in music? No one else could do it. But is that all the prospectus has to offer?

"Ha! Richard Wagner: 'A *Faust* Overture.' We always enjoy hearing that. But why not the 'Siegfried Idyll?' Why not the new Venusberg music, which we are also denied in the opera? Why not excerpts from *Der Ring des Nibelungen?* or *Parsifal?* Why? Why?

"But what? And how? Do my eyes deceive me? Berlioz? Symphonie Fantastique? No, really? That's absolutely impossible — and yet, there it is, plain as can be: Symphonie Fantastique by Hector Berlioz. No, the courage of the Philharmonic has something Spartan about it. They dare to shock their subscribers with such a thing. Oh! It's hilarious how the classical public trembles at the prospect, how the pure at heart among them lower their pious gaze because at the end comes a witches' sabbath, how the serious-minded condemn the mad substance, how the pedants rage at the free form, the free harmonies, the free fantasy and the composer's other freedoms!

"Needless anxiety! Needless rage! Exaggerated agitation. The Philharmonic can easily speak of the devil, because it lies in their power to let him in. 'Honorable public,' I would like to say, 'he will not show up. Console yourselves. You will not have to hear the Symphonie Fantastique. I could almost promise it. So, be calm.'

"The gentlemen of the Philharmonic are far too polite to concern themselves with what might be in their subscribers' interest, and far too contented to permit themselves any honorable agitation for their own sake, even if it were to displease a cultivated public. Otherwise, they would have to include a symphonic poem by Liszt in each of their concerts, and get it through their heads, at last, that among twelve symphonic poems, with which Liszt has earned first place after Beethoven in the field of purely instrumental music, the choice must not be restricted to 'Les Préludes' and 'Mazeppa.'

"If the Philharmonic Society were truly animated by an artistic spirit, their objective should be to educate an audience, to cultivate it. This can be achieved successfully only by ruthless measures. Nothing serious, nothing great, nothing significant will be gained with concessions here, concessions there. This is as true of art as of life. And with the Philharmonic everything favors a ruthless policy. It has, to begin with, no competition, standing quite alone of its kind. Herr Kretschmann's[3] Orchestra Society is hardly to be compared with it. Things are different in Paris, Berlin, London, and even Leipzig. There one can speak of competition, but in Vienna . . . . . Secondly, the public flocks to the Philharmonic not only because it has no other way of satisfying its hunger for music, but also because fashion dictates that one be seen there. Whoever can produce a season ticket to the Philharmonic concerts is to the unfortunates who cannot as are fat people, with their substantial shadows, to the tragic Schlemils who, casting no shadow at all, have no right to existence. Not to speak of the Founder tickets, whose owners are so proud of their property that our planet would long ago have collapsed under the weight of their prodigious complacency were such complacency not, fortunately, distributed among all the other planets. A concert institution, however, that regularly finds subscribers is also relieved of financial anxieties. What prevents the Philharmonic, then, from proceeding more artistically in the building of its programs than has heretofore been the case? Are there solid reasons for its inartistic policies? I think not. Had I a decisive voice in the selection of programs, I would say: We shall play something of Liszt or Berlioz in every concert, as these are two masters whose greatness and significance the public has yet to grasp. Should the public protest at first, so what? Time will take care of that. The public's indifference toward these masters will turn to attentiveness, its frivolity into reverence, its astonishment into comprehension and then into admiration, love and enthusiasm. You will be praised for having achieved through your determination that which your calling requires: to lend your resonant organ to all that represents progress in art, that announces itself as truly new, substantial and pathbreaking, that raises itself above the common and mediocre, and strives toward the ultimate, shrinking before no difficulty, and holding out to the last man when it is a matter of serving a worthy cause!"

Thus, in short, and approximately, the monologue of that nocturnal enthusiast whose views may well strike a sympathetic chord in many a reader of these lines.

1.   Hans Makart (1840-1884), Austrian painter famed for his rich and vivid coloring, and Wagner's favorite painter. The Makartplatz in Salzburg commemorates his birth in that city.

2.   A curious observation, as Wolf himself had just completed the first draft of a tone poem based on Heinrich Kleist's "Penthesilea." Was this an admission of doubt as to his own ability to bring it off? In any case, he persisted, and his score was read at a rehearsal of the Philharmonic on October 15, 1886. Unbeknownst to Hans Richter, Wolf was present. The reading, according to Wolf, was a travesty. It was greeted by the orchestra with laughter, whereupon Richter said: "Gentlemen, I should not have let this piece be played to the end, but I wanted to see for myself the man who dares to write in such a way about Meister Brahms."

3.   Theobald Kretschmann (1850-1929), Bohemian cellist, conductor and composer. At the time of writing he was first cellist of the orchestra of the Court Opera and organizer of a series of concerts with an orchestra of his own.

26.   Bülow and the Meiningen Court Orchestra

November 9, 1884

We have had frequent occasion to admire Bülow as a piano virtuoso, almost none to give him his due as a conductor. I remember him conducting his own "Des Sängers Fluch"[1] several years ago. What impressed me then, however, was something purely superficial, namely the vigor and security with which he commanded his forces. It should be different this time, for he will be conducting a considerable number of Beethoven's compositions at the head of his own orchestra.[2]

We will thus be in a position to appraise Bülow from two points of view: that of the theoretical musician (artist) in his conception of the works themselves, and that of the practical musician (virtuoso) in the extent to which he succeeds in communicating his conception as urgently and as intelligibly as possible to the orchestra. As a pianist, Bülow has solved brilliantly this problem of uniting artist and virtuoso. Encountering him now as conductor, we shall be concerned only with the virtuoso, the practical musician, and then we must give some attention to this other instrument, the orchestra, both as such, and in its relationship to the conductor.

One can be an excellent conductor and still not establish the intimate relationship with a strange orchestra that the virtuoso has with his instrument, and for a simple reason: the instrument is a soulless mechanism, the orchestra an organic body, made up of the greatest variety of individuals. It may matter little to the piano virtuoso whether he plays a Bösendorfer, a Blüthner, a Bechstein or a Steinway, assuming the instrument itself to be good and in good order. Nor will it make any difference to X that Y played on the same instrument the day before, and so on.

Not so with the orchestra, which accustoms itself, in time, to its conductor, regardless of how much it may have resisted him at the beginning. It is a wild horse, initially hostile to bridle and rider, but, in the end, responsive to both. But let a strange rider come along, who does not handle the reins just as the first rider did, and there will be the devil to pay.

So it is in the relationship between orchestra and conductor. Tradition is powerful, habit, perhaps, the strongest of all passions. Let us assume that the orchestra's own conductor has thoroughly impressed upon it the stamp of his own individuality in terms of rhythm, melos, solo playing, ensemble, the various adjustments of strings, woodwinds and brass in the constant fluctuation of accents and nuances from *ppp* to *fff*, and a thousand other refinements. For this orchestra to give to a new conductor in a few rehearsals the response achieved by its own conductor in years of careful work is as impossible as everything is supposed to be possible for God. What a cross must Berlioz have had to bear with all those various orchestras when he was introducing his works to Germany! Bülow has been well advised to travel with his own bag and baggage, i.e., with his own orchestra.

But there is still the question: What kind of orchestra is it? Berlioz says: "One must distinguish between an opera orchestra and a concert orchestra. In general, the former may be considered, in certain respects, inferior to the latter." He neglected, however, to identify the distinction and to spell out its implications. With his predilection for outsized orchestras, he apparently had in mind the size, and the normally more favorable disposition, of the concert orchestra. This would apply only in a limited degree to the Meiningen Orchestra. It plays concerts only, but it numbers not more than sixty men.

We see no great harm in that. There are reasons enough, despite Berlioz's reservations, why even a small orchestra may enjoy an advantage over a theater orchestra, even one playing concerts, be it ever so large. First and foremost is the fact that a concert orchestra, giving a concert every two or three weeks, is not so overworked as the opera orchestra, which plays almost every evening. That kind of drudgery is numbing. It leads to indifference and, in a work requiring many rehearsals, hostility. That work, without rehearsals, will succumb to routine.

Secondly and thirdly, there must be other factors favoring the concert orchestra, but they do not come immediately to mind. One must leave the reader with something to think about. There occurs to me now a second, even a third and fourth factor, but as a matter of courtesy I shall refrain from disturbing my amiable reader in his cogitation, and thus offending him. I shall keep them to myself. In any case, there is much to be said for the concert orchestra. You may rest assured of that.

But a concert orchestra is not sufficient unto itself. It is a healthy body. It eats well, drinks well and sleeps well. It is able, therefore, to withstand much and to accomplish something. But it lacks a head. The Meiningen Orchestra has a head, and no less a one than -- Hans von Bülow. That, indeed, is about all that needs to be said, and I could just as well go to bed, the ghosts having long since crept into their haunts. But my esteemed boss would hardly wish me a friendly "good night" if my contribution were so meager. So let us continue.

All the world knows Bülow as a piano virtuoso. Among virtuosos, he stands alone as an interpreter of classical music, especially of Beethoven's keyboard works. This artist is, indeed, one of the few consoling phenomena in the swarm of our modern pianists, one who concentrates his capacities in a more profound conception, a thoroughly thought out, ultimately objective representation of the substance of the great masters (and I don't mean Brahms, to whose compositions Bülow has recently turned with sheerly pathological mania) in contrast to the smart, impertinent youngsters from the Liszt school who perceive the objective of their envisioned mastery in machine-like, vacuous acrobatics, superficial glitter, leaps and capers and other such ludicrously tasteless nonsense, and imagine themselves to be working wonders while pounding the instrument like devils possessed. These marauding pianistic nine-day wonders do their great master little honor.

If we have known Bülow heretofore as one of the most ideal interpreters of Beethoven on the piano, we shall soon have occasion to admire him as such at the head of his own orchestra.

Under his baton this orchestra has become a mirror reflecting most intimately his artistic individuality, just as the musical substance of a composition, its innermost core laid bare, is reflected in Bülow's own extremely sensitive powers of apprehension. It is his most intimate friend, the echo of his voice, his heartbeat and his thoughts. This orchestra's relationship to its conductor is something like that of steel to a magnet — obedient to his will as to a superior natural force.

It is, in short, nothing other than a piano in Bülow's hands, but larger, richer in resources of tone color, and immeasurably more eloquent. It may be inferior to other orchestras in size, but in intrinsic value it probably surpasses most of our concert and opera orchestras. Bülow may proudly display as his motto: Quality, not quantity, is our specialty!

You have admired the artist at the piano. This time it will be his baton that ignites fires of rapture in your head and heart!

1.   A Ballade for Orchestra, Opus 16.

2.   Bülow accepted the position of director of music to the Duke of Meiningen in 1880, and remained for five years. On this visit to Vienna the orchestra gave three concerts in the Grosser Musikvereinssaal, on November 20 and 25 and December 2.

27. A Vocal Mystery

November 16, 1884

We have heard Herr Bötel ¹from the Municipal Opera in Hamburg for the first time as Lionel in Flotow's *Martha*. His rather small, slender, almost delicate figure, bashful in its bearing, sometimes awkward in its movements, and rather too restrained than too active, we found uncommonly appealing in its touching helplessness. Herr Bötel has only recently turned to the stage, and his modest manner becomes him as a beginner. Indeed, it is striking, especially since this amiable characteristic is rarely encountered among tenors, be they neophytes or seasoned veterans. Herr Bötel had no cause for such constraint upon the stage, as he may be only too certain both of his adequacy and of his triumph. Whoever has heard the resounding gold in this throat might well wish that his entire being were one enormous ear. Nor, had every enthusiast a good fairy at his side, ready to fulfill his every wish in the twinkling of an eye, would such an ear be a misfortune. If a nose can go for a walk as a privy councillor (see Gogol's *The Nose*), one could, as an ear, circulate in respectable society without sacrifice of station or rank.

To describe Herr Bötel's voice is a ticklish proposition. We shall hope to do it succinctly by reporting as follows: Take "The Last Rose of Summer," whose cursed popularity must answer for the greatest possible number of suicides, melancholiacs, hydrophobes (because of the enormous pressure on the tear ducts), deaf mutes, poisoners and heavens knows what else. Now, when we certify in all seriousness that, despite the obvious peril to which we might be exposing ourself in so doing, we could hear this melodious opiate sung by Bötel twenty times with delight, then our relish in this singer's magnificent organ approaches the freezing point of acknowledgement (which, as everyone knows, is as good as no acknowledgment at all). Should we, after such praise, still look for a batch of appropriate adjectives with which to depict clearly the character of Bötel's voice? Should we compare it with the sobbing of the nightingale, the song of the finch, the pealing trill of the lark, the -- heavens, with what else should we compare it?

"I could supply you," said the stranger who, I know not how, had materialized behind my back and read the last words of my manuscript -- "I could supply you with a fitting comparison. Do you have the Collected Works of Grabbe handy?"

"Yes, no!"

"If not, get them."

"And what for?"

"In order that you may learn to grasp the mystery of a shy voice, which I assume the voice of your much admired singer to be."[2]

"Shy voice! Mystery," I cried, astonished and smiling incredulously. "That sounds more like an insane billet of Victor Hugo than Herr Bötel's hale and hearty voice."

The stranger threw me an angry glance and, turning to go, said (the first two words in a contemptuous tone, the two following words with special significance):

"*Kehlkopf* | larynx | -- *Kohlkopf* | head of cabbage or blockhead |. Shy voice -- mystery."

And vanished.

I must admit that this curious exclamation sets me to thinking. What does a larynx have to do with a blockhead? Maybe the stranger wished thus to describe the insignificance of the vessel that contains the golden tones? Or to point out that it is not the larynx alone that makes for beautiful singing? Or that larynges and blockheads are alike common? Or that what is mysterious about a beautiful voice lies not so much in the audible tone as in the invisible pinions on which the very soul hovers? But why should the revelation of this mystery (O, Kralik, Kralik!) fall to a shy voice? That is the dilemma, I say with Victor Hugo. And if I now write fifty times, "I'm reflecting on it," I would be no closer to solving my problem than the French poet was to his. I'll get the complete works of Grabbe. That should help ---- .

A feminine guest, Frau Baumann,[3] from the Municipal Theater in Frankfurt am Main made her local debut as Donna Anna in *Don Giovanni*. -- What good is even the finest voice if the physical appearance does not contribute something to sustaining the onlooker's illusion? Frau Baumann's voice is strong enough to fill our opera house, but she sings without feeling, is dull, has not a trace of temperament. In appearance she can hold her own with Frau Wilt. It is a misfortune when an opera singer cannot bring to the stage a comely figure, but a Donna Anna such as Frau Baumann's casts doubts upon Don Giovanni's good taste. In such a case, the charm of Donna Anna, instead of becoming a reality, remains a fable.

How the management can assign a comedy role to Herr Rokitansky is a mystery. Herr Rokitansky as Leporello is about what Herr Meixner[4] in the Court Theater would be as Romeo. To sing Leporello it is not enough simply to be a bass. A native gift for comedy is essential. Leporello is a part for Herr Mayerhofer or, in a pinch, for Herr Scaria. Herr Rokitansky, with the best of intentions, could make nothing of this role. He simply has no gift for comedy.

Frau von Naday's Zerlina is rather coarse and fat. In the duet, "La ci darem la mano," she changes her facial expression literally with every word. It was both ludicrous and offensive. Exaggerations of that kind are much worse than indifference, on which account Fräulein Schläger (Donna Elvira) was perferable to Frau von Naday despite her apathetic run-through of the part.

The inglorious figure of Don Ottavio is made to order for Herr Perschier.[5] About his vocal accomplishment I shall say nothing. Herr Hablawetz[6] is, as we all know, a usable Masetto. I have intentionally held Herr Reichmann (Don Giovanni) to the last in order to end this review of *Don Giovanni*, which began in the minor, as does the opera, with a strong D major chord. Herr Reichmann, one of the principal ornaments of our opera stage, was the only enjoyable performer among the cast. One rejoiced at his appearance, was bored in his absence. The performance came to life only when he was on hand. Herr Reichmann makes the godless profligate too amiable, however, with the result that one is almost sorry when the devil finally takes him.

1. Heinrich Bötel (1854- ?) was a native of Hamburg, and principal tenor at the opera there beginning in 1883. He was a great local favorite.

2. Presumably an allusion to *Scherz, Satire, Ironie und tiefere Bedeutung* | see footnote to January 27|.

3. Emma Baumann (1855-1925), a German soprano especially noted as a Mozart singer.

4. Karl Meixner (1815-1888) had been a member of the Court Theater since 1850.

5. Adolph Peschier (1849- ?), a member of the company from 1881 to 1885.

6. August Egon Hablawetz (1833-1892), Vienna-born bass, a member of the company from 1870 to 1892.

28. Iphigénie en Tauride

November 23, 1884

Direktor Jahn reached down into the deepest recesses of the Court Opera's archives, where lie practically buried the works of one of the noblest composers, and what he brought forth was -- Gluck's *Iphigénie en Tauride*. The ten years' dust that had settled on the score was carefully brushed away, and now see! Gluck's sublime masterpiece again enters triumphantly into our opera house.

It cannot be said of this opera, as of so many another perfectly decent work, "If I rest, I rust." Gluck's armor (he is said to have had the habit of encasing himself in armor when the euphony began to sound within him) was, indeed, dusty, but it was not rusty, despite the 105 years that had passed since its premiere. Musical Paris at that time was as if enchanted by this work. We all know of the war between the Gluckists and the Piccinists, and with what fervor it was fought. There were bloody battles then, when opinions parted and daggers came together. Yes, in those days one contested with dagger in hand, and not with empty words, brochures, pamphlets or epigrams. As ink is spilled today about Wagner, so blood was spilled in 1774, although not, of course, in the same quantities, or mankind would have had to swim for dear life a second time, and in a flood of blood, and a Richard Wagner would not yet have been born. But wielding stout steel daggers instead of scratching with steel pens, that was something else. In those times it still paid to fight, and the Piccinists had, indeed, nothing to laugh about when Gluck, with *Iphigénie en Aulide*, walked off with the first great victory over his adversaries. Four years later, in 1778 [actually May 18, 1779], came *Iphigénie en Tauride*, and Gluck dominated the field as he does to this day (as recently demonstrated by the success of this work on our stage), and as he shall continue to do as long as there are people whose whole existence is not limited to a pair of ears.

Our public taste has declined pretty badly, but it is not yet so rotten, so utterly dulled, so coarse, as to be impervious to the grand emotions of Gluck's music, although the countless performances of *Mefistofele* might lead one to fear the worst. The audience's appreciation of *Iphigénie en Tauride* would hardly have delighted its composer more intensely than it delighted me and, perhaps, many another, similarly happy to make such a joyous observation. May the sparks flying from the incendiary lightning of Gluck's music into the hearts of listeners grow to an enduring flame of exalted enthusiasm, serving as illumination against the will-o'-the-wisps of that *Mefistofele* of the Italians, Germans and French; for the negative spirit of Mephistopheles casts its spell insidiously among the modern operas of the followers of Meyerbeer and Wagner. Let Gluck, Mozart and Wagner be our holy trinity, first consolidated from three to one in Beethoven. It is them we have to thank for life's sublimest pleasure. Profoundest pain and loveliest rejoicing, the tortures of Prometheus and the euphoria of Nirvana, every human impulse is embraced for us in the music of these masters. It is through utter involvement in this music that we first become aware of our better selves. Their melodies are genii guiding us over the dull lethargy of everyday existence to a world such as we have imagined, perhaps, only in the blessed dreams of childhood.

Now to a discussion of the participants. Everyone seemed utterly dedicated to his noble task. Frau Materna[1] was the Iphigenia. She obviously had her troubles maintaining the repose and dignity befitting the character of the priestess, even in outbursts of ultimate terror, dread and horror. She constrained herself as best she could, and succeeded to some extent in struggling with her impetuous nature. How beautifully she sang the famous aria (Act II), "O malhereuse Iphigénie!" This aria is the loveliest blossoming of Gluckian melody. The oboe ritornello is literally as if drenched in tears. What awful, heartrending grief does it not express, especially when, in the course of the aria, voice and oboe alternately or together, breathe their complaint, and when, at the words, "You suffer as I do myself," the minor seconds clutch at Iphigenia's grieving heart like icy hands until one thinks it must break? And yet the forbearance and exaltation in that heart, the sublime mourning in that eye, the gentle repose and temperance of the holy priestess in every movement! This composition is so deeply felt that even in the first four measures the picture of the true Iphigenia must take shape in the mind's eye, and the listener identify with her totally. I can think of nothing in the entire field of music to compare with this aria. It is the most sublime revelation from that realm of art. Herr Reichmann was an ideal Orestes, vocally and dramatically. How expressively, how sorrowfully, he sang the aria, "Le calme rentre dans mon coeur," how eloquent his acting! After the preceding agitated recitative, "Dieux, frappez le coupable, et justifiez-vous," which he uttered with imposing power, and in which the whole nature of the desperate man inwardly rebels, Herr Reichmann managed in masterly fashion the gradual, hesitant transition to a state of repose which he does not trust, and which, indeed, is no true repose at all, but fatigue caused by his trials. His movements were heavy, slack, his body as if broken. He was tired. This portrayal justified his expressed doubts as to whether this be truly a state of rest. And however often Orestes deceives himself that he has again found repose, he is contradicted by the orchestra, whose pulsating rhythm defines all too plainly, and in drastic fashion, the reaction of the preceding outburst.

Herr Winkelmann (Pylades) realized splendidly the aria, "Unis dès la plus tendre enfance" (Act II), a worthy counterpart to Iphigenia's G major aria. It could only benefit by being taken a little less broadly. Herr Winkelmann's voice is well suited to Pylades. His mask, too, pleased me, the smooth face giving Pylades a suggestion of youthfulness, almost childishness, in effective contrast to Orestes' sombre appearance. Herr von Reichenberg (Thoas) irritated us by his terrible enunciation. Since Thoas, fortunately, is not very prominent, it was bearable. The supporting roles were well cast with the ladies Hellmesberger,[2] Kaulich and Hauser.[3] Herr Gritzinger,[4] as Scythian messenger, on the other hand, cackled his short recitative like an agitated hen. The management should be more careful in the casting of minor roles. The opera was solicitously prepared by Direktor Jahn. Chorus and orchestra did their best. Everything points to *Iphigénie en Tauride* being taken into the repertoire. Let us hope so.

About Herr Bötel, one finds oneself saying the same thing! He has a wonderfully beautiful voice, and knows how to use it. If one overlooks his shortcomings as an actor, one can speak enthusiastically of his Raoul, i.e., insofar as the lyrical passages give the visitor opportunity to bring his opulent voice into harmony with its rather spiritless projection. Thus, he sang the first act aria very beautifully, as was inevitable. He had only to sing, without introducing any feeling appropriate to the character of the piece which would have involved his voice.

The vocal organ in the singer is like the instruments in the orchestra or the colors on the palette. If the orchestra is to express fright or terror, the composer will hardly employ flutes, harps and triangles. And if the painter wishes to produce a southern sky on his canvas, he will, in all probability, prefer a shade of blue. The correct choice of means of expression is certainly not all there is to it, but it is enough to see that the wings of fantasy are not clipped, but encouraged, at least, to follow the artist's intention, and this in higher degree the more that ends and means are mutually complementary.

When, for example, our excellent Hablawitz manages to evoke that characteristic tone for the dragon in Richard Wagner's *Siegfried*, it is thanks to his rough, surly, cavernous voice. The listener's fantasy, with the very first sounding of those barbaric tones, sets to work breathing real life into the dragon, seeing him with Mime's eyes, fearing him with Mime's fear. (I speak of Mime, of course, for where, today, does one find a Siegfried? He has gone off with the one and only Siegfried to Walhalla.[5] There are, to be sure — although not from the Wälsung race — an appalling number of Siegfrieds who are reluctant to die out, and who stand little chance of admittance to Walhalla even at a high entry fee, despite the gods' thirst for gold.) With Herr Winkelmann, on the other hand, the tearful flavor in this otherwise very competent singer's voice can be disturbing, especially in heroic roles, while the seductively mellow, flowing timbre of Herr Reichmann's voice is extraordinarily well suited to most of the roles he sings. From these few examples it may be seen how the vocal organ in itself may be an integral factor in the representation of a character, and that the organ, in harmony with personal appearance, constitutes the essential prerequisite for a truly convincing dramatic characterization.

Where passionate outbursts are required, or emphatic accents, inner convulsions or emotional representation, however they may be inspired, the performer withdraws into the backbround to the extent that the force of the emotion more or less commands the entire person. Here the presenter of character [*Darsteller*] steps in, his relationship to the actual actor [*Vorsteller*] being that of the idea to the tool that gives it life. If this tool is to the musician his instrument, so to the painter it is his crayon, not even his paintbrush. To the musician it is the least adequate of keyboards, not the orchestra. And to the singer it is not the dramatic voice used to represent character, but simply a voice.

Only in the most perfect representation can this apparently almost complete absence of the necessary requisites make the listener forget how an orchestrally conceived musical idea, if only it is strong and eloquent enough, may leave us oblivious to the shortcomings of the orchestra. Such a perfect presenter should not, to be sure, be too one-sidedly endowed. Instinctive genius is called for, such as is found only in the greatest spirits. The most penetrating comprehension on the part of a less gifted performer, no matter how cleverly he may balance contrasts, separate the essential from the unessential, calculate, experiment, etc., can never come so close to truth as the bold certainty of getting it right that distinguishes genius.

My God! Now I've started something! Where was I? I was supposed to be reviewing *Les Huguenots*. Well, we hear it often enough. The casting of the principal roles remains about the same, and about Herr Bötel, too, it seems to me that there's not much else to say — "So!" (that's a quote.)

Since I am running out of space, I shall simply attest to the significant success of Bülow's orchestra concert. A detailed discussion of the virtues and shortcomings of the orchestra will follow in the next number. I was unable to attend the Philharmonic concert.

1. Amalie Materna (1845-1918), Styrian dramatic soprano, and one of the greatest. She sang all three Brünnhildes at the premiere of *Der Ring des Nibelungen* in Bayreuth in 1876, and was also the first Kundry in *Parsifal*. She was a member of the Court Opera from 1869 to 1894.

2. Rosa Hellmesberger (1857- ?), daughter of Georg Hellmesberger, Jr. She was a member of the company from 1883 to 1889.

3. Anna Hauser (1851-1907), a Viennese soprano who had joined the company in 1880.

4. Leo Gritzinger (1851-1910), a secondary tenor who was with the company from 1884 to 1889.

5. Possibly a reference to Ludwig Schnorr von Carolsfeld (1836-1865), who sang the first performances of *Tristan und Isolde* in Munich on June 10, 13, 19 and 30, 1865, and died three weeks later on July 21, aged twenty-nine. He was to have been the first Siegfried, already knew much of the music, and had sung excerpts in concert. His last words were: "Farewell, Siegfried! Console my Richard!"

29. The Meiningen Orchestra

November 30, 1884

The first concert was devoted exclusively to works of Beethoven. There were the overtures to *Coriolanus* and *Egmont*, the First and Fifth Symphonies, the great fugue for string quartet (Opus 133, played by the orchestra's strings), and a Rondino for Winds. One sees, the table was richly set, the repast piquant and easily digested, excepting only the great fugue, which I find incomprehensible. That the orchestra accomplishes the extraordinary was especially evident in the performance of the Rondino, with the wind players distinguishing themselves as soloists. The reciprocal relationship of the orchestra to its conductor, and vice versa, has already been discussed in these columns. In order to avoid repetition, the reader is referred to that earlier discussion. The superiority of this orchestra to our own best is indisputable. One may take exception to the preponderance of the brass. All else is beyond criticism.

The second concert began with Raff's overture to Genast's drama, *Bernhard von Weimar*,[1] a far from self-sufficient piece, without color or form, utterly superficial in conception -- not an organism, just so many disjointed members. The Lutheran chorale[2] is subjected to the most intricate contrapuntal tortures with the most appalling ingenuity. The middle theme, too, with its grace notes in the woodwinds, excites memories of the Nuremberg torture chamber -- grates, pincers and other similarly edifying devices. And then the march at the end! All the cripples of the Thirty Years' War passing in review before our pitying eyes, starving and freezing. So lamentable a business is this march that one involuntarily reaches into one's pocket for alms.

From this torture chamber we were released to the open air, at least, with Brahms's Concerto in D minor, but it was a kind of liberation hardly calculated to rejoice the hearts of any but our musical critique and its rhyming counterpart, namely, the clique. Through this composition there blows a draft so cold, so chilly damp, so foggy, that one's heart can freeze, one's breath be taken away. One could catch cold from it. Unhealthy stuff. Herr von Bülow played the solo part in a masterly fashion, and the orchestra provided an immaculate accompaniment -- without a conductor! How thoroughly identified with its conductor must an orchestra be to bring off such a *tour de force*!

With the opening measures of the Overture to *Der Freischütz*, following the Brahms concerto, all present felt as if reborn. One noted it in the frantic applause. The overture was played accordingly. Even the introduction: broad and expressive, adagio, as the score prescribes. In the theater nothing is ever adagio. It's always andante. There's no time to lose in the theater. One must get on with it. But why? The devil is not yet at your heels. Wait, at least, until he gets there. It's only twenty-five measures. Then, in God's name, hurry along to the jaws of hell of the molto vivace. But all in vain, in vain. Adagio, andante, it's all the same. Keep moving! The sober listener shrugs his shoulders. Another may bite off his thumb. -- The thumb is gone, but the evil remains.

The happy mood as the jubilant strains of the overture faded away was promptly dampened by Brahms's Symphony in F. As a symphony by Herr Dr. Johannes Brahms it is, to some extent, a conscientious, respectable enough job. As the symphony of a second Beethoven it is an utter failure. For what we must require of a second Beethoven is precisely what is wholly lacking in Brahms: originality. Brahms is an epigone of Schumann and Mendelssohn, and as such he exerts about as much influence on the course of the history of art as the late Robert Volkmann, namely none. Brahms is an industrious musician who knows his counterpoint, and who has sometimes good, even excellent ideas, sometimes bad ideas, sometimes ideas already familiar, and, often enough, no ideas at all.

He calls to mind a homeless emigré from the days of the French Revolution. He is, indeed, the very image of the two emigrés in Grabbe's *Napoleon*, whom the author describes in these words: "What coattails, what puffy cheeks, what antiquated bearing and thinking, what ghosts from the good old and very stupid days! Of the revolution and its bloody course they know nothing. But they have survived, and now they stand there like a blade of grass in a dwindling mountain freshet and think that, because they have survived the torrent and the crumbling banks they are stronger than the flood. They have not budged a hair's breadth out of themselves or away from their haughty delusions."

Schumann, Chopin, Berlioz, Liszt, the leaders of the post-Beethoven musical revolution (Schumann, at the time, thought he had found the Messiah in -- Brahms!) seem to have left no impression upon our symphonist. He was either blind or feigned blindness as the eyes of an astonished mankind opened wide and overflowed with tears in the glare of Wagner's radiant genius as Wagner, like Napoleon, born on the waves of the revolution, commanded the flood into new channels, created order and accomplished deeds that will remain forever vivid in the memory of all men.

But this man, who has written three symphonies, and probably intends to follow them with another six, can remain untouched and unmoved by such a phenomenon! He is only a leftover of old remains, not a living creature in the mainstream of the time. Just as in the old days they danced minuets, or even wrote symphonies, so Herr Brahms will now write symphonies as if nothing had ever happened.

Like a departed spirit he returns to his homeland, staggers up the rickety stairs, laboriously turns the rusted key that gratingly opens the hingeless, broken-down door to his dilapidated dwelling, and notes with vacant gaze the spiders busy at their airy construction and the ivy pressing inward through the blurred windows. A pile of yellowed writing paper, a dusty inkwell, a rusted pen attract his attention. As in a dream he totters to the old family armchair and broods and broods — but nothing of any account occurs to him. Finally, he has the glimmerings of an idea. He recalls the good old days, embodied in a figure, wrinkled, toothless, jabbering away and muttering like an old woman. He listens to this voice, these sounds, for so long that it seems to him that they have taken shape within him as musical motifs. Heavily he reaches for the pen, and what he writes — well, they are certainly notes, a lot of notes! These will now be put together, properly and correctly, in the good old form, and what comes out is — a symphony.

All this may be accepted — since Herr Brahms neglected to provide one — as a program designed to assist the listener to a better understanding of his symphonies. It presumes to do no more, however, than set the tone of the symphonies. To invent a detailed program on the basis of this general outline might well prove too much for even the sincerest admirer of Brahms's muse!

1.   Eduard Franz Genast (1797-1866), a protégé of Goethe in Weimar, which was to remain the principal scene of his activity as singer, actor, composer and playwright. *Bernhard von Weimar* dated from 1855. Raff was also in Weimar at that time, and became Genast's son-in-law.

2.   "Ein' feste Burg."

30. The Meiningen Orchestra's Last Concert

December 7, 1884

The opening work was Hector Berlioz's Overture to Byron's "The Corsair." The composition does not achieve the heights of the gifted Frenchman's great instrumental works, and it is significant that Berlioz, usually capable of uniting the most vivid colors on his palette, could give so little character to the instrumental shading of this overture that one imagines him at work on his painting with a wet sponge rather than his color-saturated brush. (What does Herr Brahms use, one wonders, when orchestrating his symphonies? Compared with Brahms's instrumentation, even Berlioz's (very exceptional) wet sponge is a brush dipped in the colors of a Makart.)

But in the Overture to "The Corsair," Berlioz was unable to evoke those instrumental sounds of nature that so distinguish the "March of the Pilgrims" in "Harold in Italy," the love scene in *Romeo and Juliet* and the "Scène aux Champs" in the Symphonie Fantastique. And for a very simple reason: the sole true and characteristic motif, or theme, did not occur to him. Without the right theme, the loveliest instrumentation is of no avail.

(Herr Brahms is clever, and orchestrates badly on purpose, lest anyone think that he looks to brilliant instrumentation to disguise the poverty of his ideas. It was on that account, recently, that he was given a fanfare [a pun here on *"vertuschen"*, meaning to disguise, and *"Tusch,"* meaning a flourish].

"A fanfare?"

"Yes, by trumpets and tympani!"

"There, you see, you see? Thus is honesty rewarded."

"Yes, yes, composers, there is still justice on this earth. With the motto: 'Honor endures longest when poverty (of ideas) is no disgrace,' compose away. Fanfares will be cheap, clique pays claque, trumpets and tympani, click-clack, and longer or shorter, louder or softer, however agreed upon for cheap goods, but always honestly orchestrated! Composers! What prospects! Bring on your piano, violin and bass fiddle concertos! If one has composed a symphony in which a tragic motif occurs, slithering like a 'convulsive worm,' even if it's no good, out with it! It is still not bad enough not to be trumpeted and tympanied. Oh, an innocent in chains must put the most tender-hearted keeper into the mood of a tiger compared with the heartbreaking spectacle of poverty of invention celebrated by tympani rolls and trumpet fanfares."

"But what is all this talk about poverty of invention? You aren't so naive as to believe that a composer is going to own up to his want of ideas? Or that one salutes Herr Brahms because one finds him an uninventive composer? It's quite the contrary. He is assumed to be profound, unfathomably, uniquely, maddeningly profound."

"Maddeningly?"

"Yes, at least so the critics find it."

Hm, hm -- So that's it. Of course, of course! The critics.

"O, they are wise and clever,
And one does not deceive them."[1]

Whether they deceive themselves or the public?

Back to Berlioz.

The principal theme of the overture has, to be sure, a certain pomp, but only when the trombones lend it their splendor. In the woodwinds and violins it seems almost banal. Berlioz may well have seen the heroic figure of the corsair, but it did not speak to him. Annoyed, possibly by the conjured apparition's defiant silence, he hails it with that boastful phrase whose inner emptiness is ill concealed by the superficial majesty of the trombones. It strikes us as prosaic, and may well have diverted the phantom from the composer's enraptured gaze before he could catch the phantom's eye. One can hardly expect the corsair to accept such bumptiousness. Thus the phrase winds its way pretty miserably through the overture, and since the apparition will not speak to us directly, Berlioz is at pains to put words in its mouth that are decisively alien to its nature. As a result, he could not get the colors of his landscape right, either, and they are intimately related to the battles and vicissitudes of the hero. How infinitely superior to this Overture to "The Corsair" is Wagner's Overture to *The Flying Dutchman*! How much might be said of the latter at the expense of the former! But no more digressions.

The second number was Brahms's Piano Concerto in B flat, with the composer as soloist. Whoever could swallow this piano concerto with pleasure has nothing to fear from famine. We may assume that he rejoices in an enviable digestion, and that, in a time of famine, he would readily accommodate himself to the nutritional equivalent of window panes, bottle corks, oven screws and the like. Seen with the eyes of a worthy health council, the Brahms Concerto in B flat is certainly not to be underestimated.

But this assessment is subject, of course, to expert examination by music critics who, pious, humane and Brahms-worshipping as they may wish to appear, are a long way from attaining the truly Christian charity of my own assessment. Since there is, unfortunately, nothing to praise in the music of this work, I have called attention immediately to its innate curative potential as radical abdominal therapy, emphasizing how indulgence in the delights of Brahms's melodic fountain might serve the state in time of famine.

And since a music critic is also expected to write about music from time to time, I have thought it best to honor this work, a victim of the tortures of living death, with a reverent sign of the cross, and to pass it by in sorrowing sympathy, wishing it with all my heart eternal rest and the delights of the

Heavenly Kingdom. It might be well, however, if this charitable dispensation were deferred until the music world has thoroughly ruined its stomach, or has been so steeled by its savoring of this concerto that the prospect of famine might be greeted with jokes and laughter.

Next on the program was Wagner's *Faust* Overture. This most important work of the post-Beethoven musical era was interpreted under Bülow's baton even more brilliantly, if such were possible, than in the conductor's own excellent pamphlet on the subject.[2] What a piece it is! Not long, and not in four movements, either. Not a symphony, just an overture, but a *Faust* overture. Despite the fact that it is only an overture, it towers in the realm of music like a lighthouse over the sandy reefs of the absolute music of our four-movement symphonies, concertos, serenades, suites, etc. Who will not founder, let him follow this light. It is no deceitful enchantress that holds forth there. It is a benevolent, strong, serious spirit, sending forth its beams as the seaman throws the life-saving ropes to the drowning. That this work should be received with enraptured enthusiasm (like Beethoven's symphonies) was to be expected.

Brahms's Variations on a Theme of Haydn bear eloquent witness to his true gift: for ingenious contrivance. When it comes to making variations on a given theme, Brahms has no rival. Everything he has ever done is just one mighty variation on the works of Beethoven, Mendelssohn and Schumann. Indeed, if all Brahms's works were to be judged in this sense -- and I consider it the only correct one -- then I, too, could place Brahms and Beethoven side by side, and the multiplication table would come into its own again.

With Beethoven's Symphony No. 8, Hans von Bülow said his farewell to the Vienna public. The latter, showering the agitated conductor with thunderous applause, offered him the left cheek, having relished, apparently, the slap on the right cheek administered by Bülow at the preceding concert. But not even this demonstration of Christian sentiment could move Bülow to any further offensive utterance.[3]

A few words in conclusion about the Brahms enthusiasts. They were, primarily, people who enthuse for enthusiasm's sake. Their normal habitat is the fourth gallery at the opera. On this occasion they moved on less familiar terrain -- yet not without success. Who it was that issued the invitation -- "Come, Romans, to applaud!" -- I know not. Perhaps it was the chance appearance of Caesar and his retinue looking for "culture" -- or was it a dress rehearsal for a forthcoming battle in the opera house?

Then there are the enthusiasts who truly believe in Brahms. They are surely small in number. And there are those who never believe in him, but forever talk him up -- and write about him. They are more numerous. There are those who hate Brahmsian music with a deadly hatred but enthuse over it because the newspapers praise it. They are very numerous. And, finally, there are the ciphers -- zephyrs, really, despite the lovely bellies they often carry around with them -- who simply attach themselves to a man who is much discussed. In order, as a zero, to be counted for something, they trot along behind the unit -- it won't work with Wagner any more, so make do with Brahms! They wear a Jacobin cap today, a Jesuit habit tomorrow, white tie and tails day after tomorrow, only to run around next day as sansculottes. They change their convictions with their linen, and wear them only for display, as women wear jewellery. All is for appearance's sake, and when they wander in the sunlight they cast no shadow. They talk a lot, understand little, and can do nothing. In fact, they *are* nothing. But the human individual can bear anything rather than nothingness. They have a title. Is it genuine? I fear not. But being a nobody without profession, without an appropriate title, capable of sweetening their existence only by a fine-sounding name -- it is hard, I grant. So they look for a title at all costs in order to moderate the contempt they feel for themselves. One has to be somebody, or -- oh, wretched fate -- at least *seem* to be something or other.

1. A parody on lines from the aria "O Sancta Justitia" from Lortzing's *Zar und Zimmermann*: "O, ich bin klug und weise, und mich betrügt man nicht."

2. "Über Richard Wagner's *Faust* Overtüre" in the *Neue Zeitschrift für Musik*, Vol. 45, Nos. 6 and 7, August 1 and 8, 1856.

3. Bülow had made a speech at the first concert explaining why he wished to substitute Brahms's "Academic Festival" Overture for Beethoven's *Egmont* Overture. The audience insisted on Beethoven, to which Bülow responded that a Vienna audience in 1810, given a choice between Beethoven and Weigl, would have chosen Weigl. Joseph Weigl (1776-1846) was an Austrian, a contemporary of Haydn, Mozart and Beethoven, popular in his time, and much favored by the Court. His opera, *Die Schweizerfamilie*, held its place in the repertoire of German theaters for many years.

31. *Vogl as Tristan*

December 13, 1884

Herr Vogl, from Munich was the Tristan, or, to speak in his manner, the Trrristan. Compared with this continuous rattle, as, for example, in the upward surging expiation oath: "Tr(rr)ug des Her(rr)zens! Tr(rr)aum der(rr) Ahnung ew'ger(rr) Tr(rr)auer(rr)! einz'ger(rr) Tr(rr)ost,"etc., the most hellish racket of the most decrepit, unlubricated coach on our potholed pavement must fall upon the ear as a siren song. The listener is assailed by a sensation of chewing mill wheels, which is quite an imposition. His sensitivity to such disaster may well be somewhat dulled by now, to be sure, Herr von Reichenberg having taken every conceivable pain to accustom the public to clamorous consonants.

Half of this superfluous sibilation and rasping would stand Herr Schittenhelm in good stead, who hardly enunciates any consonants at all. Of the

introductory strains of the young sailor we caught only the following fragments: "We(st)wär(ts) schwei(ft) der Bli(ck), o(st)wä(rts) st(r)ei(cht) da(s)
Schi(ff)." The letters in parentheses were swallowed mercilessly. Whoever did
not know the text from memory, or have it in his hand, could more easily have
deciphered the language of the sparrows –– and without a preparatory elixir of
magic-working dragon's blood –– than make any sense of the mumbo-jumbo
emanating from the stage.

(Herr Schittenhelm, on this point, is conspicuously at one with the Spanish
king in Grabbe's remarkably witty and farcical libretto to *Der Cid*, in which
the king is made to say: "German recitatives are always clumsy. That's because
of the harshness of the language, which sounds like the clash of barbarian
swords in battle. Here, therefore, I simply leave mine out." Herr Schittenhelm
is more restrained than this king. It is enough for him to drop just the
consonants.

How different it would be if the lucrative situation of the opera singer were
to be united with baronial dignity in one person. Such a one would do as the
king, i.e., he would omit the recitatives or anything else according to his
pleasure. If someone were then to take his life in his hands and tell the rebel (as
happens in Grabbe's text): "You have no right to do that; you are earning
13,000 Talers a year" –– and the rebel replied: "That's just why I have no
scruples about it," it would all make sense, as we know from experience.
Things pursue their normal course, while the moral of this story tags sadly
along behind like a dog rejected by its master, pursuing justice, to be sure, but
kicked by justice and injustice alike,and driven to the devil.)

But to return to Herr Vogl. His virtues will be remembered from his last
visit. That his voice was not, on this occasion, bright enough is hardly worth
mentioning. What surprised me was that so intelligent and thoughtful an actor
would establish so little contrast between Tristan's passionate love and his
self-denial in Act I. Broad, measured, restrained movements are appropriate
to the Tristan of the scene that precedes the tasting of the love potion, the more
so in that Tristan's every word gives the lie to his true feelings. This entire
scene, indeed, is but a masked declaration of love on both sides, with Tristan
feeling himself called upon to employ the more drastic disguise. Isolde is less
adept at camouflage. Nor is she under any outside pressure. Her enemy is
within, a creature of her own will, to whom she can as well confess her true
feelings as sublimate them in hate. With the tasting of the potion the hearts are
unmasked. The passionate exclamations, "Tristan!" "Isolde!" have no more
sense and meaning for them than the preceding exchange of querulous hair-
splitting: fear and awe –– duty, license –– propriety, decency –– Tantris,
Tantris[1] (a nice quarrel duet, is it not, my critic friends?). The sensations
remained the same. Only the point of view has changed.

Now Herr Vogl, from the moment of this fateful transformation, over
which the angel of death is already spreading his black pinions, did not alter
his deportment in the slightest detail. Forgetful of self and blind to the world,
therefore reckless, and rash in his confidence of Melot's loyalty, a victim of

Lady Venus enchantment, convulsively imagining himself to have escaped into Night from a treacherous Day that he sees not because he will not -- this Tristan cannot possibly have the same outward appearance as the Tristan whom Herr Vogl shows us so well before savoring the potion.

The ever more irrepressibly burgeoning love for Isolde -- against which he has struggled, at first intrepidly, then with recourse to the sickliest of moral equivocations -- finally bursts forth like an unbridled mountain stream whose savage torrent sweeps every obstruction before it into the abyss, an elemental force denying all -- duty, honor, gratitude, loyalty! That, I say, is a Tristan quite different from the gentleman described by Isolde at the beginning of the act "who shields his gaze from mine, looking away in shyness and in shame." But Herr Vogl played him -- at least so it seemed to me -- throughout the entire act as the ill-disposed Tristan of Isolde's resentful imagining -- and thereby committed a grievous error.

Frau Materna has never sung and acted Isolde more beautifully than on this occasion. A truly refreshing achievement. If Frau Papier (Brangäne) would only sing *piano* now and then, her wonderful voice would work considerably more enchantment. Too few nuances create a monotony no matter how beautiful the voice. How is it possible that Herr Kapellmeister Richter lets Herr Sommer get away with his mutilation of "in Irenland" and "von Engeland" in the lines: "Sein Haupt doch hängt in Irenland, als Zins gezahlt von Engeland" by slurring the G upwards to D and the A to E flat? I have remarked this sloppiness previously, knowing full well that my voice would go unheard, just as I am convinced that this time, too, my admonition will be spoken into the wind.

Herr Scaria can do anything he wants to. Often he chooses not to. But this time he wanted to, "and what he wanted to do" (I trust that the variant will not be held against me)[2] "he could." His Marke is no king in a deck of cards, but a living and well-favored man, even if he didn't run the surprised Tristan right through the ribs, as many a critic would have preferred.

1. The name by which Tristan had been known by Isolde while she was nursing his wounds until she learned from his sword -- as she tells Brangäne -- his true identity.

2. The variant is of Hans Sachs's commentary on Walther von Stolzing's singing at the audition for the Meistersinger at the end of Act I, subsequently repeated to David in Act II:
    Nun sang er wie er musst'
    Und wie er musst', so konnt' er's.
    (Now, he sang as he had to, and as he had to, he could.)

32. *Vogl as Loge*

December 21, 1884

Herr Vogl's accomplishment as Loge in *Das Rheingold* by Richard Wagner beggars all description. It was a demonstration of the actor's art worthy of taking its place beside Niemann's inspired Tannhäuser or the Tristan of Schnorr von Carolsfeld (about which we must accept Wagner's testimony, as Schnorr's all too premature death prevented us from hearing him).[1]

These three characters are, to be sure, fundamentally different in disposition and development (with Loge one cannot speak of any development at all). Each, consequently, must be regarded from a different point of view. There can be no doubt, however, that the role of Tannhäuser imposes the most exacting requirements upon the protagonist. To what transformations is this erratic Minnesinger not exposed, ranging from the most intense sensuality to the severest asceticism! What a world of effects lies between these poles of human experience! And what conflicts and pressures must there be at work within him to so shatter his personality and call forth such reversals of behavior!

Faced with this role, the merely intelligent actor is lost. Artificial fireworks are not enough. A volcanic nature, even if it sometimes discharges only cinders, but one that needs no special impulse from outside to set off an eruption, containing within itself so many elements in ferment that, once diverted from its familiar course, the slightest opposition will set off a catastrophic outburst. Such, it seems to us, is the underlying characteristic of Tannhäuser's nature. Niemann's own impetuous nature was predestined for identification with that of Tannhäuser in such a degree that one need only pronounce the name of that artist to evoke immediately the image of the noble Minnesinger. Niemann's conception of the role has become the model, just as Schnorr set the standard for Tristan, and as now Vogl, as the youngest in the league, has given us an incomparably striking characterization of Loge.

It would surely not be uninteresting to draw a parallel between the three characters and these three splendid actors, each of whom gives, or has given, his best in one of the three roles. Only limitations of space restrain me from so doing. If, however, I had to suggest the relationship of the three characters one to another in rough outline, I would say this: The poet did not fix the character of Tannhäuser with a single stroke. He lets him emerge little by little before our eyes. Tannhäuser arouses our most intense interest only in the course of the drama. Just as in a painting the central figure stands fully revealed only when not another stroke is left, and possibly only when the picture itself is at last contained within its golden frame, so with Tannhäuser our interest is dependent upon his physical and spiritual relationship to his surroundings, whose frame he needs. Removed from the picture, he loses all significance. In order to grasp what goes on within, we must always have the external influences before our eyes.

This applies to Tristan, too, but in far lesser degree. When he first appears before us, introduced by the motif associated with him, he is already the person he seems likely to become. But Loge leaps into our vision immediately self-sufficient and intelligible. With Loge the composer required neither sketch nor paintbrush nor chisel. Two strokes, thus and so, and like a flash of lightning the flickering figure is there, complete and perfect, the devil's disciple, half demigod, half giant, the malevolent, crafty features, the ever-cynical smile, the slyly twinkling eyes, the darting movements -- whether with feet, head, hands or fingers -- the flame-flickering headdress, the fiery red cloak folded around a half-naked body! Yes, it was Loge, all right, god of fire and flame, never at rest, always in motion, like the element he represents.

Was it really Herr Vogl? I doubt it, for I would have recognized him by his *rr*. It was Loge himself, issuing forth from the abysses of eternal fire in response to the magic formula of Herr Vogl's summons. It cannot be other-wise explained than as the work of Herr Vogl's own special Tarnhelm. But the magic works only to conjure the god of fire; for him alone does Vogl find the right incantation. For the rest, the Tarnhelm is to him a "childish toy," as it is to Mime, the dwarf. To go further into detail about Herr Vogl's accomplish-ment, bordering as it does on the miraculous, would be presumptuous, unless one wanted to write a book about it. Enough. The name Vogl will remain branded upon Loge, one of Wagner's most original characters, in letters of fire as long as the score of *Das Rheingold* remains a human heritage (and should this inestimable benefaction ever be lost to mankind, then the time might not be far off when man returns to his forefathers in the virgin forests).

It was a pity that the roles of Freia, Fricka, Donner and Froh were not in abler hands than those of Mmes. Baier and Dillner[2] and Messrs. Frei and Gritzinger, that it was not Frau Papier as Fricka, Herr Sommer as Donner and Herr Schittenhelm as Froh. Alone praiseworthy were the ever ready Herr Schmitt[3] (Mime), who in an act of true self-sacrifice undertook his rather thankless role, and the achievements of Fräulein Meissner as Erda and of the Messrs. Rokitansky and Reichenberg as Fasolt and Fafner. One should expect more of Herr Scaria (Wotan) than he offered on this occasion. He was not quite in form. Herr Horwitz (Alberich) seemed obviously concerned to unite the singer with the declaimer. The intention is admirable. It is only that in his over-enthusiasm he went so far as not to sing at all, but only to declaim. He should try to achieve a blend of both, and he will succeed. Not to forget the Rhinemaidens. There is nothing with which to take exception in their singing, overlooking a tendency to sing sharp on the part of Fräulein Lehmann. But how hapless their movements, how contradictory of their own purpose and of Alberich's words. With the exception of Fräulein Kaulich, who plunged and surfaced in accordance with the poet's instructions, there was nothing but dull horizontal splashing around, utterly destructive of any illusion. The Mlles. Braga and Lehmann should acknowledge an admirable example in Fräulein Kaulich's self-denial. I gladly concede that see-sawing can cause uneasiness if one is not used to it. But where that is the way it must be, one must resign oneself to discomfort. Having a tooth pulled is certainly worse. So, courage!

Herr Vogl was fine as Siegmund in Richard Wagner's *Die Walküre*, too, but compared with his Loge, nothing extraordinary. He was often too preoccupied with details, unlike Niemann who paints Siegmund with a wider, bolder brush. While Vogl's details are imaginative, he neglects to develop his heroes from essential elements of their nature. There was, nevertheless, so much of interest in his conception of Siegmund that we were again aware of being in the presence of an uncommonly intelligent actor.

That Frau Materna, as Brünnhilde, and Frau Ehnn, as Sieglinde, are without peers goes without saying. Frau Papier I was hearing for the first time as Fricka, and also for the first time found myself wishing that the scene between Wotan and Fricka were twice as long, so gripping does it seem to me since she has taken over the role. Herr Scaria as Wotan was rather too sparing of his sonorous organ, and he suffered some disturbing lapses of memory. "Weihlich weiseste *Göttin*" is a crude violation of the alliteration.[4] He has done better in this role. Herr von Reichenberg, the Hunding, would do well to remember that it is Siegmund and not the audience that asks him his name. It is customary, I believe, on the stage as well as in private life, to turn toward the inquirer, and not away from him, when answering a question. There is nothing further to be said on that point. On the whole, a successful production.

Herr Vogl had another debut, as Eléazar in Halévy's *La Juive*, and indeed with much success, his voice, too, sounding especially beautiful on this occasion. The other participants did their best to do justice to their roles, among them Herr Rokitansky, who distinguished himself with his lovely singing of the effectively sustained cavatina |"Si la rigueur"|.

Now to Auber's *Les Diamants de la Couronne*| The Crown Jewels|. Absent from the repertoire for a number of years, this delightful, favorite light opera enjoyed a generally friendly reception in the recent revival. The applause, however, was in no way commensurate with the uncommonly amusing, sparkling music adorning a skilfully made, effective libretto by Scribe. It would truly be a shame if this opera were not to find a place in the repertoire. The crown of the evening was Fräulein Bianchi in the leading role of the bandit chieftainess Theophilie, revealed in the third act as the Queen of Portugal. Generous applause rewarded the faultlessly dispatched coloratura and trills. In sustained song, too, as in the lovely aria of the third act, she struck tones that went straight to the heart. Excellent, especially in his acting, was Herr Stoll (Don Enriquez). He overdoes things from time to time, but that apart, his histrionic gifts, particularly in light opera, are not to be underestimated. True, his voice sounds somewhat forced, but one soon gets used to that. He is a very capable singer. Fräulein Braga (Diana) doesn't sing badly, but her movements are wanting in charm. Beauty patches are in themselves insufficient to capture the rococo spirit. More powder, but not just on the coiffure! The ever reliable comedian, Herr Mayerhofer (Bazano) and Herr von Reichenberg (Robelledo), too, deserve special mention. The ensemble was good, the production no less so.

Just space to remember hastily Alfred Grünfeld's[5] recital. A full house testified to this virtuoso's popularity. Beethoven, Schumann, Chopin, Liszt, Rubinstein and an attractive mazurka of his own, all brilliantly played, technically perfect, but often withdrawn in conception, especially with Schumann. Grünfeld is more virtuoso than artist. The union of both in the same person is becoming ever more rare. What he accomplishes as a pure virtuoso is, indeed, admirable, and the applause went on and on.

The Wagner cycle ends this week. These have been, for the most part, successful productions, and given thus in proper sequence in a cycle, had a more earnest character than is possible when the one or the other of Richard Wagner's works is inserted into a varied repertoire. The presence of Herr Vogl, from Munich, greatly increased the interest in individual performances. In respect of this artistic policy we cannot adequately thank the Intendant, his excellency Freiherr von Hofmann. May such Wagner cycles soon be repeated, to the joy of the public and the honor of the management.

1.　See footnote to notice of November 23.

2.　Bertha Dillner (1847- ?), a member of the company from 1863 to 1865 and again from 1873 to 1884.

3.　Victor Christian Schmitt (1844-1900), a German tenor from Frankfurt am Main, who had been with the company since 1875.

4.　Wagner's text reads: "Erda, die weihlich, weiseste Wala, riet mir ab von dem Ring" (Erda, the wise and holy Wala, advised me against the ring). It occurs in Wotan's account to Brünnhilde of the story of the ring in Act II. Wolf could not have known that Scaria's frequent memory lapses were a symptom of the mental illness that would lead to his death two years later.

5.　Alfred Grünfeld (1852-1924), a piano virtuoso famous for the rapidity of his repeated notes. He was one of the earliest pianists to record.

33. Bruckner on Two Pianos

December 28, 1884

Bruckner? Bruckner? Who is he? Where does he live? What can he do?

Such questions may be heard in Vienna today, and even from regular subscribers to the concerts of the Philharmonic Orchestra and the Society of Friends of Music. If you meet someone to whom the name is not wholly unfamiliar, he will actually recall that Bruckner is a professor of music theory at our Academy. Another might add that he is an organ virtuoso -- and fix the first half-educated informant with a triumphant look. A third will believe, a fourth may know, a fifth will assert and a sixth will swear that Bruckner is also a composer, nothing special, to be sure, not a classical composer. A connoisseur will shake his noble head sceptically, observing that he has no sense of form. A dilettente bemoans the confusion of musical ideas in his compositions. Another remarks his faulty instrumentation, and the critics find it all abominable, and let's hear no more about it!

One other remains to be heard from -- the conductor. He, in fact, has good words for this composer's works, and brings his influence to bear in their behalf despite the critics' slanderous opposition. He proposes to perform them. To whom does he make this proposition? To his subordinates, the orchestra. And here his trouble begins. If the tribunes of the orchestra veto the conductor's decision, the conductor may move heaven and earth -- to no avail. Dictatorial power is not his to wield. He must abide by the orchestra's verdict.

(What can be expected from such a procedure is obvious, especially when these orchestra tribunes are as little able to grasp the deeper substance of a composition as they are capable of admirable accomplishment on their instruments. It does not follow that because a man is a good soldier he has the makings of a field commander. An orchestra musician can blow or fiddle a heavenly solo and still be far, far, very far from conceiving an expressively played solo within the context of the whole piece.)

Thus vanishes the last hope, and Bruckner, this Titan in conflict with the gods, must be content with trying to communicate his music to the public from the piano. It's a miserable business, but better than not being heard at all. And when our unlucky fellow has the good luck to find such enthusiastic interpreters as Löwe[1] and Schalk,[2] then we must count him at least partially compensated for the unjust procedure of our fashionable musical institutions.

I have just spoken of Herr Bruckner as a Titan in conflict with the gods. I could not, in truth, think of a more appropriate metaphor with which to characterize this composer, combining as it does both praise and disparagement in equal portions: raw natural forces against the predominance of the intellect. Translated into the terminology of art, it reveals an extraordinary native artistic endowment in all its freshness, incompatible with the musical sensibility, the intelligence, the manifestations of a level of cultivation, characteristic of our time. These are the principal elements in the work of this composer, and they find themselves, unfortunately, at loggerheads. Had Bruckner ever succeeded in achieving their reconciliation, he would have become, without doubt, a great figure approaching the significance of Liszt.

It is a certain want of intelligence that makes Bruckner's symphonies, for all their originality, grandeur, power, imagination and invention, so difficult to grasp. There is always and everywhere the will, the colossal strivings — but no satisfaction, no artistic resolution. Hence the formlessness of his works, the apparent extravagance of the exposition. Bruckner wrestles with the idea, but he lacks the courage to come to the point and then, fully in the clear as to his intentions, get on with it.

Thus he wavers, rooted halfway between Beethoven and the new advances of the moderns, the latter represented most successfully and vividly in Liszt's symphonic poems, unable to decide for the one or the other. That is his misfortune. I do not hesitate, however, to describe Bruckner's symphonies as the most important symphonic creations to have been written since Beethoven. They are the works of a floundered genius, like the colossal writings of Grabbe. Common to the works of both Bruckner and Grabbe are the bold, grandiose conceptions — and the confusion and shapelessness of the execution. As in Grabbe the luxuriance of his fantasy, and the genius betrayed in the flight of his thought, remind us of Shakespeare, so in all of Bruckner's symphonies we detect in the grandiose themes and their thoughtful elaboration the language of Beethoven.

It would certainly be rewarding, then, to give this inspired evangelist more attention than has been accorded him hitherto. It is a truly shocking sight to see this extraordinary man barred from the concert hall. Among living composers (excepting Liszt, of course) he has the first and greatest claim to be performed and admired.

Note: This was actually the third, and not the last, of the so-called "Bruckner Evenings" in the Bösendorfersaal, in which Schalk and Löwe sought to gain a wider following for Bruckner by playing his major orchestral works in transcriptions for two pianos. They had played the Seventh Symphony on February 27, 1883, and the Third on May 7 of the same year, before Wolf had begun writing for the *Salonblatt*. At the "Bruckner Evening" reviewed here (it took place on December 12) they played the First, and repeated it on April 23, 1885. Wolf may well have heard the earlier performances, and thus have chosen to discuss Bruckner in general terms rather than concentrate on the one symphony. His suggestion that Bruckner was virtually unknown in Vienna is a slight exaggeration. Bruckner's Mass in F minor had been performed in 1871, the Second

Symphony in 1873, the Third in 1887, the Fourth in 1881 (conducted by Richter), and two movements of the Sixth in 1883 (conducted by Jahn).

1. Ferdinand Löwe (1865-1925), Viennese pianist, conductor and pedagogue, a pupil of Bruckner, and instrumental in the publication of many of his works. He subsequently became a cherished member of the small circle of Wolf's intimate friends and supporters.
2. Josef Schalk (1857-1911), older brother of the more famous conductor, Franz Schalk (1863-1931). Both were Bruckner's students. Josef is now remembered primarily for his piano transcriptions of the Bruckner symphonies. He also became an important advocate and propagandist for Wolf and his songs.

34. Wagnerians Among Themselves

January 4, 1885

Thus, "strictly among ourselves," as Wagner liked to conclude some of his literary efforts. "Among ourselves," indeed, and whoever does not like it that way may avoid these private soirées. Since, fortunately, they have not yet become fashionable, like the Philharmonic concerts, for example, our music lovers may inspect with some composure the program of such an evening. 1. Bach. 2. Spervogel.[1] 3. An unknown composer (not of the Mendelssohn school, but, horror of horrors, Paderborn, in other words, old-German). 4. Lieder (by whom? by Richard Wagner, perhaps, or Liszt or Berlioz or even old-German . . . the singer must compensate you if the composition failed to please). 5. Romanza for Piano and Violin by Beethoven . . . . Our Beethoven (you say), that should be good -- but 6. Peter Cornelius?[2] And 7. Two numbers by Richard Wagner -- but they are two pieces to which you should not entirely close your ears since a clever critic[3] once called your attention to a pretty waltz motive alleged to occur in the scene of the flower maidens in *Parsifal*, although cautiously giving only a favorable prognosis to the Magic Fire Music.

Take it or leave it. You won't find much amusement, but you might be offered good music, and especially music, moreover, that you will not hear in any other concerts. But if you prefer to wait until these private soirées have become fashionable, you can continue to amuse yourselves at the Philharmonic concerts. I suspect, however, that you will wait in vain. An enterprise whose concern is solely artistic, taking commercial factors into account only to the extent of seeking to cover expenses, alienates the canons of fashion in the same degree that it accommodates the requirements of the age. One may already credit these private soirées with popularity if one accepts the term in its noble context as meaning not so much something that delights the multitide as rather the spiritual comprehension of a phenomenon by persons who both know and sense why they find it delightful. To popularize something is not a matter of appealing to the greatest possible numbers, but of reaching those people who are obsessed by the object of their affections and who, consequently, have convictions and express themselves accordingly, i.e., have the courage to stand up for what they have correctly perceived.

The public that attends these private soirées is composed of such people (there are, of course, exceptions). It is not large, but here one is worth a hundred. Compared with the public for our large orchestra concerts, they are a little band of Greeks against the incalculable hordes of the Persians. History offers examples enough of what a little band of inspired and dedicated souls can accomplish against a force of venal mercenaries, however superior in numbers, I say it again: a public must be characterized as truly intelligent, cultivated and true to its ideals and convictions to which one can offer programs of a special kind without having to worry about scaring it off -- far from it! With such a public one knows that with programs of this kind one is accommodating its wishes and meeting its requirements not by first improving its taste, but by sharing it ---- not, of course, in the manner of the gentlemen of the Philharmonic, who also show themselves eager to adapt their own taste to that of the public. Such a public will also be free of any partisanship as long as the matter at hand concerns an advance in the art of music (in the Greek terminology) the only art still capable of life and growth (and did not the compositions of the Minnesänger Spervogel signify an advance over the calcified procedures of the musical doctrine of the time analogous to the reforms of Gluck and Wagner, if not, of such historical and cultural significance?).

As well advised as the artistic directorship of the Vienna Academic Wagner Society has otherwise been in the selection of programs, the choice of Peter Cornelius' eight-voiced chorus, "Der Tod, das ist die kühle Nacht," [Death, that is the cool night] must be counted a decided mistake. The performance of this composition did the late composer no special honor. Anyone unacquainted, or only fleetingly acquainted, with Peter Cornelius can arrive at only a distorted notion of his truly significant gifts by hearing this chorus. Indeed, one of the outstanding characteristics of his talent, the spiritual permeation of poetry by his music, is here utterly absent. We are further alienated from Peter Cornelius by his foolish decision to set to music this tasteless, trivial and anodyne poem of Heine. One would hardly have wished the composition of this poem off on a hack composer, of which, again, we have all too many, much less on Peter Cornelius, who was equally poet and musician.

The abilities of the participants were inadequate to make the chorus of the flower maidens from *Parsifal* truly enchanting. Anyone who has not experienced this scene in Bayreuth will hardly get a clear picture from this sketch. The intention was admirable, and would have been vindicated had only Herr

Felix Mottl[4] been on hand to apply the finishing touches and conduct the performance. Since that could not be, we had to content ourselves with what was offered, acknowledging the sincere industry of Herr Schütt.[5]

1. Three Spervogels appear among the composers identified in various songbooks dating from the era of the Minnesänger, i.e., the twelfth and thirteenth centuries.

2. Peter Cornelius (1824-1874), now best remembered for his opera, *The Barber of Baghdad.*

3. Hanslick.

4. Felix Mottl (1856-1911), who had left Vienna to become conductor of the Grand Ducal Opera at Karlsruhe.

5. Eduard Schütt (1856-1913), pianist, composer and conductor, who had succeeded Mottl as conductor of the Academic Wagner Society.

35. Of Glinka — and d'Albert

January 11, 1885

The third concert of the Society of Friends of Music began with the Overture to Glinka's opera, *Russlan and Ludmilla.* The piece would seem to be made to order for our concert public — fresh, melodious, falling pleasantly upon the ear, sometimes even piquantly. What more could one want?

Yet, and despite all that (my God, here I am unthinkingly writing in Busch trochees | Dennoch, und trotz alle diesem|, our public did not take to it. Obviously,it was not in the clear about Glinka — whether he is, all in all, a good, a mediocre or a bad composer. Our concertgoers are always most thorough where they should not be. Know this: Glinka, or more precisely, Michael von Glinka, born in Novospask in 1803, is, so to speak, the founder of indigenous Russian opera. His most important work, *A Life for the Czar*, is one of the most splendid manifestations of Russian patriotism, and enjoyed an unexampled success on the Russian stage. If I am advised correctly, Bülow introduced it to great applause in Hanover [in 1878]. In any case, it would be appropriate — indeed, it is high time — for us to offer a local welcome to Glinka's compositions. One should produce *A Life for the Czar* or *Russlan and Ludmilla*, even if only to dare an experiment.

Are we not continuously experimenting on our operatic stage? And with what success? I offer *La Gioconda, Muzzedin* and *Heini von Steier* (both by that composer of the music of the future, S. Bachrich) and [Gounod's] *Le Tribut de Zamora* as examples, other disastrous novelties not coming immediately to mind. In the rush for novelty one forgets to perform [Marschner's] *Vampyr,* lying neglected these last fifty years. And see what has happened now. Old-fashioned it may be, but can the brand new, still sizzling importations from Paris and Italy, or even those born and baptized (?) right here in the inmost heart of our own city, fill the house as does *Vampyr*, composed fifty-seven years ago? What should deter the management, then, from producing Glinka's operas? Why should not we, too, give the Czar a life, particularly since Austria and Russia are enjoying friendly relations? And even supposing that we are all secretly nihilists at heart, what of it? Just so long as the Czar sings well, and nothing dull, he may be certain of our applause. Glinka's artistic patriotism offers full assurance that what he sings will not be dull.

One thing is certain: In his operas we will hear genuine, truly expressive music, and that is saying a good deal, now that our own modern composers are heading in the new direction, looking to it for salvation despite its obdurate unmusicality. One finds it smart, nowdays, as soon as one has reached the point where he can distinguish between a third and a fifth, to dive into the mainstream of the new direction, abandoning oneself to the caprices of the current, and then to wait, lulled in happy dreams, until washed ashore in the land of good opera texts. Deluded idiots! Learn first to be musicians before presuming to forget the musician for the poet. What use are lovely librettos if you can't set them to music? Music! Above all, music. Then, too, musical understanding and, if possible, poetic sensibility. But once again, music above all!

There is no want of that in Glinka. His was a musical nature through and through. One senses it immediately in this Overture to *Russlan and Ludmilla*. A fresh piece, prefaced, thank God, by no pompous introduction with empty figuration, muted violins, endless drum rolls, gruesome tremolos, would-be romantic tooting on the horns and other such clever diversion designed to evoke some farfetched mood or atmosphere. Nothing of all that! The violins set right off, perky and gay, with the main theme, the rhythm and the strongly simple but somewhat clumsy harmonization reminding us of Berlioz's compositional procedures. Even the middle theme, with its strong odor of triviality supported in the most primitive fashion by the orchestra as if it were a dance tune, recalls the middle themes of Berlioz's overtures.

Without wishing to hold up triviality as a worthy objective, still, I can hardly think of anything in the works of our modern "solid" and "serious" musicians so treasurable as the trivial passages offered with such charming and naive lack of inhibition by Glinka and Berlioz. With Wagner, in *Rienzi*, they are sheerly delightful. But enough of that, or we shall stray into awesome byways.

There is not much to be said either for or against the idea of performing Mozart's "Offertorium de Venerabili Sacramento" |Litaniae de Venerabili Altaris Sacramento, K. 243]. The piece is neither exciting nor offensive; the passing production of a genius.

Herr Eugène d'Albert[1] played Beethoven's Concerto in E flat with great refinement. His technic is complete, his touch round and soft, his conception, however, governed more by the score markings than by any imaginative grasp of the spiritual substance of this wonderful work. His playing aroused the audience to such demonstrations of approval that he felt himself called upon to oblige with an encore. The Chopin Waltz in A flat, unfortunately, charming as it is in its own right, was the last thing in the world that one would wish to hear after the magnificent E flat concerto. Predictably, a majority of the audience were not of a mind to be disturbed in their superficial enjoyment of the pianist's art by this tactlessness. Any halfway sensitive person, however, could have consigned the pianist and the Chopin waltz to the devil the minute the concerto was over.

The concert was brought to a worthy conclusion with Franz Liszt's blazing Hungarian Rhapsody in F. The audience was beside itself with unbounded rapture at this cornucopia of the most magical orchestral effects, the impulsive sweep of the melodies, the insinuating, audacious rhythms, the fevered, pulsating sensuality, all ending finally in orgiastic intoxication, and presenting us, thus, with the portrait of a nation in such perfection as only Lenau [2] could approximate.

Fräulein Klein, a new member of the resident company at the Court Opera, had a fine success as Marguerite in Gounod's *Faust*. A resonant voice and well-schooled acting are reckoned treasurable assets on these boards. Fräulein Klein has both, and in no small degree. It's quite another matter with Fräulein Köppler, a guest from the Breslau Municipal Theater, who made her debut as Elsa in Richard Wagner's *Lohengrin*. Her voice is disagreeable, hoarse in *piano*, shrill in *forte*. Her movements are hesitant and sometimes ambiguous, but not unlovely. I like her, for her singing is expressive, her movements truthful. Obviously, she was nervous on this occasion, and probably indisposed as well. She should do better another time. We shall wait.

I should like, in conclusion, to discuss Herr Walter's first| sic | Lieder recital. I confess that this is a touchy business, for however favorably one may write, it is never enough to satisfy a tenor! One would almost have to yoke Pegasus in order to accommodate a tenor's vanity with bad verses. The useful and agreeable occupation of writing bad verses has for some time now, fortunately, been a monopoly enjoyed by Herr R. K.| Richard Kralik |. I could easily recite innumerable verses by this indefatigable poet for the merriment of all. But I shall await a better opportunity. Instead, I shall make do with the final strophe of a Heine poem as a fitting tribute to the famous Herr Walter, allowing myself a small variant:

> Er sang von Liebessehnen,
> Von Liebe und Liebeserguss;
> Die Damen schwammen in Tränen
> Bei solchem Kunstgenuss. [3]

1.   Eugène Francis Charles d'Albert (1864-1932), who was to become one of the great piano virtuosos of his generation.

2.   Nikolaus Lenau (1802-1850), whose *Don Juan* was to inspire Richard Strauss's tone poem. He wrote poems about gypsy life already set by the young Wolf, hence the reference.

3. No. 79 of *Die Heimkehr*, "Doch die Kastraten klagten," which, its three verses reduced to prose, tells us that "The eunuchs complained when I raised my voice, finding it too coarse. Then they raised their own little voices, and the trilling was like crystal, so pure and fine. They sang of the pinings and effusions of love. The ladies swam in tears at such artistic delight." Wolf has merely changed the opening "They" of the last verse to "He." This was not Walter's first Lieder recital. See notice of February 2, 1884 and footnote.

36. The Blinkered on Blinking

January 18, 1885

To a professional musician concerned primarily with the vocal art of the performer, Herr Vogl's convulsive blinking would be a matter of indifference. In the opinion of the music critic *Dp* this lamentable circumstance "proved insuperable to this performer's considerable artistry."

The professional musician, destined by a dire fate to be a music critic, too, will stick to what is relevant and pertinent, in contrast to our esthetically cultivated music critics who indulge themselves so happily in abstract hair-splitting and who, when they turn to something concrete, note immediately, and with uncommon critical perception, that, for example, Herr Vogl's important dramatic talent cannot shine brightly enough because too heavily overshadowed by the unfortunate, involuntary, convulsive activity of his eyelashes -- a discovery Christopher Columbus most assuredly would have made had he not carelessly chosen to live at a time when only something so utterly commonplace as a piece of the earth was waiting to be discovered.

In the most recent performance of *Tannhäuser,* Fräulein Schläger was decked out in a pink ball gown of the most modern cut. Venus in a corset! How charming! It's a pity that Venus-Schläger forgot fan and gloves, thus giving an impression of niggardly outfitting. The Venusberg scene had, on the whole, a tolerable ballroom gaiety of the kind that always prevails before the formal dances begin. Oddly enough, the anticipated quadrille never took place, although there were certainly enough couples. But the loving couples -- nymphs, fauns, satyrs and bacchantes -- have disappeared, leaving Venus and Tannhäuser behind alone.

Aha! I thought to myself, now we'll have a *pas de deux*, a polonaise or a waltz in three-step or six-step, a French polka or something of that sort. Deceived again! Instead of the anticipated dance music we had the sensual song of the sirens. My God, what can be the meaning of that? Are we not at a *bal masqué* in the Sophiensaal or the Grosser Musikvereinssaal, or at the Opera Ball? Oh yes, we are at the Opera Ball all right, but something is wrong. We are sitting in the parterre, and separated by the orchestra from that delightful creature in the pink ball gown from whom we would like to request a dance.

But now she's singing. Heavens, is that any way to behave at a ball? And he, her gallant, is he not singing, too? Are we awake or dreaming? We pinch ourselves in the calves, rub our eyes, almost punch our noses to pieces to escape this awful delirium. With Tannhäuser's invocation of the Virgin Mary there is, as everyone will recall, a lightning change of scene. We are saved. Impetuously we thank holy Joseph for his inexpressible benevolence in ridding us of this ghastly caricature of the divine Venus.

And what do our esthetics-mouthing critics say to this masquerade, this salon Venus? They find everything in the best of order, excellent — couldn't be better. If Tannhäuser were to return from his pilgrimage to Rome with a Baedeker in his left hand and an umbrella in his right, and dressed in the togs of an English tourist — what more? And if, instead of telling us of his pilgrimage, he were to turn somersaults (although it is doubtful that an English tourist would excel in that art), no one would detect anything out of the way. Certainly not! But if Tannhäuser were just once to "blink convulsively," or wiggle his little toe, that would be the great moment to disclose to the public one's all-embracing, all-comprehending, all-knowing wisdom.

This performance of *Tannhäuser* was pretty mediocre. We are accustomed to that here. Fräulein Köppler did not entirely live up to our expectations. One may well credit her with industry and good intentions, but she lacks the resources to translate intention into deed. It is hardly praise for her if I declare her Elisabeth to have been the best accomplishment of this opera evening.

Herr Eugène d'Albert gave a most successful solo recital in the Bösendorfersaal. This extraordinary pianist performed most brilliantly in the Bach-Tausig Toccata and Fugue, the Chopin Polonaise and, even more brilliantly, in [Liszt's] "Soirées de Vienne." D'Albert belongs indisputably among the most gifted performers of the time, and one is tempted to believe that the future will belong to him alone.

Seldom have two individuals hit it off together so well as Willi and Louis Thern.[1] To prefer one to the other is impossible. It seemed to me that they played with equal perfection, particularly in their performance of Chopin's Fantasie-Impromptu, Opus 66, on two pianos. This perfect identity of touch, even in a kind of performance demanding frequent use of tempo rubato, can truly give one the shivers. — But may they in the future spare both themselves and their listeners Grieg's Concerto in A minor. This music-simulating racket may suffice for putting cobras to sleep or arousing rhythmic sensibility in bears being trained to dance. But it does not belong in the concert hall — unless one were to do as the Sudanese and be content with cultivating their melodic caterwauling. Then, maybe —

1.   Willi (1847-1911) and Louis (1848-1920) Thern, sons of Karl Thern (1817-1886), a Hungarian pianist and composer of Austrian parentage, would seem to have been the first proper virtuoso duo-piano team. There was nothing new about performance on two or more pianos, but public performance, prior to their time, had been a matter of *ad hoc* partnership for this or that occasion. Contemporary accounts of the Therns' concerts in Vienna, Leipzig, Paris and London suggest a hitherto unexampled refinement and homogeneity of style, concept and technique, sometimes exhibited in unison performance on two pianos of pieces originally written for solo performance on a single piano. Such was the unanimity of their playing that they became known as "the Siamese Twins of the Keyboard." Their father transcribed for them for two pianos the complete "Well-Tempered Clavier."

37. Lilli Lehmann
as Isolde and Leonore

January 25, 1885

Tristan und Isolde by Richard Wagner.

The Isolde was Fräulein Lilli Lehmann, from Berlin.[1]

Both Materna and Sucher have achieved a far sounder characterization. Lehmann made of Isolde a virago, which is about as wrong as wrong can be. The poet's Isolde is all woman, passionately in love with Tristan, but rejected, denied, affronted and scorned by him. Yet a woman is never more feminine than when she is in love, and Isolde is in love from the first scene right through to the "Liebestod." She seethes, rages, storms, fumes and curses -- at whom? At her beloved. Why? Because she loves him. Isolde is, moreover, far too womanly a woman, i.e., she loves Tristan far too much to be able to so alter herself as to give the impression that he means absolutely nothing to her. The cold and scornful pronouncements are at odds with the pounding of her heart, with the impetuous longing for the reconciling potion, with the futile evasions and diplomatic dodges that she employs to shake Tristan's imperturbable composure. Yes, she loves him only too well. She is only too feminine.

Why, then, these magisterial, disdainful attitudes, these icy glances, these formal gestures? Why this unbending, austere creature altogether? Lehmann's Isolde seems ever to be asking herself: "Am I still a queen? Should I not be ashamed to be a queen and yet to love -- and not to be loved in return?" Whereupon she strikes a commanding attitude and announces with utter satisfaction: "Yes, I am a queen, every inch a queen!"

Granted, the real Isolde does, in fact, recall her royal blood from time to time, but how different her reasoning from Fräulein Lehmann's Isolde! It is not against her love for Tristan that the real Isolde's pride is set, but rather against the "tribute-owing Cornish sovereign" for whom she was recruited. "Ireland's heiress he courted to honor Cornwall's dispirited king, Marke, his uncle." She who portrays Isolde may confront Tristan's heartless defiance with the woman scorned, but not with the princess offended. Fräulein Lehmann was not of my opinion about this, and I can only assume that Fräulein Lehmann labors under a misapprehension.

To certain moments in the first act this splendid artist managed, nevertheless, to attach a quite special significance, notably the death-defying expression of her countenance and her serene, composed posture after savoring the love potion. And this she accomplished with a vividness that no other Isolde has brought so effectively to this highly dramatic episode. It was the more remarkable in that Fräulein Lehmann, after her previous cool deportment, could have had every reason to interpret the love potion as a pathological charm, and to give a more emphatic representation of its effect through trembling, shuddering, convulsions, swooning, and so on.

Fräulein Lehmann's Isolde was not a rounded, fully worked out achievement, but it had many beautiful, even gripping details. The "Liebestod" was effective beyond anything ever imagined, a sublime vision of ecstasy transfigured. But it was rather by her expressive features and her patrician bearing than by her singing that she cast her spell. The voice was too often overwhelmed by the orchestra. A shame that she enunciates so badly. Not a single word was comprehensible. A serious deficiency!

Fräulein Meisslinger sang the Brangäne, and to our entire satisfaction. The best that I can find to say about Herr Sommer (Kurwenal) is -- nothing. I prefer not to give way to my periodic exasperation with this singer. If Herr Winkelmann (Tristan) would keep his hands away from his wig he might place them more often on his heart. Not that I see any particular necessity for this latter gesture, either. But it is less irritating, possibly because it is so traditional, than Winkelmann's original habit of disheveling his wig. This, I grant, looks more exciting, but it is not by so much as a single hair's breadth more sensible.

Fidelio by Beethoven. Toward the end of the *Leonore* Overture No. 3 the parterre, fortunately, remembered that Beethoven is to be taken seriously, and amused itself less noisily, although still loudly enough to sustain the impression that it did not make much of him, and had not the slightest intention of forgoing certain personal indulgences as do those simple souls who, at the first note of Beethoven or any other good music, break off even the most fascinating conversation, put their opera glasses aside and settle down to listen quietly and attentively. Such curious folk excite the sympathy of the parterre, to whom the god Beethoven, too, is merely a poor unfortunate wretch whose music is so little conducive to conversation that not even the *Leonore* Overture can restore the flow of an interrupted speech. Poor Beethoven! Oh noble parterre!

Fräulein Lehmann commands the role of Leonore in *Fidelio* far more perfectly than that of Isolde. The great aria with the recitative she sang with profound sensibility, tenderly as well as vigorously, with rapture as well as resolve. Facial expression and gestures were fashioned accordingly. There were some failures. That passage, "Töt erst sein Weib"[First kill his wife], in particular, should not be spoken. It is the following pronouncement, "Noch einen Laut und Du bist tot"[Another sound and you are dead], which, when spoken, achieves that awful effect of a bursting out of one sphere into another, cited by Wagner in response to Schröder-Devrient. In Wagner's description its uniqueness lay in the fact that the listener, as during a flash of lightning, had a brief insight into both spheres, the one ideal, the other real.[2]

Herr Winkelmann's Florestan was a thoroughly admirable achievement. Rocco (Reichenberg) and Marzelline (Fräulein Pirk) acquitted themselves well. But there was one curious item. In the libretto fashioned for the Vienna Court Opera, Fidelio addresses Florestan with the consoling words: "Was du auch hören und sehen magst, vergiss nicht, dass überall eine Vorsicht ist" [Whatever you may hear and see, don't forget that overall is a providence]. [The common meaning of *Vorsicht* is prudence, and the common term for providence is *Vorsehung*. The remainder of this notice is an elaborate play on the archaic double meaning of *Vorsicht.* Not until the reference to providence intervening in Florestan's behalf does Wolf relinquish the fun of ambiguity by coming out, at last, with *Vorsehung.*]

Yes, yes -- there is a providence. Indeed, there can hardly be anyone who should doubt the existence of a providence. Above all, it is clever diplomats and cunning tradesmen who never forget how important a thing is prudence. All sensible people concern themselves with providence, be they monotheists, deists, pantheists, polytheists, fetishists, atheists or even fatalists. They all believe that the use of prudence can be helpful in most circumstances. But despite all prudence, the Mother of Wisdom (whose natural daughter is prudence) would hardly have sustained the half-dead Florestan had not provi dence announced itself in the nick of time by an effective trumpet fanfare. Now, one may incline more toward prudence than believe in providence, but it remains a certainty that it would have ended badly for Florestan and Leonore despite the pistol that Leonore, through prudence, carried with her. In any case, it was certainly not the intention of Herr Treitschke[3] to lay so much emphasis upon prudence, and he obviously had providence in mind. I believe firmly that the guilt lies with the typesetter. Whether he erred from impru- dence, or whether providence also played a apart -- for providence is incom- prehensible -- is a question I should be able to answer, since, thanks to a similar fate, it is close to my heart. I shall make no dogmatic pronouncement, but I do believe that the blame for such deviltries rests more heavily on the conscience of the printer. If misprints occur in this review -- and I am sure that they will -- I wash my hands in innocence, like Pontius Pilate. For if I may say with Philip II, "I have done my part. The Cardinal, the traitorous wretch, has left me in the lurch,"[4] and I gnash my teeth horribly [*entsetzlich* another pun derived from *setzen*, meaning to set type], but still in vain. . . . . Oh!!!!!!

1.   Lilli Lehmann (1848-1929), one of the most remarkable singers of her own or any other generation, was, at the time of this guest engagement in Vienna, just beginning to move from a previously lyric and coloratura repertoire into the dramatic. Wolf may have been unaware that her Isolde, discussed here, was only her second appearance in the role, her first having been in London in July of the previous year. Her Leonore in *Fidelio,* reviewed here, was also new, her first appearance in the part having taken place in Berlin only ten days before. During this visit to Vienna she also sang her first Donna Anna and her first Norma, as well as Konstanze in *Die Entführung aus dem Serail.*

2.   In "Über die Bestimmung der Oper," *Gesammelte Schriften und Dichtungen,* Vol. IX. It was Wilhelmine Schröder-Devrient (1804-1860) whose performance as Leonore in the Vienna revival of 1822 led to general popular acceptance of Beethoven's only opera. Wagner heard her in this part in Leipzig in 1829, and wrote her a letter afterwards, saying that "as of that day my life had acquired its meaning, and that if she were ever to hear my name mentioned as of consequence in the world of art, she should remember that on this evening she had made me what I herewith vow to become." She was subsequently Wagner's first Adriano (in *Rienzi*), his first Senta and his first Venus.

3.   Georg Friedrich Treitschke (1776-1842), who revised Joseph Ferdinand Sonnleithner's text of *Fidelio* for the second revival of the opera in 1814.

4.   In Schiller's *Don Carlos.*

38. *Welcoming a Cancellation*

February 1, 1885

Thanks to Fräulein Lilli Lehmann's sudden hoarseness, the scheduled performance of *Don Giovanni* did not take place.

This sentence -- so it must seem -- could all too easily give the gentle reader a false impression as to what moved the critic to express so tersely his gratitude for Fräulein Lehmann's hoarseness and the consequent cancellation of *Don Giovanni.* From the pithy content of that sentence one might well assume that the critic despises Mozart's *Don Giovanni.* Good sense should have warned me never wantonly to allow such an awful suspicion to arise, even if boundless admiration for this work is something to be taken for granted, and any criticism of it something to be passed off as a more or less bad joke.

Your critic assures you that he intended neither a sad joke nor a dogmatic pronouncement as to the merits of *Don Giovanni,* nor even -- and here such an assumption cannot be excluded -- an unfavorable and even malicious assessment of Fräulein Lilli Lehmann, thus making of this sentence a miracle of condensed significance. He would not have dreamed of such a thing. All he had to do in order to prevent erroneous inferences was to write: "The cancellation of the performance of *Don Giovanni* due to the sudden hoarseness of Fräulein Lilli Lehmann is greatly to be regretted." Who then would have dared to question my admiration of Mozart? Who would have dared to read into it a vote of no confidence in Fräulein Lilli Lehmann? Who would have found even any special significance in this version? Certainly no one. So, there must be another reason for the provocative sentence at the beginning of this article? Yes, of course! And so, lest your fantasies stray into even more tortuous byways, I shall withhold no longer the one and only true reason for my pleasure in the cancellation of the performance.

Many of my musical friends envy me my — seat in the parterre, from which, in their view, I can follow the course of a performance in comfort. They should, in fact, mourn the fate that places me there as a critic, and daily give thanks to heaven when no opportunity is afforded them to visit the opera. Even should an especially beautiful work, or an especially gifted performer tempt them to do so, they should be thankful that they are spared this direct and easy way (which also leads to hell) and have to take the zigzag route to the galleries, step by step, and the higher the more taxing, arriving finally at that point where one may say, with Dr. Marianus [in *Faust* II]: "Here the view is free, the spirit uplifted," as can be said, indeed, of the fourth gallery.

But what business has a critic in the fourth gallery, he who dare not miss the slightest happening on the stage? To how many optical illusions would he not be exposed? The most important things would escape his sharp eyes. He would not see the illumination of the evening star in *Tannhäuser,* that one gripping moment when the parterre comes to life, remaining alive until, with increasing darkness, the evening star [Abendstern] is extinguished, whereupon, exhausted by such strenuous concentration, one gives oneself to blessed repose, if not to a refreshing snooze. One may prefer, by way of contrast, and with the help of the opera glass, to search out a Lichtenstern or Morgenstern, shining happily into the world. For such observation the critic, despite his weighty responsibilities, has opportunity enough. The ordinary music lover will find such agreeably touching manifestations in the conduct of the parterre less obtrusively distracting, for if he is sufficiently engrossed in the work being performed, neither the bad performer nor the distracted audience will tear him away from his illusions. But the critic! He must concern himself primarily with the performer, and only via the performer with the work. How often would he gladly look away from a bad performer! He may not. On the contrary, armed with the opera glass, he must follow the si ger's silly antics, and direct his two eyes diligently and open them appropriately wide in order afterwards, in his review, to shut one of them.

Now, if through continuous attention to externals, the critic, as a rule, remains detached, and, as a consequence, never achieves a full enjoyment of the work, it will be understood that during those intervals where the orchestra alone is heard, and the singer as such is silent, although with much to do as an actor (which, naturally, he neglects, preferring to rest his hands in his lap, untroubled by the forceful exhortations of the orchestra), the critic, distracted from the stage by such absurdities, will instinctively turn his attention to the behavior of the audience. And here he is offered a spectacle to stand his hair on end, even without being absorbed in "the devil's elixir."[1] One knows the heartless scenes taking place in the parterre and the loges during the most shattering events on stage: the smiling faces, the gay glances, the friendly discourse, the jokes, the apathetic finger-drumming, etc. Truly, for a music lover a seat in the parterre is an ominous gift, and to sit next to a subscriber a great honor, possibly, but no great pleasure.

Let's have a look at this subscriber. His very attitudes single him out. He sits, I will not say with his back to the stage, but still so markedly sideways that with a very quiet inclination of his noble head he can inspect the entire auditorium. This positioning of the body does not strike me as being notably courteous, but it obviously offers very special advantages and agreeable rewards, especially since the subscriber, as a being of culture and rank, can blithely disregard the idea of propriety in the more noble sense of the term. In this attitude he sits it out for an act or two, in order, after the third or fourth, to take his leave. And here we encounter an evil that cannot sufficiently be abhorred, that is painfully felt throughout the whole house, but against which, so far, no steps have been taken. Munich, Dresden and even the Czech National Theater in Prague have seen fit to put a stop to it. Can it be that we in the Court Opera House in Vienna have never been able to bar latecomers from the beginning of the overture to the end of the act of whatever is being played? Should the knowledgeable and attentive among the audience be disturbed by the noise of ushers showing latecomers to their seats? Or by the even more offensive racket made by the latecomers slamming down their folding seats with as much weight as a lackey brings to bear in slamming shut the doors of a noble carriage. In this connection, I should add that the lackey raises no claims to cultivation, and that he does his job in the street or in the courtyard without background music, unless it be the accursed wailing of an out-of-tune barrel organ. Such external nuisances, and adding to them the internal mishaps about which it is impolite to speak, are well calculated to sour the theater attendance of anyone who takes art seriously.

Now, let him mourn the cancelled performance of *Don Giovanni* who will. Your critic does not -- and rejoices!

1.   Properly *Die Elixiere des Teufels,* a book by E.T.A. Hoffmann, published in 1816.

39. Das Andreasfest
Romantic Opera by Karl Grammann[1]

February 8, 1885

Our contemporary German composers all suffer from an *idée fixe*. They believe that they can set only librettos that deal from the beginning to end with matters utterly German.

(It sometimes happens, to be sure, that in the course of an ever so German opera, among peasants and burghers, in the forest or on the meadow, a swarm of light-footed short-skirted sylphs will make their presence abundantly conspicuous by their shameless and at the same time infinitely ludicrous antics, just as in the very un-German French grand opera. This seems not in the least to compromise the German patriotism of the composer and his librettist colleague, for both proceed, thereupon, to carry on more Germanically than ever, which is to say, more tediously, more heavily, more mindlessly, more incompetently than before. One need not, therefore, reckon it a denial of an audience's patriotism, however German that audience may be, if the Germans in its ranks, attesting their lively gratitude for the composer's patriotic sentiments by sincere applause, find it convenient at the opportune moment, i.e., just after the interpolated ballet, to take to their heels in all haste, and thus, by swift flight, salvage those vestiges of their wit and humor not melted away under the leaden roofs of such Germano-operatic boredom in order to defy with what remains of such precious gifts more serious castastrophes than deadly German opera evenings.)

For such composers anything not having to do with German sagas, German myths, German fables, does not exist. History books too, are industriously examined, but not without circumspection so far as the grandeur of the forefathers is bound up with the destinies of alien peoples. Welcome treasures, too, are the old German chronicles, and many a composer who has hunted vainly for a historical Minnesänger or Meistersänger has settled finally for a mythical rat catcher, just so long as the tale is German and, if possible, romantic, for on the romantic element all depends. But no, that's overstating the case. Romanticism alone is no longer enough for them. They find it too incredible that one should set off into the blue yonder in search of the marvel of Peru [2] without a historical setting. They know their public, and they know perfectly well that it is not a child, and that it will not easily be satisfied with colored soap bubbles without something substantial to go with them. It wants to feel solid ground under its feet in order that its powers of imagination may wander the more freely in the enchanted realm of romanticism. That is only natural, and by no means presumptuous. One would assume, then, that the librettist will breathe so much humanity into his creatures that we perceive at least a tolerably natural complexion, if not a beating heart and an expressive eye. -- But far from it! He is content with a narrow, precarious, malodorous and hazardous emergency exit when he could bestride a splendid highway with a wonderful view of a whole world -- splendid, that is, for poet and musician, but not for hacks. To the latter the highway looks damned rocky, and still more hazardous than the emergency exit to which they now utterly entrust their well-being.

This emergency exit is historical perspective. "Historical perspective" sounds well. It has a certain pompous ring. In fact, it does not amount to much. In a moment of dire peril, when the art of the costume designer no longer suffices to animate the pale marionettes and shop window dummies of the librettist and his musical assistant, when one piece of their tawdry finery after another falls away and we begin to see the miserable wood or wire frame -- the soul of this soulless scarecrow -- at such a critical juncture there emerges the histor-ical perspective. That means a historical duke, king or emperor, high on horseback or gravitationally afoot, who hides the confused creatures of the "romantic plot" under the cloak of his ducal, royal or imperial benevolence and holds forth to them interminably about patriotism, loyalty, trust in God, almighty providence [*Vorsehung*], not to be confused with prudence [*Vor-sicht*], etc. That is the mighty coup to which the librettist of a romantic opera has recourse in order to provide the public, assisted by the most elaborate theater machinery, with a horribly frail and rickety footstool.

That *The Flying Dutchman* as a romantic opera text without the slightest historical background, and not even bound to any certain time, can still stimulate our imagination, and transport us to a world of fantasy without disturbing the utterly enraptured listener's sense of equilibrium -- such a phenomenon should by rights inspire in our opera-composing romanticists some misgivings about their all too ingenuous procedures with respect to "romantic opera." In normal life clothes may make the man. He needs only to button his elegant coat up to his chin and put his hands in his pocket, and he will not be taken for a fool, although at the same time he dare not expect to be thought intelligent. From people, however, who tell all their secrets out of school, and blare out their passions and convictions in love and vengeance arias, drinking and hunting songs, romances and ballads, recitatives and endless melodies as on the stage, one might reasonably expect that they would seek to draw our attention to their personalities, not to their clothes. As a rule, however, it works the other way around. Mere armor, not the person within it, leads us to assume that we have to do with a knight or soldier. It's just like a masked ball. The mask is decisive. If a German dons a Turkish costume and, on top of that, squats cross-legged on the ground, his Islamic authenticity is no longer in doubt. Let a Turk try it with a German costume, and ape German comportment, and without doubt, he is a German, at least as far as his dress is concerned. But the minute either of them opens his mouth, the foreign accent unmasks him. This may be why the Turks of Herr Bachrich's famous opera, *Muzzedin,* appear too Viennese to the Ottomans, which does not mean that his *Muzzedin* could be taken by the Viennese for a genuine Turk. They would be more likely to suspect a Lapp, despite the Turkish costume and the Turkish music, were it not that certain droll characteristics in Herr Bachrich's music suggest that his Turks are really disguised Phoenicians or some related strain. Or do we err?

Should the gentle reader who has followed my evasions thus far be growing impatient, and ask when I may get around to reviewing *Das Andreasfest,* let him accept with composure and serenity my earnest assurance that I have already come to the end of it. Still, I seem to recall having treated the musical part of it too fleetingly. And so a postscript: Why does Herr Grammann call his *Andreasfest* a romantic opera? Could he not have called it a "romantic harp concerto" with orchestra obbligato and garnished with an utterly super-fluous apparatus of solo and choral song? What needless reflections are not prompted in the head of an operagoer by so inaccurate a designation as "romantic opera." He thinks immediately of solo roles, male and female, of choristers and corps de ballet and stage designers, of the theater mechanic, the stage director, the prompter, the conductor and the orchestra. In defining this resounding body he is not, to be sure, very thorough, but he does imagine all the instruments, from the contrabass tuba to the piccolo, one after another, and he is no more delighted by his knowledge than by the number of the instruments. How soft, how awesome, how splendid, how rippling they will sound, either singly or together. And a harp, too! Ah, a harp! The mere sight of this instrument transports him to the blessed state of nirvana. During the performance, however, his predilection for the harp will be noticeably dimin-ished, and in the fourth act he curses the instrument in *ffff* ten times more angrily than Bishop Ernulphus who, as old Shandy maintains, passed on to us anathema, and that is saying a lot, since anathema, in the view of Dr. Slop, is the father of curses. . . . Condition of a lost soul in the ninth circle of Dante's Inferno. If folk harpists henceforth complain of bad takings, the blame lies with Herr Grammann. He should have thought of this while scoring *Das Andreasfest.* A revolution of harpists would be the natural consequence of his carelessness, in view of which, and in the interest of peace, it would seem indicated that *Das Andreasfest* be laid quickly *ad acta.*

Fräulein Lilli Lehmann continues her guest appearances on our opera stage with great success. As Donna Anna she might well have been more passionate, but as Norma hardly more majestic. We would like to experience her Iphi-genia. Her noble, restrained and ever expressive acting qualify her very specially for a role of this kind. If only she enunciated more distinctly. This baby talk is unbearable.

Effective support was rendered by Fräulein Marie Lehmann and the other principals, notably Herr Peschier who, as Ottavio, evolved an eye language that can hardly have been surpassed by Saint Lawrence on the griddle. One saw, indeed, only the white of his eye, producing a not unseemly lighting effect in contrast to the hero's black attire.

1.   Karl Grammann (1842-1879), a minor German composer resident in Vienna 1871-1884. *Das Andreasfest* had first been performed in Dresden in 1882.
2.   Wunderblume, an exotic flower.

40. Die Entführung aus dem Serail
Bianchi as Lucia

February 15, 1885

Just before curtain time, Herr Reichenberg took over the role of Osmin for the suddenly indisposed Herr Rokitansky, and he carried it off very well, musically. He was less successful dramatically, and yet only the slenderest resources are required to achieve an absolutely truthful realization of this original character. A couple of bold strokes, and it's done. The singer who undertakes this role should, above all, avoid becoming too concerned with detail. Osmin is carved from a single slab (and a pretty rough one, too), and the fundamental tonality of this character should, therefore, be suitably shaded, vocally and dramatically, by discreet modulation into the nearest related keys only at the most appropriate moments. Once, and only once, does Osmin shed his forbidding bearskin: when the effect of the wine catapults him into such a -- for him -- exotic tonality of utterly uninhibited jollity that he loses all sense of identity. For the rest, Osmin is a grumbler throughout the entire opera, and no good-humored grumbler, either. He's a thoroughly irate, malicious and surly grumbler, full of poison and bile. He is envious, too, and eager to gloat over the misfortunes of others, lustful without being able to experience pleasure, cruel, cowardly and cunning. Despite all that, he is stupid and loutish -- and the incarnation of impotence. Yes, if all were to come to pass as this fine fellow pictures it: "first beheaded, then hung, then impaled on a hot spit, then burned, then shackled and held under water, and finally flayed."

Obviously, this conscientious harem warden might have assisted the Holy Roman or Spanish inquisitors with a very edifying and salutary recipe. Fortunately, in this instance, it got no farther than the pious wish. We cannot be too grateful for the fact that [Selim] Bassa closed his ears to his faithful servant's well-intended but, in their design, rather bold and extravagent suggestions, and thought it better to reward bad deeds with good, thereby certainly winning the hearts of all Christian elements in the audience and assuring himself of their most sympathetic and warmest reception — if, of course, only insofar as the Christians were sufficiently numerous.

To return to Herr Reichenberg, he did not entirely manage to endow Osmin's character with the requisite consistency. Now he smiled, now he was brusque, now he cast friendly glances, sometimes was good humor itself, as, for example, during Blondchen's aria: "Through tenderness and coaxing." Herr Rokitansky understands this character far better. The peevish, surly manner in which this otherwise very able bass goes about his tasks — his unexampled indifference could drive a newborn baby out of its mind -- his only helps him here to overcome his evident inability to act, but even enables him to create a character, possibly quite contrary to Herr Rokitansky's intentions, of an authenticity rarely achieved on any stage. Herr Rokitansky's Osmin is a masterpiece, owing nothing either to the singer's good will (more likely to his ill will) or to his histrionic capacities.

For a dramatic soprano, Fräulein Lilli Lehmann has more coloratura than she needs. But with less emotion both in sustained song and spoken dialogue Kostanze could still have given the excellent Bassa to understand that declarations of love in the imperative mode are unbecoming even to one of his station. Selim, moreover, was clever enough to grasp this, if not gentleman enough to forgo certain rudenesses toward Konstanze. In view of his other virtues, we shall not hold it against him. The amiable Blondchen (Fräulein Marie Lehmann) managed both skillfully and effectively to give her anxious swain tangible evidence of her love and fidelity. It may be assumed that the lively Pedrillo [Herr Schittenhelm], by recourse to a strong antidote, has been relieved of his doubts -- at least until the next performance. For the rest Herr Schittenhelm was droll enough. We liked particularly his smart appearance, much enchanced by the two-pointed beard. One should not underestimate the effect of a beard so elegantly fashioned. It has a fascination of its own. One must reckon it an act of irresponsible folly if such a product, conspicuously encouraged by nature itself, and given the finishing touches by the virtuosity of the barber, should be subjected, on one's own authority or through caprice or -- and this would be most unpardonable of all -- because of unfavorable criticism, to any alteration, and accordingly disfigured, or surrendered to the iniquities of the razor and therewith destroyed. Truly, man is as thankless in his innermost impulses as thoughtless in his public actions.

Lucia di Lammermoor. We have no wish to quarrel with Herr Filippi, who sang Edgardo in this opera, because of his Polish accent. Herr Filippi seems, to judge by his perenially satisfied demeanor, to be an amiable gentleman. Moreover, he is forever placing his hands on his heart, as if to assure us most ardently of his amiability. We gladly take him at his word. His appearance is sympathetic, and since he has an agreeable voice, and uses it well, he cannot fail to please. The main interest of this evening centered on the contribution of Fräulein Bianchi. Her agile throat excited the audience's amazement and admiration. The applause lavished on her accomplishment was unending. Tasteless as coloratura singing may be, simply as a means of displaying a singer's virtuosity. it can also serve the opera composer in developing a dramatic situation. The "Mad Scene" in Act III of *Lucia* provides an example. This senseless up and down vocalizing on the vowel *a,* does it not resemble the nonsensical stuttering of a lunatic? Might one not also conclude, on the other hand, from these ludicrous vocal capers called coloratura that the solemn, noble figure of Norma at the sacrificial alter in the first act of the opera that bears her name had already lost her wits? For me, at least, she was clearly out of her head. Whether others felt as I did, I know not.

41. La Gioconda — *In Absentia*

February 22, 1885

Whoever could not attend the German performance of *La Gioconda,* as I, for example, could not, but who would like to talk about it, as I would not, or who has to describe it (however unwillingly), as I do, finds himself in a rather critical situation. It becomes less critical, however, if he who would like to talk about it possesses some degree of imagination, as I do, for example, who must write about it. For there are very, very many things, as demonstrated daily, that one can talk about and write about without having seen them, heard them, felt them or understood them, especially a performance of *La Gioconda* There is nothing in it to feel or to understand, although there is more to hear than is tolerable to the most hardened eardrum, and just enough to see to distract one's aural attention from the great spectacle of the orchestra.

This apparently critical situation becomes manifestly so, however, when a critic in such a critical situation is supposed to criticize. Under such dubious circumstances a critique, no matter how good, might be beneath criticism insofar as the critic's intention is to be properly critical, that is, objective, as the critic's calling requires. The perceptive reader may, without jeopardizing his judgment of character, of which he doubtless holds, and rightly, a high opinion, credit me with enough sense on this occasion to write anything but a critique of the performance of *La Gioconda.* Nothing is more foreign to my nature than to deceive myself wittingly, and thus to deceive my readers. I shall be on my guard, accordingly, against serving up assumption about which I can offer only a surmise, and facts about which I can hand down a verdict (and possibly a false one) as one and the same dish.

About this opera, to be sure, I have reached a verdict. Since my task now, however, is a critical discussion of the performance, I must restrict myself, through the medium of fantasy and previous experience of the capacities of the participating singers, to surmise. And thus I surmise that the success of *La Gioconda* on this occasion can be justified solely and exclusively by the inspired performance of Frau Lucca. One can vividly imagine with what brilliant colors Pauline Lucca endowed and even beautified the pale, yes, repulsive figure of the street singer Gioconda, how, with her eminently dramatic endowment, she could so raise this now passionate, now tender, and then again alternately presumptuous and self-denying female, now snorting vengeance and then deeply touched, in short, this bloodless, soulless creature, forever swept from one extreme to another, that one might easily imagine oneself in the presence of a truly human being and not the utterly common, ordinary stage puppet of the librettist.

It is regrettable that Frau Lucca dedicates her finest resources to the most unworthy tasks. In reviving from apparent death such operas as [Gounod's] *Le Tribut de Zamora*, [Goetz's] *The Taming of the Shrew*, *La Gioconda* and the like by the enchantment of her dramatic art, she resembles exactly the instrumental virtuosos whose vanity is never more completely satisfied than in the realization that by their arts alone they have rendered the worst muck appetizing to the public. That, however, is a sorry distinction.

Herr Müller, in my opinion, may well have made far more of Prince Enzo Grimaldi than the Italian tenor Valero, and the same may be said of Fräulein Braga relative to her Italian predecessor, Signora Giuli. On the other hand, it may be assumed with some degree of certainty that the Barnaba of Herr Sommer was as superior vocally to Signor Dufriche's as the latter's lively acting was superior to Herr Sommer's hapless deportment.

Still, one may assume, thanks largely to the effective participation of Frau Lucca, that this German production was no inconsiderable improvement on last season's Italian production. But we see no grounds for self-congratulation, being of the opinion that repeated performance of such rubbish is an unworthy enterprise for even the worst Italian company.

42. Cascading Coloratura

March 1, 1885

Frau L'Allemand was the Rosina. At first we thought this must be a doll. Beginning in the middle register, her voice sounded like that of a squeaking child. But very soon there was an unexpected turn of events in the singer's favor. As soon as Frau L'Allemand headed for the higher regions of the vocal range, the voice gained in intensity, incisiveness and even in euphony. She is a virtuosa in coloratura. Unfortunately, she is only too well aware of her virtuosity, never passing up an opportunity to put her trickery on display for better or worse. Every rest, every fermata, is used to interpolate cadenzas, trills, roulades, etc. It's coloratura wherever you look, wherever you listen, wherever you reach.

A persistent downpour in the mountains is horrible, frightening, destructive. In people it excites ennui, impatience and melancholia. One becomes a misanthrope, a pessimist, a cannibal. One begins to pay more heed to the devil than becomes a gentleman, for one curses in every possible key -- the key of F is most appropriate. One offers vernacular curses and scholarly curses, drawing upon quotation or upon one's own invention, in pithy aphorisms or in broad metaphors and similes. A master of many languages enjoys, moreover, the advantage of being able to translate the same curse into Italian, Spanish, French, Turkish and Dutch (although the Dutch, thanks to their notorious stolidity, may not be on an especially good footing with diabolic grammar), and may thus relieve his spleen six times over. Or one may, under such circumstances, driven by desperate boredom, busy oneself with poetizing and composition or, indeed, with both at the same time.

But great, significant, monumental as Herr Richard Kralik may stand in his own estimation, I fear, yes, I fear that his poetic fantasy has been under water for too long, that the soporific effect of an inexhaustible downpour is so faithfully relfected in his "Verselein" that his prospects of rivaling Hafis, Pindar and Walter von der Vogelweide, or even to surpass them, will have to turn into water. While a substantial rainfall can be fruitful after a long drought, with too much of the fluid element the opposite is to be feared. Now I gladly concede that Herr Kralik's so-called poetic vein suffers severely from drought and aridity, a perfectly natural phenomenon with which we have no quarrel. The more painfully, then, must every sensitive person be affected -- and it is they to whom the *Büchlein der Unwesenheit* [1] is directed -- when so

well-ordered a nature as Herr Kralik's is so little at home with the barometer
of his moods that, passing up the opportune moment for maybe halfway
tolerable production, it first spreads the wings of his dear poet's soul when
they must collapse under the weight of the most desperate boredom and, thus,
come to resemble the misshapen stumps of the penguin.

Oh, what crises, what horrors, does a steady downpour in the lonely
countryside not have upon its conscience. It reduces mankind, and distorts it.
But (and this is what I have been leading up to) I would rather make a pact
with the devil, or stand under a shower for the rest of my life, than listen to
coloratura for a whole evening of opera. As graciously, as charmingly as it
flows from the throat of Frau L'Allemand, one grows tired of it after a while.
Frau L'Allemand is, on the other hand, a delightful actress, and looked the
jealous Bartolo so innocently and at the same time so roguishly in the eye, that
it was an utter joy to see. Splendid as always in comical roles was Herr
Mayerhofer (Dr. Bartolo). His worthy compatriot Basilio (Herr Reichenberg)
was in an almost exuberant mood. A respectable accomplishment. Herr
Horwitz has no talent for comedy, and so his Figaro was pretty cold.

In *The Daughter of the Regiment* Frau L'Allemand sang the Marie with the
same bravura she had brought to Rosina in *The Barber of Seville*. Again, it
was her acting, and especially her facial expression that impressed me most
favorably. The rough heartiness of Sergeant Sulpice was well echoed in Herr
Reichenberg's characterization. Herr Schittenhelm [Tonio], too, found his
role congenial. Finally, a word of praise for the 21st Regiment for its disciplined behavior toward the defenceless Swiss [Tonio]. In *Mignon* Frau
L'Allemand bade farewell to our public. She could hardly have chosen a better
role than that of Philine. How charming she looked, how coquettish. If
Philine is the only natural figure among the other cripples of this ghastly piece,
she was, thanks to Frau L'Allemand's excellent performance, absolutely
consoling. The achievements of the other singers in this opera are familiar.

In the festively illuminated Grosser Musikvereinssaal Handel's "Saul" was
performed to commemorate the 200th anniversary of his birth. If much of this
work impresses us as old and pallid, as, for example, the arias and the
recitatives, the choruses disclose a verve, a dramatic vitality, a titanic force, an
irresistible power of expression that still fills us with astonishment and
admiration and will continue to do so as long as music is played and sung.
Among the participants Frau Papier stood out over all. Frau Schmid-Csasny
discharged her difficult task not badly. Herr Winkelmann and Herr Reichenberg lack the broad tone appropriate to oratorio, but they both had fine
moments. What pleased me most was that Herr Schittenhelm sang the Witch
of Endor. Was that a funny witch! And how beautifully she sang, the evil
witch! And how amiable she looked! A sight almost as elevating as amusing.

1.   Either a malicious garble or a typographical error. The proper title is *Büchlein der Unweis-
heit* [Booklet of Unwisdom]. Wolf, with *Unwesenheit*, makes it *Booklet of Nothingness*.
One suspects malice rather than error.

43. About the Philharmonic Concerts

March 8, 1885

What of the Philharmonic concerts?

They are obviously headed for disaster. And could it, under the prevailing circumstances, be otherwise? The gentlemen of the Philharmonic, whose motto is by no means Robert le Diable's "Ah, gold is but a chimera," but rather the philosophy of the villainous Iago, "Put money in thy purse," cannot easily make any claim to be taken seriously from a purely artistic point of view.

Granted, man is commonly a slave of circumstances. He must earn money in order to live, and to assure such earnings he must make concessions. Now concessions constitute restrictions of one's freedom, a consequence of insurmountable circumstances. And so we are back where we started: earning money, concessions, restrictions, slavery. But if we look to see in how far this paramount evil, the earning of money, has exercised a damaging influence on the impending artistic crisis of this concert institution, and on the dependent relationsip into which the Philharmonic public could fall as a result of it, we find a phantom, a mirage. For the Philharmonic is, in truth, in the fortunate position of being able to earn money without making concessions. If, despite that, they have not become millionaires, and do not rule the world, or do not own all the shares of the Northern Railroad and all other railroads of Europe and America as yet not nationalized, if despite all that they are still slaves, is that any reason for offering ever worse programs? Is this Philharmonic Society not just as sovereign as any of the thirty-two monarchies of old Germany? Are they under any outside pressure? Is there a competing orchestra? Are they not free and independent? No. They are slaves, less free than the blacks on the plantations of South America. They are slaves of the vanity and their indolence.

They are slaves of their vanity in that they wish, on the one hand, to be judged according to their virtuoso accomplishments, and on the other, by favoring the works of certain composers who have come to the fore through publicity, to solicit the flattery of a "famous" and "feared" critic [Hanslick]. They are slaves of their indolence in that they lack the courage to ignore this "feared" critic, and because they treasure nothing above comfort. They have a powerful ally, one whose loyalty is not determined by critical notices, good or bad. This ally is little embarrassed by its confederate's vanity and indolence. Let the Philharmonic play what it pleases, it offers no criticism, except maybe of ladies' hats. It complains of nothing, except possibly excessively hot weather. It listens with opera glass in hand, sits on its ears and is, on the whole, of a harmless nature. It is, in short, fashion.

It is hardly to be assumed that the gentlemen of the Philharmonic are the last to whom this fact has remained a secret. It would be truly mad, if not presumptuous, to see in the hectic rush for tickets to the Philharmonic concerts anything other than a manifestation of the most absurd fashion. The gentlemen of the Philharmonic will surely not flatter themselves that the public streams to their concerts in expectation of artistic delights. We know that Herr Kapellmeister Richter is anything but malicious, but the devil himself could not have behaved more maliciously than our genial Herr Kapellmeister in the choice of such a program as we were offered at the most recent concert: Gade,[1] Dvořák, Molique[2] and, as an act of mercy -- what a stupendous undertaking -- a symphony by Mozart. Bravo, Herr Kapellmeister! You display taste, good will, industry, dedication, earnestness, stamina and a goodly portion of ambition. Whither will it all lead you? You won't, for God's sake, aspire to the dizzy heights of performing Haydn's childrens' symphonies? Beware the strain of such works, the sleepless nights, the bloody sweat! O, insatiable one! The laurel and palm branches that will cool your fevered brow in recognition of your indescribable contribution, the world-shaking heroic deed of performing string or woodwind serenades by obscure composers! -- How is that? They have only inspired an even greater urge for great deeds, for Herculean labors? Icarus, Icarus! Beware of thy fall!

No, Herr Kapellmeister. You must take care of yourself. Spare yourself. You need a rest. Spare us your precious life. It is not yours alone. It belongs to art, to the battle against the Philistines, to the struggle for freedom, for an emancipated view of the world. Continue to favor us with Dvořák rhapsodies, Gade overtures, cello concertos by Molique. But don't overdo it. Why, as the final number, a Mozart symphony, and, indeed, the marvelous one in E flat! This piece is too complex, certainly requiring countless rehearsals. These may be agreeable to you, given your pronounced love of rehearsing, but to us they are a horror, a catastrophe, for you will destroy yourself, and we shall forever be denied the prospect of hearing just once at a Philharmonic concert under your direction Czerny's "School of Velocity," whose orchestration Herr Bachrich would doubtless undertake as a favor -- and for a commensurate fee.

1.   Niels Vilhelm Gade (1817-1890), Danish composer, a protégé of Schumann and Mendelssohn, succeeding the latter as conductor of the Gewandhaus concerts in Leipzig in 1847. He returned to his native Copenhagen in 1848, and spent the remainder of his life there, much honored as organist, conductor and composer.

2.   Wilhelm Bernhard Molique (1802-1869), a renowned German violinist, who settled in
     London in 1849 and remained there until shortly before his death, highly esteemed as
     virtuoso, chamber musician, composer and pedagogue. His compositions include six violin
     concertos and the single cello concerto referred to here.

44. Voice Alone Does Not the Singer Make

March 15, 1885

Tannhäuser by Richard Wagner

Frau Papier sang Elisabeth for the first time[1] and, we hasten to add, with great success. The virtues, as also the shortcomings, of this highly gifted singer were more distinctly in evidence than ever before. They balanced each other out, so to speak, insofar as a compromise between the predominance of vocal expression on the one hand, and the reticence of dramatic expression on the other, may be regarded as possible without leaving an unsatisfactory impression upon the audience.

A notable defect, it seemed to us, was the curious sense of distraction conveyed by gaze and countenance at certain moments when Frau Papier was achieving the most moving projection of the musical expression. We must remark therein a considerable want of dramatic capability. As securely as Frau Papier was master of her role musically, just so insecurely did she command it dramatically. The effect of her singing upon anyone listening with eyes closed will be convincing. But one may also feel, at times, that he is enjoying a mere comedy. Since, in opera, we cannot separate the singer from the actor, nor give the former the slightest priority over the other, we can grant the voice itself, lovely, ample, bell-like, crystal clear (and all the other familiar descriptive adjectives) as it may be, only a secondary consideration in the assessment of an opera singer's qualifications. Thus, only those can enter a claim to perfection who are equally at home in the arts of singing and acting. Not that we have anything against lovely voices. -- Quite the contrary, so long as the lovely voice is used as a means of enhancing the musical expression, or to lend it a certain coloration. By and large, however, it is the lovely voice that counts, i.e., a means becomes the end. This turns a means into an end.

It is from this perverse point of view that public and critics alike assess the sing-song of Herr Sommer. The lovely voice means more to them than lovely song. And yet, how inferior are Herr Sommer's accomplishments to the largely ignored accomplishments of Herr Ley. Herr Ley has humor enough, in the favorite drinking scene in *Der Vampyr*, to make fun of his own voice when he sings: "I, too, sing, but not always beautifully." Would that Herr Sommer might sing half so beautifully, and demonstrate some of Herr Lay's other virtues. I know as well as anyone that Herr Lay's voice is not to be compared with Herr Sommer's. But what Herr Lay sings preserves its characteristic stamp, and therein is to be sought the principal merit of an opera singer.

Fräulein Schläger (Venus) surprised us this time with a fanciful costume to which, unfortunately, I must take exception. The slit on the one side should be sewn up. Such unworthy devices are all very well for a faded coquette bent on exciting a jaded worldling. But they are not for a Venus. She is, after all, the goddess not of lechery, but of love.

Tannhäuser is certainly Herr Winkelmann's most successful role. A word or two, however, about his fussy business after the scenic transformation in the first act, which displeased me. In moments of utter astonishment, people are overcome by a kind of petrifaction. Herr Winkelmann understands this well enough, for he remained quite a while rooted in an enraptured attitude. But was it called for, time and again, to set his hands in motion in order to express a sensation of joyous amazement? Do we not have eyes, facial expression, attitudes? A hesitant or vigorous or wavering step, forward or backward or to the side, etc. -- can it not make conventional hand wringing superfluous, or at least relieve the hands of the total burden?

In this respect, Herr Schittenhelm, who sang Walter on this occasion, was more adept. He followed the song contest with facial expressions by turn serene or sombre. Mostly he smiled roguishly, like the sun in April, but often too, as I have said, he followed developments with the threatening mien of clouds heavy with storm. The whole contest was mirrored in his countenance, which was the more significant in that he was acting not only for himself but for his colleagues. Heaven only knows, there may be a genius tucked away in Herr Schittenhelm.

Faust by Gounod

Herr Baer,[2] from the Court Theater in Darmstadt, made his local debut as Faust. A run-of-the-mill opera tenor, not good, not bad, "respectable". In his fantastic *The Damnation of Faust*, Berlioz allows the hero of the legend to sojourn in Hungary, on the banks of the Danube -- for the sake of the "Rakoczy" March which Berlioz, as we all know (although the gentlemen of the Philharmonic and their conductor may not), elaborated and orchestrated in his ingenious fashion, and eventually incorporated in his *Damnation of Faust*. The librettists of Gounod's *Faust*, as they certainly held quite strictly to Aristotle's unity principle,[3] could not permit themselves a luxury similar to that of Berlioz. Herr Baer, on the other hand, accomplished something that would have seemed inadmissible to the better judgment of the librettists. He stuck a warrior-like mustache under his nose, although not with the intention of competing with Berlioz's inspiration, and achieved something not unlike the aspect of a pandour.[4] This was something that might have left the librettists, as well as the composer, of *Faust* pretty much unmoved. For us Germans, such "piquanteries" provide a bit of merriment.

1.   A lamentably brief, if glorious, operatic career was thought by many to be accountable to the assumption by Papier, a contralto or mezzo-soprano, of soprano roles.
2.   Ludwig Baer (1844-1900), who, before embarking on a singing career, had been a good enough violinist to be concertmaster of the Gewandhaus Orchestra in Leipzig.
3.   As summarized by Will Durant in *The Life of Greece*: "Beauty is unity, the cooperation and symmetry of the parts of a whole. In drama this unity is primarily a unity of action; the plot must concern itself with one action chiefly, and may admit other actions only to advance or illuminate this central tale."
4.   A South Slavonic irregular in the Austro-Hungarian Army.

45. Concerts

March 22, 1885

It cannot be my intention, today, to review recent concerts — if for no more valid reason than the fact that I have not been to any.

Now, the gentle reader might well be entitled to ask why I have not led off these lines with a more appropriate heading, since I myself, and right at the outset, have announced my intention not to attempt a concert critique in the usual sense of that term, the customary heading, "Concerts," implying plainly enough just such a critique.

Scholarly discussion of this debatable matter would serve no useful purpose, either for my readers or for me. So with that let's break it off, and rather cast an eye over our concert life, asking ourselves why it should be that our public, despite a surfeit of concerts, still has time, stamina, courage and self-denial enough to wander into concert halls?

What can dictate such sacrifices and hardships? Certainly not the urge to hear good music, since for some time now the repertoire has been determined not by those who give the concerts, but by the press. Or are there really still those who can discern in the frequent reiteration of the name Brahms anything more than the glistening fruits of indefatigable publicity? Indeed, I doubt that even ever-enthusiastic, idealistic music dealers, who might wish to assimilate Brahms "in bulk" would see in such melancholy symptoms any convincing evidence of Brahms's popularity.

No singer, male or female, no fiddler, no pianist, indeed, no orchestra, dares put on a concert in which at last one Brahms composition is not played or sung. Has there ever been anything so ludicrous? Beethoven, Schubert, Schumann and Mendelssohn, not to speak of Liszt and Berlioz, are given short shrift, while the press, hovering above the head of Herr Johannes Brahms like the Holy Ghost in tongues of fire, empties the cornucopia of propaganda over him, urging his compositions upon virtuosos and concert institutions with fire and sword, or, to put it more elegantly, commending his compositions to their attention.

One cannot hold it too much against the virtuosos if they capitulate without resistance, and unconditionally. A poor pianist or violinist, too, must live, and the press is the indirect source of his daily bread. From his behavior toward the press depends his weal and woe. The press commands: "Play Brahms, or we shall not come to your concert, we shall not review you. And if we do not mention you, or if we speak ill of you, then you will see where and how you dispose of your tickets."

Since we can hardly expect of vocal and instrumental virtuosos as much, or anything like, the heroism of the Roman Consul of old, Regulus[1] we should not be surprised if they pursue a path paved with gold and, in a certain sense, with honor and glory. It is a path on which one soon achieves a goal, but promptly trips and stumbles if one treads it with the soles of artistic conviction. The difficult situation of the virtuosos, often rendered desperate by ever-growing competition, may halfway excuse this betrayal of one's own faith. But in cases where artistic honor is in no conflict with petty concern for one's livelihood, it is absolutely unpardonable to accept the directives of our critical Holy Trinity.[2] This complaint concerns, above all, the conductor of the concerts of the Philharmonic and the Society of Friends of Music.

We think far too highly of this conductor, risen to eminence under the precepts of Richard Wagner, to believe in the sincerity of his attitudes toward Brahms's manner of composition, just as we also regard the influential critic of the *Wiener Presse* [Max Kalbeck] as too intelligent, logical and clear-headed to see in his eternal protest against the art form of Wagner and Liszt anything but a hobby horse that he mounts, now with charm, now with dignity, but always with evident pleasure.

I have observed in the course of these articles that nothing so astonishes me as the courage of our virtuosos, composers and singers in giving concerts, and the lamb like patience and the positively touching characteristics of human kindness of those who attend them. What demon plagues those miserable creatures? Is art served, or can the public find refreshment when, for example, cellist X seeks effects on his instrument appropriate to the piccolo, or when violinist Y tries to imitate on his E string the rough voice of the double bass, or when a contralto reaches for the high C and a soprano for the low G, not to speak of pianists? Things can hardly be madder in a lunatic asylum than in a concert hall. And yet, it is precisely this wretched nonsense that principally draws the public, leaving the true artist in a predicament like that of Dr. Aylmer,[3] Bishop of London, who, when he noticed that the majority of his congregation slept through his sermon, began to read from a Hebrew bible. Suddenly the congregation was all attention. And the Bishop said: "What a fine lot you are! You are attentive when I read something of which you understand not a single word, and you sleep when I speak in your mother tongue of matters concerning the salvation of your souls."

Does not this anecdote, as passed on by C. Ch. Lichtenberg,[4] fit our concert going public to a T? But there could come a time when Hebrew music will sound more intelligible to these people than some musical sermon by Brahms. By that time, however, the long-awaited and true messiah may well have made his appearance. I hope it will no longer be my lot to review him.

1.   Marcus Alilius Regulus, third century Roman general and statesman, who was captured in Africa toward the close of the first Punic War. According to tradition, he was sent on parole to Rome to negotiate either a peace or an exchange of prisoners, and urged the senate to refuse the proposals, also insisting on being returned to Carthage to fulfill the terms of his parole. Upon his arrival in Carthage, the legend has it, he was tortured to death.

2.   Presumably Hanslick, Speidel and Kalbeck.

3.   John Aylmer (1521-1594), Bishop of London in the reign of Elizabeth I, a controversial and contentious clergyman characterized as "Morrell, the bad shepherd," in Edmund Spenser's *Shepheardes Calender* (1579).

4.   Georg Christoph Lichtenberg (1742-1799), German aphorist and physicist. Two visits to England resulted in a book, *Letters from England*. Wolf's source for the Bishop Aylmer anecdote, however, was more likely a Brockhaus selection, *Georg Christoph Lichtenberg's Gedanken und Maximen* [Thoughts and Maxims], Leipzig, 1871, in which Bishop Aylmer's words appear almost exactly as Wolf gives them.

46. Advice to Operatic Visitors

March 29, 1885

Every opera singer who takes it upon himself to appear as guest on a foreign stage would do well to remember that he is entering an enemy camp, that he is necessarily declaring war on that singer whose roles he chooses for his debut. I say "necessarily" because the rare exceptions among singers and actors, those whose characters are not composed of vanity, envy and narcissism, prove the rule. Since, however, and fortunately, every singer regards himself as an exception (to the rule) -- whether from vanity and narcissism need not concern us for the moment -- there remains no danger for the individual.

Now, a sensible person will hardly deceive another without nurturing the desire or wish to defeat his adversaries. To this end he may or may not be justified according to the availability to him of the ways and means of fulfilling his wishes, of turning hope into reality. A clever fellow, accordingly, attacks only when sufficiently sure of himself. Will he also rely solely on his own strength and superiority? If there were only two persons on this planet, or two nations, certainly! But matters being as they are, he will be forced to play politics, too. What can the best-trained army under the most heroic of commanders accomplish against the intrigues of a wily diplomat. Thus, politics, politics, politics, unless one chooses to commit suicide.

Herr Ondry, from the Municipal Opera in Pest, was unpolitical enough to make his debut on our opera stage in [Ambroise] Thomas's *Hamlet*. This was a grave mistake. Herr Ondry should first have acquainted himself with *Hamlet's* standing with our public and our critics. He would have learned that this opera is almost never given, that the public dreads it as if it were cholera, and that the famous scholarship of our critics has already advanced to the point of despising it.

Subsequently, Herr Ondry took another bow in Gounod's *Faust*. This was a real mistake, if only because Herr Baer recently made a guest appearance in this opera, and the critics have thus had to hear it twice in rapid succession. The audience that gorges itself today on *Faust* may tomorrow, perhaps, have its digestion restored by *Mefistofele*. But the critics will take care to avoid any undertaking with *Mefistofele* except in the line of duty. Nor can one blame the critic if, after two hearings of *Faust*, he finally loses patience.

To retain, under the most profoundly depressing circumstances, sufficient objectivity to give due attention to the singer, to assess his achievements according to their merits, i.e., to recognize them if they are truly good, to savor vinegar with honey, and discover that the honey is excellent, instead of wishing the whole witches' brew to the devil, spiced with a thousand curses, as one would dearly love to do -- to go along with all this is, I frankly confess, a miserable business. We shall not assume, not even for the fun of it, that Herr Ondry's motive in including *Hamlet* and *Faust* in his repertoire was malevolent. Or was it an exaggerated confidence in his own capacities that led Herr Ondry to be heedless in his choice of the operas in which he saw fit to appear? Or was it simply the old familiar routine as it is cherished and fostered in opera houses (those absolute hothouses of routine), which because a bit of thought is required, regards a serious preoccupation with higher things as useless and unfruitful, even when it would be of obvious benefit to those concerned. Be all that as it may --.

Enough. Despite all misgivings and complaints, we can give Herr Ondry a pretty good testimonial. A well-schooled and powerful voice, rather monotonous in its utterance, sometimes even raw, but sometimes very effective; unaffected movements, although not always appropriate to the situation, and often quite operatic or, in plain language, puppet-like; lively play of facial expression, mostly correct, and in general a good bearing -- all this, in short, a characterization of Herr Ondry's accomplishment. The same was true of his Solomon in Goldmark's *The Queen of Sheba*.

The appalling demands Goldmark makes on the singers' voices were easily mastered by our local forces. Frau Kupfer was surprisingly good as Sulamith, and Herr Winkelmann splendid as Assad. Frau Papier should invest her Queen of Sheba with a bit more inner fire, so that bearing and gesture, as the tangible expression of a truly felt emotional experience, might capture at least a suggestion of immediacy, if not of beauty. She would then shine without a rival in this role. The transfigured, lovely image of the fabulously enchanting queen is wafted toward us with the first note that Frau Papier attacks. But it is important, too, that the sensual appearance be sustained, and for that the mere mask is not enough, as well as that mask was chosen, and as beautiful as she looked in it. That Frau Papier should have used a red slip of paper to announce her indisposition and request our indulgence I find inexplicable. If indisposition means to be thoroughly in control of the situation, to be in as good voice and spirits as ever, then I would love to experience the evening when Frau Papier informs the public that, on this occasion, she is especially well disposed.

47. Berlioz's Symphonie Fantastique

April 5, 1885

About the performance of the Symphonie Fantastique of Hector Berlioz at the seventh subscription concert of the Philharmonic Society:

Whatever may have moved the Philharmonic to make an exception, and deviate, at least this once, from their traditional policy vis-à-vis the works of Berlioz, I am content to probe no further for the secret mainsprings that wrought the miracle. Suffice it to say that, at this time, the Symphonie Fantastique was not only announced, but actually was played.

Two factors encourage me to see myself exempted from an analysis of this work, no less gigantic in its plan than in its execution: (1) It may be assumed that Schumann's famous critique[1] is familiar to every music lover, and that (2) the meager success the work enjoyed in the most recent concert calls for a more intensive consideration of our concert life, both in general and in detail.

Before attacking this subject (and it will be an attack, you may rest assured of that), let me call attention once again to Schumann's admirable essay. His unbiased attitude toward this work, his intimate grasp of its poetic substance, his acute analysis in terms both of form and of musical content -- in which Schumann delivered a very model of music criticism -- and, finally, the generous insights that led him to recognize in Berlioz's procedure, originating in the most intimate compulsion, a decisive advance in instrumental composition honor Schumann the critic no less than Schumann the composer.

Remember, moreover, that Schumann, in preparing this critique, as just as it is intelligent and enlightening, did not even have an orchestral score to assist him in his analysis. He worked from the piano reduction, if Liszt's, to be sure.

With any other composer, this might have mattered little, but it matters much with a musician like Berlioz. His notes, in the piano reduction, resemble dried-up mummies, whereas the orchestra scores of this master call to mind the magic books of Prosper Alphanus in *Klein-Zaches,*[2] head and stem, periods and pauses, clefs and bar lines leading a ghostly existence. Despite all that, Schumann recognized at a first glance the beauties, the colossal dimensions, the daring strokes, the inspired off shoots, the depth of feeling, the strength of the ideas, the cogency of the expression, the command of form and the structural logic of this violent sorrow-child of Berlioz's muse.

Where, however, all this had to remain hidden to him, he did not cry out for help, nor cover his perplexity in the cloak of critical authority (that ragged cloak from whose holes the vanity and ignorance of our critical one-day wonders simper loathsomely at the outside world), but, instead, once arrived at the end of his examination, he confessed frankly that without a score he found the last pages of the symphony bad. As a matter of fact, you will hardly find an admirer of Berlioz's compositions to whom the fifth movement of the Symphonie Fantastique, in the piano reduction, is sympathetic. The orchestral effect of this movement, however, with the basic theme of the "Dies Irae" in the trombones beneath the encircling witches' sabbath is overpowering, shattering, catastrophic. It stands to the same passage in the piano reduction as does a real hurricane to one badly painted, or badly described, whichever you prefer.

How seriously Schumann took this critical mission can be inferred by way of example from his own words: "In the firm conviction that certain academic theoreticians (does that not remind you immediately of the matadors of our daily criticism?) do more damage than our practicing Titans, and that with their encouragement of miserable mediocrity (does not one think instinctively of our famous but unfortunately old-fashioned symphonists of today?) create far more mischief than does praise of poetic extravagence, we call upon our successors, once and for all, to attest in our behalf: that, with regard to the compositions of Berlioz, we did not, as is customary, lag ten years behind with our critical wisdom, but pronounced ahead of time that a genius resides in this Frenchman."[3] O, how I admire, how I worship Schumann, if only for this critique!

And now to the attack. I mentioned at the outset of this article that the majority of the audience reacted negatively to this Berlioz symphony. And so I ask: Does our concertgoing public deserve to hear anything but Diabelli childrens' pieces[4] and Brahms symphonies and concertos? Do these two masters not wholly suffice to meet the musical requirements of our concertgoing public? If, for example, one would awake gentle sensations of quiet rapture, tender pining -- play Diabelli. If the public wishes to experience ascetic seizures, to be melancholy, to abandon itself to despair -- play Brahms. In case the compositions of both these famous successors of Beethoven, contrary to all expectations, excite the opposite sensations among the audience -- well, that's all right, too. If Meister Brahms would like to appeal to the light of heart, and Meister Diabelli trouble the belly, what does it matter? But what of Hector Berlioz (you will note that I did not venture to apply to this composer the euphemism, "Meister," however advantageous it might be for him in the eyes of our public)? What is this porcupine to our refined, distinguished Viennese public? Does he have human sensibilities? Is his art respectable? Does he know law and order? Is his manner of expression intelligible? Is his world not a graveyard of all reason, of all wholesome human understanding? Yes, yes, yes, yes! Our reply herewith:

Does Berlioz have human sensibilities? You lunatics! Do you think that the eternal community of those exalted spirits who, speaking in a voice of thunder, and wearing the radiant wreath of divinity, reveal to the clear and wonder-hungry eye of the inspired artist the never-heard, the never-seen, the never-dreamed, the never-imagined — do you think that they bear your misshapen form, speak in your squeaking voices, carry your tiny clockwork in their bosom? Who are you that you presume to remonstrate with the divine? If your eyes are stupid, your mind confused, your head turned, must it be the same with the artist (not counting the "Meister," of course)? Do you suppose that your Beethoven wrote his melodies right out of your heart? Now, that would be a good one! You, the Philharmonic audience, have never grasped him, never felt him, never understood him. You have chewed him over, then spat, then chewed again until you have persuaded yourself that he tastes good. But he doesn't really appeal to your taste, and if, one day, the glorious Vienna critics tell you (and why shouldn't they?) that Beethoven is, after all, a miserable composer, his intellectual nourishment eminently unhealthy, you will, without further reflection (or I am a Chinese), vomit, and wish to hear nothing further from Beethoven.

Is Berlioz's art respectable?

Has not the concept of respectability long since lost all its relevance for you? You, who form your views and your taste from the sediment of trashy French novels and insipid French comedies; you, who are so respectable that you would gladly hang a bit of clothing around the loins of the Medici Venus or the Venus de Milo, but only because naked beauty leaves you unmoved, because your dulled senses are no longer susceptible of natural reaction, because only the commonplace is appetizing, because, in a word, you are indecent — should you, of all people, pose such a question?

Does Berlioz, in his creation, have regard for law and order?

How do you clever people come by such thoroughly intelligent reservations? Are you not beasts of burden, going about your business or profession in dull stupefaction, either coaxed, raised up, trod upon, jostled or enslaved according to the dictates, favorable or unfavorable, of circumstance? And have you ever taken the trouble to reflect seriously about law and order? Do you know any order beyond that of the police, or any law other than fear of fine or imprisonment? The comet-like course of genius does not accept restriction to traditional paths. It creates order, and elevates its will to law. And Berlioz is a genius. Bow before him, you all-knowing ladies and gentlemen. And you critics, be more modest in the future, and do not think that because the eagle looks down upon you from the highest heavens, you can also see him.

Does Berlioz express himself in an intelligible manner?

To obtuseness, certainly not. Is his artistic world a burial ground for all healthy good sense and intelligence? Ah, if one could only bed down all Berlioz's adversaries in this burial ground, that they might, at last, lose all their damned reason and their cursed intelligence. For what mischief do clever people commit, especially those dealing, by the by, with esthetics and who are, God help us, critics, too? That would be too much even for a Job.

The Philharmonic have finally mustered their strength for a deed. Unfortunately, their conservative policies are largely responsible for the spoiling of our concertgoing public. Let them not despise the applause of the young, who, from the galleries and from among the standees, jubilantly hailed the orchestra's grandiose achievement no less than the wonderful work itself. It has always been the young, whenever there was something great afoot, who moved ahead as pathbreakers. Let us not be led astray by the wrath and deceitful behavior of our critic opponents. We have the shield of truth to protect us, we carry the sword of dedication with which to wound our enemies. War against the Philistines! War against the critics! Let those be our watchwords from now on!

1. In his *Neue Zeitschrift für Musik* (No. 3, 1835).

2. *Klein-Zaches Alias Zinnober*, a fairy tale by E.T.A.Hoffmann. The story concerns Paphnutius, who introduces enlightenment into his petty principality and bans all that is wondrous. The fairy Rosabelverde takes refuge in a convent as Miss Rosenschön, while the magician Prosper Alphanus, in the role of a benevolent physician, withdraws to a country estate, there to protect poesy from the "cultural police" of the prosaic world of the bourgeoisie.

3. The quotation is from an article by Schumann in the *Neue Zeitschrift für Musik* (Nov. 4, 1836) on Berlioz's Overture to *Les Francs-Juges* in which Schumann, speaking ill of the work, recommends a German performance "if only to demonstrate the extremes of the French schools of music, that of Auber and this, the one as featherweight as Scribe, the other as uncouth as Polyphemus. Our worthy cantors," Schumann continues, "will faint dead away at such harmonies, and scream about sansculottism. We certainly do not intend to compare the Overture to *Les Francs-Juges* with the Overture to *The Marriage of Figaro*. In the firm conviction, however. . . ." Then follows the passage quoted by Wolf, but with a curious variant on Wolf's part. Where Wolf has "Auszeichnung poetischer Extravaganz," or "praise of poetic extravagance," thus implying a general connotation, the Schumann original has "Auszeichnung *solcher*[such]poetischer Extravaganz," referring specifically to the Overture to *Les Francs-Juges*.

4. Anton Diabelli (1781-1858), a protégé of Michael Haydn in Salzburg, subsequently so successful as teacher of piano and guitar that he was able to found a publishing firm that prospered and long bore his name. He is now remembered, as composer, solely for the theme of Beethoven's 33 Variations on a Waltz, Opus 120. Wolf refers here to piano sonatas and sonatinas for two and four hands composed by Diabelli for instructional purposes.

48. *Another* Stagione

April 12, 1885

Carl Theater: Italian Opera Performances.

The Italians are always welcomed among us with open arms. I suspect, however, that they excite far less enthusiasm in their own country than in ours, and that especially the company now playing here would arouse the indignation rather than the applause of Italian audiences.

Viennese operagoers appear to have looked forward to these birds of passage, who do more cawing than singing, with a longing hardly less passionate than a drowning person entertains for the nearest beach. The crisis must, indeed, have been desperate if we are to comprehend the boundless delight inspired by the eventual deliverance. One who has just escaped drowning thanks his lucky star that he is, at least, still among the living. But, alas, the inhospitable beach is just large enough to give him a running start for a fresh plunge into the water to escape, through a swift death by drowning, the cruel tortures of starvation.

Our operagoers are more fortunate, since they live from delusion, and delusion, on this occasion, seems to have survived every challenge of fact. They imagine themselves to be hearing divine Italians in their heavenly language, and the sweetest melodies sung *con amore*. Nor can one hold it against them, considering that even a Herr Polack, despite his prominent nose, now that he rejoices in the mellifluous cognomen of Polacco, can no longer turn up his nose at imagination.

Having thus reestablished the exterior harmony of this opera company, and agreed once and for all about the authenticity of Signor Polacco, let's have a look at the accomplishments of its other members. *Lucia di Lammermoor* was given with Signora Fohström[1] in the title role. I could see the Signora because I have good eyes and a good opera glass (although not so good as the one I had before someone traded his for mine at the opera). Whoever is nearsighted, however, or the possessor of a bad opera glass, will have to be guided by his ears if he would know whether the Signora is stage right, stage left, in the foreground or in the background, for see her he will not. Signora Fohström is so dainty, so delicate, so ethereal, so transparent as can hardly be imagined. And this most especially as soon as she begins to sing. Then her mist-shrouded presence practically disappears, and the more so as the tones swell out. She sings nicely, and, as with all coloraturas, is strong at the top and weak in the middle. She sings easily, but without charm. Her coloratura is clean and adequately cultivated. On the whole, a notable — apparition.

Signor Pantaleoni[2] sang Lord Ashton. This singer kept the audience's hands almost continuously busy, and this preferably by some effectively bawled-out high notes whose sound could by no means be reckoned beautiful. There is no denying him a certain ardor, but his acting has an irresistibly comic effect. He moves his hands in the same funny manner by which Herr Rokitansky has so often put us in the most cheerful of moods — only the forearm is involved, bent to the right, then to the left, and vice versa. Signor Ravelli,[3] as Edgardo, pleased me far more, if only because his engaging appearance, his unaffected bearing, his bright countenance and his embonpoint were suited so well to the music and so badly to the words of the grief-stricken, deathly pale and emaciated Edgardo. For the rest, Signor Ravelli has quite a sympathetic voice. Others may find it unsympathetic. That is their affair. The outstanding characteristics of Signor Polacco have already been noted in the most appreciative terms.

The next production, *La Traviata*, enjoyed a better attendance, but the performance was just that much worse. With the exception of Signor Polacco, who again provided an amusing background, all the singers were new. The Traviata was Signorina Theodorini. [4] Her voice squeaked like an ungreased wagon wheel. It may have had a softer sound at one time, but that is of little concern to us today. To speak of her appearance and acting would be to fill the cup of censure to the brim, and that is not at all my intention. Giovanni di Negri, as Alfredo Germont, was supposed to play the tender lover, and he would have fully accomplished his objective had not a rival appeared in his (Alfredo's father, sung by Signor Mariano Padilla.[5] This Signor Padilla, who, with his hollow, sepulchral voice, cooed like a dove, then twittered like a hummingbird or snorted like a whale, only to lose himself in a barely audible murmur, made the evening for me. The audience, too, was visibly enchanted by him, but for other reasons, as I could assume with some certainty. What the others achieved was too insignificant to warrant the expense of another word. Our operagoing public, now arrived at the goal of its most ardent longing, knows full well how to treasure its good fortune. Its gratitude knows no bounds. Every sound, no matter from which throat, is applauded. The enthusiasm is indescribable. Glovemakers may take heart!

1.   Alma Fohström (1861-1914) joined Colonel Mapleson's company at Covent Garden shortly after this Vienna engagement, and toured America with him in 1886. She was a leading soprano at the Imperial Opera, Moscow, from 1890 to 1904.

2.   Adriano Pantaleoni (1837-1908), baritone brother of Romilda Pantaleoni.

3.   Luigi Ravelli (1848-?) sang with Colonel Mapelson for many seasons, and made operatic history of a kind by objecting to a scene in Baron Bodog Orczy's *Il Rinnegato* in which the tenor is killed by the baritone in a duel, an indignity, he argued, intolerable for a tenor. His inability to distinguish between conduct on the stage and conduct in real life also led to unpleasantness between him and Minnie Hauk in a performance of *Carmen* at the Academy of Music in Philadelphia on February 8, 1886.

4.   Helena Theodorini (1858-1926) had created the title role in Massenet's *Herodiade* at the
     Italian premiere at La Scala in 1883. She later taught in Paris, Buenos Aires and New York.
     Among her pupils was Bidu Sayão.
5.   Mariano y Ramos Padilla (1824-1906), a Spanish baritone who sang for many years with
     Colonel Mapleson. He was the husband of the soprano Désirée Artôt.

49. Of High Cs and Turks

April 19, 1885

Herr Mierzwinski shot off his high C successfully. It made a fearful noise,
answered each time by a crackling echo from every part of the house. I
suppose I should mention in passing that it was as Arnold in *William Tell* that
Herr Mierzwinski opened fire on the audience. It struck me as rather superfluous to mount a well-staged battle when nothing mattered but the thunder of
Herr Mierzwinski's cannon. And the audience, too, would have been adequately served had it been offered that awesome weapon alone, situated appropriately before the prompter's box and, from this strategic position, exploding
its high C a few dozen times at its own convenience.

The simplicity and originality of such a procedure did not, unfortunately,
occur to the management, much to the disadvantage of any sense of unity in
this performance. Because Herr Reichmann took Tell very, very seriously the
audience's previous concentration on Mierzwinski's 24-pounder was diverted
to his [Mierzwinski's] Arnold. That was, of course, a sorry situation, and since
Herr Reichmann threw more than enough of his splendid voice at its expressive best into the breach, the scales were tipped dangerously against Mierzwinski. The audience, caught in this cross fire, grew more serious, and the 24-
pounder, in the audience's opinion at that moment, weighed at least twenty
pounds less. The last of Herr Mierzwinski's high Cs came from a 4-pounder. It
had almost no effect whatsoever.

Herr Mierzwinski had a better time of it in *Les Huguenots*. He had no rival
to fear. In the first Romanza he trilled decorously and amiably from A to B
flat. Having arrived at the B flat, he tarried a while, smiling and surveying his
surroundings, before plunging to lower regions. He struck me as being rather
tired on this occasion, but he fought off fatigue with stamina and good
fortune. Fräulein Klein, as Valentine, left us acutely aware of what we were
missing in Frau Lucca who, unfortunately, cancelled. With what other singer
in this role would it not be the same? Fräulein Bianchi (Marguerite) was
greeted with rich floral offerings, and had many recalls. She will, henceforth,
and like Frau Materna, grace our stage as guest. [1] I wonder of in the future we
will have guest orchestras and guest choruses?

The Philharmonic celebrated the 25th anniversary of the orchestra's continuous existence with a performance of Beethoven's Ninth Symphony. It was a gala occasion, and the grateful public demonstrated its jubilation by occupying, at a price of course, every seat in the Grosser Musikvereinssaal, not only on the day of the performance, but at the dress rehearsal too. The concert began with a sacred overture by Otto Nicolai, who conducted the first Philharmonic concert in the Redoutensaal on Easter Monday of the year 1842.[2] (Actually, following Nicolai's departure from the Kaerntnerthor Theater, there were no regular Philharmonic concerts until Otto Dessoff[3] took over their direction in 1860, at which time it was decided to renew them in a certain sequence annually, as has been done consistently to this day.)

Hardly anyone will have recognized in this sacred overture the witty composer of *The Merry Wives of Windsor*. It is only a *pièce d'occasion*, as the program notes told us, and as such good enough. The counterpoint to the chorale "Ein' feste Burg ist unser Gott," however, smacked damnably of the schoolroom, although the combining of orchestra and chorus is accomplished with some skill. And so on. There is no reason to linger with it. The symphony was played perfectly. The soloists, Fräulein Lehmann, Frau Papier, Herr Winkelmann and Herr Mayerhofer, took on their difficult task with resolution, and held together with one accord, something not always possible even with the sincerest and most sympathetic intentions. Truly, it went beautifully. Herr Reichmann, on the other hand, sang his recitative with a conspicuous lack of expression, and then -- was it really necessary to apply to Beethoven's [sic] heavenly naive words the absurdities of operatic diction? Did Herr Reichmann really have to follow the more agreeable and more joyful "more joyful," with an emphatic "Yes, more joyful!?" To hell with that "Yes!" It may be all right in a famous Turkish opera when Yussuf yells at the renegade: "Be damned in all eternity, yes et . . . . ty!" Turks are godless fellows, who, for the sake of a mighty curse, could mercilessly disfigure the German language if they were given many vengeance arias to sing. But Herr Reichmann! He would not, in heaven's name, want to be a Turk?

1.   She remained with the company until 1887.

2.   Otto Nicolai (1810-1849), Prussian-born, Italian-schooled composer and conductor, now remembered for his opera, *The Merry Wives of Windsor* and, in Vienna, where he was Hofkapellmeiser of the Court Opera at the Kaerntnerthon Theater from 1841 to 1847, as the founder of the Philharmonic Concerts. A so-called "Nicolai Concert" for the orchestra's pension fund is an annual event in Vienna to this day. The overture played at the concert reviewed here was known as "Ein' feste Burg" after the famous Lutheran chorale on which it was based.

3.   Felix Otto Dessoff (1835-1892) was Hofkapellmeister at the Court Opera and conductor of the Philharmonic from 1860 to 1875.

50. *Anton Rubinstein's* Nero[1]

April 26, 1885

To call *Nero* a grand opera simply because of the pretty sets and, too, because there is singing shows how far one can go, taking the French *opéra* as a starting point, building on its least edifying aspects and thus heading for ruin. If in Meyerbeer's operas there were, at least, individuals so skilfully costumed that one could from time to time imagine them to be real persons, later fashioners of grand opera have concerned themselves solely with the costuming of supers, with luxurious pomp and ceremony, with conflagrations and voluptuous dances, leaving the principals to figure out how to spin the thread of the plot amid all this senseless hubbub and unholy spectacle.

In bringing a *Nero* to the stage one cannot proceed too cautiously. One cannot delve deeply enough into this character, nor adequately interpret it. Still, I do not find this material utterly unsuited to dramatic exploitation. The world about Nero is so corrupt that it gains thereby a certain definite physiognomy whose reflected image is concentrated in Nero's mad conduct. Everything is rotten, miasmatic, apathetic, bored, and going mad from boredom. In such an atmosphere, however, the spectator cannot survive for long. A cleansing contrast is needed. The librettist of the opera at hand has understood this very well, and has, as was to be expected, sought refuge in Christianity.

But Christianity cannot be embodied less effectively than in the person of the converted Chrysa, or less effectively as spectacle than in the cold astonishment of the Roman legions at a visible cross in the heavens at the close of the opera. What does Christianity do for Chrysa in face of the daily mounting horrors of Nero and his companions? Trembling and hesitant, she confesses to Vindex, a commander of the Gallic legions, that she is a Christian, and is mightily relieved to find the excellent Gaul so little disturbed by what was at that time a rather daring disclosure. The excellent Vindex, in love with Chrysa, finds in this case the religion of love preferable to that of renunciation, and replies: "I admire Him (in the admirable translation from the French it goes: "I Him admire") as a god of love whose mercy has granted me your love."

In the third act, when Nero courts Chrysa, the librettist had the opportunity to dramatize the superior power of Christianity -- as opposed to Nero-Dionysius, madly and vaingloriously asserting his divinity -- by giving the maiden's confession that burning ardor of the first Christians, who conceived of death as a special mercy. Nero, in this scene, should have come to the realization that above him, the god, there exists a higher being, representing not mere selfishness and pleasure, but love and renunciation. Nero could not, of course, be converted, but he could be shaken. He need not believe in the wonder of a Christian god, but he could begin to doubt his own divinity. And could Chrysa have found lovelier words than those of love, of love of man, with which to reply to the love-thirsty tyrant?

Instead of that, Chrysa insults the soft-hearted, sentimentally whimpering Nero (he is, after all, an operatic hero) in a most un-Christian manner, and Nero who throughout the entire opera has worn the fool's cap and bells, presenting himself as no more than a good-for-nothing, a dissolute rake, a drunkard and womanizer, is not a little put out by his shameful defeat -- as luckless suitor. There is, in Jules Barbier's libretto, not a trace of diabolical grandeur, that blasé, elemental force, that scornful contempt of the world and all its works, and that lunatic arrogance that gives to even the most atrocious crimes and depravities of this inspired libertine a titanic stamp. The hero's character fluctuates between that of a fop and that of an ordinary, demented profligate.

One could easily cite other examples to illustrate the shortcomings of the libretto, but it is truly not worth the trouble. I count heavily, moreover, upon the reader's gratitude for sparing him a description of the plot. He would be well advised to pay no attention whatsoever to the text, and further to provide himself with cotton wool in order to savor the only worthy element in this opera, the setting and the scenic arrangement, undisturbed by anything heard. This assumes, of course, that he feels moved to attend this spectacle opera, and I gladly encourage him to do so.

The score is to be numbered among the sorriest phenomena since the creation of the world. Chaos is music by Rossini compared with this muddy mass of hazily crawling rhythms and modulations. This music could kill the Wandering Jew from sheer boredom. If things had looked so desolate, so dead, in Nero's world as in this score, there would never have been any martyrs, and a Nero so tortured deserves to be canonized.

The singers, first and foremost Herr Winkelmann as Nero, did all that was humanly possible to extract a spark of life from these stuffed creatures. Love's labour lost! Frau Papier, Frau Kupfer, Frau Schläger, Herr Stoll, Herr Sommer, Herr Schittenhelm, etc. (another twenty-odd are involved) may have been good or bad (they were all good) -- there was nothing to be done, and for the same reason that the dead cannot be recalled to life.

1. First produced in a German translation of the French original in Hamburg on November 1, 1879. This Vienna premiere took place on April 20.

51. Farewell to Bertha Ehnn

May 3, 1885

Because of the absence of Herr Sommer, suddenly moved to offer an exhibition of injured vanity, the management saw fit to summon Herr Dr. Krückl[1] from Hamburg in order to make possible the second performance of *Nero*. Why all the to-do? Why this conscientiousness in so unworthy a cause? Why engage a singer from Hamburg when one could simply have eliminated the role of Vindex from the score? Or would one find such a procedure too daring? What? With this *Nero*? Or have we not already seen the Hermit in *Der Freischütz* ignominiously deprived of his achievement in having brought the opera to a satisfactory conclusion? And, if I mistake not, right here in our own Court Opera!

Now it seems to me that the sudden appearance of the Hermit is no less decisive for the fate of the young hunter and his fiancée than the comportment of Vindex in the last act for the fall of Nero. There is one distinction, to be sure, in that for the absence of the Hermit we are offered no compensatory conflagrations, triumphal marches, ghostly apparitions, etc., and that we identify the more heartily with the fate of the engaged couple because what unfolds before our eyes is a picture of purely human events, something that cannot, unfortunately, be said either of the libretto or of the music of *Nero*. We tremble for the destiny of the engaged couple in *Der Freischütz*. Will the powers of darkness prevail? Will innocence fall victim to diabolical knavery? Should a crime committed in desperation, and in a weak moment not find clemency, even forgiveness? Not according to the law, or prejudice. But now the devout Hermit has his say. His gentle and admonitory words succeed in reconciling the prince — we again breathe more easily.

Do we ever warm to any person or scene in *Nero*? What is Vindex to us? What is Nero? Or the twenty-odd other supernumeraries with resounding Roman names? They are mere letters from which we strive in vain to produce a coherent word. Everyone seems eager to press forward when it comes to submitting important works to major surgery. Why let the choice opportunity pass when the time came to make a virtue of necessity? Well, conductors and directors are an unregenerate lot. And so Herr Dr. Krückl sang Vindex. If I offer the opinion that the singer, whatever the circumstances, made more of the role than the authors, it signifies neither praise nor blame, if for no other reason than that I did not hear him.

Frau Berta Ehnn made her last public appearance on April 29 as Mignon in A. Thomas's opera of that name. With her departure from the roster of the Court Opera we lose the most poetic actress and singer among the entire female personnel of the Viennese operatic stage. Others surpass her in passionate dramatic accents, in opulent vocal resources, in vocal schooling, even in personal charm. But all these attributes, treasurable as they may be in themselves, pale before the truthfulness emanating from the innermost core of the characterizations realized by the dramatic art of Frau Ehnn.

In this sense, and assessed from this point of view, she created Elisabeth, Sieglinde, Agathe, Elsa and Eva. What admirable things she achieved in other roles I know only from hearsay. Her Mignon, however, is not unfamiliar to me. It is held to be her most congenial role, and to represent her at the very summit of her powers. That may be. The manner, however, in which the highly poetic Mignon of Goethe has been reduced to a ludicrous caricature in Thomas's opera has always so outraged my esthetic sensibilities that I could not achieve sufficient objectivity to separate the virtues of the interpreter from the ghastly distortion offered us in the opera. I may even have withdrawn my attention arbitrarily from the actress in order to avoid having to receive from her hands a better picture than that afforded by the librettist's poetic rubbish heap. Were it even another creature -- Juliet or Ophelia -- but Mignon! And in this farce! Singing Styrian songs to gypsy music rhythms and bleating "Kennst du das Land?" -- actually only a trivial chansonette tune in a perfumed dinner dress with a long train to make it look like something! To hell with it. As I said, I have no critical judgment to offer on Frau Ehnn's Mignon.

Now we have heard her for the last time, the sweet, warm, intimate tones that lay deeper than in the throat, tones that poured forth from her heart. For us there remains, however, the bittersweet realization that what once spoke to our heart so immediately, with such ardent vitality, will henceforth be heard only in the ghostly echo of remembrance until that, too, gradually dies away and only the name, Ehnn, will remain. Then, however, Fama will appear to tell the future that Frau Ehnn was a great artist whom Vienna greatly loved and admired.

1. Franz Krückl (1841-1899), a Moravian baritone who had come by the "Herr Dr." legitimately. He had already begun a career as jurist in the civil service when he decided to turn to singing. He appeared in many German opera houses, but principally in Hamburg, where he had participated in the world premiere of *Nero*. Following his retirement from the stage, he wrote two books, *The German Theater and its Legal Protection* and *The Contract between Director and Actor in the German Theater*.

52. Rosa Sucher and Jenny Broch

May 10, 1885

Frau Sucher is to be numbered among the consoling few whose guest appearances on foreign stages always guarantee something good (our resident Court Opera singers are foreign guests on their own stage). She belongs among those who do not display themselves with a glittering trinket on their miserable dresses, who do not impose upon us, for the sake of a few effective arias or scenes, Italian or -- now pouring from the solicitously administered opera factories in ever greater abundance -- "international" operas with Old Testament settings. She belongs among those who, because they shine like precious metal, do not scorn a gold setting, in contrast to those who seek to prove that the brilliance of the stone is sufficient unto itself, and that whether the setting be of precious metal or base is of no consequence, or that -- to abandon metaphor -- it is all the same whether one's talent be lavished on good works or bad.

It is not all the same. An extraordinarily endowed artist may blind us however totally to the faultiness, if not the faultless tedium, of a piece (if tedium itself is not to be reckoned a crime). He may focus our attention however intensely upon his person. He may raise our powers of imagination however infinitely above the marshy lowlands of some wretched work. He must, in the end, return to his point of departure, to the work itself. In this he is not different from the jumper who cannot escape the pull of gravity. There he lies (not the jumper but the artist) in his swamp, as tiny and insignificant as a frog that has happily survived a near-fatal inflation. What do we now see? Swamp. What do we now hear? The ever so varied and melodious chorus of its worthy inhabitants.

Ah, a highly precarious terrain for the vainglory of performers is a bad piece of theater. The attraction of the characterless, the false, works magnetically in drama on even the most brilliant genius of the performer. And quite naturally so, since in the end he is displaying only himself and not his role. There is a contradiction here, rendered the more sensible the more the performer tries to bring the character into its own, thus falling into ever greater confusion, and leaving the audience with a sense of having lost all contact with both the role and the performer. The latter, in a work of art, on the other hand, has an easy time of it. Granted some talent and a sense of the genuine, he will succeed in finding the right interpretation, the appropriate gesture, the proper bearing.

He need not resort to excessive force or overacting when the best effect lies in utterly spontaneous naturalness. He need not rack his brains when all he has to do is feel, nor suffer confusion when there is no need for it, or when a clear head is called for. He need only perceive what his role is, not what is to be made out of it.

Frau Sucher was recently the Leonore in *Fidelio*. Heaven knows when we might have heard this opera had she not come to us. And that is what I wished to emphasize as a good omen for her visit at the beginning of this article. Last season, already, Frau Sucher silenced our critical pen with Leonore, Isolde and Brünnhilde. It is to be hoped that in the course of this visit, too, that glowing triad of womanly ideals will find in her an inspired interpreter. A beginning has already been made. Frau Sucher, fortunately, does not possess the kind of voice that appeals to the taste of our operagoing public. If, nevertheless, she was able to ignite the audience with her achievement as Leonore, it was thanks to her eminent dramatic talent, that urging the listener on irresistibly to participate in the loving woman's desperate act of rescue.

Among others in the cast, a special word for Herr Schrödter, whom we are hearing for the first time this season. He is our man. We have not had his like before. How well he sings, acts and speaks! What indestructible good humor! What an agreeable, carefree, unaffected manner! And how fine he is in characterization! He was only singing Jaquino. But just let anyone try to follow him.

In *La Sonnambula* we heard Fräulein Jenny Broch[1] for the first time. Hearing her was not easy, for the voice is as thin as the thread of a cobweb. There were times, indeed, when one had to trust to the eye to perceive that she was singing at all, which was not hard, to be sure, as she opened her mouth pretty wide. Her singing is very clean, very secure, and very dull. In meeowing she can hold her own with any pet cat. Her tones sound like the echo of a flute. Of acting not a trace. It was amusing to note the way she balanced her head on her shoulders. One more than half expected her to do a juggler's trick with it. Unfortunately, it did not come to that. During the French Revolution such shaky heads exercised a considerable fascination. Fräulein Broch would have been ill-advised to audition for Marat or Robespierre. Nowdays we simply shake our own heads at such absurdities. Other times, other customs.

Lack of space forbids a detailed discussion of the most recent of the Bruckner concerts presented by the Wagner Society. I shall reserve a thorough-going review of the String Quintet and the Te Deum for a more favorable occasion. For the moment I shall note only the accurate performance of the former by the Hellmesberger String Quartet and of the latter by the chorus of the Wagner Society, conducted by the gifted composer himself. The impression made upon the listeners by this work was utterly overwhelming, even without the supporting orchestra. We shall have much good and beautiful to report about this concert.

1.　Jenny Broch (1860- ?), An Austrian coloratura, a member of the company from 1884 to 1886. She sang briefly with Colonel Mapleson in Great Britain in 1887.

53. Le Prophète *without Honor*

May 17, 1885

Signor Mierzwinski ended his guest engagement at the Court Opera as prophet, i.e., as Meyerbeerian prophet. If there is precious little that is prophet-like about this Meyerbeerian hero, Signor Mierzwinski robbed him even of the semblance of any such thing. This is said rather as praise than as criticism. Anyone does a praiseworthy deed who, for example, exposes a swindler. Meyerbeer's Jan of Leyden should have remained a publican. As such he could have disposed of all Anabaptist riff-raff in a perfectly natural way by recourse to his sturdy fists. He would have remained a man, and spared us the unedifying spectacle of a second Damocles over whose anointed head swing the drawn swords of three vagabonds (so-called apostles of the heavenly kingdom). He should have used a stout club, first to clear the premises of the three Anabaptist wretches, and then, after the noble Obertal has played a nasty trick on him, instead of putting his head between his legs, look up bravely and think how best to pay him back, not with the help of other scoundrels, but on his own.

Such a Jan of Leyden would, to be sure, hardly have become a prophet, or, if he had, then a hero, an inspired prophet who believes in himself and who, because he believes in himself, exerts power over others. But this Meyer-beerian prophet has control neither over himself nor over others. Arrived at the summit of his power, with all the emblems of supreme authority, a crown upon his head and a sword in his hand, surrounded by an adoring populace, radiant in royal attire, he suddenly becomes a coward, a flyswatter too weak to defend the tail of an ass, for purely out of fear he denies his mother. Why out of fear? Because the three pitiless dagger tips tickle his nose. What, in front of all the people praying for the prophet's health and welfare, an attempted assassi-nation? A fine idea, indeed! But what is all that to the librettist, to the composer, to the audience? It's effective, and that's that. (The kind reader may wonder how in this day and age one can get worked up over the subject matter of *Le Prophète*. My only excuse is that the performance which it is my pleasure to review was, for me, a premiere.)

Thus I also heard for the first time Frau Papier as the famous prophet mother, Fidès. I had already -- I say this without further ado -- formed the most horrible visions of the ridiculousness and absurdity of this musico-dramatic forceps delivery. The text of the role goes with the music no less intimately than water with oil, two fluids, as everyone knows, that get along well enough together until someone tries to mix them, in which case they become mutually hostile and seek to go each his own way. One could compare Fidès' words and their musical expression with a couple who hit it off tolerably but cannot love each other. The stern papa comes along, insisting that they should love each other, too, and then begins a conflict destined to end in comedy, farce or tragedy. Papa Meyerbeer made a tragi-comical figure out of Fidès, which is why the role has become so famous. For whoever cannot go along with the tragic Fidès will probably find the comic one appealing. The singers all know perfectly well that the role is also a feast for the most varied palates, and they like to sing it, especially since it leaves every "artist" free to spice the stew with fermatas and cadenzas to her heart's content.

So, Frau Papier sang Fidès, and after a very short prelude of dubious sensations I was able to decide definitely for the comical Fidès. Frau Papier, to put it plainly, sang cadenzas and even the fermatas in such deadly earnest, and with such loving devotion, that I was hard put to it to keep from bursting out laughing, although, truly, one should rather be sad when a singer of the best intentions, and sometimes of the best ability, can so far forget herself as to court the favor of the audience, like an Italian tenor, with long drawn out fermatas, the most preposterous hamming, vocal exhibitionism and other such nonsense. There is no reason why Frau Papier should resort to that kind of thing. She possesses an inestimable treasure in her voice. Let her be generous with the gold of that voice if she so chooses. We have nothing against generosity, even in the wrong place. But squandering, a squandering that knows no bounds, that is conscious and intentional, and all for the applause of an ignorant audience! That is blameworthy, and unworthy of a singer of Frau Papier's eminence.

In the most recent performance of *Tannhäuser* Frau Rosa Sucher was the Elisabeth. Frau Sucher knows how to find the characteristic keynote for each of her roles, and how to make each an individual. She often errs in the sketching of this or that detail, but she never departs from the frame of a homogeneous conception. She can trace the most contradictory emotional currents ever so cleverly to a common source, and reveal to the audience a psychological portrait accomplished in broad strokes. Only one thing displeased me thoroughly in Frau Sucher's Elisabeth, and that was her indifference to the postlude after the A-flat cantilena in the second act. Wagner prescribes exactly what the interpreter of Elisabeth has to do in order to give this postlude its artistic justification, and when Wagner felt called upon to enliven a musically silent scene by prelude or postlude he had his own good reasons. Frau Sucher should have taken the trouble to move a few steps farther into the background, the while following with her eyes the departing beloved, and thus giving to the postlude the character of an unspoken fond farewell, which is what the composer had in mind. Where, in such cases, is the stage director when the conductor nods?

Another guest, Herr Dr. Krückl, in the first act, attracted my attention in no small measure. Consistently distinct enunciation, vigorously projected, if with a voice weakened by age (no matter), free, natural gestures, a manly conception (in contrast to our own baritones), a singer in a thousand! What do the next acts hold in store for us? Well, that was a pretty surprise. Like a stone apostle, he fixed the audience with a flinty stare and apostrophized it from the prompter's box with the flattering verses: "Blick' ich umher in diesem edlen Kreise" [I look about me in this noble circle], etc. Now what on earth moved Herr Dr. Krückl, contrary to his role, to render such compliments to the parterre? How dare he offend the sensitive parterre by calling it a proud oak, a forest of heroes, brave, German and wise? And all that in deadly earnest, without the trace of a smile! O, God, why was no teasing gremlin flitting around Herr Dr. Krückl's lips? Had he but smiled, the parterre would have known that the harangue was intended ironically, in which case it would have had no choice but to consider itself insulted by the singer. If, at its next opportunity, it revenges itself for Herr Dr. Krückl's ambiguous behavior in the time-honored fashion, it will serve Herr Dr. Krückl absolutely right. For the chorus and the principals, too, it is insulting when Herr Dr. Krückl turns his back. From them, too, he may expect some unpleasantness. Wolfram von Eschenbach was, moreover, a master of courtly deportment and good manners. Herr Dr. Krückl, therefore, also provoked his august shade. Subsequently, Herr Dr. Krückl appeared to be addressing the star in the medal of a beribboned gentleman in the chamberlain's box rather than the evening star, for his eye gazed ecstatically in the direction of this exalted neighborhood. In short, our expectations were horribly deceived.

Herr Schrödter, who sang Walter exceptionally well, was also guilty, unfortunately, of Herr Dr. Krückl's misdemeanor. This was doubly painful, as, on the previous day, we had had an opportunity to acknowledge him as an excellent actor in *Carmen*. Herr Schrödter should be on guard against such derelictions. They are uncommonly disturbing, and the evil of violating a natural procedure far outweighs the advantage of getting a couple of tones better across to the audience. Fräulein Lehmann was the Venus this time -- very good. Herr Scaria the Landgrave -- very good. Herr Frei was the Biterolf -- very mediocre, even offensive. Was Herr Direktor Jahn's baton loaded with lead? The tempi sometimes dragged intolerably.

Just a few word about Scribe's *Yelva* or *The Russian Orphan*.[1] This rather crude melodrama was well received, thanks largely to Fräulein Abel's[2] splendid, utterly convincing performance. Fräulein Abel happily combined the gracefulness of the ballerina with the most expressive pantomime of the actress. Her harmoniously rounded, gripping performance was warmly applauded. The other participants supported Fräulein Abel most effectively.

1.　The music by Karl Gottlieb Reissiger (1798-1859), who succeeded Weber as director of German Opera at Dresden.

2.　Katherina Abel (1856-1904), Viennese pantomimist, a leading member of the *corps de ballet* at the Court Opera from 1880 to 1892.

54. Lohengrin

May 24, 1885

Herr Vogl from Munich is unquestionably the most intelligent of all Wagnerian singers. Not a glance, not a gesture, not a vocal nuance that is not relevant
to the drama in progress. Everything he does has significance, breathes real
life.

There are times, admittedly, when one notes a suggestion of purposeful
design in his actions, as though Herr Vogl wished to call the audience's
attention to a certain subtle nuance in his performance. Miming, however, as
Börne [1] says, is like the face of a clock, indicating inner movement, but not the
actual clockwork revealing its own movements. In the present case, the
clockwork is the music, which certainly leaves nothing undisclosed, especially
since the Leitmotifs constantly hold the listener riveted, directing his attention
to the scenic happenings on the stage. Herr Vogl would do well to content
himself with being the face of the clock. Another thing: Herr Vogl sang the
passage [in Act III] from "Dein Lieben muss mir hoch entgelten" [Your love
must compensate me richly] to "Böt mir der Konig seine Krone" [Were the
king to offer me his crown] in such sharply accented rhythm and, at the same
time, so casually that it bordered on street balladry.

If there is anything about Herr Vogl's vocalism that might disturb me, it
would probably be the abrupt breaking off of a tone after a strong crescendo.
This vocal procedure can, under certain circumstances, be incomparably
effective, especially in recitative and in rousing episodes of a violent character,
but not in cantilena, not in sustained song, where every tone must be nicely
rounded, i.e., no crescendo without the compensating, complementary dimin-
uendo. Herr Vogl, a great vocal artist, knows all that better than I, but he
doesn't always know when he errs.

The narrative at the close of the opera, too, could have been quieter, gentler,
softer, more mysterious. He put too much passion into it, was too much the
mortal. Lohengrin's eye, during this narrative, is directed above and beyond
the circle of his immediate environment. His spirit dreams of the wonders of
Monsalvat while his earthly self tarries among ordinary mortals long enough
to address them for the last time. So, too, should his voice be none other than
the instrument expressing ecstatically his spirit's unworldly dream. What
tenderness, what lyrical poesy, is not required to realize such demands! Herr
Vogl's Lohengrin fully deserves, nevertheless, the most cordial acknowledgment. If the audience showered him with applause on this occasion, it was for
once entirely justified in so doing.

Frau Sucher, as Elsa, was not wholly in her element. The astringency of her voice, as well as an all too vehement accentuation in her vocal delivery, does not especially qualify her for this role. Shakespeare's "Frailty, thy name is woman" is especially applicable to Elsa. Frau Sucher's conception of the character was too heroic.

Frau Papier undertook Ortrud with commendable zeal, i.e., she made every effort to encourage in the audience a low opinion of Ortrud's character. Right from the start, Frau Papier's earnestly malevolent appearance showed us in Ortrud the embodiment of evil. Only once did she feel compelled to give the sinister expression of her countenance and getures an advantageous shift to a friendlier aspect -- in my opinion a premature move that I feel the more impelled to correct in that the majority of those who take on this female evil genius make the same mistake.

"Wie er durch Zauber zu dir kam" [How through enchantment he came to you], Ortrud whispers in the credulous Elsa's ear [Act II]. Elsa, outraged by this scandal-mongering, first draws away from Ortrud in horror. But soon the voice of compassion suppresses her growing displeasure. A short interlude of three measures illustrates this change of mood with moving eloquence. The impersonatrix of Ortrud, however, appeared to have associated this musical phrase with herself, for she cannot have been prompted by any other to justify the sudden change from an attitude of certain victory to one of hypocritical submissiveness.

This interpretation is fundamentally wrong. Not only does such an interlude, when appropriated by another, lose its significance for the rightful proprietor; the filcher himself lands in an equivocal position. To the hypocritical bearing of Ortrud, who, in this situation, seems to say: "I beg your pardon if I have been too presumptuous," Elsa could only reply: "Think nothing of it. You went too far, to be sure, but essentially we understand one another. Let's speak no more about it. Give me your hand, most worthy friend." Instead of that, Elsa, as everyone knows, does just the opposite. Why? It's simple enough. Ortrud must sustain her darkly threatening, maliciously lurking, watchful attitude until Elsa, with an amiable gesture, invites her to enter. Then the episode, and the pronouncement, "Du ärmste, kannst wohl nie ermessen" [Poor dear, you will never know], fall into intelligible and significant context.

Since Herr Scaria has grown tired of Europe, he has also lost his enthusiasm and love of art. What's Hecuba to him? There's little business to be done here. The clanging cash registers of virgin soil mean more to him. America is a good school for artisans, but a bad one for artists. [2] After Herr Scaria had taken it easy for two acts, he finally felt moved in Act III to salve his bad artistic conscience, if not to overdo it, for he flung out his address to the German cohorts peremptorily with such fire, such force, that we were absolutely stunned by this sudden transformation. Even the chorus, who had hitherto been most sparing of their throats (who can hold it against these good people, considering their daily slavery?), were so enthralled by Herr Scaria's example that they seemed for a moment to forget their choral status. A fresh breath of enthusiasm swept through their ranks, and a storm of applause coming from every corner of the house rewarded their exertions. There is a lesson to be learned from all this which every conductor and chorister might well take to heart. It speaks to them eloquently enough from the phenomenon I have just described.

Herr Horwitz (Telramund), should be more sparing of gesture. He fences, punches, cuts and saws the air until it seems that he is battling with phantoms. Otherwise, he was good. Herr Felix, this time, was the Herald. A Herald should not only sing forcefully; he should also be able to articulate distinctly. Herr Felix can do neither. We might have forgiven him the first shortcoming, but not both. An opera singer who does not also speak distinctly is fit, as best, for solfeggios or yodeling. Whoever wishes to sing Wagnerian roles should first learn to speak.

The stage director should see to it that the darkness at the beginning of Act II is more intense. Intrigues as black as those Ortrud plots prosper only in the darkest night.

One cut in the score [in Telramund's confrontation of Lohengrin and King Henry at the close of Act II] struck me especially. It does signal honor to the integrity and the comprehension of the conductor. from Lohengrin's "Nur eine ist's — der muss ich Antwort geben"[There's only one — to her I must reply] to Telramund's "Vertraue mir" [Trust me]. Now I ask a moment's attention. Friedrich von Telramund, rejected by Lohengrin, turns to the King, urging him to direct the question to Lohengrin. How Lohengrin will reply to the King — we assume — must command Telramund's attention. Nothing of the sort. Telramund has no time to listen, for the fatal cut [of 130 measures] forces him to scurry to Elsa's side and with a "Vertraue mir" get things going again, while Lohengrin, at the outcry, "Elsa," finds it necessary to wink at the King slyly, as if to say, "Well, now do you get it at last, you clever fellow?" And this utter idiocy for no other reason than to win a few minutes!

1. Ludwig Börne (1786-1837), German critic famous — or infamous — for his attacks on Goethe.
2. Scaria may have entertained the idea of singing in America, but he never did.

55. Mischief with the Red Pencil

May 31, 1885

Tristan und Isolde

Herr Vogl's Tristan was from beginning to end a masterly accomplishment. But the art of the actor has not yet reached the point where it can make good the ravages of the red pencil, however earnestly conductors may try to persuade themselves of the contrary. I am speaking here of conductors of the better sort. The worse among them cut from pure egotism, without regard for singer or work.

I tend even to believe that cutting constitutes an essential element in conductorial gratification. Judging by the most exquisitely outrageous cuts, this gratification would seem to be of a diabolical order. To cut an especially important motif, indispensable for the understanding of the drama, is a tasty bonus for upright, worthy conductors. Young aspirants from now on, in order that their qualifications may be firmly established, should be tested for their cutting rather than their conducting. In which case, let them betray no embarrassment, shame, or pangs of conscience. By God, no! It would go badly for them even if they were all geniuses. Just wield the red pencil boldly and nimbly. All else will take care of itself.

Among the American Indians, he enjoys the greatest esteem who can display the greatest number of scalps. Among conductors, certainly, he is regarded most highly by his colleagues who is the greatest butcher of scores, who can boast of shaving with his red pencil not only the scalp, but the whole head and feet of the drama. (How characteristic, come to think of it, the term "red pencil"; if applied to the nobler parts, the pencil reddens itself in the heart's blood of the score.) Indians content themselves with the scalp, and are savages. Conductors butcher their victims, and are usually civilized, even aspiring to be artists. Artists!

Herr Vogl, in any case, could not work miracles. The ingenious cut, of which the conductor must have been more than a little proud, required the singer to behave as artlessly as possible, for which, of course, not Herr Vogl but solely the conductor was to blame. The cut begins after Tristan's question, "müht euch die?"[Does that trouble you?] and ends three measures before the words "War Morold dir so wert?" [Did Morold mean so much to you?] Etc. The passage, "müht euch die?" sounds like quiet mockery coming hard upon Isolde's cry of "Rache für Morold!" [Revenge for Morold!].₁

What, then, could have made Tristan suddenly pale and sombre, and have moved him to offer Isolde his sword for the avenging stroke? Certainly not Isolde's impassioned outburst, "Rache für Morold!" for this has prompted in him only quiet scorn. On the other hand, Tristan's dark concern is perfectly understandable when Isolde confronts him with the excellence of her gallant Irish hero, her fiancé, who entered the battle in her defense and with whose fall her own honor fell. This confrontation and discourse motivates, moreover, the sadness and resignation in Tristan's words, "War Morold dir so wert?"

But it was found perfectly in order to cut this passage, violating not only the score, but also the poem, and making a sad mess of the latter, too. Now if a conductor wishes to introduce some light into this darkness, even while retaining the cut, let him take away Tristan's mocking reply, too. Give him a bit of time in which to become pale and sombre, and all is well, the performer winning time to adopt a sombre expression in a natural way, without writhing and grimaces. Might not Herr Vogl have been better advised, at the close of the act, to direct his exclamation, "O Wonne voller Tücke!" (Oh rapture full of deceit!), as an aside for himself, or directly to the audience, rather than to Isolde?

Frau Sucher (Isolde) was excellent in the first and second acts, less good in the third. She seemed distracted, and even in the "Liebestod" not wholly involved. Herr Horwitz sang Kurwenal for the first time. He might have memorized his role rather better in order not to be so obviously at odds with the orchestra. And is it clever that Kurwenal, during Tristan's vision, should give the audience to understand by appropriate gestures that Tristan has lost his wits? If Herr Horwitz thinks that he can lend this role some spice by recourse to such "piquanteries" (I borrow this lovely word from a music critic), I would even prefer the unsalted Kurwenal of Herr Sommer [a pun, or possibly an ambiguity, *ungesalzen* meaning both "unsalted" and "homespun" or "forthright"]. Herr Fuchs may be an excellent time beater -- but to conduct *Tristan?* Herr Fuchs is a metronome.

Rienzi. Herr Vogl lacked the resources to give this imposing personality even the outward stamp of imperial authority. Still, he always looked majestic [possibly a pun, *stattlich* meaning both "majestic" and "portly"], and if he lacked the power to fly at the nobles like a thunderbolt, he was not wanting in the lightning of eloquence to inflame the populace. Together with Herr Vogl, it was above all Frau Papier who stood out, bringing to the rather ill-defined character of Adriano distinctive contours as well as warm coloring. The manly bearing, the vigor of her movements, even the effective costuming of the part, along with all her other virtues, did their bit in the creation of an interesting and even sympathetic figure. Adriano is beyond question one of Frau Papier's best roles. Had she, in the passage, "It was a Colonna," sung more to herself rather than *ff* because of the low tones required, there could not have been the smallest detail in her accomplishment with which to take exception. The trumpeting of one's misdemeanors to the world is for penitents and lunatics, and Adriano is neither one nor the other. For the rest, the cast was in tried hands and true.

1.   And it is so interpreted by Isolde in an immediate response, "Wagst du zu höhnen?"[You dare to mock?], lost in the cut. This cut, as defined by Wolf, covers the seventy-odd measures in which Isolde tells Tristan about her Irish hero, her betrothed, who fell by Tristan's hand in her defense, and whose death she had solemnly sworn to avenge. She had, indeed, at the time, had the wounded Tristan in her power, and could have slain him then and there. But a look in his eye had stayed her hand, and she had nursed him back to health. Tristan is deeply affected by her account, and, saying "Did Morold mean so much to you?" offers her his sword that she may fulfill her oath of vengeance. It was especially the fact that the cut imposes upon Tristan an instantaneous and textually unmotivated metamorphosis of attitude and mood, from apparent mockery to profound and troubled sympathy, that aroused Wolf's indignation, as elaborated in the succeeding paragraph.

56. Materna as Elisabeth

September 6, 1885

Tannhäuser by Richard Wagner

The performance, except for the Venusberg scene, was better than anything we have experienced on our opera stage in a long time.

Frau Materna, returning after a long absence,[1] sang the Elisabeth. It was not her dramatic talent, however, that so delighted me on this occasion. It was rather the stylistic propriety of her interpretation, the discreet employment of her vocal resources, the sensitivity with which she shaped a melodic line, the flooding warmth (far removed from all sentimental wallowing), the lovely restraint, the evidence of good taste in her vocalism -- these were the virtues that left me firmly convinced that Frau Materna is unquestionably the finest of contemporary Wagnerian sopranos. There was nothing arbitrary or capricious, nothing ugly or fumbling or absurd. The purity, the exaltation, of her performance was unsullied. She may well have sung more excitingly on other occasions, but never, certainly, more beautifully. This time the graces listened entranced to her song.

Herr Scaria, who sang the Landgrave with astonishing devotion, combining power and dignity, may well have thought to himself before the performance: "Today I shall show the folks once again what I can do when I set my mind to it." What a pity that Herr Scaria is not more frequently subject to such self-indulgent seizures! Everyone would gain: Herr Scaria, if he were to sing decently; the public, if it got something decent to hear, and I, if I got something decent to write about, which unfortunately doesn't happen often.

Tannhäuser is generally thought to be one of Herr Winkelmann's most congenial roles. That may well be. But an actor whose hands dangle like the blades of a broken-down windmill, who is incapable of resolution, who -- but why get worked up about it? Nothing's to be done. And as a singer he was excellent.

Herr Schrödter (Walter) earned unqualified applause. Herr Reichmann (Wolfram) would be well advised to take Herr Schrödter as a model of how to sing into the auditorium without turning his back on precisely the person he is presumably addressing. It was really too much that Herr Reichmann should sing his "Song to the Evening Star" directly to the audience without by so much as a bend of the body acknowledging the object of his lyrical effusion. One accepts that kind of thing from an Italian tenor. If I could persuade myself that Herr Reichmann belongs in that category then there would be no grounds for carping about such transgressions.

1. She had been in New York for the Metropolitan's second, and its first German, season. Her accomplishment there is worthy of detailed notice. Beginning on January 5, and concluding on February 20, she sang four Elisabeths, three Valentines, four Rachels and seven Brünnhildes. She was the Brünnhilde of the American premiere of *Die Walküre* on January 30, and repeated the performance on January 31 and February 2, 4, 7, 12 and 20, or seven times in three weeks, in the course of which she also sang Elisabeth on the 11th and 19th. The New York critics unanimously echoed Wolf's boundless admiration of this remarkable artist.

57. Die Meistersinger

September 20, 1885

Why, one wonders, must our theater management's destructive impulses toward defoliation and erosion achieve their masterpiece with precisely the most fragrant blossom in the wreath of Wagner's creations, *Die Meistersinger*

As if it were not sufficient, zealously to abolish every relevant and artistically treasurable detail, the vandalism is extended even to the plot and the development of the characters. The odious town clerk, for example, must content himself with playing a village idiot. Now Beckmesser is no idiot. He becomes one only through the droll situation in which he eventually finds himself. He is, in fact, a crafty scoundrel, and he thinks like one. The scene in Hans Sachs's workshop in Act III makes it plain enough. Suspicion whispers words of warning to him from each most secret nook of his bitter heart. Only when every misgiving has been exposed to his inquisitive skepticism is he content. What scoundrel, under the circumstances, would not have become as ridiculous a figure as Beckmesser? In the abridged scene customary in our productions, however, Beckmesser walks into the trap like a booby, and the fine touches with which Wagner so richly endowed this character are irresponsibly sacrificed.

What the cast accomplished in an opera so grievously cut was almost too good. Special praise, first and foremost, for the apprentices, and especially for

David, their crowning glory. Herr Schittenhelm, to whom this role has been assigned in the past, always knew how to make the most of it. David, although an apprentice, must be able to sing like a master, for the vocal demands upon the singer are more formidable than they seem. But the actor, too, is offered opportunities to distinguish himself in every way. Herr Schittenhelm lent his endowments to both departments with all possible perfection. If, despite all that, we prefer the accomplishment of Herr Schrödter, it is thanks to his forthright, sincere manner, as well as to the melting sweetness of a sumptuous voice combined with fluent articulation, two attributes that cannot be taught, whatever a singing teacher may say to the contrary. Herr Schrödter was so completely the "trusty countenance,"[1] and even had he not been supported so effectively by his vocal and dramatic interpretive talent, he would still have been sure of our applause. In short, Herr Schrödter strikes us as the pre-destined David.

Herr Reichmann was in every respect an admirable Sachs, and no less admirable in his category was Herr von Reichenberg (Pogner). Far less admirable was Herr Horwitz (Kothner), who sang the reading of the tabula-ture with such an affected manner that the knight might well have concluded that he (Kothner) wished rather to learn spelling than acquaint him with the rules of the Meistersinger. Walther von Stolzing was sung by Herr Müller, and tolerably well acted, too. We should, in any case, be content with his achieve-ment, as no better is to be had from the resident company. But how is it conceivable that so lovely a role as that of the night-watchman can be entrusted to an obscure singer when we have a Rokitansky? The bronze organ of this bass would surely be ideal. Herr Rokitansky strikes me, indeed, as the only singer worthy of so grateful a part.

And who sang Eva? Well, we may be grateful, at least, that it was not Fräulein Braga, whoever else it might have been. Fortunately, it was Fräulein Lehmann, and there could not have been a better choice, not, at least, since the departure of Frau Ehnn. How eloquently she acted, how expressive the eyes, how plastic the facial expression! And what a conception of the role! The Evchen of Frau Ehnn has been restored to us in that of Fräulein Lehmann, which is not to say that Fräulein Lehmann copies Frau Ehnn. Not a bit of it. She goes her own way, "determined and imperturbable,"[2] and we follow her with the utmost pleasure.

Should one discuss the Beckmesser of Herr Lay? Superfluous. The world has only one Beckmesser, and if the world would like to meet him, the world must come to Vienna.[3]

1.   The allusion is to Hans Sachs's retort to Beckmesser's critique of Walther von Stolzing's
       audition for the Meistersinger in Act I:
              Verliess er uns're G'leise,
              Schritt er doch fest und unbeirrt.
       (If he departed from our conventions, at least
       he proceeded with determination, and imperturbably.)

2.   "Treues Gesicht," as he is described by Magdalene in Act I, Scene I.

3.   The reference is to Hanslick. In the cast of the third draft of *Die Meistersinger* the name of
       the town clerk was listed as Veit Hanslich.

58. Alceste

October 11, 1885

There is nothing especially astonishing about our operagoing public's indifference toward the works of Gluck. It was, after all, a full seventy-five years before the artistic sensibility of our Court Opera management found the time ripe to serve up *Alceste* as a novelty for the multitude.¹ And so there was a full house for this odd resurrection ceremony. To most of those present it must have seemed odd, indeed.

What was one to make of this severe, austere music, of this plot progressing in solemnly measured rhythm? Nothing but weeping and wailing from beginning to end. Unhappy Admetus! Unhappy Alceste! Unhappy people! Unhappy children! Miserable oracle! But patience. The second act begins more brightly. Admetus lives, the people are cheerful. Alceste, to be sure, looks far from happy, but there is no time to waste upon her woes, for already the ballerinas are hopping about, and forgotten are Admetus and Alceste, plot and music. Calamity is put aside, all pain is extinguished, all dangerous compassion suppressed, and connoisseurs and dilettantes, smirking triumphantly, set to the bridges of their noses that indispensable instrument of all operagoers -- and extol Gluck's splendid *Alceste!*

There can, indeed, hardly be anything more ludicrous than our delighted opera public at the first peformance of a new production of an opera by Gluck. How far such enthusiasm reaches can be determined at a second performance, or a third, or, if it comes to that, a fourth. Only curiosity and the self-satisfaction of being seen at a premiere drive the people into the theater. True admirers of Gluck's music can be counted on the fingers of one's hands. Were Gluck's operas given more frequently, one would be more circumspect in the choice of novelties. One would aspire to artistic rather than commercial success, an aspiration within the range of a theater so generously subsidized as ours. Much might be said, then, and said seriously, about the production of noble works of art such as Gluck's, or, indeed, all talk rendered superfluous. But that is still a pipe dream.

Frau Materna projected the title role beautifully, if not quite fully in the idiom of Gluck. More restraint, more repose, are to be recommended to one who undertakes this role. Unduly heavy accentuation is also to be avoided. None is indicated in the score. Herr Sommer (as the High Priest) sang as if nothing more were afoot than an examination by a jury of singing teachers.

Herr Scaria, as Hercules, was adequately absurd. One would, indeed, be hard put to accept this symbol of muscularity as other than a figure of fun. The final tableau is marvelous. Dear parents, if you want to give your little ones a treat, don't fail to send them to the finale. This peep show cannot fail to delight them.

1.   This revival, on October 4, was the first since 1810, when the opera was mounted for Pauline Anna Milder-Hauptmann, the first Leonore in *Fidelio*. It was sung in the Italian original, and was a disaster. At the third performance, according to the Vienna correspondent of the Leipzig *Allgemeine Musikalische Zeitung*, the theater (the Kärntnerthor) was empty. Milder-Hauptmann subsequently sang the title role with great success elsewhere, notably in Berlin.

59. Roster Problems

October 18, 1885

The approaching season heralded itself on the stage of our opera house in the form of a farewell performance. Frau Kupfer,[1] as Marguerite in Boito's *Mefistofele*, appeared for the last time upon our local stage where, for a good many years, she has moved with tolerable competence. We suffer in her departure no irreparable loss, for Frau Kupfer was only rarely able to raise her achievement above a certain respectable mediocrity. She is replaceable.

But where is the replacement? One must look around, but will a replacement be found immediately? Was it clever, then, to abandon a serviceable singer before being assured of another, presumably better? We have finally grown accustomed to Frau Kupfer's less than perfect accomplishments. It might be noted in so saying that our sensibilities have gradually been dulled over the years, if not quite to the point where we could remain unreceptive to the improvement of her modest talent, especially in recent seasons. This last consideration need not have been thought overriding by the management had they been able to substitute better for merely good.

As of the moment, however, nothing has been done. Or does one think to have found better in Fräulein Klein? In that case it hardly promises well for the visible aspect of those Wagnerian heroines to whom Frau Kupfer has heretofore lent the outer contours [a pun derived from the fact that *klein* in German means *small?*]. No, we would prefer to await succor [*Sukkurs*, a play on the name of Rosa Sucher] from Brünn or Olmütz, where so many lovely nightingale eggs have been hatched, not a few of them subsequently recognized on foreign boards as cuckoo eggs, and dispatched in due course to the cuckoo [*Kuckuck*, in German, serving also as a euphemism for the devil].

The continual engagement and disengagement of singers seems almost to have become a habit with the management of our Court Opera. Where will it all lead? What is its purpose? One fears seriously that our situation may come to resemble that of the free city of Frankfurt. I, at least, have noted in a very amusing report by Börne on the character of the theater management there a striking resemblance to the management of our own opera house. In a *Carefully Considered Statement to the Honorable Public* he quotes the theater management. May this witty statement be found appropriate as a lighthearted disposal of this odious subject:

To the Honorable Public

If our constant endeavor to maintain the stage entrusted to us in a condition of inner dignity and outer brilliance has not been generally acknowledged, the fault lies with the modesty of our subscribers, if only because they are reluctant to admit that so much was rquired to satisfy their demands, i.e., the maintenance of the finest and highest artistic standards. But we can no longer remain silent without placing ourselves in a compromising position, and hazarding Germany's high opinion of the Attic connoisseurship of our beloved citizens. We shall abjure all rhetorical flourishes, which confuse rather than elucidate, and tell in simple language what improvements we have quietly wrought in our theater, and what we propose to do in the future.

Other theater managements, and, indeed, the best, content themselves with having good artists, and no more than that. We, however, have always gone much farther. We knew from experience, or have inferred from human nature, that familiarity breeds contempt, even for the best and most beautiful, and that it may leave one utterly without feeling of any kind. We have not been content, therefore, merely to see that our stage was provided with good personnel. We have been concerned rather to have on hand an adequate number of incompetents, the intention being that the public should never want for objects of comparison and thus not lose its delight in better artists. Not satisfied to let it go at that, we have engaged as guest artists, insofar as they were available, and for the same reason, the very worst, knowing full well in advance that they would be hissed off the stage. We can say without boasting that we spend annually more money for bad guest artists than other theaters do for resident artists who are consistently good.

1. Frau Kupfer turned to Italian opera, and continued her career with success in Italy, Spain and South America, returning to her native Vienna in 1898 as a teacher of singing.

60. *Unanimously:* No!

October 23, 1885

Music?

Hardly anything can be more depressing than to be denied the fulfillment of a wish, even a modest one. And yet nothing preoccupies a man more than anxiety or confidence about the fulfillment of his hopes and wishes. One is driven to lunacy, drunkenness, misanthropy, astrology, starvation, treasure-hunting, indebtedness, exorcism, the penning of lyric poetry, loitering, unhappy love affairs, yes, even to music criticism (as in my own case, for example), and to God knows what other useful and pleasurable pursuits.

Indeed, one should, in order to evade such evil circumstances, place oneself on the coolest footing with one's wishes and aspirations, and pay them as little heed as possible. One should set office hours for such importunate guests, and then observe those hours as unpunctually as may be compatible with the self-esteem that every scoundrel entertains of himself. He comes off best, of course, who can shake off these radical agitators of the human heart as we shake off a bad habit, once and forever. The surprise, then, when something good, something welcome, comes along is the more agreeable, the anger the more moderate when the opposite occurs. When I offered a piece of my chamber music[1] to the Rosé Quartet, I was reckless enough, unfortunately, to entertain the wish that they might play it. This estimable ensemble thought better of it (as one says), and voted "unanimously"(according to an authoritative communication) to forgo a performance of my composition.

(When I think about this awesome "No!," and how it was uttered by four powerful male voices in the purist *unisono* so that the very walls trembled, then a similar passage in Gluck's *Orfeo* strikes me as truly feeble by comparison. That this distinguished quartet could rise to such dramatic accents in the field of vocal music I would never have thought possible. Such versatility excites admiration and awe, however grudging, and the realization of how superior this enterprising quartet is to all competitors even in this respect can bring us only quiet joy, to the quartet itself, however, honor and glory.)

I do not, I hasten to add, hold it in any way against this admirable quartet that they, probably acting on a sudden inspiration, should decide against my poor piece unanimously. A two-voiced rejection, to be sure, in gentle thirds, a third voice associating itself with the others in decorous contrapuntal turns ("coils" might be the more appropriate term in this case) with the fourth, a neutral power, counting rests, would have affected me far more sympathetically than this barbarically rough, inquisitorially stern and utterly inhuman, unmusically unanimous condemnation from the mouth of an awesome assemblage of four acute and experienced judges of high art. I can vividly imagine the ghastly effect that such appallingly lovely unanimity might have on a spirit less resilient than mine. Indeed, I still detect a gentle tremor when I recall how close I came to being undone by this unanimous death sentence for my composition.

Gentlemen! Have pity on us poor composers! Never bellow in unison when you condemn a work. Split yourself into atoms, if you are capable of such a thing, but desist from sending hopeful authors such blasphemous absurdities as unanimous decisions against this work or that in writing. Practice courtesy and moderation. Fill your pockets with onions, or, if you are imaginative enough to set your fountains to work by such means, just think for a moment of the story of the prodigal son, of Absalom left hanging by his hair in an oak tree, of Joseph in the pit, of Jonah in the belly of the whale, of that drunkard Noah's hangover, of Cleopatra's sorry end, or of any sad event of biblical history. This will enable you, when an author rendered desolate by your abominable unison comes within view for the first time following such a catastrophe, instantly to produce a pretty shower and, from a mask smiling through tears, inform the sensitive fellow that an irrevocable decision has brought down a horrible fate upon his innocent head. That would be humane, noble, worthy of emulation, and would in no way run counter to other statutes of an artistic institution.

I reiterate that I entertain an indomitable respect for the accomplishments of the Rosé Quartet. How, indeed, could I have any but the friendliest feelings for so useful an ensemble, guided as it is by artistic principles of the purest water (please don't misunderstand me), concerned only to spread out the finest new toys at the gaily colored annual fair of each musical season as attractions for a brilliant circle of customers. Can there be anything more reasonable than making things as agreeable for people as possible? I mean from the idealistic point of view, which most certainly is that of the Rosé Quartet.

My own work, unfortunately, is not of an order to satisfy the highest requirements of art, and least of all in the most essential detail: -- Whether the Rosé Quartet's cultivated public would find pleasure in it is most doubtful. I myself am almost of the opinion that this highly competent audience (for everyone fortunate enough to possess two ears assumes himself competent to pass judgment, and rejoices in the assumption), would have found my work a bad bargain, and I bow my head accordingly before the acuity and sure critical instincts that this justly beloved quartet has shown so exquisitely in the fashioning of its program, fashioned, as was to be expected: *unanimously*.

---

1.   The posthumously published String Quartet in D minor. The letter Wolf had received read as follows: "We have attentively played through your D minor Quartet and unanimously resolved to leave the work for you with the doorkeeper of the Court Opera (Operngasse).

Will you have the kindness to send for it as soon as possible? He could easily mislay it. With heartiest greetings." The letter, and the four signatures, too, were in the handwriting of Siegmund Bachrich, the violist and the senior member of the Rose' Quartet. As the composer of the operas *Muzzedin* and *Heini von Steier* he had appeared frequently in Wolf's notices as a figure of fun.

61. Routine Triumphs Again

November 1, 1885

When Wagner came to Vienna during the winter season of 1876 to hear his *Tannhäuser* and *Lohengrin,* [1] first having personally prepared them thoroughly, his statement following the performance of *Tannhäuser* that his objective as producer had been to make his works intelligible to the public "insofar as the available forces would permit" was felt by the entire press to be offensive. [2]

The critical dwarfs with their clever, guileful formulations found this utterance from the mouth of the Titan altogether rude, and so they whined and struck angry attitudes and rushed in closed ranks against the indomitable Wagner (poor wretches), and huffed and puffed and sweated and croaked and generally behaved so comically and oddly in their awful indignation -- the dear little fellows against the all-powerful -- that they seemed, each and every one, to have taken leave of their senses. All hell, as I have said, was let loose by this statement of Wagner's to the public, a statement, moreover, thoroughly called for. Or was Wagner supposed to acknowledge in Herr Labatt[3] (of singular memory) an artist uniquely predestined to realize his ideals?

If the performances of *Tannhäuser* and *Lohengrin* at that time had a more consecrated character, if they did away, at least, with the most glaring absurdities, it was primarily Wagner's doing, the singers' only insofar as they were either intelligent enough to allow themselves to be taught by him, or bright enough to take his hints, or, finally, talented enough to carry out his instructions. Only Frau Ehnn may well have been numbered among the latter. Still and all, Wagner must have recognized in the "available forces" the obstacle preventing the performance of his works in a degree of perfection that would be possible under more favorable circumstances, and should be possible in a theater of the first rank.

Adequate forces were available, it should be added, to master the new Venusberg music and setting.[4] One could bring off this daring enterprise even today, but to demand effort, time, industry and money from the management of our Court Opera when something serious is afoot would be a far more hazardous venture. And so it's the same old story all over again. Wagner wanted to offer us an ideal performance despite inadequate resources. He could not do it. The management of the Court Opera today, blessed with the richest resources, could easily restore the new Venusberg music to its rightful place. It does not wish to do so. Wagner's forthright acknowledgment that the available forces were inadequate to satisfy the high requirements he set for art was found at that time to be presumptuous and offensive. Today, the squandering of adequate forces upon the least worthy objectives would probably be thought praiseworthy. Who, under the circumstances, might not give way to despair!

Once Wagner had departed, no one had anything more urgent to do than forget as soon as possible, and come what might, every bit of tradition stemming directly from him. People shied away from high principles, were concerned only for their trivial amusement. Thus it happened that the new Venusberg scene, since it involves, unfortunately, sensuous rather than nonsensical elements, was shelved with admirable dispatch, and without regard for other considerations that loudly bespoke the shamefulness of such a procedure. But perhaps I am overstating the case. One did not want to go so far as a total break with the new Venusberg scene, for it was not entirely ineffective. It was decided, accordingly, to retain from the new version the cupids shooting a hail of arrows into the amorous throng, while making do with the music of the old. Thus Punch and Judy come again into their own, and small children -- and big ones, too -- will be heartily grateful to the producer for this favor.

1. It was this visit and these performances that made a Wagnerite out of the fifteen year-old Hugo Wolf. As recounted in letters he wrote to his family in Styria at the time, he hung around the stage door during rehearsals and around the lobby of the Hotel Imperial (where Wagner and his retinue were staying in a seven-room suite) at other times, seeking an opportunity to meet his new idol. This, with the connivance of a sympathetic hotel manager and servants, he actually managed to do. The meeting, in Wagner's reception room, was brief. Wolf produced some compositions for Wagner's inspection -- according to Wolf's biographer, Frank Walker, they were almost certainly the Piano Sonata, Opus 1, and the Variations, Opus 2 -- and Wagner, short of time, deferred judgment courteously, and wished the young Wolf well. Wagner said, according to Wolf: "I wish you, dear friend, much fortune in your career. Go on working hard, and when I come back to Vienna again show me your compositions."

2. The fatal words fell during a curtain speech following the first *Tannhäuser* performance on November 22. Wagner expressed himself with less restraint in a letter to King Ludwig, recounting his Vienna experience (January 26, 1876): "I achieved miracles there, but with a trouble which I could hardly bring myself to go through again! Wretched singers with huge salaries, who openly said I was there to ruin them, because I pointed out to them the bad habits into which they had fallen, without endowing them with the strength to shake them off for ever! They admitted I was right, but asked me what use this sudden re-baptism would be to them, seeing that they would be bound to revert to the old belief again!" (As translated in Ernest Newman's *The Life of Richard Wagner*, Vol. IV.)

3. Leonard Labatt (1838-1897), a Swedish tenor who sang at the Court Opera from 1869 to 1883, and of whom Wagner had no high opinion.

4. According to Newman, "It was at these performances of *Tannhäuser* that the opera was given for the first time in the definitive revised version, the new Venusberg music not following upon the complete Dresden overture, as it had been done in Paris, but being dovetailed into it in the fashion now familiar to concert- and opera-goers."

62. A Dream
From the Diary of a Chinaman

November 8, 1885

I would not wish to be the Intendant of a court opera house.[1] Not now -- nor ever! It's a galling occupation, a Sisyphean job, a burden calling for the mighty shoulders of an Atlas. I can talk about it, because I speak from experience. For one entire night I was the central figure of this story. I was Intendant of the court theater in a large city of my native land -- whether it was Peking or Tonking or Nanking or some other city of the Heavenly Empire with a name ending melodiously in "king" I truly cannot remember. Suffice it to say that I was Intendant, and I knew that it was I because the image reflected in my mirror after the unhappy day of my entry upon this dreadful office confirmed it.

I was somewhat astonished at first by the changes taking place in my outward appearance. How, I exclaimed aloud, is it possible that in so short a time vexations, anger, troubles, cares and disillusionments could affect me so horribly? This complexion, alternating between the most luscious sea green and the loveliest brimstone; this bald pate with its dirty-white wisp of hair waving in the breeze like a *parlementaire's* flag of truce; these sunken eyes, this lifeless expression, these revolting wrinkles, these pendulous ears, this crooked back -- my God, what an appalling sight! But to this imposing visible aspect was added, I soon had to note, to my horror, a similar frame of mind. This curious external and internal transformation dated, as I recall it now, from shortly after the memorable address I delivered, announcing, so to speak , the program for the great concert I proposed to conduct in discharging the responsibilities of the high office to which I had been called.

Ah, well, it was a sorry concert. I may say that the difficult score from which I had to conduct was familiar to me. I made improvements, introduced cuts where they seemed called for (and there were many), added some music of my own where I found additional measures necessary, changed text and music -- in short, I began to institute a pretty thorough reform of that superficial, frivolous score.

But of what account was my industry, my enthusiasm? No one understood me. I decided then to sack the entire company. With personnel freshly engaged, a new spirit would enter the desecrated temple of art, heretofore a temple of moneychangers. Fees were to be distributed more justly. Leading sopranos, altos, tenors, baritones and basses, with their absurd pretensions, were to be banished instantly, and with them their creatures, the claque, whose prosperity the so-called top singers had always supported so industriously (for it is the vulgar stamping and clapping of such a mercenary multitude that inspires many a noble singer to sing his throat out, and not any enthusiasm for the work, great and noble as it may be).

Further, it was decided to reduce the ballet by half, and to throw out all the parasites throughout the company who were being well paid for their idleness. Only truly fine works were to be performed, and these only in the most nearly perfect manner possible. In order to make this feasible, the theater was to be closed twice a week to give the conductor an opportunity, on such days, for less hectic rehearsal. Latecomers, moreover, were to be denied admission during the overture, or when a scene was in progress. Similarly, the attendants would be directed to eject all unruly elements then and there, whoever they were –– but quietly. Beyond that, the entire fitting, furnishing and decoration of the auditorium was to be done over. Etc., etc.

What were the consequences of these sound proposals? First, a conspiracy, then a revolution. The "Son of Heaven" in a move designed to quiet the storm, sent me, as a token of his high esteem, a handsome sabre, along with a polite request that I test the keenness of its blade. I knew perfectly well how to honor the significance of this royal initiative, but still, I was rather hurt by so indiscreet a presumption, especially as I had not the slightest desire to disembowel myself. This unwelcome situation was resolved, however, thanks to the intervention of powerful sympathizers. The Emperor conceded me not only my life, but also my office and status. But, concerned for my welfare, he appointed an assistant to take over the actual conduct of affairs. Since that time, I have experienced no happiness, for my assistant was abominable.

Where once there resided in me gaiety and peace of mind, were now only melancholy and a certain bitterness. My former enthusiasm gave way, in the low company of my new colleague, to cynical scorn. My earlier industry, dedicated to the highest achievements, degenerated gradually to idle time wasting. I was irresponsible, lazy, arrogant, undiscerning, unavailable to those of good judgment, and the more susceptible to every kind of flattery and nonsense. I grew hard of heart, and unjust. I began to think of art as mere entertainment, and took any art work seriously, as did my colleague, only when it demonstrated a commercial potential. I was stubborn and dull-witted. My only creative occupation consisted in instigating intrigues among the female personnel. Finally, I even began to read newspapers. It was not long, however, before I awoke to the horrifying realization that my broken spirit could produce a spark of life only when reveling in our famous music critics' prose.

That scared me out of my wits. Sweat streamed from my forehead. I wished to die. I begged to be killed, but no one listened. In desperation I even laid hand upon myself, and was just in the act of self-strangulation when my violent and clumsy exertions –– thank heaven! –– restored me to consciousness.

My first act was to dash to the mirror. I looked a bit confused. My eyes were somewhat swollen. But for the rest I resembled not in the least that hot-blooded and subsequently melancholy Intendant whose fate I had so taken to heart. It was all perfectly clear: I had dreamt. Overcome by the emotion of this happy circumstance, I shed the sweetest tears of thanksgiving and compassion.

1.   A certain poignancy about this fanciful piece resides in the fact that almost exactly a dozen years later, it would be Wolf's delusion of having become the new director of the Court Opera that would reveal to his friends the onset of insanity.

63. Haydn's "Creation"

November 15, 1885

"The Creation" by Haydn. What a spirit of childlike faith speaks from the heavenly pure tones of Haydn's music! Sheer nature, artlessness, perception and sensitivity! It is the mark of his greatness as an artist that when we hear his music we are utterly unaware of the art, and yet what a variety of musical structures encloses his charming tonal pictures!

His extraordinarily keen artistic perception is most conspicuously evident in the field of tone painting, much cultivated in recent times, and now falling into disrepute. And, indeed, we would shudder at the very thought of what a modern composer might do in the handling -- or mishandling -- of a subject offering such opportunities for tone painting as "The Creation" or "The Seasons." There would be so much depiction that we would hear no music. If a modern composer wished, for example, to illustrate chaos, it is certain that we would encounter no triad, unless possibly an augmented one. It would probably fall to a perfect fifth to defray the musical expenses of such a vision.

(If we could suppose that the good Lord had consecutive fifths ringing in his ears at his first glimpse of chaos, then it would follow that justified self-defense rather than wantonness or malice, as some philosophers have suggested, prompted his desperate decision, in the ridiculously short span of seven days, to inflict so much evil upon the world. An ordinary piece of cotton wool to be sure, could have rendered the same service, but there were no trees at that time, nor plantation owners. The cotton wool industry still dreamt peacefully in the womb of chaos, and Jaeger shirts rightly were still a chimera.[1] O, happy days of chaos!)

Still, one could live with this diabolical expressive device if only that had been the end of it, for today dissonances and shrill instrumental effects fall like hail about our ears, and the orchestra moans and groans until one is ready to believe that chaos has become a wild beast with a toothache. If a composer's intention was, indeed, to portray the tumbling about of contentious air currents, or the hissing ascent of a fiery rocket, or some other natural phenomenon, his motives may have been of the best, but he has achieved nothing, and we retain, moreover, a very low opinion of his good intentions.

To such extremes can confusion go, however, when tone painting is so dominated by the purely external, that from all the atmospheric no atmosphere emerges, no mood, and from all the characterization no character. There is always the occasional detail, but never an effective whole. How different was Haydn's procedure. Just look at chaos in his "Creation." The very first measures, with the muted violins, awoke in us the sensation of being in the presence of a mysterious something. A magician, he evokes the sombre picture of chaos. Gray fogbanks roll slowly on in disordered masses, illuminated by iridescent lights. Listen! What manner of voices were those, cries of distress and despair, gently solemn strains? They intertwine, dissolve, melt away. Another apparition emerges from the darkness, radiant in magical beauty. The soul thrills at the sight of this enchanting phantom. With serene movement it pursues its course. It drifts upward. The atmosphere is suffused with deep red. It falters, falls — a flash of lightning out of the black abyss — and the apparition has vanished. Seas of mist again envelop the richly colored scene. The tone poet has awakened from his dream.

That is, to be sure, a pitiful sketch compared with the fantastic world conjured up by the tone poet in his prophetic vision. But had Haydn wished to turn into music exactly what he had seen, one may assume with reasonable certainty that his chaos would have remained the more unintelligible in just the same degree that it speaks the more intelligibly to us now. Why? Because the composer has given us not his vision, but rather the impression made by the vision upon his musical sensibility.

Enough of that. The performance, under the direction of Kapellmeister Fuchs was a good one. Of the performers, too, there is only good to be said. It was quite the opposite with the Mozart Requiem, as far as the performers were concerned. It got off to a sad start with Herr Sonnenthal,[2] so overcome by emotion in his declamation of a prologue by Eduard Mautner[3] as to be rendered well-nigh speechless. None of the soloists, Frau Niklas-Kempner, Herr Winkelmann and Herr Rokitansky, was in especially good form. Only the chorus and orchestra, under the direction of Hofkapellmeister Hellmesberger, measured up to their requirements.

At the memorial service for Hoftheater-Intendant Freiherr von Hoffmann it did not escape notice that those ladies of the Court Opera most indebted to his good offices for their present artistic standing graced the occasion by their absence. But others, too, who in former times sought his favor invited a charge of ingratitude by remaining away from the solemn occasion.

Among the most interesting activities of our musical life are the Renaissance Concerts promoted by Dr. Robert Hirschfeld[4] and Franz Köstinger. It is a wholly praiseworthy enterprise, quite beyond commensurate acknowledgment, and certainly not to be dismissed by a shrug of the shoulders as some of our critics ill-disposed to renaissance concerts have tried to do.

About the Schütz Festival (commemorating the 300th anniversary of Heinrich Schütz's birth), which offered rich stimulation and rare pleasure to historian and musician alike, I must reserve a more detailed account for a future time.

1. Jaeger-Hemde, literally huntsman's shirts, a brand name for a type of pullover then fashionable.

2. Adolf Ritter von Sonnenthal (1832-1909), a very famous Court Theater actor and, at the time of this notice, the Court Theater chief stage director. Distinct enunciation had never been his strong point, nor was it assisted by a slight Hungarian accent. Viennese theater goers used to say that he spoke as if suffering from a cold.

3. Eduard Mautner (1824-1889), Hungarian-born Viennese journalist and poet.

4. Robert Hirschfeld (1858-1914), instructor in musical esthetics at the Vienna Conservatory, a music critic of the *Wiener Zeitung*, and founder of the Renaissance Concerts, who shortly before his death became director of the Mozarteum in Salzburg. Wolf's reference to ill-disposed critics reflected the recent publication by Hirschfeld of a polemical booklet, *Das kritische Verfahren Hanslicks* (Hanslick's Critical Procedure), provoked by Hanslick's observation in his review of a Handel festival that "Prior to Handel and Bach there were living musicians, but no music that lives for us today."

64. The Cunning Peasant[1]
Comic Opera by Anton Dvořák

November 22, 1885

There may be those serious enough —— heaven help them! —— to find this opera comical, just as there are those comical enough —— God preserve them! —— to take Brahms's symphonies seriously. Your critic, in the interest of his health, would gladly have laughed. He had, indeed, reason enough to let the anesthetic merriment of all genuine comedy work its balm on his bronchitic chest. He confesses, however, that despite the most awesome dedication and lively attention to this work, there was not a moment when it touched that string in his ailing breast whose benevolent vibrations he so fervently wished to detect. Quite the contrary, there is in the narrative substance as well as in the music of this comic opera an amiable prompting to melancholy reverie. This fortunate circumstance may well have brought many an infatuated lieutenant and many an ardent maiden closer together in spirit, but that aside, let no one at the risk of his job, his life and his immortal soul expect us to fathom the still deeper significance of this gentle, melancholy mood. Now to the matter at hand. The story, unless I am greatly mistaken, is fascinating, well made and original. Regina, daughter of the rich peasant, Martin, loves a poor devil, the shepherd, Gottlieb. The rich peasant, Martin, loves the money of another rich peasant's son, Konrad. Pay close attention now, for what is about to occur is, unless I am greatly mistaken, absolutely without precedent. The rich peasant, Martin, proposes to his daughter that she marry the other rich farmer's worthless son, Konrad. Regina -- who would have dreamt of such a thing? -- declines, whereupon Martin -- who could have imagined it? -- scolds his daughter and makes a frightful scene. The daughter bawls, the papa curses, his protégé bungles a declaration of love, and scratches his head, and the house-keeper, Gertrude, the *enfant terrible*, can think of nothing better to do for the moment than to bawl along with the daughter. The quartet is complete. Now, musician, fiddle up what you can.

But we prefer to stay away from the music for a while, and get along with the story. Martin and Konrad remain behind on stage. They vent their depressed spirits in vulgar jokes. Finally, to cheer up the moody presumptive bride-groom, Martin hits upon a devilishly cunning plan. They will have some fun with Gottlieb, who is given in his idle hours to walking up and down beneath his beloved's window. Martin and Konrad resolve, the very next night, to give the unsuspecting Gottlieb a sound thrashing. Wonderful idea! The two con-spirators lick their chops in happy anticipation as they go off. But man proposes -- the cunning peasant disposes. Gertrude, like all women, cannot resist eavesdropping. Suspecting mischief, she makes a quick decision, and hides behind the first likely bush (which, thanks to the lighting, was singularly ill chosen), and becomes a voluntary witness to the dastardly plot. Nothing must happen to the dear, good Gottlieb. Naturally. She exits in high dudgeon.

Enter now the Count and Countess, he with valet, she with chambermaid. Village dignitaries and the townsfolk, as is customary, escort them to their residence. Regina presents the Count with a bouquet, and he deigns to find her attractive. All leave, whereupon Konrad and Martin undertake to solicit, without success, the Count's intervention in the matter of Regina's marriage to Konrad. Exeunt Konrad and Martin. Now Regina and Gertrude seek the Count's intervention in behalf of Regina and Gottlieb. The Count is most attentive to Regina, but Gertrude -- now what can she be up to while this is going on? She gives herself up entirely to the delights of eavesdropping, cursing roundly from time to time at certain tender utterances of the Count, to which he gives the proper weight by offering Regina a property if she will accommodate his wishes. Regina seems to go along with the idea. The Count will await her at night after the party to be given in honor of his arrival.

Our two worthy pearls have not yet recovered from the Count's infamous behavior when the valet, with intentions similar to his master's, makes a play for that poor lamb, Regina. But to the valet Regina is no lamb. She has become a cat, and she scratches. The eavesdropping nightowl, Gertrude, not shunning the glare of daylight, lays about her furiously with talons and beak.

Unfortunately for the amorous valet, the jealous chambermaid catches him during one of his persistent assaults on Regina's innocence. Obedient to her peremptory dictation, the languishing servant distances himself from the scene, having first arranged with Gertrude to come the next night to Regina's house. Now the Countess and the chambermaid are informed of the Count's treacherous conduct, and of the valet's, too, and the opera closes with a final scene from — Figaro!

That final scene was, in fact, the only surprise in this wonderful libretto. The music, put together from Bohemian national melodies, is, in the long run, soporific. The instrumentation is abominable, brutal, absurd. To dress up anything as miserable as this libretto with a pompous noise of snare and other drums reflects the utmost tastelessness. It is bad enough to meet Dvořák in the concert hall. That this embarrassment should insinuate itself into the opera house is truly deplorable.

Anton Rubinstein is in Vienna to offer, on the piano, a historical review of the keyboard literature from its beginnings to its crescendo in our own time. The first recital, with William Byrd, Dr. John Bull, François Couperin, Jean Philippe Rameau, [Domenico] Scarlatti, J.S. Bach, Handel, C.P.E. Bach, Haydn and Mozart in the program, pursued, as was to be expected, an interesting course. The important thing, for the most part, was simply that Rubinstein played. For who, excepting the historian, will be concerned as to whether Byrd is to be played one way, or Bull another, or whether the "hen" [Rameau's "La Poule"] should cackle sentimentally, joyously or angrily, or whether the Carman's Whistle [Byrd] should blow wantonly or languishingly? In any case, the cat in Scarlatti's "Cat's Fugue" glided with velvet paws over the A string, and the Haydn Variations in F [minor] could not have been better played.

For me, however, Rubinstein seemed to play Mozart's Fantasy in C minor too fleetingly, too soberly, and with a certain pedantry. And that fast tempo! That was no adagio, hardly a moderato. But how eloquently how charmingly, how utterly in a Mozartean vein was the delightful Rondo in A minor and the "Alla turca" from the Sonata in A major, how doubly splendidly did the warm colors of the orient blaze in this masterly bit of musical characterization, with Rubinstein drawing the most vivid shades from the keys! It is more agreeable to hear the artist than to criticize him, wherefore I desist betimes.

1.   Selma Sedlák, originally produced in Prague in 1878. The Vienna premiere was on November 19.

65. Opening with Berlioz

November 29, 1885

The Philharmonic concerts may well claim a place of honor in a chapter on the world's miseries. We are tolerant folk, not given to haggling. Let the concerts take their place of honor and, with the help of God, Brahms and Dvořák, establish their right to it.

But to consort, for God knows what reason, with that devil Berlioz, that archfiend, Beelzebub, Belphegor, Astaroth and Mephisto, and thumb their noses at the critical Holy Trinity -- I withdraw that metaphor and substitute a three-headed hellhound standing guard, vainly to be sure, at the portals of musical misery, and granting admittance only to utter ruin, death and decay of good taste -- to wantonly tickle with a prickly Berlioz the snout of that monstrous creature, that allegorical horror, the friendly wagging of whose tail is their most fervent concern in their pursuit of that place of honor, and thrust into its jaws, instead of a mush compounded of Brahms and Dvořák, an armor-clad Berlioz on whom it will rip out its teeth -- that, dear reader, I call either foolhardy or tactless or both. The Philharmonic, with this first concert of the new season, has brewed a dainty soup for the critics. I shall help them to lap it up, and I'll enjoy it, too, even if no one chooses to grace my repast by intoning a blessing.

The Philharmonic opened this first concert with the Overture to *Benvenuto Cellini*. Mentally and in lexicons I review the masterpieces of all ages and places, endeavoring to find a work better suited than this Berlioz overture to introduce the season of 1885 A.D. In vain. Had the Philharmonic enjoyed the privilege of being able to reflect for a thousand years upon the best possible choice, they would still have had to come up with this *Cellini* overture. Naturally. Just name me another overture that takes off more festively, more jubilantly, than the opening twenty-two measures of the *Cellini* overture -- including Weber's overtures, which are certainly not wanting in inflammatory matter. And then the sudden tension, entering with the theme of the Cardinal, pizzicato in the basses (what lies ahead?); and the way the woodwinds, later the violins, violas and cellos, intone the delicious melody which, in the course of the opera, lifts a grotesque farce far above its wonted lowly estate by its irresistible enchantment -- can this melody, so beautifully easing our tense expectation, be heard as a harbinger of glad tidings for the further progress of the Philharmonic concerts? What I mean is this: Can a sudden happy occurrence (in this case the entrance of a heavenly melody), coming after expectant silence, be regarded or felt as a promise for the future?

I'm only speculating. Pronouncement and subsequent disputation are not at all what we want. But I will say this, and no power in heaven or on earth will divert me from my course: Whoever understands me, understands me, and whoever does not understand me, and this I proclaim categorically, understands me not. And whoever is disposed to question the extraordinary lucidity of that sentence, too, is neither Christian, Turk, heathen nor Chinese. I despise him when I can no longer hate him, and I shall do him in.

But once again let me say: The choice of the *Cellini* overture as opening number was extremely happy. If critics find this work confused, abstruse and so on,[1] then the odds are 100:1 that it is precisely the opposite. To understand this splendid overture fully, one must, to be sure, as with every overture, hear it in the context of the drama for which it was composed. But that does not deter the critics. There is the matter of form to be considered. What is not composed according to the rules of quadrature -- it is not given to just anyone to write "academic" overtures -- will be denounced as absurd, unpalatable, extravagant, and so on in the same key. Once more: the *Cellini* overture was a good choice, and it was gracious of Hofkapellmeister Richter that he should open the season with -- of all people -- Berlioz!

The Hellmesberger Quartet, to the satisfaction of just about everyone, has returned to the small hall of the Musikverein. It should never have left. How enchantingly Hellmesberger has been playing Beethoven lately. Certainly no one approaches him in the Adagio of Opus 135. His playing is at once penetrating and charming, and his sons, the professors Josef and Ferdinand, know exactly how to anticipate and pursue their teacher's intentions, and to play, so to speak, into his hand. The violist, too, is excellent.

It was the turn of Schubert, Weber and Mendelssohn in the third Rubinstein recital. Rubinstein's playing does not provide unalloyed pleasure. His extraordinary technic tempts him to extreme tempi. This fatal idiosyncracy is calculated as no other to destroy any given piece of music. A composition played at the correct tempo, even without a trace of imagination or sensitivity on the part of the player, can give the listener a more accurate picture of its character than the most exquisite shading at a tempo ill chosen. The second movement of the "Wanderer" Fantasy, thanks to the hectic pace, was sheerly unrecognizable. All of Rubinstein's virtuosity could not win us to this music, while the unskilled hand of any decently accomplished dilettante can set our sensibilities aflame if the right tempo, far slower than Rubinstein's, is maintained. In the "Moments Musicals," on the other hand, Rubinstein gave of his best, simply because his always fascinating playing was uninhibited by improper tempi. Similarly, the effect of Weber's "Polacca Brillante" was utterly electrifying.

1. Hanslick, reviewing this concert, seized the opportunity to lump Berlioz's *Benvenuto Cellini, Les Francs-Juges,* "Waverley "and "The Corsair" overtures together and characterize them collectively as "tortured, without style, unmusical, melodically trivial, and abstruse in their development" in contrast to the Overture to *King Lear* and the "Roman Carnival" Overture, of which he thought highly.

66. On Applause

December 6, 1885

If one could persuade the Philharmonic's subscribers -- that is, if one could persuade them that it is fashionable -- to subscribe to concerts hitherto provided gratis by nature and without endorsement of an enthusiastic impresario -- an eclipse of the moon, for example, or a thunderstorm, or a prairie fire, a sunrise, a sunset, a splendid rainbow, an earthquake, a fata morgana, the eruption of a volcano, or some other of nature's spectacles, either awful or lovely -- what do you suppose would be the first reaction of these amiable people? Would it be horror, admiration, reverence, terror, bliss, anxiety, pleasure, contrition, exaltation or any other powerful sensation that sets the pulse racing, or stops it altogether, that sends a shudder through the soul, beguiles the spirit, shatters the mind or stirs up passion? Nothing of the sort. Their first reaction would find expression in a characteristic itch in the palms of their hands, to rid themselves of which they would decide forthwith to give the good Lord a round of applause for having staged such a splendid show. It is maddening.

Must then, in the name of heaven and all the angels and archangels, the incendiary lightning of enthusiasm always travel to the hands and feet? Must there be clapping and stamping? Must our hands and feet function as portable lightning rods for the electrified spirit? Is applause, I ask, appropriate under all circumstances? Is it a law of nature? Or is it only a foolish, iniquitous habit characteristic of universal thoughtlessness?

When a French soldier, at the victorious sounds of the last movement during a performance of Beethoven's Fifth Symphony, impulsively shouted "Vive L'empereur!" this music must have awakened in him the sensation that the eagles of the victorious legions were swirling about his head, and that it behooved him forthwith to advance with fluttering standards to die for the emperor. The sanguine Frenchman showed that he had grasped this music correctly. It had, in any case, made a powerful impression on him. Something similar, according to Richard Wagner, occurred in Leipzig when, during a performance of Liszt's "Dante" Symphony, at a climactic passage in the first part, a desperate cry of "Holy Jesus!" was heard from the audience. I do not believe, indeed, that this chirping, petty Leipziger had grasped the "Dante" Symphony as correctly as our brave imperial guard had grasped the Fifth Symphony; but that drastic soul may well have made a great impression upon the impertinent Leipziger, especially if this bold hare was a rascal, or even a "profound" critic. The horrors of the first movement of the "Dante" Symphony are nicely calculated to make hell hot for such a fellow.

Now, I would not wish to give the impression that I am opposed to all applause. Go ahead and applaud, but only where the work itself invites it: at thundering closes and with compositions of gay, festive, warlike or epic character. And yet, in compositions of kindred character, when they express a specific poetic idea, intelligible to the listener, the ending can either call for applause or render it disturbing -- always assuming a natural reaction and not a stupid prejudice. Or would one deny that the ending of the *Coriolanus* Overture affects the sensibilities quite differently from the close of the *Egmont* Overture? The dawn of freedom for an oppressed people, reddening over Egmont's grave and bursting out in the brightest sunlight, grabs powerfully at the listener's heart. He feels lusty, exalted, free. He would like to join in the general rejoicing. He applauds, and shouts a "bravo!" or two. We all join in because we sympathize with the liberated people. Applause in this case is in order. But if there is no other way than hand clapping and foot stamping to express our sympathy for the self-destroying Roman, then there is something wrong with our involvement. After this frightfully tragic destruction of his defiant ego, could Beethoven's Coriolanus awake in us no other sensation than the desire to be freed as soon as possible from a more profound impression? The eye still stares straight ahead in stupefaction, as in a magic mirror in which the gigantic shadow of Coriolanus slowly disappears from view. The tears still flow, the heart pounds, the breath is short, every limb caught in a cramp. And yet, hardly has the last tone faded away, and there you are, already happy and gay, chatting, criticizing and clapping and -- Oh, you have gazed into no magic mirror. You have seen nothing, felt nothing, heard nothing, understood nothing, nothing, nothing.

But you applauded well. The wonderworld of the most passionate drama, the Prelude to *Parsifal* -- now, if only it had pleased you as much as the Piano Concerto of Saint-Saëns. Well, there was no want of applause for each.

Rubinstein's fourth recital, devoted to compositions by Robert Schumann, was uncommonly enjoyable. Again, it seemed to us that Rubinstein is at his greatest when measuring his strength against the slightest. Irresistibly beautiful were the "Phantasiestücke," including "Traumeswirren" and "Vogel [Bird] als Prophet" (not to be confused with the Munich Vogl [i.e., the Munich tenor, Heinrich Vogl] as Meyerbeer's Prophet) — and was "Carnaval" less so? Or the Adagio from the Sonata in F sharp minor and the dreamy pieces from "Kreisleriana?" Many another blossoming piece lost, to be sure, its characteristic luxuriance in the hurricane of a hectic tempo, notably Nos. 1 and 3 of "Kreisleriana." But all in all, we could rejoice wholeheartedly in the gifts offered to us from Robert Schumann by Anton Rubinstein in this delightful way.

There was a lot of variety in the last concert by the Hellmesberger Quartet. Two string quartets, a piano trio and two vocal numbers. We musicians would have been content with Beethoven's Opus 127 without the rest. We are, of course, gourmets, not gourmands, and what does not taste of nectar and ambrosia gives us a bellyache. A musical menu spiced by two Brahms compositions cannot but make us thoroughly ill. To avoid that misfortune we were clever enough to let one of those pieces, the Quartet in A minor, fall under the table, sensing that the other would be hard enough to keep down. Thus we heard only the "Ständchen, " sung by Herr Winkelmann. What with Herr Winkelmann's distinct enunciation, it was not surprising that we lost the sense of the poem. The lover, presumably, is complaining to his beloved about his boredom, his despair and his toothache. Herr Brahms, who has hardly a rival when it comes to the characterization of such moods and afflictions, has again given a brilliant example of his eminent ability to master a situation with a few short strokes. How beautifully, in this "Ständchen," is boredom expressed! How eloquent is its language! The effect was also surprising. One yawned to one's heart's content. And with what mastery was the transition from boredom to despair prepared and executed! One would have liked to tear one's hair out by the roots in sheer delight. Now despair, now boredom, and this in a degree of perfection possibly only with a master of Brahms's significance.

Volkmann's Trio in F (probably a posthumous work) is better suited to the classroom than to the concert hall. Volkmann wrote much better things than this. One should choose from among them. Schubert's "Auf dem Strom" was pretty exhausting. Herr Winkelmann's monotonous interpretation contributed no less than the ghastly length of the composition to a feeling of utter fatigue. What complaints had not to be overcome, how long had we to grope around in spiritual darkness before the long-awaited E flat triad brought light? But the sun rose, and Beethoven spoke to the congregation, and disclosed to them the wonders of his fantasy.

67. *Chopin Recital*

December 13, 1885

"As popular as some of the works of that master may already be whom we propose to discuss, and whose strength had been broken by severe illness long before his end, we may assume that in twenty-five or thirty years his music will be accorded a less superficial and lightweight assessment than it enjoys today. Whoever is concerned with the history of music in the future will grant him a place appropriate to one who distinguished himself by so melodic a genius, by such marvelous rhythmic inspirations and by such felicitous and substantial extensions of the harmonic system, and whose creations will rightly be given priority over many a work of larger dimensions played again and again by major orchestras and sung again and again by innumerable prima donnas."

About that today, surely, there can no longer be any disputation. In the thirty-five years that have passed since the publication of the book from which that quotation is drawn [Frédéric Chopin, by Franz Liszt, 1852], there has been, in fact, so pronounced a swing in favor of Chopin's compositions in the concert halls that public and critics alike have almost reached the point where the capacities of a piano virtuoso are measured by the level of achievement he has attained, or not attained, in playing Chopin. A piano virtuoso not fully up to the playing of Chopin is numbered among the pianistic pariahs. I am not exaggerating. One forgives the artist a spiritless, inadequate performance of a Beethoven sonata, but the dry, academic playing of Chopin allows of no pardon. Woe be to those unfortunates who today make our concert halls insecure if they cannot establish their credentials with an "authentic" Chopin. An authentic Chopin is not to be found, however, in any music store. He is not tucked away in the notes. He may be recognized only in performance. How is this genuine fantasist to be played? Let's hear what Liszt has to say about that in his book:

"In his playing, this great artist captured charmingly that excited, shy or breathless trembling that affects the heart when one has the sensation of being close to a supernatural being that one cannot identify, grasp or contain. He used to let the melody rise and fall like a boat borne on a mighty wave, or he gave it an indeterminate movement as if some merry apparition were straining into this tangible and comprehensible world. He first introduced into his compositions that device which gave his virtuosity so individual a stamp, and which he called tempo rubato: a stolen, irregularly interrupted time-measure, desultory and languishing, then flickering like a flame in a draft, or swaying like corn under a soft breeze in the field, or like treetops leaning this way and that according to the capricious whims of the wind. Since, as it happened, the designation [tempo rubato] taught nothing to him who knew it, and meant nothing to him who did not know it, who did not understand its meaning, Chopin subsequently stopped using the term, convinced that whoever had an understanding of it could not help but divine the law of this license. All his compositions must be played in this hovering, characteristically accented and prosodical manner, and with that morbidezza whose secret is elusive when one had not often had the opportunity to hear him."

Liszt had heard him often enough. How deeply Liszt penetrated into the characteristics of Chopin's genius is well known. It is said that in the playing of Chopin's works one could not distinguish between the one artist and the other.

Liszt was also the one qualified to bring to practical realization the theoretical treatise on the performance of his works projected by Chopin but never executed. All the important pianists of recent time have, at least, studied with Liszt, among them Tausig and Rubinstein.[1] That the latter plays Chopin with such a sense of style is certainly due in no small degree to Liszt's influence.

How does Rubinstein play Chopin? I doubt that he plays otherwise than Chopin played, although far more accomplished technically. How wonderfully conceived was the Funeral March from the Sonata in B flat minor! A theater setting could not have realized this mournful picture more vividly. But above all the last movement, which bursts like cutting scorn upon the voice of love, of melancholy, of resignation in the softly fading funeral music! Away, away with your plaints and sighs, with your devotion, with your memories, your incurable nagging pains! -- That is its awesome message in the howling storm of the triplets, whipped along as if by the whirlwind. Above the fresh burial mound the winds whistle and play with the fragrant wreaths, bedewed by hot tears. Tomorrow, perhaps, the teary veil will turn to dust before the beneficent smile of the rising sun. Oh, a far too mournful philosophy speaks from the monotonous strain of this dreadful postlude.

1. Rubenstein played for Liszt in 1846, but was never a pupil.

68. Russians

December 20, 1885

"Everything in moderation." This maxim, redolent of worldly wisdom, works as well in ordinary life as in art. It can be applied just as aptly to an excessive indulgence in pigs' feet (as attested in a poem, "Alles mit Mass" [Everything in Moderation] by E. Mörike[1]) as to an over-indulgence in musical pleasures, as demonstrated in no small degree by Anton Rubinstein's piano recitals.

But we are not among the apostles of moderation. We have never preached abstemiousness, self-laceration and mortification. No musical Trappist we. But to listen for an entire evening to Russia's hopeful music of the future might well sour the most nihilistic patriot of the Czar's realm. Sour is the right word. I would as soon be transformed by magic into an old bassoon as endure another such evening. I was so soured[2] that not even the most harmless triad could relieve my distrust of "the power of music."

If the Poles have had the worst of it wherever and whenever they have opposed the Russians, this time it was the Russians who came off badly, despite numerical superiority. Yes, yes. Chopin did them in. Eleven etudes by Chopin opened the hostilities at this last of Rubinstein's recitals. It was a hot encounter — eleven etudes. But the spectacle was bloodless. Melodic cries fell upon the ear. The spirits of exotic flowers danced their now dithyrambic, now languishing rounds in pronounced, original rhythms. One can be stunned by this music, but it causes no pain. But the Russians! Above all, the mad Balakirev![3] There is a note hog for you. He downs everything, skin, hair and all. A Jacobin if ever there was one. Poor, much abused, long suffering Berlioz! What an innocent lamb you are compared with this ghoul Balakirev. The bloodthirsty villain is not content merely to murder music. He even makes fun of the corpse, and jokes about the thousand wounds he has inflicted in spells of madness (composing spells). Happy Russia that brings forth such progressives! Only Tchaikovsky, among the Cuis,[4] Liadovs,[5] Rimsky-Korsakoffs and whatever their names may be, makes an honorable exception. Tchaikovsky is concerned to make not only Russian national music, but, above all, music. His "Song Without Words," waltzes and romances are attractively imagined and as attractively executed. Even his "Scherzo à la Russe," pleases me, although the Russian national element in this work roughly disfigures its beauteous contours to the point where they are no longer recognizable.

The most favorable impression, after the Chopin etudes, was made, unquestionably, by the compositions of Michael Glinka. He is the classicist, as opposed to the new hyper-romantic tendencies of modern musical Russia. His operas, *A Life for the Czar* and *Russlan and Ludmilla*, are also known and esteemed in Germany. His piano pieces are melodious, nicely felt and not without imaginative touches. The program ended with compositions by the brothers Rubinstein.[6] The celebrated virtuoso betrayed no special talent in the selection of pieces for this occasion. He could have done better for himself. A Waltz and an Albumblatt by Nicholas Rubinstein, two grateful salon pieces, are familiar items in Rubinstein's programs.

Anton Rubinstein has a nice piece of work behind him. Such an undertaking, and of such dimensions, stands alone in concert history. One may call it a well-nigh superhuman accomplishment if one thinks about the "what." The "how," of course, is a question of genius, and Rubinstein carried off his self-imposed task as becomes a genius. But in another respect, too, Rubinstein offered an example that put his humanity, his nobility, in the finest light. Allowing an exception for the proverbial *noblesse* of Franz Liszt, there can hardly ever have been anything similar. Seven recitals for the benefit of indigent musicians and music lovers gratis! This noble streak in Rubinstein's nature is no less an ornament for the man than is his genius for the artist. So, if the public at large proffer the famous man the splendid laurel, the small community in the Bösendorfersaal gratefully slips in a modest spray of evergreen, consecrated to the faithful memory of noble humanity.

1.   Eduard Mörike (1804-1875), Swabian poet, whose poems were set by many composers including Schumann and Brahms, but which were to find their most congenial composer in Wolf, who set fifty-seven of them.

2.   Wolf is punning here on the verb *verstimmen*, which means both "to sour" in the sense of "to put out of sorts" and "to put out of tune."

3. Mily Alexeivitch Balakirev (1836-1910), generally regarded as the founder of a Russian nationalist school of composition, now remembered as a composer chiefly for his oriental fantasy, "Islamey."

4. César Antonovitch Cui (1836-1918), a protégé of Balakirev, a prolific composer and also, probably unknown to Wolf, a music critic.

5. Anatol Constantinovitch Liadov (1855-1914), an associate of Balakirev in the research of Russian folk music and a minor composer, chiefly for piano.

6. Anton Rubinstein's younger brother, Nicholas (1835-1881) is remembered not so much as a pianist and composer, but rather as the founder of the Russian Musical Society in Moscow (in 1859) and of the Moscow Conservatory (in 1864), both of which he headed until his death, and as an early sponsor of Tchaikovsky.

69. Patti's "Adieu a Vienne"

January 3, 1886

If Fräulein Abel must be given an opportunity to play a leading role once a year, why not *La Muette de Portici*? Is it, then, so difficult, as between two objects, to choose the better? Or are there really those who could prefer this miserable farce, *Yelva*, to Auber's masterpiece? Must our Court Opera be reduced to the status of a sanctuary for the most worthless junk? How can one in all seriousness set about staging so silly a subject? I would not have the heart to recommend this piece for a booth in the Prater.[1] So, Fräulein Abel created the role of Yelva. That is no reason to mount the work. The Court Opera is not there for the convenience of singers and dancers. It's the other way around. The Scribe potboiler was boring despite its tension-inducing devices, and despite Fräulein Abel's industrious efforts to sustain our interest in the Russian orphan. Fräulein Abel was, indeed, only too industrious. Her movements surpassed in agility those of a weasel. Repose is also movement. The most powerful emotions find expression in utter stillness. If the crescendo of passion were to be reflected in the movements of the actors, when even the slightest suggestion of emotion sets off a cyclone in their limbs, would they not, at the *dénouement*, have to be carried from the stage with shattered bones?

Adieu à Vienne! Ten years ago, this sentimental heading to the announcement of a concert by Patti would have left the heart of fashionable society unmoved. One would have smiled incredulously, ambiguously or, indeed, even maliciously. One would have smelled "Europe-fatigue," and expressed surprise that such a celebrity as Patti should so soon be paying homage to the American concert ticket system. One could have asserted, and with some justice, that here in our country, German and Italian nightingales (whether

Swedish, too, I know not) sound such melancholy summonses only when they have sung themselves hoarse in America. But these reproaches, that one could have addressed to the diva ten years ago, could be repeated today, and on the same grounds, namely, that they are groundless.

Adieu à Vienne cannot, however, deny its character of "just dropping by." Some day it will, indeed, be an *Adieu à Vienne*. In this farewell greeting there is a suggestion of self-criticism on the part of the famous singer. Unfortunately, we must add our voice to hers, much as we would have liked to contradict her. True, the tones pour forth silvery clear from the diva throat, but only on the level terrain of the middle voice. She can no longer climb the precipitous heights of the high E and above, nor roam those perilous paths from which trill upon trill once poured down on the delighted ears of enraptured listeners in a fine golden shower. That's all a thing of the past. The fastidious taste of her singing, however, the agility and refinement in the execution of fioritura and mordents, excite admiration now as before. A pity that she cut the dialogue (I mean in *The Barber of Seville*), as a result of which her acting could not develop freely enough. Rosina/ Patti did, indeed, right at the beginning, make a brave stab at German, addressing Dr. Bartolo in a purr by his pet name, "alter Brummbär" [old grumbler]. This bold attempt was eminently successful. Too bad that it remained an isolated episode. That the audience did not spare its hands may be taken for granted at a Patti evening, likewise the all too obligatory downpour of flowers.

Lohengrin. The debut of Fräulein Minna Walter[2] was attended by a cordial success. This gifted singer has a well-schooled voice, if none too strong. A speech impediment that occasionally gives to her utterances a somewhat childlike character is of no assistance to her virtues. Her acting reflects little routine, if any, and so, at least, nothing has been spoiled. Much came off well, notably the lively play of facial expression during Lohengrin's arrival (Fräulein Walter was the Elsa) and during the duel. There were, on the other hand, things that went wrong. Elsa's shock and apparent self-possession at the scandalous outpourings of the insidious Ortrud during the bridal procession were barely outlined. The inner transformation in Elsa's credulous nature, indicated plainly enough by the sudden change in the situation, cannot be sufficiently vividly projected. Feelings hitherto foreign to Elsa now rage in her bosom. She fears that Ortrud's charges may be true. Her faith falters, her confidence is shaken, her love appears to her as an unworthy sacrifice, and doubt, rising like a sinister demon from her bosom, spreads its dark pinions over the anxiety-tortured spirit of the loving woman. This significant inner process cannot be too articulately realized. The other roles were in the best of hands, and almost without exception well performed. Herr Scaria, however, is gradually becoming intolerable. The applause of the mob means more to him than the judgment of connoisseurs. His every thought and action seem directed at obtaining a fictitious "farewell." Is that any way for a born Wagner singer to behave?

Don Giovanni. Close your eyes, and those warm, sensuous tones conjure up the vision of Donna Anna's luxuriant beauty. It is as if one were wandering in orange groves, drinking in their enchanting fragrance and dreaming of fabulously beautiful women. A divinity speaks from those tones, emerging from the mortal frame of Frau Wilt. Capricious fate! Envious gods! Prudent caution, yes, prudent caution shall I call you who separated voice and appearance, as sharply contrasted as night and day. For if the two were merged harmoniously, Frau Wilt would have been the apple of discord of all nations, and a modern Iliad would surely have come to pass. Time has not been unkind to her voice [she was fifty-three]. Only the artificially induced showiness from time to time contests the brilliance of her voice, but ever and again the warm gold shines through in all its magic. Minute-long ovations. The singer was honored as she can hardly have been at the peak of her career. And she thoroughly earned it.

1.   A famous Viennese amusement park.
2.   Minna Walter (1863-1901), who became a full-fledged member of the company in 1887, and remained through the season of 1888-1889. She was the daughter of Gustav Walter, the tenor.

70. The Bruckner Quintet —
Sarasate

January 10, 1886

Anton Bruckner's Quintet [1] is one of those rare artistic phenomena blessed with the capacity to utter a profound secret in a simple, sensible way, in contrast to the usual procedure, much favored by our modern "masters," of clothing simple, everyday thoughts in the enigmatic utterances of oracles.

Bruckner's music flows full-bodied and rich from the clear fountain of a childlike spirit. One can say of any of his works: "It sounded so old, and was yet so new." [2] This is thanks to a strong, popular strain that emerges everywhere in his symphonic compositions, sometimes overtly, sometimes hidden. How charming, for example, is the Ländler-like trio of the Quintet! How well the composer, for all his earthiness, knows how to play the gentleman of distinction, sometimes by a harmonic deviation or a bit of ingenious counterpoint, by a more richly colored instrumentation or a surprising inversion of themes, etc.

Never is Bruckner commonplace or banal, a virtue he shares with Schubert. But neither do Bruckner's compositions ever seem to be contrived. His harmonies are bold and new, and they lend the melody an utterly characteristic finery, a definite physiognomy that impresses itself upon the listener's sensibility with adamantine incisiveness. His thematic invention is the product of an extraordinarily fertile fantasy and a glowing perceptiveness, hence the lucid imagery of his musical language. The sentence structure, however, seems too dependent upon rapid progress, well-ordered periods and a certain well-rounded formal equilibrium. One is reminded from time to time of Victor Hugo's lapidary style, whose short, detached sentences bear, in fact — formally, at least — some resemblance to Bruckner's musical sentence structure. Granted, one can elaborate a subject just as well, and just as exhaustively, in chopped-off sentences as in a long caravan of the best-ordered periods. Epigrammatic brevity of form can allow thoughts to emerge more powerfully, more plastically, but also more one-sidedly and often less clearly. Here, in any case, a happy medium is preferable to either extreme. That this composition, at its repetition, was greeted with still greater applause is no less a credit to the audience than to the composer.

The innovation of introducing vocal numbers between the individual chamber compositions will hardly earn the public's gratitude. Frau Amalie Joachim[3] sang songs of Brahms and Beethoven, of the latter, three Scottish songs [from Opus 108]. For the singing of Brahms's songs Frau Joachim's voice is eminently suited. Her singing was as cold and heavy as the compositions. For the Scottish songs she lacks utterly the hearty sound, especially for the last, "Das Bäschen in dem Strässchen" [The Gossip in the Alley]. Following the nightmare of Brahms's gravedigger songs, the effect of the Schumann Quintet [in E flat, Opus 44] was extraordinarily refreshing and enlivening. Frau Rappoldi-Kahrer[4] at the piano played her part with fastidious insight and warmth. Schubert's String Quintet in C [Opus 163] provided a worthy ending to this evening.

The famous fiddle virtuoso Sarasate[5] is to his instrument pretty much what Patti is to hers. He is, if one may say such a thing, a coloratura fiddler. His muted, sweet, insinuating tone assigns him to an area remote from the dramatic, from the forceful accents of passion. In his genre, however, he is probably unique. Trills, arpeggios, octaves and passages in thirds, in the highest and lowest positions — everything is played with fabulous security and elegance. In cantilena he is buoyant, noble, simple, and without any superfluous embellishment. A sensitive, highly admirable artist. Participating in the recital was Frau Wilt, who sang the ocean aria from *Oberon*, and unleashed, at its close, a truly deafening ovation. There was lively applause, too, for the excellent piano offerings of Frau Marx.[6]

That Herr Walter, next to such minstrels as Orpheus and Ibycus,[7] is the most famous Lieder singer in the city of Vienna and its environs will readily be conceded by everyone who atttends his recitals. How beautifully he sang on this occasion, with his gently veiled voice. It was a rare pleasure. If we cannot yet say of our modern Orpheus (for as such we must name him) that his song softens stones, but only that it drives men mad[8] -- from sheer delight, of course -- the blame rests solely with Herr Walter. Why does this bold singer not hazard, gratis, a recital in a quarry? It would be only an experiment. How much nitroglycerine might not the state be spared annually if Herr Walter's claim to fame was the ability to undermine highway-obstructing rocks with the sound of his voice! What could approach such a patriotic undertaking? And music! What honor to her! May the example of the heroes of antiquity yet kindle Herr Walter's courage to an eternal deed for the well-being of mankind and his own immortal fame!

1. The String Quintet in F, dating from 1879, Bruckner's sole venture into chamber music, first performed by the Hellmesberger Quartet, who also played it on this occasion, in 1881.

2. "Es klang so alt, und war doch so neu," as Hans Sachs, in the Act II "Flieder" monologue, remembers Walther's singing in his audition for the Meistersinger.

3. Amalie Joachim (1839-1898), wife of Joseph Joachim (1831-1907), the great violinist. Amalie Joachim (née Schneeweiss), a contralto, along with the baritone Julius Stockhausen (1826-1906), was a pioneer in bringing the German Lied into the public concert hall, just as her husband, with Brahms and Clara Schumann, was largely responsible for bringing chamber music out of the chamber. She and Joachim were divorced in 1884.

4. Laura Rappoldi-Kahrer (1853-1925), a highly regarded Viennese pianist whose teachers and sponsors had included Liszt, Henselt and Bülow. Her husband, Eduard Rappoldi (1831-1903), was one of the finest violinists and pedagogues of his generation, and was for a time second violin in the Joachim Quartet.

5. Pablo Sarasate (1844-1908), Spanish violinist, one of the great virtuosos of violin history and composer of the still widely popular "Zigeunerweisen."

6. Berthe Marx (1859- ?), a distinguished Paris-born pianist, long associated with Sarasate. She transcribed a number of his violin compositions for the piano.

7. A Greek poet of the sixth century B.C., and one of the "Nine Lyric Poets" chosen by Alexandrian critics as the best of ancient Greece.

8. See footnote to notice of June 1, 1884.

71. Oberon

January 17, 1886

Stage designers and theater engineers regarded this opera, when it was new, as their domain. It was up to their art to realize from without what could only be reached from within. Stage sets and machinery should take over from the poet. Much wit and ingenuity, accordingly, was brought into play by designers and engineers to help this opera to its feet. Fantasy was awesomely taxed when the most luxuriant splendor of the sets proved inadequate to the task. The wheels and cylinders of the stage machinery were greased and greased again in the hope that they might do their job more punctually, for one knew that upon their proper functioning the success of the opera depended. And in fact the engineers, in league with the designers, had something to show for their efforts. The trouble was that what they accomplished would have better served another work that needed them less. It was of little use to *Oberon*, and for the same reason that has frustrated, even in our enlightened and inventive century, the experiment of pumping life into a dead body with a bellows or giving to an automaton, despite all mechanical contrivance, the free self-sufficiency of a human body. Stage sets and machinery worked, but the whole thing did not work. The opera was a bore despite the lovely music.

Let the reader, if so inclined, imagine himself in a waxworks. Now watch. The wheels begin to turn, and the marionettes move. Imagine some beautiful music to accompany the spectacle. As long as the music plays, you will surely forget the deceit. You see it, of course, but it does not concern you. It suggests nothing, and that perfectly naturally because all your attention is held in the thrall of that which appeals most strongly to your sensibilities. The ear is now the only organ whose activity impinges upon your consciousness. Suddenly the music breaks off, and a harsh voice intones its abominable solo, identifying the characters being played by the marionettes in a common, vulgar manner. What pain! What a contrast! But that is how it is with *Oberon*. The characters in this opera are hardly more than marionettes. They represent the various types of voice: lyric, heroic or buffo tenor; soprano and mezzo-soprano. For the rest, the librettist trusted to the *deus ex machina* [a magic horn] that turns up in the nick of time, works its miracle and brings the story (?) to a happy end.

But despite the happy ending, and despite the beautiful sets, the opera had no popular success. The engineers gradually grew skeptical of the effectiveness of the wonders with which they had hoped to transfer one and all to a state of bliss, and the opera was bedded down in the archives as incurable, along with her similarly incurable sister, *Euryanthe*. In such a dire situation, a German conductor decided on one last rescue operation. He thought he had identified the fundamental affliction in the spoken dialogue, and had nothing more pressing to do than set it to music, hide and hair. Herr Wüllner,[1] composer of the recitatives for *Oberon*, in so doing forgot two things: first, the impropriety of such a procedure in a work whose musical effectiveness, aside from the substance of individual pieces, is to a large extent calculated against the time spaces filled by the spoken dialogue, and, secondly, the inadequacy of even a successful transformation in view of the utter vacuity of the poetic material. It would almost seem that Schumann's aphorism, namely, that a proper musician should be able to set a restaurant menu to music, had inspired Herr Wüllner to the composition of the unhappy *Oberon* recitatives. It would further seem to have escaped his attention that Schumann's utterance pertained to the uncommonly fruitful fantasy of Schubert,[2] compared to which,

Herr Wüllner's powers of imagination do not show up especially well. What garrulous, obtrusive, impertinent recitatives these are! And how they overgrow the frame. Weber's music can hardly get a word in edgewise. It is very difficult, to be sure, even impossible, to extract any lyrical implication from the common, everyday speech of this dialogue, as Herr Wüllner's recitatives purport to do. But who told Herr Wüllner to bring *Oberon* into further disrepute through well-intended improvements? And nothing annoys us more in these recitatives than the hypocritical attempt to create a daydream atmosphere by a so-called "characteristic" mask. Only *secco* recitatives would have been appropriate to the flatness of the dialogue. Even Herr Wüllner's talent might just have sufficed for that undertaking.

Herr Wüllner, in any case, presumed with his musical enrichment of Weber's score to have wholly cured it of its affliction. In fact, he only made matters worse. No one thus far, apparently, has thought of thoroughly revising the libretto, as obvious as is the need for such a revision. Well, as things stand we could warm to the music and be diverted by the sets. If only the characters of the opera will engage our attention, then the effect will be complete. Heretofore, it has been fragmentary because the opera as a whole lacked unity in multiplicity: the poetic idea. It was denied the poet to accomplish the ideal in the master's last work.

The performance left much to be desired, less on the part of the soloists than of the conductor and the chorus. Fräulein Schläger carried off the extraordinarily difficult role of Rezia well. Her voice is adequate, and mastered with apparent ease the vocal requirements, if not exactly leaving the listeners ecstatic by its inner warmth. New was Herr Schrödter as Scherasmin. The remarkable utility of this singer, particularly in comedy roles, has been noted previously. He is, along with the Messrs. Mayerhofer and Lay, the most useful and talented singer on our stage. The dragged tempi in the Allegro of the Overture and in several places in the first and second acts were absolutely painful. A Weber allegro cannot be taken at too fiery a tempo. More drive, more spirit! What we heard was enough to put one to sleep. I would like to know why it is that the opera chorus cannot manage a pianissimo. The introductory slumber motive of the first act would have awakened a deaf man, let alone so gentle a spirit as Oberon. "Die Quelle tönt, der Zephyr stöhnt zu laut" [The fountain sings, the zephyr groans too loudly], and the elves who sing those lines roar like ten thousand hurricanes. It was no different with the closing chorus of the second act, whose strain can descend to the commonplace if it is not sung with the ultimate delicacy and tenderness. The scene with the mermaid was evocatively arranged. The picturesque setting, encompassed by an enchanting melody, could not but have gained much if someone could only have seen to it that the song of the mermaids reached the auditorium as if born on the breath of the wind from a great distance. A pertinent thought that might also be obvious to our stage directors if it were only a bit less obvious.

A delightful variant on Senta's final verses recently provided me with no little amusement at the last performance of *The Flying Dutchman*. As everyone knows, Senta plunges silently into the sea after the words: "Preis' deinen Engel und sein Gebot! Hier steh' ich, treu dir bis zum Tod!" [Treasure your angel and his command, I remain true to you until death!] Now, Fräulein Klein felt called upon to develop this scene in a more piquant manner. She let the last word, "Tod," fall into the sea, and then followed it in, first having startled the unsuspecting listeners from their accustomed repose with a ghastly shriek. Fräulein Klein probably wished to indicate by this shriek that Senta had suffered a sudden attack of hydrophobia. This conception is, at least, original, although I cannot suppress some mild doubt as to its propriety. Herr Reichman, on the other hand (his was an especially beautiful performance as the Dutchman) was content with more harmless emendations. He prefers the more conventionally operatic *Allmächtigen* [Almighty] to *Allewiger* [eternal] and happily confuses "Ach!" with "O!" and "O!" with "Ach!" Herr Reichmann, however, is a leading baritone, and leading baritones are great men, and great men do not concern themselves with trifles. Oh, would that I were a leading baritone!

1. Franz Wüllner (1832-1902), German pianist and conductor. He conducted the premieres of *Das Rheingold* and *Die Walküre* in Munich in 1869 and 1870. He supplied the recitatives for a new German version of *Oberon*, first produced in Vienna in 1881.

2. The reference is to an aphorism not by Schumann, but by Georg Philipp Telemann (1681-1767), cited by Schumann in a discussion, in his *Neue Zeitschrift für Musik*, of Schubert's last works: "And if Telemann demands that a true composer should be able to set to music a placard [Torzettel], then he would have found his man in Schubert." (Vol. 8, p. 177 [1838].

72. Brahms's Symphony No. 4[1]

January 24, 1886

A lucky thing for the famous sculptor Thorvaldsen that his good genie gave him the happy notion of sculpting a scene from the life of Alexander the Great.[2] The prospects for this artist's enduring celebrity might otherwise not have been bright. But now that he has had the unearned distinction of having inspired the famous Kopi,[3] i.e., the composer Johannes Brahms, to write a new symphony, he is assured of immortality for all eternity.

Unfortunately, no information has been forthcoming from reliable sources as to what kind of sculptures may have imposed upon Herr Brahms the awesome obligation of writing three symphonies. If we were to indulge in idle speculation, inclining greatly to the assumption that Friedländer's old disabled veterans[4] constitute an essential element of those symphonies — at least as far as freshness of invention and variety of expression are concerned — one might see in it no more than an honest endeavor to get on the track of those providential external influences and impressions which, in Schumann's opinion, are not to be despised.[5] The fact remains, if we are to give credence to Kalbeck's assurances, that the immediate cause of the first suspicious symptoms of that cold artistic fever that has so troubled Herr Brahms for some fifteen or twenty years, and to which, as with his previous three symphonies, a fourth has now fallen victim, was the chance impression made upon him by Thorvaldsen's "Alexander."[6]

The Fourth Symphony, in E minor -- "But stop! Already the choice of tonality belongs to the distinguishing characteristics; for, curiously, neither Mozart, Beethoven or Schubert, nor even Mendelssohn or Schumann, ever wrote a symphony in E minor."[7] Now in the name of the garden spider, that's a colossal discovery! What an original, profound artist Herr Brahms must be when he can compose symphonies not only in C, D and F, as Beethoven could, but even, unprecedentedly, in E minor! Heavens! I begin to stand in awe of Herr Brahms's uncanny genius. Ben Akiba's notorious pronouncement that there's nothing new under the sun[8] must now be regarded as an old wives' tale, and merit no more than a compassionate smile. But what an accumulation of wisdom is not required for such a discovery!

When Richard Wagner, discussing Beethoven's Ninth, expressed doubt about the development of new art forms in the symphonic field, it was Franz Liszt's works that relieved his anxiety. But it never occurred to him that something strikingly new could emerge, anchored in the traditional form, simply through the clever choice of tonality. Yes, indeed, there's nothing new under the sun; only a symphony in E minor. It is to Herr Hanslick's undying credit to have called attention to this fact with appropriate emphasis. Ben Akiba's awesome assertion, so discomfiting and discouraging to all who would be original, is suddenly gone without a trace, as if it had been only a breath of air. A new field is now opened to all modern composers, and a grateful field, too, the cultivation of which requires nothing more than the denial of all those disciplines without which, unfortunately, not even a Beethoven could write a symphony. Equipped with a good nose for tonalities not previously employed by major composers in their symphonies -- what further need for the melody of graphic representation and similar nonsense? Whoever now, and in the future, writes symphonies in the tonalities of A flat minor, E flat minor, F sharp minor, C sharp minor and B flat minor, which those fine masters forgot to exploit in their symphonies, will not have to wait for his hair to grow long before knowing whether he is original or not. He is, even if he remains a baldpate for the rest of his days. But to leave nothing to chance, try the following tonalities: B sharp major, A sharp minor, C flat minor. Even C flat major is not to be despised. But if some genius of the future wants to pile Pelion on Ossa and storm Olympus, he would be well advised to turn to more complex tonalties such as E double flat minor, G double sharp major and the like. Since Herr Hanslick is, as everyone knows, a very objective critic, as amply demonstrated on the one hand by his reviews of Richard Wagner, and on the other hand by his reviews of Brahms, he will have no choice but to remark the extraordinary in this procedure with increasing emphasis and seriousness, the more emphatically and the more seriously in the same degree that the tonality of E sharp minor is more complicated than E minor, and F double sharp major more complicated than E sharp minor, and so on.

Conspicuous is the crab-like progress in Brahms's output. It has, to be sure, never reached beyond the level of mediocrity, but such nothingness, emptiness and hypocrisy as prevails throughout the E minor symphony has not appeared in any previous work of Brahms in so alarming a manner. The art of composing without ideas has decidedly found in Brahms its worthiest representative. Just like the good Lord, Herr Brahms is a master at making something from nothing. (This opinion is shared even by Herr Klabeck -- ah, pardon! Herr Klobeck, I mean Herr Kalbek. Anyway, why should I not be permitted a typographical slip? After all, Herr Hanslick "first" started it with his "austere frost." [9]

In this sense, at least, one may call Brahms's art divine. Certainly it is not human, unless one chooses to recognize in the composer's musical impotence, and in his vain struggle against it, a trace of human weakness, and sense therein, perhaps, some human feeling. In truth, all four of Brahms's symphonies speak the language of mute despair. Therein, too, may lie the cause of the ghastly monotony in the last larger works of this composer. Herr Brahms attempts, indeed, to bring life to his symphonies by contrasts. He is not very successful at it, unfortunately, for to the fundamental tone of these symphonies, deriving from "can't do," he can offer only "wish I could" as a contrast, which comes to the same thing. But to let the dead-tired fantasy run the gauntlet between "can't do" and "wish I could" through four movements is, in the end, no joke. Nor does the audience have much to improve its spirits, what with little crumbs of melody, limping rhythms and arid harmonies, the sum total of Brahms's riches. How easily, however, might both be assisted if Herr Brahms could bring himself to have done with his self-laceration. Enough of this awful business. May Herr Brahms be content to have found in his E minor symphony not only a tonality in which, heretofore, tolerable fare was produced only in smaller forms, but also the language giving most eloquent expression to his despondency: the language of the most intensive musical impotence.

The Lieder recital by our greatly beloved Court Opera singer, Frau Rosa Papier, achieved a resounding success. The singer was rewarded for her exemplary accomplishments in the most flattering manner by the large audience.

1.   Wolf is reviewing the first Vienna performance, by the Philharmonic under Hans Richter, on January 17. The world premiere, by the Meiningen Orchestra, had taken place the preceding October 25, with Brahms conducting.

2.   Bertil Thorvaldsen (1768-1844), Danish neo-classical sculptor, known as the Scandinavian Michelangelo. The work referred to by Wolf is a 30-foot frieze, "The Entry of Alexander the Great into Babylon," commissioned for a wall in the Quirinal Palace in Rome.

3. Apparently a word play on Kopist (copiest) and Komponist (composer). In Wolf's view, Brahms's symphonies were modeled on the classics of European music just as Thorvaldsen's sculptures were modelled on the Greeks and their Roman copiests.

4. Friederich Friedländer (1825-1901), a minor Viennese painter whose best known work is "Invalides à la Cantine" in the Vienna Art Museum.

5. As elaborated by Schumann in his review of Berlioz's Symphonie Fantastique, previously cited by Wolf (see footnote to notice of April 5, 1885).

6. In his monumental *Johannes Brahms*, published in eight volumes between 1904 and 1914, Kalbeck has Brahms protesting strongly against this supposition.

7. Wolf is quoting from Hanslick's review in the *Neue Freie Presse* of January 19.

8. Joseph Ben Akiba (40-135), the greatest biblical scholar of his time, often called "the father of Rabbinical Judaism." He was a pioneer in the collection, collation and ordering of Judaic oral tradition. The insight attributed to him by Wolf did not originate with Akiba, although Akiba may have been responsible for its preservation and dissemination in Ecclesiastes 1:9.

9. Wolf is having malicious fun at the expense of both Hanslick and Kalbeck. In his review, Hanslick had been the victim of a typographical error. What he wrote, defining or identifying the fundamental characteristics of Brahms's larger works, was: "männliche Kraft, unbeugsame Consequenz, ein ans Herbe streifende Ernst" [masculine strength, unbending consistency, a seriousness bordering on austerity]. In the paper, however, *Ernst* [seriousness] appeared as *Frost* [frost]. The error was corrected in Hanslick's *Collected Works*. Wolf continues his word play by substituting "erst" (with the quotation marks) for "Ernst." The German reads: "Hat doch Herr Hanslick mit dem 'herben Frost' es 'erst' gemeint."

73. Der Trompeter von Säkkingen[1]

January 31, 1886

Opera in three acts, with a prologue, by V. Nessler.

The libretto is fashioned with reasonable fidelity upon the Scheffel[2] original i.e., the cast of characters is about the same, although what transpires among them is rather different. In order to set up an effective (?) ending, the librettist has seen fit to deviate somewhat from the Scheffel poem. This involves not so much the rechristening of Margareta as Maria, the daughter of the Baron, but rather the introduction of two persons of whom Scheffel's poem makes no mention. These are the soldier, Konradin, and the divorced wife of Count Wildenstein. To the first falls the task of giving Werner's career a bad turn by provoking a fight that leads to Werner's banishment. The job of the Countess is to see to a "satisfactory" conclusion. Let's have a closer look at this lady, and eavesdrop upon her at work.

A sister-in-law of the Baron, Countess Wildenstein is Maria's aunt [*Base*].

Every aunt, if only for the sake of the rhyme, has a nose [*Nase*], for what opera librettist could resist the temptation and speak of *Base* without some slighting reference to her *Nase*? That is indispensable in writing opera librettos. Very well, then. Maria's *Nase*, too, is severly criticized by Countess Wildenstein. That her *Nase* is introduced in the diminutive (*Näschen*) simply makes it (figuratively) that much bigger. Now, when the Countess advises Maria to keep her nose out of such things, kissing for example, we, in turn, would have preferred that she make better use of her own nose in matters no less important to her than Werner's kisses to Maria. We might then be spared the silly farce based on that old, worn-out wheezy device beloved by all librettists concerned for a happy or unhappy ending: the child stolen by gypsies and, usually, happily restored. Just think of it. Werner, a count's son stolen by gypsies, Werner the Kapellmeister and, finally, Werner promoted to Marchese of Camposanto through the benevolent intervention of the pope!

Anyway, Werner, as we have indicated, has been stolen by gypsies, and has grown up among them. The Countess Wildenstein knows all about that. But she also knows more. She knows that her own son was stolen by gypsies, and she finds in Werner's features a remarkable resemblance to her own. That the trumpeter's age, too, is exactly the same as her own child's, astonishes her. But it never remotely enters her mind to look into Werner's background and personal history. For "my son would be just as old, and of just such fine figure had he not, as a child, been stolen from us by those wild hordes." That's nice logical thinking for you! A stolen child — is it out of the question that he might reappear? Has anyone sent the good Countess a death certificate? We know from the ending that this could not have been the case, because eventually she recognizes in Werner her long lost son. That in the first and second acts she plots against Werner is still no proof that her child must be dead. Why, then, does the Countess fail to hearken to the voice of her heart? Because Werner is a peasant, and not of noble birth. How's that? Mother love would have perished instantly in the face of Werner's lowly station? She would not have dared to recognize her son in the uniform of a common soldier? Her humanity would have involuntarily revolted against such a thing? May we be spared such nonsense.

— The business about the mole is pretty childish, too. It had to be left to chance to bring about the recognition scene between the Countess and Werner. The latter had to be wounded before the Countess could be reminded that her stolen child had been distinguished by nature with a mole. Indeed, she has even spoken about that in the first act when Werner met her for the first time. How much more logically things would have gone had the Countess simply walked up to Werner and asked him if he had a mole on his right arm. The plot, in case the answer was affirmative, would have come to an end two acts sooner. But were that, too, not to be regarded as a fortunate happenstance?

Indeed! One would have done better to make one huge cut from the first note of the first act to the last note of the third. What we have, in fact, is a number of motley scenes without inner cohesion, extracted arbitrarily from the Scheffel epic, individuals without character and situations without substance. As compensation we are offered processions and battles, cannon fire and church bells, soldiers' songs, farewell songs and welcome songs, but no lullabies. There are no drinking songs, either, but there is an aria about gout, and then peasant dances, mocking choruses and a splendid ballet. The naive listener misses only two things: plot and music. Each must limit itself to utterly external considerations if they are to be noticed at all, the first to the occasional change of scene while the dramatic progress remains unchanged, the latter to noisy instrumentation of the most vulgar sort in the absence of any trace of melodic invention. It moves along melodiously, to be sure, and makes a show of conciseness and plasticity. Love's labor lost! One can no more make original melodies out of antiquated phrases than make a new gown out of old rags. Every melodic figure betrays its threadbare condition. Every melody is stillborn. A decent burial – that is all that *Der Trompeter von Säkkingen* may expect.

Among the cast (I speak of the second dress rehearsal), Herr Mayerhofer (Baron) came off best. His humor is well suited to catch the dryness and woodenness of the role, and he succeeded as far as humanly possible. Frau von Naday (Maria) and Herr Sommer (Werner), however, outdid themselves in histrionic incompetence and vocal inadequacy, insofar as beautiful singing is concerned. Herr Stoll was quite a comical Damian. Fräulein Meisslinger played the Countess Wildenstein with much dignity and great energy, Herr Hablawetz the Count with military bearing. The suitor Konradin, as played by Herr Horwitz was not wanting in joviality. The character might profit from greater virility. About the ballet we shall write in the next number.

1. *Der Trompeter von Säkkingen*, by Viktor Nessler (1841-1890), an Alsatian composer who spent most of his professional life in Leipzig. He wrote many operas and operettas, of which only *Der Trompeter von Säkkingen* won an enduring place in the repertoire. It was first performed in Leipzig on May 4, 1884.

2. Josef Victor von Scheffel (1826-1886), now remembered only for *Der Trompeter von Säkkingen*, an epic poem written in 1854.

74. A Tenor Messiah

February 7, 1886

Emil Götze,[1] the famous tenor from the Municipal Theater in Cologne, has become the overnight idol [*Götze*] of the Vienna public. For some time, now, we have heard mysterious rumors about the emergence of a fabulous tenor. Such a one has been craved as manna by the people in the desert. One has had dreams and visions in broad daylight of the future tenor messiah -- but has contented oneself, before resorting to idolatrous violence, with entrusting the result of these visionary habits to the small lottery. The belief in a tenor wonder was especially concentrated in the Coachmen's Guild, from which, as we all know, many a forerunner of the longed-for tenor savior has emerged. Now, however, he seems finally to have arrived, the long anticipated, the passionately yearned for -- not from the House of David, to be sure, nor from the heights of the coachman's box -- but then should the tiresome coachman superstition endure forever? We believe, indeed, that the newly discovered tenor is the man to put an end to it for all time.

Herr Götze, who, after the cathedral, is the only notable rarity in Cologne -- since bad music, as it was cultivated there by the late Ferdinand Hiller,[2] is nurtured with the same solemnity and industry in other localities -- aroused the curiosity of our public in no small degree. The sold-out house was proof enough of that. One was in a fever of anticipation to make the acquaintance of a singer whose fame has already spread well beyond the borders of Germany. Nor did one have long to wait. One fine day the theater bulletin announced: *Martha*, by Flotow: Lionel -- Herr Emil Götze, of the Municipal Theater in Cologne. The great moment had come, all yearning was stilled, all curiosity satisfied. And the best of it was: every expectation was surpassed.

A distinguished presence, with a touch of embonpoint, youthful, virile in bearing, bright-eyed, free and natural in his movements, Herr Götze won every heart just by the way he looked. Nor was it long before the listener was surprised by a high B flat, incomparable in its tonal splendor, brilliance and warmth. Herr Götze is certainly anything but a crooner. His full-throated voice is without subtlety. Those many nuances between *pp* and *ff* that enliven singing, and make many a listener assume more voice than is there, were not evident to us in Herr Götze's singing. There was not even a true *mezza voce*. He sings either in falsetto or in full chest tone. The latter sounds better, and about that Herr Götze himself is in no doubt. One notes this in his modest use of head voice. If his singing is, nevertheless, irresistible, it is thanks to the inner warmth, the immediacy of expression, and to a certain simplicity in the phrasing that enable him to make good the shortcomings enumerated above. Correct and distinct enunciation is not the least of his attributes. The impression made upon the expectant audience by the guest's achievements bordered on the magical. Applause, both during the performance and at the close of every act, was unending.

Fräulein Bianchi was as distinguished a Lady [Harriet] as she was a charming Martha. Just as it is given to a chosen few to lend, through the enchantment of personality, a special fascination to the most commonplace occurrences, so is it given to Fräulein Bianchi, as a true artist, to ennoble the trivial, to transfigure the base, and to render the repulsive beautiful. What dull, sugary melodies engulf every line of the libretto of *Martha*! We would perish miserably in the swelling flood of this fresh water were it not that Fraülein Bianchi's restrained and tasteful singing, from time to time, turns the tide, absorbing all the hyper-emotional, tear-drenched sentiment of this abominable score.

Perfectly in their element were Frau Papier (Nancy) and Herr von Reichenberg (Plunkett). But what a wooden knight was Herr Felix! This kind of
humor could freeze the marrow of one's bones. Lord Tristan is a good role for
Herr Mayerhofer.

1. Emil Götze (1856-1901), a German tenor who enjoyed a great success first in Dresden (1878-
    1881), then in Cologne, whence he travelled as guest artist to all the more important German
    opera houses. Shortly after this Vienna engagement, a throat ailment imposed a long
    interruption in his career.

2. Ferdinand Hiller (1811-1885), German pianist, composer, pedagogue and author, was a
    pupil and protégé of Johann Nepomuk Hummel, an intimate during a long residence in Paris
    (1828-1835) of Cherubini, Rossini, Chopin, Liszt, Meyerbeer and Berlioz and later, in
    Dresden and Leipzig, of Spohr, Mendelssohn and the Schumanns. In 1850 he founded the
    Conservatory in Cologne, remaining its director until his death. Schumann's Piano Con-
    certo is dedicated to him.

75. Götze as Lohengrin and Faust

February 14, 1886

The favorable impression Herr Götze made upon us in *Martha* has not been
reinforced by a more intimate acquaintanceship with the Rhenish artist. He
has, certainly, a brilliant vocal endowment, cultivated with equal strength in
all areas of its range, but, unfortunately, only athletically. With *piano, mezzo
forte* and the entire gamut of expressive song he is on as hostile a footing as
many a "Germanist" upstart with the use of the cases in grammar.

Herr Götze seemed to us, upon his appearance [as Lohengrin], probably as
a result of too severe supervision on the part of his manager, to be in such an
irritated mood that he sang his farewell to the swan for the throng on the
banks of the Scheldt in a gruff voice. I feared for the poor creature. After this
grim farewell he introduced himself to Elsa not as the celestial knight to whom
we are accustomed, but rather like a gendarme dispatched by the grail to
attend to public law and order in Antwerp. We wish to note immediately that
our mysterious Lohengrin, at every last quarter note of his farewell, gesticu-
lated a downbeat in contradiction of the upbeat of the conductor. This
embarrassing conducting by the knight of the grail recalled Herr von Bülow's
extemporization in Berlin when from the podium he begged a lady in the first
row that, if she must use her fan, she do so in time with the music.

Herr Götze sang the now popular "Never must you question me" so rudely that an intimidated Elsa/Lehmann, from this moment on, sang the whole opera consistently a semitone flat. Herr Rokitansky, too, withdrew into his stiff collar, and decided forthwith to have nothing further to do with acting. And, indeed, why act King Henry? The audience knows him well. That is the standpoint of singers who combine incompetence with intellectual indolence, the most dangerous enemy of all art.

And the finale of the first act! Oh, oh! But Herr Götze sings above the tumult and goes off as the victorious hero. The audience is content, and applauds, but Wagner's muse veils her face, and weeps bitter tears. Never have I heard the orchestra sound so brutal, both in ensemble and in detail. But no one notices, no one complains. The public's critical faculties can only decline when art is continually maltreated, and it loses all sense of the beautiful.

In Gounod's *Faust*, that "Gallic whispered endearment," as Herr Hanslick used to put it in his droll way,[1] we noted in Herr Götze, more even than in *Lohengrin*, the want of vocal artistry. And if Herr Kalbeck claims that Hanslick's pen draws its ink from the urn of Uranus, we cannot, even at the risk of offending Herr Dömpke,[2] agree with the characterization of *Faust* as "Gallic whispered endearments." In any case, we are concerned with Herr Götze, who gave his Faust so indignant and defiant a tone as to suggest a determination to stop at nothing, not even, for example, at singing Hanslick's songs from his golden-curled youth to Herr Dömpke without interruption to the end of his days.[3]

But our task is to speak of Herr Götze. In a word, he "trumpeted" Faust. May we be forgiven the adoption of this stylistic blossom that, as the saying goes, insinuates its fragrance into my pen. Its recent gallant employment does it all honor. I prefer, nevertheless, to restore it to the gardener. May he put it in his buttonhole. Besides, to return to Herr Götze, Herr Dömpke, leaving the concert hall in the company of others a few days ago, said: "Tell me with whom you consort, and I will tell you who you are." How right he was! Thus, too, Herr Götze, idolized by the aristocracy of Cologne, the nervous vibration of his soul, only exceptionally sensed that contact between singer and listener. (A notable exception, however, was the art and manner in which Herr Götze conceived and executed the role of Walther von Stolzing in *Die Meistersinger*, an observation that would make us infinitely happier if it did not apply to an exception.)

We can regard an all too healthy, robust female with pleasure, but that does not mean that we love her or would give our life for her. The sum of our impressions remains, then, that nature has endowed Herr Götze with abundant resources, but that art has usually been only a platonic spouse. To conclude, as Herr Kalbeck says, with our excellent and always usable Herr Horwitz, be it further noted that Herr Sommer sang the Valentine.

1.   "Gallisches Liebesgeflüster." If Hanslick ever so described Gounod's *Faust* in writing, there
    is no suggestion of it in the several lengthy and, on the whole, sympathetic discussions of
    Faust and others of Gounod's operas as they appear in Hanslick's *Collected Works*.

2. Gustav Dömpke (1851-1923), an East Prussian critic who, thanks to Hanslick's urging and sponsorship, had come to Vienna in 1879 as critic of the *Allgemeine Zeitung*. He was a great admirer of Brahms (and Hanslick), and an outspoken anti-Wagnerian. He returned to Königsberg in 1887 to become music critic of the *Hartungsche Zeitung*, in which position he distinguished himself as a propagandist for Bach and Brahms.

3. As a student of Johann Wenzel Tomaschek (1774-1850) in piano, theory and composition (in his native Prague), Hanslick had composed a number of small piano pieces and songs. From the latter, some thirty years later, and with the assistance of Brahms, he selected a group of "the relatively most successful," and had them published (by Simrock) in a volume titled "Lieder aus der Jugendzeit" [Songs from the Time of Youth]. The title was made a condition for his blessing of the project by Brahms in order, as Hanslick explained in his autobiography, *Aus Meinem Leben*, "to account, to some extent, for the now old-fashioned simplicity of the melodies."

76. Alfred Grünfeld

[Undated]

The recital given by Alfred Grünfeld, brother of the well known impresario [Ludwig], came off brilliantly, as it does annually. One rejoices with him in noting that his pianistic activity is accorded the recognition it deserves. To repeat that his technic has reached the ultimate would be carrying coals to Newcastle.[1]

Grünfeld is, in the better sense of the term, a darling of the public. He is no unprincipled libertine, no compiler of fashionable esthetic trends whose socially and technically developed culture extends to the choice of his tailor. How I detest the traveling salesmen of music, those international gigolos who turn up here today, there tomorrow, knowing a bit of every language, and truly so well equipped that in newspaper offices -- those cornerstones of world history -- they can accompany their obeisance with an appropriately elegant turn of phrase. What disturbs me, however, is the instant recognition of Grünfeld by Hans von Bülow, that immortality-seeking clown convulsively clambering up and down the ladder of fame. If Bülow, that surly constable of the artistic turnpike, suddenly sings Grünfeld's prize song, it may be assumed that he did so only in order, cost what it might, to get somebody else's goat. Bülow remains the pure musical hedgehog. Quills perpetually raised, he thinks the entire world must inevitably prick itself on them. But that is not the way it is. Blood flows only from those who tap them fearfully. Grünfeld tapped them forthrightly and cheerfully, and the tiny hedgehog duly released a little manifesto which, settling on the editor's desk in the guise of a dove of peace, cooed sympathetically in Herr Grünfeld's direction.[2]

Let's have a look at Grünfeld's program. A rather mixed bag! Schubert and

Moszkowski,[3] Bach and Grünfeld, Beethoven and Brahms. We applaud this kaleidoscopic benevolence, by which every listener takes home a morsel of satisfaction and -- whether through Moszkowski or through Brahms or through Grünfeld -- feels the harmonic or unharmonic side of his heart vibrate. There is no accounting for taste. The music critic of some Allgemeine Zeitung or other said to me not long ago that when he hears Brüll's *Goldenes Kreuz* [*Cross of Gold*] he feels a delightful tickling in his blood -- odd enthusiast! And I once knew a famous musical esthete who was a confirmed cheese hater and yet relished the music of Brahms. Another, a writer on music, could listen with pleasure only to those composers who set his poems to music. Ah, narcissism! But love is, indeed, blind. Sometimes it is taciturn, too, as, curiously, a well-to-do contemporary discovered, quoting Shakespeare freely. "Love and be silent,"[4] he wrote in a critical concert review of his love's dawning. Most remarkable!

But to return to Grünfeld, for the vagaries of taste have led us too far afield, we were especially delighted with the interpretation of Robert Fuchs's Praeludium. What a splendid piece of music! What healthy, fresh and invigorating strength! A blue Italian sky smiles, too, over Moszkowski's Barcarolle No. 1, and even more so in the following Barcarolles which Grünfeld passed over -- how we missed them! The impression made by Fuchs's Praeludium, on the other hand, was complete, despite the omission of the fugue. In Moszkowski's Barcarolle we find that amiable touch of flirtatiousness that doubtless characterizes the other Barcarolles in even greater degree. Robert Fuchs's Praeludium is, in D major, if we are not mistaken, a beautiful and secure tonality unlikely to prompt us to the stale joke, "E minor and never again"[5] (a Leipzig connoisseur muttered it into his socialist beard after hearing Brahms's Symphony No. 4).

Let us conclude with our sincere acknowledgment of Grünfeld's artistry. That he denied us the further Barcarolles of Moszkowski would be the only thing we might venture to hold against this greatly beloved pianist. May he find absolution for this miniature sin of omission in his next concert.

1. "Eulen nach Tarnopol tragen" in Wolf's text, a curious variant, for which Wolf offers no clue, to the German idiom, "Eulen nach Athen tragen" (carry owls to Athens).

2. Wolf is referring to a letter written by Bülow to the editor of the *Allgemeine Musik-Zeitung* (Charlottenburg) under the heading: "Un po' più di giustizia" (a little more justice), protesting an unfavorable notice given by the journal's St. Petersburg correspondent, who had found it presumptuous of a "salon pianist" to concern himself with Bach, Mendelssohn, Schumann, etc. Grünfeld had given two recitals in St. Petersburg, and Bülow had attended both. Bülow, who had just met Grünfeld for the first time in St. Petersburg, closed his letter by begging the editor to "grant citizenship to Grünfeld among the pianists worthy of being taken seriously despite the fact that his playing is not at all boring."

3. Moritz Moszkowski (1854-1925), Polish pianist, composer and conductor, now remembered mainly for his salon pieces.

4. *Twelfth Night*: "She never told her love," etc.

5. A pun derived from the almost identical sound of "E moll" (E minor) and "einmal" (one time, or once) as elided in Saxon and other German dialects.

77. The Wagner Society

March 14, 1886

One must credit the Vienna Academic Wagner Society with knowing how to make programs. Grown to maturity in an evolutionary phase whose significance remains to this day, understandably enough, a mystery to our distinguished music critics, this wholly contemporary artistic society has already achieved among the better element of the public a popularity that, as the last big concert demonstrated, places at least the visible success of its endeavors beyond question.

A concert of so serious a nature as that here under discussion, given during the carnival season, without subscription support, a concert that could justify its rather sudden scheduling with the credentials neither of the Philharmonic Society nor of the Society of Friends of Music, looked at askance by our distinguished music critics, heard by them with deaf ears and reviewed by them with distorted understanding -- that such a concert would attract a numerous, attentive and enthusiastic audience incomparably different from the shady mob at our subscription concerts, is a significant indicator to be noted in happy astonishment by all ordinary, extraordinary and disorderly (to whom I belong) members of the Academic Wagner Society, namely, to emerge more often than heretofore from the narrow confines of the "private soirées," and put on concerts in the grand manner. Why forever address the congregation in the catacombs of the Kleiner Musikvereinssaal? That congregation is adequately resistant to bad music, beef and modern liberalism.

To make the policy of its master the property of all is the present task of the Wagner Society. This policy has as its goal, as we all know, the maintenance and activation of the Festspielhaus in Bayreuth. One has gone further, recently by giving concerts whose proceeds go toward covering the cost of travel to Bayreuth and admission to the Festspielhaus for indigent musicians and other impecunious enthusiasts of the Wagnerian art. Until recently, however, such concerts could be attended by only a small number of Wagner devotees. This was much to be regretted, since, as I have said, the Wagner Society exhibits immeasurably greater artistic discretion in the composition of its programs than any other of our capital's musical institutions.

When, at last, it became necessary to exchange the Bösendorfersaal for the Kleiner Saal of the Society of Friends of Music, it became apparent all too soon that this operation, also, was a smokescreen. The Bösendorfersaal would still have sufficed for the "private soirées." The urge for larger quarters was purely superficial. The Society had far more substantial matters in mind. The "private soirées" had already lost their private character, and were hardly distinguishable from public concerts. One found oneself forced, involuntarily, into a gratifying position without being quite consciously aware of it. The memorial concert in the Grosser Musikvereinssaal following Wagner's death was an example, as was the most recent big concert.

Must the Wagner Society, then, always await the opportunity of this or that pretext to put on a concert? Do artistic events such as the large orchestra concerts of the Wagner Society require an excuse or a justification? And if, in the future, this excellent society intended to give four big orchestral or choral concerts instead of the "private soirées," or in addition to them, what would it be risking? At most the jolly yelping of some music critics. And what does that matter? Whoever has an ounce of sense is certainly bright enough not to sacrifice it to the opinion of a critic.

We were recently able to determine that Vienna's musical public is not so corrupt as intimate acquaintanceship with the Philharmonic and opera audiences tempts one to assume. The audience at the concert of the Wagner Society displayed an attentiveness, an understanding and an enthusiasm such as one is accustomed to observe only in certain individuals. An audience concerned only with music, eager to let music refresh heart and spirit, indifferent to whether or not a concert by the Wagner Society is fashionable -- such an audience, surely, will welcome most eagerly every future concert of the Wagner Society. There should be no want of attendance for the projected undertaking, and since money, as we all know, is a powerful charm, there should be no difficulty in assembling a good orchestra. But of this, more at another time --

The program was devoted exclusively to works of Richard Wagner. The stately Kaisermarsch, whose triumphant strains got the proceedings under way, was followed by the Prelude to *Götterdämmerung*, with Frau Wilt and Herr Winkelmann assisting. Frau Wilt did not entirely satisfy our high expectations. Her performance, correct enough musically, was too lacking in dramatic fervor. Thus, many a significant passage went by the board, although fluently dispatched from a purely musical point of view. Frau Wilt has heretofore kept herself too aloof from Wagnerian roles, and it is not surprising therefore if, in this unfamiliar terrain, she stumbled more than one would have wished.

The performance of the Grail Scene from the first act of *Parsifal* was perfect on the part of both soloists (Reichenberg and Winkelmann) and chorus and orchestra. With this the concert might well have ended. But the final scene from *Götterdämmerung* was still to come, beginning before Brünnhilde's entry. Of Frau Wilt's accomplishment I can only repeat what I have just said. It was the orchestra under Hans Richter that provided the high point of the evening. Never, for us, has the final scene of *Götterdämmerung* unrolled so plastically as in this most recent orchestral achievement. The effect was at once crushing and exalting.

78. The Damnation of Faust

March 21, 1886

Dramatic Legend in Four Parts by Hector Berlioz.

Among the multifarious musical compositions inspired by *Faust*, Berlioz's *The Damnation of Faust*, along with Wagner's *Faust* Overture and Liszt's *Faust* Symphony, must indisputably be awarded pride of place. Granted, Berlioz failed to achieve an organic work of art, congruent in terms of form and substance, such as the two compositions of Wagner and Liszt. His *Faust* is a fragmentary mosaic, a haphazard structure replete with the most beautiful details, but without a clearly conscious aim. The Faust idea, in its purely human features an inexhaustible source of artistic inspiration, is dissolved with Berlioz in an idle play of capricious fantasies, admittedly ingenious and admirable in themselves, but destructive of the unity of poetic intention, and inhibiting any full enjoyment of the totality of the work. This criticism can be made of Schumann's *Faust*, too. Inner incoherence is common to both, and if Schumann's *Faust* adheres with greater sensibility to the Goethe model, Berlioz's work surpasses it in musical substance. However one may feel about Berlioz's approach to the Faust idea, one thing is certain: almost every number in this work excites our most fervent admiration. Let us examine this remarkable opus more closely.

The Introduction places Faust -- oddly enough -- in a Hungarian plain. Justifying this curiosity in a preface to *The Damnation of Faust*, Berlioz says: "Why, some may ask, does the composer have his hero wandering through Hungary in the first part? Very simply because he wanted to introduce a piece of music based on a Magyar theme. He confesses it with utter candor. He would have taken his hero anywhere, and have given the matter not another thought if prompted to do so by the slightest musical motif. Did not Goethe himself, in the second part of his *Faust*, take him to Menelaus's palace in Sparta?"

Well, the reference to Goethe's "arbitrary" procedure is truly naive. Berlioz obviously lacks a proper understanding of the profound symbolism of the classic Walpurgis Night and the bond of love between Faust and Helen. Nor does Berlioz's frank admission of willingness to transport his hero anywhere for the sake of a musical motif speak well for his dramatic intentions in dealing with *Faust*.[1] The concept of a *symphonie descriptive*, in any case, occupied him more intensively than that of a "grand opera," just as the *légende dramatique*, despite its outward appearance, is closer to the *symphonie de-*

scriptive than to an opera. But to return to the work's musical aspects --

A marvelously atmospheric instrumental movement (Introduction) evokes the mysterious surge and flow of reawakening nature: "Rivers and creeks are freed from ice by spring's pure, animating glance."[2] -- Fragments of the Hungarian ["Rakoczy"] march and the peasant dance flash through the delicate fabric of the orchestral hymn to spring. Soon we hear the hearty strain of the peasant song, "The Shepherd Primped for the Dance,"[3] a piece full of vitality and high spirits. Then come horn and trumpet fanfares. The Hungarian army moves across the stage to the sounds of the "Rakoczy" March. The elaboration of this motif is no less admirable than its instrumentation. The audience demands a repetition, but the conductor proceeds without pause to the second part.

A melancholy, gloomy motif, repeating itself in contrapuntal intricacies at ever higher levels, and thus practically prompting Mephistopheles's words, "Have done with your melancholy rumination, gnawing at your vitals like a vulture,"[4] announces Faust in his study. The utter dreariness of Faust's spirit, his disaffection, his world-weariness, are here grippingly articulated. The Easter hymn following upon Faust's monologue contains rare beauties, especially toward the end. A short recitative leads to the words, "Tears flow, earth reclaims me" [Mes larmes ont coulés, le ciel m'a reconquis].[5] A shrill chord -- and Mephistopheles stands before Faust, ready at once to offer assistance. The scene passes so swiftly that Mephistopheles does not even find time to conclude the expected contract. They go straight to Auerbach's cellar, where merriment reigns. Berlioz has not overlooked Siebel's subtle hint: "With open heart sing and drink and shout."[6] The wild singing of the revelers leaves no doubts as to their condition. And now the "Song of the Rat." What an original, reeling rhythm! Only a drunk can strike up such airs. At the end a requiem is sung for the rat, with a fugue on the *Amen*. In his book, *Les Grotesques de la Musique*, Berlioz describes in a humorous manner an incident in connection with that fugue. Under the heading, "Is that a Joke?" [Est-ce une ironie?], he relates:

"I was conducting the second performance of my *Damnation of Faust* in the theater in Dresden [in 1854]. In the second act, in the scene in Auerbach's cellar, the drunken students, after the 'Song of the Rat,' call out *Amen*! 'A fugue on the *amen*,' says Brander, 'a fugue with chorale! Let's strike up a properly scholarly piece.'

"Thereupon they take up the theme of the 'Song of the Dead Rat' again, at a slower tempo, and make of it a proper, scholarly, classical fugue, with the chorus now singing only the first syllable, now rapidly singing the entire word, *amen, amen, amen*, accompanied by tuba, ophecleide, bassoons and double basses. This fugue is written according to the strictest rules of counterpoint, and despite the mad brutality of its style, and the sacrilegious and blasphemous contrast between the music and the significance of the word *amen*, the audience is not shocked in the least, if only because such horrible distortion is now common to all schools. The harmonic effect resulting from the tissue of notes in this scene is always and everywhere applauded. Following the pedal point and final cadence of the fugue, Mephistopheles steps forward and says: '"By heavens, gentlemen, you fugue is most edifying, so much so, indeed, that one imagines oneself in a holy place. Allow me to observe that the style is scholarly, truly religious. One cannot imagine a better expression of the pious sentiments with which the church, in a single word, terminates its prayers."'

"During an intermission, a music lover sought me out. This recitative had caused him some misgiving, for he asked me, smiling shyly, 'Your fugue on the *amen*, it's a joke, isn't it?'

'Ah, my friend, I fear that it is.'

"He wasn't sure!"

Delightful, inimitably amusing, is Mephistopheles's song, "There Once Was a King" [the "Song of the Flea"]. Berlioz's melodies are anything but popular ballads, which is why men grown gray in the engaging handicraft of music criticism shake their heads dubiously over them to this day. I, who for some time now, have been flourishing the "critics' bloody scourge," driven to do so by necessity rather than desire, confess candidly that I find Berlioz's melodies agreeable, even at the risk of being a violator of their noble craft by my illustrious colleagues. The "Song of the Flea" is a special favorite of my degenerate taste, and I cannot warble it to myself too often. But to business --

Faust, who has had enough of such noisy revelry, demands other pleasures. Mephistopheles charms him into a deep sleep on the banks of the Elbe. Sylphs and gnomes sing him a lullaby ["Dors, heureux Faust"], with its concluding "Dance of the Sylphs," is the high point of the work. The magical beauty in the handling of voices and orchestra defies any description. Whoever has not heard it is to be pitied. Faust awakes from his blissful dream of love. He has dreamt of Marguerite. He must see her. Mephistopheles promises assistance. The scene changes. Soldiers approach, and strike up the lusty chorus, "Castles With High Walls and Battlements" [Villes entourées de murs et ramparts].[7] A high-spirited chorus of students ["Jam nox stellata"] interrupts their song, and then joins in. The strict working out of these simultaneous choruses is a contrapuntal masterpiece. Berlioz has a penchant for this kind of counterpoint, as demonstrated in the *Cellini* Overture, in *Romeo and Juliet* (the ball at the Capulets), and even in songs, as in "The Captive."[8]

Beating of the tattoo. The crowd withdraws. Faust in Gretchen's room, a scene full of sweet serenity and spiritual happiness. Mephistopheles alerts Faust to Marguerite's approach. They withdraw. Now comes the recitative, "It is so sultry, so musty here" [Que l'air est étouffant!][9] and the "Song of the King of Thule," with viola obbligato. This song has a unique atmospheric charm that one cannot resist even if, for cogent reasons, one wished to. That is evidence of the genius in Berlioz's compositions. They may not be immediately pleasing. They are often initially offensive. But if one spends some time with them, and studies them, digs into the idiosyncrasies of their character, then they reveal their magnetic force. In order to make sure of Marguerite's infatuation, Mephistopheles summons the will-of-the-wisps. The dance that these spirits now execute belongs among Berlioz's most charming inspirations. And then comes Mephistopheles's Serenade! The very devil of a piece. Conspicuously weak, however, is the subsequent duet between Faust and Marguerite ["Ange adoré"], thoroughly unworthy of Berlioz. The reappearance of Mephistopheles, to be sure, erases the regrettable impression, but only with the entrance of the chorus, "Hola, mère Oppenheim" (the French version of Marthe Schwertlein), does the music raise itself to a level where we again recognize the composer of *Benvenuto Cellini.*

Part IV. Gretchen alone. A doleful melody from the cor anglais constitutes the ritornello of the song, "D'amour l'ardente flamme consume mes beaux jours."[10] This yearning, longing, hoping, this resignation, these tears and sobs, these mute plaints of a tender heart, this gentle melancholy, this angelic goodness -- never have they been depicted more touchingly than in this most deeply heartfelt melody. Neither previously nor subsequently did Berlioz write an air at once so intimate and so simple. It was given to him by a god that he might delight mankind. Compared with this ritornello, the song itself amounts to little, charming us only when the cor anglais repeats the elegiac strain. Gretchen awaits her friend in vain. With her last sob the ritornello, too, dies away. Profound silence.

The next number, the "Invocation of Nature" [Nature immense, impénétrable et fière], belongs among the utterly exalted manifestations of music. One senses in it the beating wings of an ominous destiny. It is as if the Holy Spirit were addressing us from eternal space. It is a grandiose piece of music. Mephistopheles appears and tells Faust of Gretchen's predicament. Faust demands his assistance. Mephistopheles agrees on condition that Faust bind himself over. The deal is made, the black horses chafe at their bits, off, away, with the speed of the wind. But it is not to Gretchen's cell that Mephistopheles guides him, but to hell. In the spectral journey and the ensuing pandemonium the orchestra celebrates its orgies. The grotesque is just as mighty as the mighty is grotesque. Everything is gigantic, cyclopean, bordering upon the boundless, the monstrous. An infernal chorus ["Has! Irimirukarabrao"]greets Mephistopheles in his realm. It suggests mad neighing and gnashing of teeth -- ghastly, but glorious. Hell's mouth falls silent, and one hears only crackling of subterranean flames. A stifled lamentation is heard from the depths. Then utter silence. Faust's damnation is complete. The gates of heaven open. Seraphim hover aloft, singing hosannas and addressing their prayers to the Lord. Marguerite enters the realm of the blessed to heavenly strains rising like fragrant clouds of incense.

The performance, except for a few details, was satisfactory. Given the small number of rehearsals, it must surely be reckoned a miracle that it took place at all. Kapellmeister Richter thus gave new evidence of his eminent enterprise. Frau Papier sang Marguerite very beautifully. Herr Hill was a praiseworthy Mephistopheles, a bit heavy, especially in the songs, but still very, very creditable. Herr Walter may have been a good Faust in 1866. We find it otherwise today. Herr Nigg sang his modest role [Brander] modestly enough.

It seems recently as if one were now disposed to make good our earlier injustice to Berlioz. I speak of conductors and the public, of course, not of the critics. They are incorrigible. The rapid succession of performances of the Requiem and the Te Deum, the repetitions of the Symphonie Fantastique, *Romeo and Juliet* and the Overture to *Benvenuto Cellini*, and now finally *The Damnation of Faust* provide the foundation for a future prosperity, for a noble popularity of Berlioz's works in our city, which accorded them the warmest sympathy in the great composer's own lifetime. Now, too, the success was complete. The applause, which could refer only to the work, was enthusiastic. It would be a splendid victory for it if this performance could be repeated in this season. It could not be other than successful.

1. Hanslick, reviewing the same production, takes Berlioz severely to task for distorting the Goethe epic, "a sometimes barbaric butchery," much as Wolf had taken Boito to task on the same grounds.

2. "Vom Eise befreit sind Strom und Bäche," as Faust says to Wagner in *Faust* I, Scene 2.

3. "Der Schäfer putzte sich zum Tanz, mit bunter Jacke, Band und Kranz," etc., sung by the peasants in the same scene.

4. "Hör' auf mit deinem Gram zu spielen, der wie ein Geier dir am Leben frisst," as Mephistopheles offers to place himself at Fausts's disposal.

5. "Die Träne quillt, die Erde hat mich wieder."

6. "Zur Tür hinaus, wer sich entzweit! Mit offener Brust singt Runda, sauft und schreit," breaking up a brawl between Frosch and Brander. Siebel does not figure in the Berlioz work.

7. "Burgen mit hohen Mauern und Zinnen," sung by the soldiers in *Faust* I, Scene 2.

8. "La Captive," composed in Subiaco in 1832 to a Victor Hugo text while Berlioz was a Prix de Rome laureate in Italy.

9. "Es ist so schwül, so dumpfig hie."

10. In *Faust* I "Meine Ruhe ist hin," set by Schubert as "Gretchen am Spinnerade."

79. *Bruckner's Seventh*

March 28, 1886

For a whole month now no work by Richard Wagner has been given in our opera house. Instead, *Der Trompeter von Säkkingen* has been striding across our stage, proudly and grandly, three times a week. Who knows how long this situation might have endured had not the sudden visit of Fräulein Schöller,[1] of the Bavarian Court Opera, brought a temporary interruption of this musical sans-culottism.

Fräulein Schöller has just about everything required to be a good Elsa: a gracious figure, a gentle eye, a feminine bearing, a fresh, pure voice with an especially well cultivated top, a lovely *piano*, a straightforward projection and natural gestures. Thus equipped, she could not fail to arouse the audience's warm sympathy for her achievement. The performance as a whole left much to be desired. Herr Walter, substituting for the suddenly indisposed Herr Müller as Lohengrin, did nothing to heighten the delights of this evening at the opera. We can assert with much pleasure, on the other hand, that Herr Rokitansky assumed the role of King Henry earnestly and industriously, and came pretty close to taking it to heart.

Anton Bruckner's Symphony in E, No. 7, following its triumphant entry into various German cities (Munich, Leipzig, Hamburg, Hanover), has now been heard in Vienna, too. Bruckner has not been spared the age-old painful experience of the prophet without honor in his own land. Struggling for decades in vain against the obtuseness and the hostility of the critics, rejected by the concert institutions, pursued by envy and ill will, he was already an old man when fortune kissed his brow and the thankless world pressed laurel wreaths upon his head. Not even Berlioz had so bad a time of it as Bruckner. Berlioz was denied by his countrymen, but abroad he enjoyed successes, and in his creative prime, too, that must have brought a measure of consolation for his misadventures in Paris. For Bruckner the doors of foreign concert halls were first opened late in his life, and the transient attention given his works under Herbeck's influence was neither serious nor thorough enough to reveal his full worth in the spotlight it deserved. Only most recently, thanks to the efforts of some young musicians and the Academic Wagner Society has there been a favorable turn in the public attitude toward his works. His Te Deum was performed to applause in the concerts of the Society of Friends of Music, and now the Symphony No. 7, in E, so jubilantly received in Germany. The ice of our concert institutions' severe reserve has been broken. The great success enjoyed by our countryman abroad could no longer be contemplated with the indifference heretofore most generously accorded Bruckner's works by our Philharmonic Orchestra.

"We who set the fashion in Vienna know how to appreciate the man who wrote the Symphony No. 7. We shall play it whether critics and audience like it or not, for Bruckner is a genius, and his music lovely and noble." I can imagine the gentlemen of the Philharmonic saying something of this sort as they went about the preparation of this symphony. All well and good, and utterly praiseworthy. But, gentlemen, you are a bit late in achieving this insight, and we even venture to entertain some doubt as to your fine intentions, clothed as they may be in exemplary rhetoric. Or is it really because the symphony pleases you, and not, as I suspect, because it was found pleasing abroad, that you have honored it with a place in the programs of your illustrious concerts? Be that as it may, the symphony was played. The success was complete, the public carried away, the applause deafening. The gentlemen of the Philharmonic would do well to remember, however, that there are still half a dozen

Bruckner symphonies awaiting performance, and that among them even a less significant one than the E major is still a Cimborasso[2] compared with the mole hills of the Brahms symphonies.

The concert by Jean Lassalle,[3] who has already enjoyed a successful debut in our opera house as Rigoletto and William Tell, was notable for a very dreary program. Two big arias by Massenet, and sundry songs by Gounod, constitute a dreadful imposition on any musical person. Still, Lassalle's singing pleased us more than the compositions. He sang the arias with much theatrical flair, and the songs, especially "Le Soir" and "Medjie," with taste and feeling. -- Among the participants in this concert, Herr Ferdinand Hellmesberger gave us pleasure with his sensitive playing of an aria by Pergolesi, and Herr Brüll diverted us with his interpretation of piano pieces by Schumann, Chopin and himself. About the latter, what pleased me most was that I did not hear them. What an amiable composer is Herr Brüll, who does not force his audience to listen. How I admire him. He will have many imitators!

And yet a second baritone, who is also a first, namely first baritone of the Lamoureux Concerts in Paris, is among us at the moment, Herr Émile Blauwaert,[4] has just given a recital in an unfortunately sparsely attended Bösendorfersaal. The "unfortunately" applies not to the recitalist, but to the absent audience whose non-attendance cost them delights of the rarest sort. Herr Blauwaert, who has been here a full month with the intention of giving a recital, has remained a fairly unknown quantity despite the reputation he enjoys in Paris and Brussels. It would appear that he is merely a bad drummer (beating your own drum is part of the business), for, drumming with skill and grace, he might easily have extracted from the hide of his newspaper a benevolent and resonant grunt that would quickly have found a sympathetic echo in the hearts of the public and have given the hall a more friendly appearance.

Continuing, now, with the singer's achievements, mention should be made, first and foremost, of his versatility in the stylish conception and interpretation of compositions of the most heterogeneous character. Herr Blauwaert struck the diabolical tone in the Serenade from Berlioz's *The Damnation of Faust* in the same masterly fashion in which he established the childlike folk character in the Flemish songs, and he sang the declamation in Hans Sachs's address in the third act of *Die Meistersinger* just as expressively as the purely vocal aria [of Momus in "Phoebus and Pan"] of Sebastian Bach. Especially admirable in Blauwaert's singing is its accuracy, its rhythmic precision and its lively expression. In this sense, he sang the Serenade of Mephistopheles, especially, with a perfection of which a German singer can hardly have a notion. Herr Hill, excellent as was his recent Mephistopheles in Berlioz's *The Damnation of Faust*, would be well advised to get a recipe from Blauwaert for the singing of Mephistopheles's Serenade.

May Herr Blauwaert decide to give a second recital. The unanimous applause enthusiastically accorded him in this first concert should encourage him to do so.

1. Pauline Schöller (1862- ?), a Viennese soprano who sang principally in Dresden and Munich. As Pauline Schöller-Haag she sang at the Metropolitan in the season of 1890-91.
2. Properly Chimborazo, a mountain in Ecuador 20,702 feet high.
3. Jean Lassalle (1847-1909) succeeded Jean-Baptiste Faure as principal baritone of the Opéra in 1872. He was also a familiar and greatly admired visitor in all the major opera houses of Europe and America.
4. Émile Blauwaert (1845-1891), a Belgian bass-baritone, especially noted for his Gurnemanz in the Bayreuth production of *Parsifal* in 1889.

80. Rhapsodies by Brahms and Liszt

April 11, 1886

"Who brings a lot will have something for many, and so everyone goes away contented." The Society of Friends of Music may well have been guided instinctively by the amiable philosophy of the theater director [in the Theater Prologue to *Faust* I] in putting together the fourth and last of its concert series. It was a stew, as motley in its constituent elements as the taste of our public.

There was a symphony by Haydn for that species of easygoing pensioner who shakes his head disconsolately at every locomotive whistle, at every newly constructed coffee machine, at Schopenhauer's philosophy, at Liebig's beef extract, at music drama, and so on. They are decent folk, hospitable and uncommonly garrulous. They love to talk about the good old days. Their favorite composer is Haydn.

Then came a Psalm [117] for double chorus [a cappella] by Robert Franz, presumably as a favor to Herr Professor Schuster.[1] The Rhapsody for Alto, Male Chorus and Orchestra by Brahms will hardly have sent the Corybants of this musical idol into the usual state of ecstasy, as this composition has not yet reached the freezing point of fantasy and sensibility, as have the most recent works of this industrious composer. The Rhapsody is to be numbered among the best of Brahms's productions. One does not note in this piece the determination to be "serious" music. The classical toga drapery falling loosely about the crumbling frame of ideas in his symphonies, this *tour de force* of the tailor's art, is not yet evident in this Rhapsody. Its thoughts have no need to hide behind a mask. They have no need to arouse curiosity, which, in such cases, and naturally, is never satisfied. Either they are there, or they are not, for in art one must declare oneself immediately. In his Rhapsody, Brahms has done it, however hesitantly. Since I like this piece, I am truly sorry that I cannot raise my panegyric in praise of Brahms to so high a pitch as that achieved by Eduard Hanslick, the amiable critic and fervent admirer of his friend Johannes, in his enthusiastic notice of the latter's Fourth Symphony. I refer specifically to his curiously euphemistic recognition of its fundamental character as "frostiness bordering on the austere."[2] It is an assessment to which we most happily subscribe, and which would have required no modification, not even a feigned one.

Did the admirers of Robert Schumann not find the musical ballast of the "Schifflein" (chorus with soprano solo, flute and French horn) [Opus 146, No. 5] too light? So it seemed to me, at least. Schumann wrote such wonderfully beautiful choral pieces. Why choose an inferior one? And finally, something for the club folk, and it is to be hoped that Herbeck's "Das Fischermädchen," a simple glee club item, satisfied their Philistine tastes.

Up to this point, the concert had hardly been exciting, but -- "All's well that ends well." Liszt's Hungarian Rhapsody No. 2 (dedicated to Joachim)[3] compensated us generously for what we had suffered thus far. Gone all boredom and drowsiness the instant the wild fantasies, the bold rhythms, the exotic primitive utterances of the homeless Gypsy strains struck the ear. The Rhapsody is only a sketch, but in these fleeting strokes of the pen one recognizes the hand of the master. The narcotic charm of these sounds is hard to resist, least of all when Liszt endows them with color and form! Kapellmeister Richter is quite right in giving his special attention to this category of Liszt's creative activity, and in the *tempo rubato* of this rhapsody he brought to bear a sensitivity that may well be unequaled. The rhapsodies constitute, to some extent, the hellish vestibule to the heaven of Liszt's symphonic poems. In seeking to awaken in the public a lively sympathy for the works of a composer stupidly and vulgarly insulted by our critics, and to blunt the edges of the public's still cherished prejudices, he is well on the way toward achieving his admirable objective in offering, from time to time, works such as the Hungarian rhapsodies. -- May he not be led astray by the yelping of the hostile critics!

1. Heinrich Schuster (1847- ?) was a Viennese jurist, author of many books on municipal law and administration and two books on copyright law as applied to music. As a musical amateur he had studied piano with Julius Epstein, esthetics of music with Hanslick, and harmony with Bruckner. He had published a biography of Franz in 1873.

2. See footnote No. 9 to the notice of January 24, 1886.

3. No. 12 in the series for piano solo.

81. A Tale of Two Tenors

April 18, 1886

Two Meyerbeer operas one right after the other! Why not a Meyerbeer cycle, or an Excelsior Week, or a *Trompeter von Säkkingen* Olympiade? Such excursions cannot be denied our opera house simply as incompatible with its artistic standing, since for that institution everything has become a chimera, the only exception being money. One hears a lot of talk about the artistic sensibility of the present general director [Wilhelm Jahn]. There may be some truth in it, but it is not reflected in the repertoire.

In the most recent performance of *L'Africaine* the Selika was Fräulein Tischler.[1] The role imposes considerable demands on singer and actress alike. Fräulein Tischler acquitted herself admirably on both counts. The overall impression was highly favorable. She sang the lullaby at the beginning of the second act very beautifully. It was the upper register, especially, that touched off spontaneous demonstrations of approval. Her coloratura, too, is admirable.

Herr Mierzwinski appeared next day as Raoul in *Les Huguenots*. Whether Herr Mierzwinski sings the Prophet, or Arnold in *William Tell*, or Raoul, it's all the same. Each of these roles provides him with opportunity to show off his high chest tones, and that is all that matters. His conception of a role, and his acting of it, are not worth talking about. The voice, in its high and highest reaches, has lost none of its brilliance. In the Act III aria he easily took the trill from A to B flat, and then moved on to a resounding high C as if there were nothing to it, which, when viewed from another and even higher standpoint than high C, is true. The casting of the other roles was as usual except for the page, sung not by Frau von Naday, but by Fräulein Baier, a welcome change that should have been effected long ago.

The concert given by the tenor Darewski went off smoothly enough, I am happy to say, although it might easily have been otherwise. Here is what happened. In order to make room for a temporary stage for the productions of the opera class of the Conservatory, a considerable number of rows of seats had to be removed from the hall.[2] Instead of the usual twenty-two, there were only fifteen, while tickets had been sold for the full house. Those then, who, like myself and many another worthy homunculus, entered the hall with an ideal placement in the sixteenth row could choose between standing or grabbing any unoccupied seat. For practical reasons, I chose the latter course, and experienced not the slightest twinge of conscience about the cold-bloodedess with which I occupied alien terrain. It was fortunate that Herr Darewski's European fame did not extend beyond the equator, and that the available seats were sufficient to accommodate the gentle surge of the public, since otherwise there would surely have been a catastrophe, with consequences reaching well beyond the fifteenth row to the entrance and even to the steps. It was well, too, that among the Shylocks in attendance none insisted upon the seat indicated on his ticket. Everyone found it more advisable to lend an ear to the blandishments of the sympathetic ushers than to insist in blind rage upon his rightful place. One chose to see the confusion in a humorous light, and the offerings of the artist likewise.

I do not know for certain that Herr Darewski intentionally gave Eléazar's great fourth act aria from *La Juive* so comical a character, but it seemed to me that he was bent on parody. If this was truly what the singer had in mind, then, while his intention was deplorable, the performance was admirable, for he unquestionably possesses a talent for parody. In this he is most wonderfully supported by his organ, which makes a mockery of everything we are accustomed to expect from a voice. The sweet-sour expression of his singing, combined with a brilliantly cultivated grotesqueness of facial expression, and then the languishing *smorzandi* and the sobs, now half strangled, now utterly toneless, now furious -- all this was irresistibly funny. Less parodistic accomplishment was demanded in an aria from Rossini's *Otello*, if only because it is droll enough on its own account. But the singer knew what he was about in putting the number on his program. He probably wanted to do a satire on coloratura singing. And, indeed, he could hardly have sung it more satirically. That was a rumbling and rattling and clattering[3] suggesting a minor earthquake. The audience acknowledged this charming *tour de force* according to its merits, and demanded a repetition. I, however, concerned for my life, escaped by hasty flight into the great outdoors. Herr Darewski pursued me -- in thought, of course. Reflecting conscientiously on the impressions left by the concert, I became ever clearer in my own mind about the significance of Herr Darewski, just as greatness always exercises its overwhelming power only at a certain distance in time and space. I came to the conclusion that Herr Darewski is a very bad singer, but as one at the service of humanity, an excellent and, in his own way, possibly unique satirist. Hats off to him!

1. Charlotte Tischler (1863- ?), only briefly a member of the company before moving over to light opera.

2. Presumably the Bösendorfersaal.

3. "Das war ein Gerumpel, Gepurzel und Getrampel . . ." There are no quotation marks in Wolf's text, but he is certainly quoting from Mörike's "Abschied," which he was to set in 1888 as the last of his Mörike Lieder. The poem, at this point, reads: "Alle Hagel! Ward das ein Gerumpel, ein Gepurzel, ein Gehumpel!" The substitution, in Wolf's text, of *Getrampel*, a dictionary word, for *Gehumpel*, a Mörike coinage, may well have been an editorial "correction."

82. A Hot Time at the Philharmonic

April 25, 1886

Things got pretty rough at the last Philharmonic concert. A bitter battle broke out over Liszt's "Mephisto Waltz." It was the standees and a part of the gallery, resolved to give their all, against the parterre, the mountain against the marsh. On the one side we had youth, intelligence, idealism, good judgment, enthusiasm and conviction; on the other dullness, frivolity, debility, ignorance, arrogance, materialism. Such were the contending forces.

There was a lot of applause, but a lot of hissing, too. Since, as we all know, these Semitic hissing sounds traditionally served the "chosen people" as shibboleth [to distinguish Gileadites from Ephraimites] in combat with their neighbors, it was not hard to determine who it was that so emphatically proclaimed both their dissent and their identity. Indeed, these "chosen people" habitually make a great show of their exquisite taste. They are always ready to recognize in Beethoven a good composer. And yet there are those who see nothing heroic in the courage of such convictions. What, then, can we call courageous? Let it pass. These excellent and generous souls will surely enrich the National Guard with a doughty legion of tailors, and thus be of service to the state. You can take an oath on that.

To take seriously the ludicrous behavior of these worthy parterre subscribers toward the works of a genius such as Liszt would be like punishing children's bad manners with the rack. We are not so cruel. But it is well to look for what it is that causes the public to behave like an ill-mannered child and to think like a well-groomed cad. How is it, we ask, that Liszt's compositions are rejected by the majority of our degenerate public? The answer is made uncommonly easy for me, since it is contained in the question. But then why, someone could object, do Beethoven, Mozart, Haydn, etc., appeal to this same degenerate public? The objection is so banal, the answer so obvious, that any blockhead could handle it easily. But should someone choose to ask me what I mean by a degenerate public, I accept the challenge gladly, and am ready with the answer: a degenerate public is one that is content to be the ward of a degenerate press.

It is a public of newspaper readers. That is the source of all other evils. That is the source of the thoughtlessness, frivolity, dependence, distraction, insensibility and, above all, the bias against those works condemned to death by the press. If this were an ingenuous public, it would not tolerate for another day the shameful chains it now fastens to itself voluntarily. But the habit of cud-chewing has already become too delightful to permit the slightest effort to use one's own teeth. Thus, this public receives its impression of a work of art not directly, but from the review in the newspaper, to be had in concrete form for a few pennies as a stimulant for stomach and spirit complete with certificate of patent. Go then to the apothecary, and buy yourselves some *nux vomica* or some other purgative if you want to have an impression. The effect remains essentially the same, and you spare yourselves the price of the ticket. And so a public, the despicable tool of a despicable press, will pass judgment on the works of a genius! A sluggardly mob that enters the concert hall as if it were a toy store, reduces the noblest possessions of mankind to idle diversions, and then, if that is not satisfactory, arrogantly turns its back on the work of art and ceremoniously hisses . . . fie, fie, and once again fie!!!

Given such circumstances, it is hardly surprising that Liszt's original com-positions have excited a lively "for" and "against" whenever they have been played in Vienna. This time the applause from the standees was still far from constituting a demonstration when a few hot headed Philistines signalled, stu-pidly enough, the shibboleth. That was pouring oil on fire. The applause grew louder, and rightly so, since it was directed no less at the splendid accomplish-ment of the orchestra and its conductor, Hans Richter, than at the work itself. And did not the wonderful performance of this Lisztian composition merit the most extravagant praise? What did Liszt's admirers do to excite the drowsy parterre to a counter-demonstration? They were simply giving due honor to service rendered.

Beethoven's "greatest and most successful work," the "Missa Solemnis," concluded the great works offered in this concert season. The performance confounded most brilliantly any fears of inadequacy that may have been prompted by frequent interruptions at the general rehearsal. The uniquely dif-ficult work, making hair-raising demands on chorus and soloists especially, was precisely played under the sure hand of Hans Richter. Much praise is due Herr Hellmesberger, Jr. - along with Mmes. Wilt and Papier and Messrs. Walter and Ney - for his lovely playing of the violin solo in the Benedictus.

83.   The Marriage of Figaro

May 2, 1886

It was on May 1, 1786, that *The Marriage of Figaro* first came across the footlights, and today, April 30, 1886, we celebrate the 100th anniversary of this masterpiece's premiere. Inevitably, we look back to the time in which such a work could originate, and then cast a critical glance at the present, which still -- or, if you prefer -- only now enjoys the works of Mozart.

These general reflections we owe to an article, "Das Publikum in Zeit und Raum" [The Public in Time and Space][1] by Richard Wagner. Among other matters it contains a detailed discussion of the precarious position of Mozart's works in Mozart's own time and of their no less precarious position in ours. I pass some of it along herewith.

Calling attention initially to the fate of works for the musical theater as determined by the strong fluctuations of public taste, Wagner says: "In Mozart's operas we can plainly see that what raised them above their own time placed them in the curiously disadvantageous position of going on to live outside it, deprived of the social circumstances that determine their conception and performance. All other works by composers of Italian opera were spared this curious destiny. None survived the time to which alone it belonged and from which it sprang. With *The Marriage of Figaro* and *Don Giovanni* it was otherwise. They could not be regarded as tailored only to the requirements of a few Italian opera seasons. The stamp of immortality was impressed upon them. Immortality! -- a fateful votive offering! To what a torturous existence is the departed soul of such a masterpiece not exposed when dragged forth by a modern theater medium for the edification of a latter-day public! Attending a performance of *The Marriage of Figaro* or *Don Giovanni* today, would we not wish for the work that it might once have lived completely and fully, leaving us its memory as a lovely saga, instead of which we see it forced into a life utterly alien to it like a martyr resurrected for further maltreatment. In these works of Mozart are united the elements of the full bloom of Italian musical taste with the spatial circumstances of the Italian opera house to form an utterly definitive idiom, beautifully and amiably expressing the spirit of the closing years of the last century. Wrenched from their native environment, and transplanted to our own time and circumstances, the eternal element in these artistic creations suffers a distortion that we vainly seek to correct through new disguises and conversions of their realistic form."

The cogency of such a pronouncement is hardly to be denied. A look at the audience, pursuing with the utmost complacency, the events of *The Marriage of Figaro* as they take place tells us all we need to know about how much has been lost of the more intimate understanding of a work gaily reflecting the moral corruption of the society of that time. Beaumarchais' comedy, whose political satire accounts for the extraordinary effect it had when new, would probably leave us rather cold today. We, on the other hand, should be offended by the contradiction between what we see and our own views and experience, since thus the immoral in *The Marriage of Figaro* would emerge the more brazenly and candidly. That we have not, however, progressed even that far demonstrates how much we remain below the standard of the spirit of the age.

As we all know, *The Marriage of Figaro* had a great success at its first performance. Most of the numbers had to be repeated, so that the opera's running time was almost doubled. Mozart was stormily applauded and recalled. The performance is said to have been excellent. But the opera quickly disappeared from the repertoire. Martin's *Una Cosa Rara*[2] crowded it from the stage. Shortly thereafter Dittersdorf[3] triumphed with his homespun operettas. The Emperor Josef II, and the public, too, opted for Dittersdorf over Mozart, who then accepted a call to Prague, where the enthusiastic reception for his *Figaro* made up sufficiently for the cabals of the imperial stage in Vienna. But the stamp of immortality was impressed upon the work, and despite listless performances and lamentable castings, *The Marriage of Figaro* delights the receptive listener now as then.

This time, too, a good deal was left to be desired, although the performance was to be numbered among the better. Herr Hablawetz is suited neither by temperament nor artistic capacity to represent a cunning and suave fellow such as Figaro, but still he emerged with good grace from all the affairs in which the opera's hero becomes involved in the course of this lively plot. But the page, Cherubino? What has happened to this tender Don Giovanni embryo? Fräulein Braga played him, and that suffices. A darling, coquettish, charming and still lovable Susanna was Fräulein Bianchi. She sang enchantingly. Following the garden aria there was endless applause. Appearance, action and song were united by her accomplishment in a harmony whose mellifluousness and beauty seemed to compete with Mozart's music. The repose and lucidity of a noble woman, so intimately expressed in the Countess's two arias, were most splendidly realized in Frau Papier's inspired singing. She, too, was accorded hearty applause. Herr Reichmann was an imposing Almaviva. Excellent performances in secondary roles were offered by Fräulein Baier (Marcelline) and the Messers. Lay (Bartolo), Stoll (Antonio), Schittenhelm (Curzio) and especially Herr Schmitt (Basilio). The opera was carefully prepared by Director Jahn. The scenic arrangement was pleasing, the audience very large.

1.   This article had only recently appeared (1883) in the tenth and last volume of Wagner's collected writings, *Gesammelte Schriften und Dichtungen*.

2.   Vicente Martin y Soler (1754-1810). *Una Cosa Rara* was first produced in Vienna on November 17, 1786, and Mozart responded to its success by quoting a theme from it in *Don Giovanni.*

3.   Karl Ditters von Dittersdorf (1739-1799). The most enduring of his many operas, *Doktor und Apotheker,* was produced in Vienna on July 11, 1786.

84. A Salute to Suppé

May 9, 1886

It seems as though the Tilaresa sisters will have had the last word in the concert season now drawing to a close. As far as the eye and a good tracking nose can determine, there is not a concert announcement to be seen.

The kiosks, usually so colorfully adorned with advertisements of coming events, have a monotonous, gloomy look. It is the lovely season when a music critic can assess these cultural installations in terms of harmony of color. He may now enjoy inner satisfaction in approaching these ominously oracular edifices, the mere sight of which, at other times, arouses fear and revulsion. Now his gaze rests peacefully upon the melancholy physiognomy of these round monsters. The secret charm they previously possessed, by which anyone thirsting for music was basely lured from the straight and narrow into their cursed circle, is gone. The language they now speak falls strangely upon the ear. With the last concert announcement they have played out their role -- and it was the Tilaresa sisters who administered the *coup de grâce.*

What about these amiable Samaritans? Although outwardly not at all like the Siamese Twins, the two ladies in their accomplishments had such an intimate relationship to one another that it was impossible to decide which of the two was the superior. They always sang together, presumably in order to rob the audience of any opportunity to make those comparisons that must inevitably have favored the one or the other -- a touching example of sisterly affection and artistic selflessness. The voices sounded like canaries and nightingales, but as to which was canary and which was nightingale I haven't a clue. I suspect that each was both.

And what did these charming songbirds sing? A lot of nice things: a duet from Nicolai's *The Merry Wives of Windsor*, Mendelssohn's "Migrant Birds' Departure"[1] and a duet from Suppé's *Boccaccio.* One was surprised to meet Suppé, an operetta composer, in the concert hall, as if the "serious" music of our "modern" classicists, destined for the concert hall in the truest sense of the term, were in the slightest degree preferable to Suppé's gay airs. One is boring, the other entertaining.

Is it a disgrace to compose entertaining music? That's all we need to render our already much abused temples of art exclusive havens for boring music simply because the muse of our modern Handels, Bachs and Beethovens, with their gouty legs and moldy cheekbones, simulate a dignified aspect.Lively music should find a welcome everywhere, regardless of genre. In music too, as in all other arts, Voltaire's maxim applies: "Every genre is permitted except the boring."[2] So let us show due respect for the amusing genre of Suppé in the concert hall, too, where certainly its role will not be the worst.

It is true, to be sure, that operetta composers very rarely find their way into the concert hall, but is that anything to be proud of? An out-and-out rascal, as far as I am concerned, is always preferable to a hypocrite. And if the music of the operetta entertains much loose and fickle company, there are to be found around the crumbling toes of the decrepit goddess of our art music hypocrisy, prudery and boredom -- three reprehensible characters stationed menacingly at the portals of the concert hall and screeching in a ghastly language intelligible enough to the sophisticated musician: "Lasciate ogni speranza, voi ch'entrate!"

It was, thus, a happy thought of the recitalists to find a place for Suppé in their program.

A welcome contrast to the vocal pieces were the piano offerings of Herr Emil Weeber. Herr Weeber happily plays the stopgap role in Vienna. The artist overdoes his modesty in putting so low a value on his accomplishments. His fiery playing, and a technic not to be underestimated, might well encourage him to place his capacities more in the foreground, to appear more often and more conspicuously in public, to undertake tours, etc.

With a light heart I lay aside the pen which, in this season, has so stubbornly resisted its employment in the reviewing of concerts. One hopes that this will be the last.

1. "Abschiedslied der Zugvögel," one of a set of six two-part songs, Opus 63.
2. "Tous les genres sont bons hors le genre ennuyeux," from the Preface to *L'Enfant Prodigue.*

85. *Materna in* L'Africaine

May 16, 1886

The way in which our opera repertoire is chosen begins to be quite witty, although the wit in the stereotyped scheduling and cancelling of the Wagner operas is neither exceptionally good nor new. The persistence and regularity with which the joke has been played over a long period of time makes it, indeed, rather funny. But playing fast and loose with the public remains a bad joke. Those responsible for the direction of our opera house would be better advised to recruit and retain good singers than to make bad jokes.

What is one to say when in the course of an entire month no Wagner opera is given, while Meyerbeer is played three times a week? Are we in Palestine or a German city? Can there be anything more ridiculous nowdays than to play — as it would seem — Meyerbeer off against Wagner? To what end? Is our opera public not already decadent enough without being brutalized? We suffer under no such lack of spiritual nourishment, thank God, as to suggest that our musical hunger might be stilled by an exclusive diet of the filth of Meyerbeer operas and, more recently, the pap of *Der Trompeter von Säkkingen.* Where, then, are the German masters, of whom that nation truly has no shortage? O, deluded populace, infamous theater directors! We live amidst plenty, and while we cannot indulge we must starve. Wagner's admirers are no better off than the tortured Tantalus.[1] They can enjoy the works of the master only with their eyes on the playbill, not with heart and soul in live performance. A Wagner opera is announced. One heaves a sigh of relief, pulls oneself together, makes ready, buys a seat in the parterre. At last, at last, they mean business — with what? With a cancellation. Is that not amusing?

Frau Materna, our opera house's resident star on tour, appears for once and, by chance, in Vienna. Good. Now we shall hear a work of Wagner's. And, indeed, *Tristan und Isolde* is announced. But Herr Winkelmann falls ill, and the performance is called off. How about trying *Die Walküre?* Since Herr Winkelmann, fortunately, is really sick, there is no danger in announcing it. How would it be if Herr Winkelmann were recovered by then? Never fear. The cancellation of *Die Walküre* was, in a sense, the bulletin on the state of Herr Winkelmann's health. But since things were already well under way, and one chose not to pull up in mid-career, *Die Walküre* was set for Saturday despite Herr Winkelmann's indisposition, but the *Siegfried* scheduled for that date indefinitely postponed. One hopes that by that time Herr Winkelmann will not have died, and that our grandchildren may possibly still hear a performance of *Siegfried.*

Frau Materna, in the meantime, sang — in *L'Africaine,* naturally. For when Wagner is silent, Meyerbeer has the word, and the *Neue Freie Presse* cries happily, "Hear, hear!" Frau Materna, who will appear only four times in this season, has already made a very agreeable beginning. We assume that her second role will be Valentine in *Les Huguenots,* her third [Sulomith in] *The Queen of Sheba,* and her fourth the famous Fidès [in *Le Prophète*]. Therewith is the purpose of her short visit, in the eyes of the Intendant or director, fully accomplished. At long last – but not until Frau Materna has fulfilled her engagement – Herr Winkelmann will be restored to his precious health, and who can then hold it against him if he indulges, with ironic satisfaction, in giving us the ailing Prince Assad in *The Queen of Sheba?*

And so Frau Materna began her engagement with Selika in *L'Africaine.*

The artist got a lot closer to the essential character of this ridiculous figure than the grotesque posturing with which actresses of only moderate gifts achieve such cheap effects. Nevertheless, as played by Frau Materna, Selika retains her shy savagery and raw sentimentality, but far less obtrusively than we are accustomed to experience them in the work of bad actresses. Frau Materna gives more emphasis to the jealously loving woman than to the native primitiveness of the African. She takes this exotic plant by its roots, not, as others do, by its brightly adorned tuft of hair.

The audience rewarded Frau Materna with applause and flowers for a performance which, musically, too, provided perfection. We shall not trouble to sing the praises of the other particiapants one by one, but simply applaud them collectively in the most respectful, charitable, appreciative, affectionate, sympathetic, flattering, restrained, obliging, ardent, conciliatory and Christian manner.

1. Tantalus, son of Zeus and greatly favored by the gods, outraged his benefactors by killing his only son, boiling him in a great cauldron and serving him up at their table. As punishment he was made to abide near a pond whose waters receded whenever he stooped to drink, surrounded by fruit trees whose fruit he could not reach. Hence "tantalize."

86. Der Ring des Nibelungen

May 23, 1886

We have had, contrary to all expectations, the Nibelung Trilogy — without *Das Rheingold* — and with it I have lost, apparently, all credibility for my powers of divination. So be it. Since it is not impossible that the clever reader may have taken the irony of my last article at face value, he will certainly not deny me his sympathy in this critical week when all has conspired against my art as prophet. I thank him for his compassion.

I could not, indeed, have enjoyed my success. I am even glad that my assumptions proved to be erroneous. While never for a moment in doubt, I secretly hoped that those who guide the affairs of the Court Opera would turn out to be right. I will gladly accept the charge of faulty insight and judgment when my incendiary words are contradicted by deeds in good faith, as has now happened. May I have further occasion to commit injustice. The proofs thereof are all too precious. May I always set up false premises, and may it be reserved for our artistic institutions to draw the proper syllogisms. Above all, may the dramatic works of Wagner be performed often and well, and to this end may our company, subsidized by the state as it is, be at full strength at least once a year. There would be then, and for a long time to come, nothing further to be desired, and on such modest peace proposals a truce could be agreed upon.

Whether we owe the performance of *Die Walküre,* rendered problematic by the sudden indisposition of Fräulein Braga, to the management's good will or to the industry of Frau Papier, or to an already sold-out house (and the last weighs heavily as gold), I would not venture to decide. I assume that all these factors together played their part in bringing about the direly threatened production. Welcome as were the withdrawal of Fräulein Braga and the hasty readiness of Frau Papier to take on the orphaned role of Sieglinde, and well cast as were the other roles by our best singers — if, indeed, Frau Materna may be counted as ours — there was a catch. With Herr Winkelmann restored to health, with Frau Materna having tamed her impatience, with Fräulein Braga having declined and Frau Papier having accepted, with the orchestra having even played a rehearsal, and with all else in order, someone was missing. Who? Only the conductor.

Herr Fuchs, too, is a conductor, of course, and he beats time as well and precisely — if hardly as beautifully — as any. But to beat time well and precisely, and even beautifully and impressively, is not evidence of conductorial talent, any more than a sound knowledge of thorough-bass makes a composer, or the most sovereign command of language a poet. All that is only a craft, which must be learned and practiced if the artist is to realize the images of his fantasy in convincingly concrete form. Now, Herr Fuchs has the craft. He has learned it very well, and he has no little opportunity to demonstrate it. but what he demonstrates is always that he remains no more than a decent craftsman, a good, honest time beater. Herr Fuchs gives a reasonably accurate translation of musical symbols into the language of the baton, but the translation is dry, stiff, schoolmasterly, as if he were drilling a horde of recruits, Herr Fuchs beats his *alla breve* measure with military precision, without allowing himself ever to be diverted in the slightest degree by a *ritardando* or *accelerando* from the trot at which he has set out. The born corporal: one, two, one, two — halt!

Kapellmeister Richter, however, is on leave, sits comfortably in London[1] and makes the most of his talent [*Pfund*], happily adding both to his renown and his weight. That's only just. But it hardly does us any honor that Richter's merits are rated more highly in every respect in England than here, and it is greatly to be regretted that we should be deprived of his capacities at a time when his absence is more keenly felt than ever. And so we have had a very inadequate, listless production of the Nibelung Trilogy, for which the singers, to be sure, were not in the least to blame.

Interest centered on Scaria's successor,[2] Herr Reichmann, who was singing Wotan for the first time in Vienna. The role was no easy assignment, as Scaria's superb accomplishment was still fresh in everyone's memory. Herr Reichmann had, nonetheless, a resounding success. His conception was virile and noble, and at the same time free of all the precious coquetry in which this singer is sometimes wont to indulge. The heroic aspects of the role, curiously, came off better than the lyric. It seemed as though he were especially anxious to shine as dramatic singer, as if he wished to discredit the charge that he is better suited to lyric roles. Herr Reichmann succeeded handsomely, but almost at the expense of lyricism.

Frau Materna's eminent accomplishment as Brünnhilde is renowned the world over. But never in all my life have I heard sensitive people utter such sighs as those emitted by Frau Materna during these two performances. Brünnhilde's fate moved and shook me, too, but the artist's prolonged sighs struck me as comically odd. Why all this nonsense? In *Götterdämmerung,* however, Frau Materna's Brünnhilde was unsurpassably beautiful, a proof that the least pretentious acting is the most exciting.

Frau Papier, who took on Sieglinde with commendable zeal, and projected the role very sympathetically, delighted us, too, as Waltraute in *Götterdämmerung.* Surprising was Herr Winkelmann's incomparably vivid characterization of Siegfied. In *Götterdämmerung,* especially, his acting and his conception were enchanting. Had Winkelmann suddenly grown utterly hoarse, he could not have pleased me more.

As I am not disposed to let myself get unnecessarily worked up, I shall pass over the characteristic merits of Fräulein Klein (Gutrune) and Herr Sommer (Gunther) with pregnant silence. I am sincerely delighted, on the other hand, to have noted how Herr Rokitansky (Hagen) visibly warmed to his part in the course of the performance. That's saying quite a lot, and merits acknowledgment. Herr Schmitt's Mime is unique. The singer's deficiencies stand him in good stead in this original role. Herr Schmitt, despite his terrible voice, is still the best Wagner singer.

With that, I hope, I have spoken the last word for a long time.

1. Richter had first appeared in London sharing conductorial duties with Wagner himself at the historic concerts in the Royal Albert Hall in 1877. He was a frequent May-June visitor thereafter, conducting what came to be known as the "Richter Concerts" and causing something of a sensation by conducting the Beethoven symphonies from memory. He also conducted, in 1882, the first London performances of *Tristan und Isolde* and *Die Meistersinger.*

2. During the second act of a performance of *Tannhäuser,* Scaria, who had recently had an alarming history of memory lapses, whispered to his Elisabeth: "What opera is it that we are singing?" He had to be led from the stage, and died insane shortly thereafter, on July 22, 1886.

87. Franz Liszt, August 1, 1886

August 8, 1886

Once again, a Titan has been summoned to eternal repose. A star has expired by whose victorious radiance all artifice and plagiarism were blinded, whose brilliance offered friendly guidance to the afflicted, pointing out where strug- gle and hostility lay in store, but victory and consummation, too; whose sacred fire, strewing lethal lightning, demolished the altars of the idolatrous and, flaming aloft, ignited the torch of enthusiasm, protecting and encour- aging the truly great.

Yes, the eye of this radiant phenomenon has closed forever, but it was the eye of an immortal. Legend and history will share in the recital of the spendid deeds of the greatest of virtuosos, but to sustain his memory for future generations not in the image of recollection, nor through the medium of the biographer, but in vital reality, the great deceased has left us an inestimable inheritance: his works.

A Faustian nature, forever dreaming up something new, and restlessly surging forward, the master exercised a reformative influence in every area of vocal and instrumental music. Intelligence, depth of thought and feeling, and an incomparable sense of beauty in musical forms are the characteristic distinguishing features of his creations. In this respect the symphonic poems, including *Faust* and the "Dante" Symphony, stand out above all the rest. The whole romantic enchantment of Liszt's demonic personality pours out to us in these compositions. They are his most personal works. He stands here at the peak of his creativity. On this eminence, reigning alone, he remains incompre- hensible to the crowd. Indeed, that was how he wanted it, as he made clear in his famous Preface to the symphonic poems, stating that he wished no everyday popularity to be accorded them. But to whoever lovingly submerged himself in this unique personality there was opened a work splendid and ideal as only a poet could conceive it.

Now the restless one rests. The universally life-giving spark has expired. The hand that once fashioned worlds and then destroyed them is stiffened in death — dead, dead, the man who, as a second Orpheus, lavished only life, blossoming life, upon the world.

To future generations the extravagant transports of those who rhapsodized rather than reported on his piano playing during his career as a virtuoso — for enthusiasm makes poets of sober souls, too — will seem a half-forgotten fairy tale. And now Liszt! The indefatiguable champion of Wagner and Berlioz, not to mention other excellent composers, forever at work with pen and baton, standing firm, patient and, in the end, victorious against all envy and slander.

Who could fail to admire such selflessness, such unenvious devotion to the work of similarly motivated rivals? Must we not love him, honor him? Therefore let us treasure faithfully his sacred memory, gather around the banner that the master flourished so successfully and victoriously against the insignificant skeptics, and above all: Let us follow resolutely in the paths the immortal trod during his earthly existence; let us preserve the heritage of his genius, protect the precious treasure, and may his spirit reign benevolently over us!

88. Fidelio *with Materna*

October 24, 1886

Rarely does a critic have a chance to cover an evening at the opera and enjoy it, too. For that you need two things: a good work and a good production. We had both, as a welcome curiosity, in last Sunday's performance of *Fidelio*. Beethoven's only opera, as a glance at the repertoire will tell you, cannot be numbered among our public's favorites, spoiled rotten as that public is by *Der Trompeter von Säkkingen*. Still, it filled the house in a manner most welcome to the box office.

Frau Materna's Leonore was not so good as usual. It was much better. The consistency with which she approaches utter perfection is truly astounding. The crude theater cloak on which, until recently, she was wont to ascend to a considerable altitude, assisted by a small quantity of hydrogen (colophony in the language of the theater), has shrunk noticeably. But her wings have grown, and however high she now soars above the valleys of the false and the conventional, reveling, too, in the purest ether of the eternally true and beautiful, we shall wish her well.

Whoever saw and heard Frau Materna on this occasion, and who followed her performance attentively, will surely not find this praise excessive. I am not speaking of details, nor of the lyrical warmth and dramatic fire with which she sang the big aria, nor of the unearthly radiance of the reassuring human tones flooding the dark prison walls, nor of how an entire heaven settled over the rescued pair in the joyously pulsating duet with Florestan, in which all the artist's wild impetuosity exploded. Neither do I speak of the uncommonly discreet character of her impersonation, in contrast to the now customary histrionic excesses of most singers undertaking this role. No, it was none of all that. Other singers share such virtues with Frau Materna. What made her achievement so treasurable for us was the overall impression, her purposeful procedure. She always knows exactly what she intends to do, and what she intends she can. This consistently implemented harmony of can and will is of a piece with the repose and freedom of her musical and dramatic characterization, and it lends to everything she does the charm of individuality and self-sufficiency. This artist can err in her conception of this role or that, but she will stick to that conception, once grasped, with the utmost consistency, and see it through to the end. She will never be out of character.

On this occasion, luckily, Frau Materna hit the nail on the head right from the beginning, and with this comforting assurance we can turn our attention amiably to Herr Reichmann, just as amiably, indeed, as he played the villainous Pizarro. And since it is generally known that Herr Reichmann possesses a beautiful baritone, and goes about his business conscientiously and skillfully, we can leave it at that, and go on to render our most sincere congratulations to Herr Reichenberg for his excellent Rocco. The same goes for Herr Winkelmann, whose voice brings the characteristic tone to the thirsting and hungering Florestan. We cannot, unfortunately, warm to Frau Naday (Marzelline). What airs and graces, what posturing and mincing, what pompousness. Good heavens, how is it possible to spend an entire evening spreading one's peacock's tail, and in every corner? Naturalness and modesty! Look at Herr Schrödter. If it is fatal for one to depart from the place in life ordained him by providence, and to make a show of oneself without good reason, it is doubly fatal on the stage. Whatever is a playwright to do if everybody wants to play a lord? Herr Schrödter understood the role very well, placing himself, as Jaquino, modestly in the background, and thus all was well.

There is only good to report of Frau Staudigl's[1] visit. She sang the Amneris in *Aida* with much verve, and disclosed a not unexceptional dramatic talent. Her voice, if a bit veiled by age from time to time, is strong and agreeable. Exceptionally effective were certain attitudes in the second act, especially in the "Vieni, vieni" passages. The audience was well disposed, and generous with its applause. For the rest, the roles were excellently cast, with the Messers. Müller (Radames), Rokitansky (Ramfis), Sommer (Amonasro) and Hablawetz (King). Fräulein Schläger (Aida), who did not spare her awesomely powerful voice (to my utmost regret), was especially loudly applauded. But why does not Fräulein Schläger clothe herself in a more human costume?

1.   Gisele Koppmayer-Staudigl (1864-?), an Austrian pupil of Mathilde Marchesi, and a contralto much admired in many German opera houses, including Bayreuth. She had just married Joseph Staudigl (1850-1916), baritone son of the famous Austrian bass of the same name (1807-1861), and a former pupil of Rokitansky at the Vienna Conservatory. Joseph Staudigl, Sr., created the role of Elijah in Mendelssohn's oratorio at the Birmingham Festival of 1846, singing the music at sight at the final rehearsal. Like Scaria — and Wolf — he died insane. It is odd that Wolf should speak of Frau Staudigl's voice as betraying the ravages of time. She was twenty-two.

89. Remembering Liszt and Weber

October 31, 1886

In observance of the centenary of Carl Maria von Weber's birth and of Franz Liszt's death, both the Society of Friends of Music and the Philharmonic Society felt called upon, in the selection of their programs, to depart at least a hairsbreadth from memory's well-trodden lane, and to offer, by way of a change, something "new."

As far as Weber is concerned, so rare an undertaking had some success. One plunged courageously into the enchanted forest of romanticism. Was that not Oberon's magic horn? And once again, how sweetly alluring — do we not wish to listen? — "gone, gone!" But there: glistening weapons, chargers, brave knights, modest ladies, the din of drums and timpani, the rustling of leaves, the ripple of waves — do we not wish to tarry by Euryanthe's side? *Allons enfants!* Truly, such resolution would do honor even to the bravest Indian at the martyr's stake. After some vexation, we arrived finally at the extreme edge of the romantic wilderness. We dug hurriedly, and the treasure was quickly recovered. "Kampf und Sieg" ["Struggle and Victory," a cantata (Opus 4) commemorating the Battle of Waterloo] was the reward of this daring expedition. (There's a moral in it for our worthy Kapellmeister. If he has lost the capacity to understand it, "he makes me sad, and I feel sorry for him."). In all the haste one forgot, unfortunately, to recover the Jubel-Overture [Opus 59], too, and that was stupid. This overture would have been uniquely appropriate as the opening number for the festive occasion. In its stead we had a "Funeral Oration" by Richard Wagner.[1] It is not, indeed, a funeral oration, but, announced as such in the program, it was found fitting to inaugurate a jubilee.

But to find a perverse world illustrated in the crassest manner, just look at the program for the Liszt memorial: "Les Préludes," a Hungarian Rhapsody, Piano Concerto, etc. If the intention was to clothe Carl Maria von Weber's centenary ceremony in funeral attire, the idea with Liszt would seem to have been the utmost gaiety. Everything was there except the "Soirées de Vienne" and a *czardas* or two. Thus Vienna and the Society of Friends of Music chose to honor the men to whom they owe so much, who so often labored in their behalf. And so again, "Les Préludes," and again and again, and after thousands upon thousands of years, and for all eternity, in heaven and hell, in purgatory, in outer space and in limbo, — again only "Les Préludes!" And again and another myriad times the played-to-death "Les Préludes?" Have mercy, Herr Hofkapellmeister! Mercy! Give us, if you want to play the villain, Brahms. Play Dvořák. Play note-writing Englishmen, as many of such as there may be. Play what you want and what you don't want, but withhold from "Les Préludes" that hand weighing so heavily upon your victim, grant a moment's rest to that lovely piece, so abused by your merciless whip, even if that rest were to be eternal. Do that, dear Kapellmeister, and God's blessings be upon you.

It is only with a heavy heart that we remember the days when the Society's concerts were entrusted to Kapellmeister Gericke, now active in America. How different would the memorial have been. He would at least have been tackful enough to include the "Heldenklage" [Heroïde Funèbre"], a sombre tone painting as yet unperformed in Vienna, as suited to the solemn nature of the occasion. Or we might have had the little known, grandiose "Dante" Symphony, or even "Christus." Who knows? But at just the wrong time it was seen fit to release so able a man. With him we lost an industrious, unbiased, enthusiastic artist who went his own way, undeterred by the critics or the crowd, recklessly standing up for everything that was not diametrically opposed to his musical faith.

But what is the credo of our Kapellmeister? Art is commerce, and the press a useful agent. Just play along with the critics, and business prospers — a practical point of view, and especially rewarding in England. But such a business cannot be conducted without compromise. For tit there must be tat. And so both Brahms and Dvořák have been performed twice to keep the business afloat. It is just possible that it may soon be riding a flood — on condition that nothing but Brahms and Dvořák be performed at the Philharmonic concerts. Beethoven will be degraded to the rank of a Weigl, and stricken from the repertoire, which would be no great blow to our critics. Nothing impossible about it, and whoever has time and patience may yet see it come to pass. As things now stand, a healthy cultivation of art is unthinkable. For that we lack the right man, one who could squash the head of the critical Hydra, and make musicians aware of their lack of judgment. What he might do about the public — ah, the public! That is a ghastly subject. We refrain from further comment.

---

1.   Presumably "An Webers Grabe," Wagner's male chorus written for the home-coming of
      Weber's remains to Dresden from London in 1844. See footnote No. 1 to notice of February
      17, 1884.

90. *The Kretschmann Concerts*

November 7, 1886

The greatest musical event of this season is the series of thirty orchestra concerts under the direction of Herr Theobald Kretschmann.

Thirty orchestra concerts! Might one not as easily believe in the wonders of "A Thousand and One Nights" as in the feasibility of so adventurous an undertaking? A foreigner utterly unfamiliar with the circumstances of musical life in Vienna, were he to fall victim to such a sublime idea, would be an object of pity or the target of bad jokes, assuming that anyone took the slightest notice at all. Beyond that, he would hardly arouse the curiosity of our amiable public as to the why and wherefore of such an improbable enterprise. One would say: He is unfamiliar with local conditions, and, in this case, that would be "wisdom's last word." [1]

With Herr Kretschmann, however, a veteran member of our opera orchestra, one may assume that he is sufficiently initiated in the mysteries of our cultural life to be fully aware of the perils — one is tempted to say even the lunacy — of such an unheard-of (but, one hopes, not unheard) project. Herr Kretschmann knows how things stand, musically, in our city. He knows, for example, that of ten Philharmonic concerts nine are packed to the rafters and that the tenth will usually be played to empty seats, even if all the angels in heaven were participating and the composer the dear God himself. He knows that things are not much better with the non-subscription concerts of the Society of Friends of Music. He knows that only such music is found interesting as is played in subscription concerts, and that the quality of such music, as far as it affects attendance by the greater part of our enlightened public, is, as the jurists say, irrelevant. He knows that if fashion dictates bowling at Gause's or ices at Demels on Sunday between one oclock and two-thirty, all will stream to those places, always assuming that such delicacies are to be had on subscription.

What, then, can have moved Herr Kretschmann, under such suspicious circumstances, to put on thirty orchestra concerts? Not, certainly, faith in all-benevolent art! Any such presumption, today, has about it, for musician and public alike, something too offensive to be taken seriously. But maybe Herr

Kretschmann hopes to gather concertgoers to his banner by an exceptional choice of program. Wide of the mark! Instead of hoisting the blood-red flag, determined with it to win or lose, he has preferred the mild white flag of truce. He deals with the critic dictators of fashion, and bows to popular taste. That's also a point of view. But, to take liberties with Goethe, why wander far afield when the right thing lies so near at hand?[2] Is Herr Kretschmann not giving thirty subscription concerts? Can anyone, today, ask more of an impresario?

And so, go ahead and subscribe. A proper person must also be a subscriber, whether of newspapers, rail or streetcar tickets, lending libraries, fasting cures or concert tickets, and so on *ad infinitum*. The first successful step would have been taken. If Herr Kretschmann can only succeed in crowning his orchestra concerts with the halo of fashion, he can give sixty concerts, and he will find his audience regardless of program and performance. We wish him the best of luck, although we can personally muster little enthusiasm for the new enterprise. It's all the same to us whether Brahms violin concertos and Fuchs serenades are to be heard at Kretschmann's concerts or at the Philharmonic. Since the program for all the concerts is as yet unknown to us, we shall withhold judgment, and restrict ourselves for the moment to a discussion of what has been offered thus far.

The concert began with Mozart's Symphony in G minor. This symphony requires no large orchestra, but it does require ultimately schooled musicians, especially winds. And it was precisely in this respect that the Kretschmann Orchestra proved inadequate, most distressingly so in the tender thirty-second note figure of the Adagio, played in such a creaking and bumpy manner that we found it difficult, despite the delicacy of the situation, to repress our smiles. The other three movements went with a good deal of zest, and were technically in order. Following this, Herr Nachez,[3] a young violinist, played the Brahms Violin Concerto in D, Opus 77, an utterly repulsive piece (forgive the rude expression, Herr Hofkapellmeister!), full of platitudes and vapid profundity. The virtuoso accomplished his ungrateful task with great bravura, and did his best to breathe warmth and life into the icy composition, for the most part successfully. I left before the last number, by Jensen,[4] reflecting that I might have done so more profitably after the Mozart.

1.   From *Faust* II

        Das ist der Weisheit letzter Schluss:
        Nur der verdient sich Freiheit wie das Leben,
        Der täglich sie erobern muss.
        (That is wisdom's last insight:
        He alone earns freedom as, indeed, his life
        Who wins it for himself in the daily fight.)

2.   The allusion is to a poem, "Erinnerung" (Remembrance):

        Willst du immer weiter schweifen?
        Sieh, das Gute liegt so nah,
        Lerne nur das Glück ergreifen,
        Denn das Glück ist immer da.
        (Would you ever wander far afield

When goodness lies so near?
Learn to grasp happiness revealed,
For happiness is always here.)

3. Tivadar Nachéz (Theodor Naschitz) (1859-1930), a Hungarian violinist, pupil of Joachim in Berlin and Léonard in Paris, long resident in London, whose technical virtuosity earned him international renown.

4. Adolph Jensen (1837-1879) an East Prussian composer best known for his Lieder.

91. Liszt on Two Pianos

November 14, 1886

However far we have progressed in the neglect of the works of the great Franz Liszt, however absurdly the grand inquisition conducts itself against all that is new, bold and splendid, however childishly our "elite" public reflects the viewpoint of our conservative and hypocritical press at the concerts of the Philharmonic and the Society of Friends of Music, however quickly, too, the upstanding, well-behaved young John becomes little Johnny when the amiable or snarling — as the case may be — Grand Inquisitor wrinkles his brow, and however quickly, again, little Johnny swells up to John when the exalted patron, delighted with the canine tricks of his most humble client, favors him with a benign wink — in a word, however bad it is, and has long been, with respect to the recognition of Liszt's works, there are still those who, disregarding the threatening constellation on the critical horizon, hurry bravely to their positions and, defying public opinion and its organs, throw down the gauntlet.

The Messrs Göllerich[1] and Stradal[2] did just this when, on the occasion of the Liszt memorial, they put six of their departed master's symphonic poems on their program. The public picked up the gauntlet and descended in hordes upon the battleground, the Bösendorfersaal. And see what happened. Saul became Paul, and the Messrs Göllerich and Stradal, the anathematized, the pitied, the scorned, ended as the heroes of the day. To do a concert of six symphonic poems, and play them on the piano one after another, takes a lot of courage. In no other city than Vienna, however, would one have seen in it anything so unusual. But here, thanks to the loving care of our staunch Hofkapellmeister, we have not progressed beyond "Les Préludes" (and once, by inadvertance, "Mazeppa").

Just think, now, how strange to the public was the highly individual language of so profound and spiritual a nature as Liszt, especially hearing it only in piano transcription, and in far too long a program. And yet with what stamina and concentration, with what lively interest and enthusiasm the listeners followed the performances! One inclines to the hope that in this rather unusual way, interest and, eventually, appreciation for the works of Liszt may be nourished. One needs, to be sure, two such initiated and devoted interpreters as the Messrs. Göllerich and Stradal. Which is not to say that their interpretations were wholly faultless. But shortcomings were so rarely in evidence, the virtues so brilliantly conspicuous, that we would find it ungracious to put nettles in laurels well earned. Since, moreover, I was in the fortunate position of being able to discuss with Herr Göllerich personally the pluses and minuses of his and his colleague Stradal's performances, I see no need to repeat it all here.

The second Kretschmann Orchestra concert was incomparably more rewarding than the first. Bizet's charming and lovely *L'Arlésienne* Suite was, among all the offerings, the best played. The public has Herr Kretschmann's sagacity to thank for the opportunity of making the acquaintance of this ingenious, adroit and imaginative piece. Herr Kretschmann is said to be showing much industry and persistence in his hunt for novelties, assisted, we are sorry to hear, by the redoutable Herr Dömpke as beater. We may expect a lot of feeble game and drooping fowl. God give us strength! Fräulein Hermine von Feyrer sang an aria from Mendelssohn's "Elijah" to the not inconsiderable astonishment of the audience. It wasn't all that bad — Herr Benno Schönberger has many of the talents that go with being a pianist, but they were of little help to him on this occasion. To play Chopin one must be a poet. Otherwise the greatest strength and virtuosity are useless.

One may credit Herr Heuberger,[3] whose "Night Music for String Orchestra" [Opus 7] brought the program to a close, with every imaginable virtue — except originality. It's good run-of-the-mill stuff, reciting commonplaces in an obliging and courteous manner. Herr Heuberger is an agreeable conversationalist who can entertain an unsophisticated and well-disposed gathering in a very respectable sort of way, never at a loss for a word, never digressing from the chosen subject — boring as it is — never stepping on anyone's toes even by accident, nor giving anyone even the gentlest poke in the ribs, but rather going out of his way to avoid giving offense, and ready with a healing plaster for every wounded little heart. He wishes to hurt no one, and will go to any length to avoid creating excitement and tension. Herr Heuberger is, in a word, an amiable composer, and he is fully entitled to the flattering distinction of being the darling of the public.

The concert given by the famous violin virtuoso Franz Ondřiček[4] drew a large audience to the Grosser Musikvereinssaal. Three years have passed since he last played here. He has made amazing progress in the interval. At that time we greatly admired his imposing virtuosity, the fullness of his tone and the refinement and variety of his shading. New, or at least far closer to perfection, was his stylistic grasp of the Beethoven Violin Concerto. The mere virtuoso is at a loss with this composition. It offers him little opportunity for the display of technical wonders. And yet what treasures are not there for the taking! This performance was enchanting, especially the way in which the artist went to the heart of the marvelous Adagio, his playing absolutely simple, without a trace of superficial embellishment, intimate, but with no aftertaste of sentimentality. It was a masterly accomplishment. The vocal offerings of Fräulein Steinbach were nicely sung and warmly received, so that nothing disturbed the harmony of this enjoyable evening.

1. August Göllerich (1859-1923), Austrian pianist, educator and author. He was a pupil of Bruckner and Liszt, and an early biographer of each.
2. August Stradal (1860-1930), a pupil of Bruckner and Liszt, who made many transcriptions of Liszt's orchestral music.
3. Richard Heuberger (1850-1914), an Austrian composer subsequently better known as a music critic in Vienna and Munich.
4. František Ondříček (1859-1922), Prague-born violinist, a student of Massart at the Conservatoire in Paris and subsequently widely acclaimed as virtuoso and pedagogue (in Vienna). He founded, in 1908, the Ondříček String Quartet and, a year later, published a "New Method for Achieving Technical Mastery on the Violin Based on Anatomical and Physiological Principles."

92. *Goldmark's* Merlin[1]

November 21, 1886

The legend of the magician Merlin dates from the earliest Middle Ages. Merlin's prophesies, in particular, to which historical significance was attributed, were held in high esteem. The tale grew taller with the passing years. The legends of King Arthur and of the Holy Grail were drawn together, and a mystic-religious element came increasingly to the fore. It was in this form that the romantic saga of Merlin came down to us in an old French fable,[2] the source for modern poets and poetasters.

The imaginative Immermann[3] adhered strictly to the French model in his myth, *Merlin*, the rather less imaginative Lipiner[4] [librettist of Goldmark's opera] only in part. While Immermann, working from Friedrich Schlegel's[5] abridged translation of the French original, includes almost every épisode in his poem, even making foundation pillars out of what appears in the fable only as ornamentation, Lipiner is content with the fundamental idea, and builds on enormous ashlars a miserable shanty of free invention. But before showing the libretto its due reverence, let us tarry first at the sources of the legend and listen to their song.

The devils were not a little put out about the redeeming mission of Him born of the immaculate Virgin, and in order to paralyze the power of His calling, they resolved to emulate God in dispatching a mortal representative into the world.

So wollen wir gleichfalls uns zeugen den Erben,
Der Mensch ist nur durch den Menschen zu werben.

[And so we, too, shall have an heir,
'Gainst man 'tis only man can set the snare.]

To this end Satan took to himself a devout, beautiful virgin who had entrusted herself to the care of a hermit (Blasius). In order, however, that he might have her in his power, she had to have made herself guilty of a sin. He succeeds, eventually, by recourse to all sorts of diabolical device, in bringing this about, whereupon he takes her in her sleep. "But Satan has foolishly deceived himself, for by betraying her in her sleep, he had failed to seduce her soul, which belonged utterly to God. . . . Thus it happened that the foul fiend once again lost what he thought to have won." The child, who came into the world with hair and teeth, was christened with his grandfather's name of Merlin, and grew to boyhood under the eyes of his mother and the hermit Blasius. He could talk immediately, and was altogether shrewd and wise. "The child of the virgin," the fable says, "was like his creator, the devil, in that he knew everything that happened in the present, or was spoken. But thanks to his mother's piety, the purification of baptism and the grace of God, he received from God the gift of divination. Thus it was that the child could commend himself to God or the devil, or give back to God what he had from God, and to the devil what the devil had given him. The devil had given him only the body. God had given him soul and intelligence, and to this child more than to any other because he needed them."

After Merlin had buried his mother, whose execution he had forestalled by his omniscience, and having dictated to the hermit on to a slate the mystery of the grail, along with all manner of prophecy, he went to the court of Vordigern in England, where he astonished all and sundry with his wisdom. For a favor he had done King Uther Pendragon, he demanded as his reward a boy, the issue of a sinful liaison between the king and the wife of one of his vassals. The child was the future King Arthur. The request was granted, and Merlin resolved to dedicate Arthur to the service of the Holy Grail, and to establish him as king on Monsalvat. But the meeting with Nynianne [Viviane, the Lady of the Lake] at the fountain in the forest of Briogne frustrated forever the accomplishment of this objective.

Nynianne was the daughter of Diona, the latter so named after Diana, the Sicilian siren, whose godchild he was. Her beauty touched the heart of Merlin from the moment that he, having assumed the form of a handsome knight, rode into the fateful forest. There promptly began between them a teasing interplay, mixed with magical wonders by Merlin who, to please her, conjured up a castle complete with knights and their ladies. Little by little he became so ensnared in her toils, although knowing full well that he dare not touch a woman, that he became "the fool." He revealed to Nynianne, in the face of her complaints that he would one day leave her, the existence of a charm that would chain him forever to her side. Zealous to learn the charm, the artful lady now went at him with flattery and threats, to get him to disclose the secret. Merlin held out for a long time, for he well knew the destructive power of the charm if used against him. But under the hawthorn hedge he blurted out his secret, and Nynianne promptly enveloped him in her veil. Merlin goes mad, is bound forever to that fateful spot, and is lost to King Arthur and the Grail. Thus the fable. According to Immermann, Satan will redeem him in return for a profession of faith. Merlin refuses, and dies at Satan's touch with the prayer on his lips: "Hallowed be Thy Name!"

From this fantastic saga, striking in its symbolism, Lipiner has drawn an opera libretto as trivial in its language as it is banal in its substance. Let's look first at the plot. Act 1. Before Arthur's castle. Lancelot reveals to Glendower the situation of Arthur rendered perilous by the treason of a Briton. Merlin, harp in hand, puts their fears at rest, assuring Arthur of victory. But the devil must have a hand in it. So, at Merlin's summons, the Demon appears, and after a weak show of defiance, declares himself ready to give Arthur his protection. There is some will-of-the-wisp activity and haze to disconcert the enemy. Merlin goes confidently into battle. Only the Demon remains rather disconsolately behind. After ranting in very eclectic verses about the fate that places him in Merlin's power, he has a good idea, and summons a creature molded of fire and water, but nevertheless the spit and image of Erda in Wagner's *Der Ring des Nibelungen*. But that by the by. Morgana, as this rare hybrid is called, appears, first announcing herself in the form of a live fountain colored green and red appropriately to her nature. She is to give the Demon a recipe for getting the better of Merlin. Morgana dallies a while, and finally comes up with it. So, a woman can be your undoing, happily croaks the reluctant Demon. Now just wait!

The scene changes. Dawn. The king and his soldiers return victorious from the battle. Merlin, the all-conquering predecessor of Professor Hansen,[6] mesmerizes the traitor, Bedwyr by name, and then indulges in some acrobatics on his harp, as if preluding a hymn of victory, when suddenly: "Hallali, hallali! Hirschlein fein, streck dein Bein, Bogen kommt doch hinterdrein," etc. [Tally ho, little doe, time to go, beware the bow.] Viviane appears with her virgin attendants and plays up to Merlin. His feigned indifference so infuriates the tender-savage huntress that she tears to shreds the oakleaf wreath which, at Arthur's behest, she is to place on Merlin's head, and throws it at the astonished magician's feet. Arthur, however, knows how to conduct himself as a proper gentleman. To the satisfaction of all, he adorns Merlin's brow with his own wreath. Once more, noisy jubilation and curtain.

Act II. Merlin's magic garden. Modred, Arthur's nephew, plots against the king. Lancelot accuses Modred of treason. Furious confrontation. Merlin is called in as arbiter. But this time the medium is more resistant to magnetic influence, and Merlin disgraces himself, as we shall see. Half his powers have been dissipated since he looked too deeply into Viviane's eyes. To make matters worse, the Demon now brings Viviane to him. At her request, the portal of the temple is opened, and one sees an altar, over it a veil. Viviane, delighted, takes the veil from the Demon's hands, and playfully tosses it aloft. But, wonder of wonders, the veil remains hovering radiantly over her head, while, at the same time, spirits emerge from every corner and execute a charming dance to old-fashioned *Ländler* music.

The scene comes to a speedy end as Merlin enters the garden. He is astonished to see Viviane, and tells her rudely to be gone. As she turns to go, he notices the veil. "The veil? Oho! Who dares come thus to me?" Viviane: "To thee? Forgive, I knew not 'twas to thee." Merlin: "And then the door — by whom am I betrayed?" Vivianne: "I bade the portal ope, and it obeyed." Merlin: "It opened itself — to you? Oh, eternal power!"

He knows now that his fate is sealed. Unwittingly he betrays to Viviane the magic power of the veil, and when, following the love scene, Merlin makes as though to leave, she tests the power of the magic by throwing the veil around his head. The scene changes immediately to a wild, rocky landscape. One discerns Merlin chained to a rock, while in the background the Demon rises up and breaks out in shrill, mocking laughter. Viviane falls to the ground with an awesome shriek.

Act III. Scene as at the end of Act II. Viviane regrets in pitifully inadequate language her impetuosity. Thereupon she lies down and goes to sleep. Morgana appears, and utters comforting words. There is still a way whereby Merlin may be saved. "When at the crossroads in the night, the gloating villain comes in sight, love shall put death itself to flight, and break the evil spell. Yes, love shall prove a savior bright, to rescue him from hell." No objections to that charming, pretty ditty, especially as the rhyming is faultless. Viviane awakens, delighted with her charming dream and pretty verses. Her attendants, too, who have in the meantime sought her out, are likewise delighted. They are modest harmless creatures.

After their departure, Merlin, Lancelot and his warriors take over the stage with their reciprocal clamor. But nothing good comes of it all. Merlin rattles vainly at his chains, and it looks as if Arthur will, in all probability, get the worst of it against Modred. But no! Merlin reaches a desperate decision. He commits himself to the devil. The Demon appears instantly, highly pleased by Merlin's perspicacious conduct, and providing the composer with the eagerly awaited opportunity to loose an orchestral volcano of the most destructive sort. Merlin is freed, and proceeds with his companions against the treacherous Modred. Viviane and her attendants, meanwhile, prepare for the festive reception of Merlin. The dialogue that now develops between Viviane and the chorus, because of its unadorned simplicity, and the compelling power of its expression, deserves to be quoted:

Viviane: "Say, am I beautiful, and will he love me?"
Ladies: "Yes, you are beautiful, and he will love you."
Viviane: "Woe, that my teardrops should profusely flow."
Ladies: "Your grace and beauty most profusely show!"
Viviane: "Is there no trace of tears remaining?"
Ladies: "No, not a trace of tears remaining." Etc.

Reading such verses, one is moved to exclaim with that famous belletrist, Konrad Dithorn of Nuremberg, author of "Battle in the Arena": "Since Freiligrath's time, none has come forward in this genre."[7]

While Viviane and her attendants continue in this extravagantly mysterious vein, the knights bring in the dying Merlin on a stretcher. Immediately there appears, in the appropriate background, the Demon, and demands his booty. But Viviane, mindful of Morgana's words, "When at the crossroads in the night, the gloating villain comes in sight," etc., stabs herself with a dagger, much to the discomfiture of the Demon, who sees himself robbed of his victim by Viviane's sacrifice. He lurches off, cursing. Anyone who finds this opera text attractive will not easily resist the poetic power of this final scene. Let everyone achieve blessedness in his own fashion.

Had the librettist, instead of giving us battles and festive processions, which interrupt and flatten the story, allowed the drama to develop out of the mysterious duality of Merlin's nature, and had he, furthermore, added to the basic theme of the legend an ethical motive, and thus given it depth and inner substance, one could speak in all seriousness of an opera text with no less a hero than Merlin. But nothing decent has ever been done with trumpet fanfares and saber rattling, with will-of-the-wisps and the apparition of spirits.

As for the music provided for this fine text, it confines itself to a few Wagnerian themes for the sophisticated listener, and to some vulgar dance tunes, much loved in Upper Austria and Styria, for the less enlightened. The rest is taken care of by chromatic scales, contrived modulations, some meager crumbs of the composer's own earlier melodies, some desperate struggles with musical impotence and inarticulateness. It seems hardly conceivable that Goldmark, who revealed invention and skill in *The Queen of Sheba*, could write so miserable a score. The principal motif, with which the Prelude begins, we hear in almost every measure of the second act of *Tristan*. Despite that, Herr Goldmark does not hesitate to play around with it through three acts (not including the Prelude) without a trace of shame or embarrassment.

Goldmark seems to have been altogether too close to *Tristan* in this score. But echoes, too, of *Der Ring des Nibelungen*, *Die Meistersinger* and *Lohengrin* are not only not avoided, but even thrust forward with a certain ostentation. Nor are borrowings from Schumann and Flotow scorned. The score, like the text, is nothing if not eclectic. Lest I seem unjust, I would like to observe that the absurd Wagner-aping in other operas with which we are familiar has reached its highest point in *Merlin*. Finally, it should be mentioned that the opera is scored with great knowledge and care. Unfortunately, the art of instrumentation, these days, is the least of a composer's accomplishments, although not even this distinction can be credited to so "serious" a composer as Brahms.

In order to assist the opera at the box office, the management did its utmost in respect of scenery, costumes and staging. If despite all that, the work does not survive, the stage director may, like Pontius Pilate, wash his hands in all innocence. The principals did all they could, for better or worse, to fulfill the composer's wishes. A true bit of fortune for *Merlin* that Frau Materna created the role of Viviane. Without her inspired accomplishment the opera would have been sheerly impossible. Herr Winkelmann developed the title role admirably, and brought down the house with his spirited delivery of the Hymn, although it is a piece more appropriate to a street singer drunk on brandy than to the exalted seer, Merlin. One hopes that the applause was for the singer and not for the piece, whose triviality would be hard to match. Herr Sommer prattled away bravely as King Arthur, a part far too miserly treated by the composer. Lancelot was Herr Horwitz, whose acting could make a stone nervous, let alone a sensitive critic. What the devil inspires Herr Horwitz to hop around like a galvanized frog?[8] I am always afraid he may finally lose his balance, and fall and break his nose. Would that he might "cultivate more sweet repose," a diet that would be very good for his acting. To give Herr Schrödter (Modred), with his innocent countenance, the role of a traitor was a bad idea, and to see our excellent buffo, Herr Mayerhofer, in armor (he was Glendower) was no less amusing. Absolutely outstanding, however, was Herr Reichenberg (Demon). His mask was truly infernal, his facial expressions diabolical, his costumes hellish, his silver claws satanic, his singing demonic — in short, the very devil of a devil.

The performance under Direktor Jahn's authoritative direction was excellent. Singers and composer were recalled again and again. But despite all that, it is our belief that *Merlin's* sojourn upon our stage will be brief.

1.   Wolf is reviewing the world premiere, which took place on November 19. *Merlin* was produced at the Metropolitan Opera House in New York during the season of 1886-87 with Lilli Lehmann as Viviane. It had five performances, and has not been heard of since then.

2.   "Merlin," by the thirteenth century French poet Robert de Boron, linking the Grail and Arthurian legend, with Merlin as the link.

3.   Karl Leberecht Immermann (1796-1840), German dramatist, novelist and poet. His *Merlin*, a drama, dated from 1832.

4.   Siegfried Lipiner (1856-1911), Austrian poet and playwright.

5.   Actually, Dorothea Schlegel (1763-1839), née Mendelssohn, Friedrich's wife, and sister-in-law of August Wilhelm Schlegel, the German translator of Shakespeare. She was Felix Mendelssohn's aunt.

6.   Possibly Gerhard Armauer Hansen (1841-?), a distinguished Norwegian physician and zoologist who had studied in Bonn and Vienna.

7.   Ferdinand Freiligrath (1876-1910), German poet and translator (Victor Hugo, Alfred de Musset, Robert Burns and Thomas Moore). I have been unable to trace Konrad von Dithorn. H.P.

8.   See footnote No. 1 to the notice of April 6, 1884.

93. Discovering Smetana

November 28, 1886

Theobald Kretschmann and his orchestra, as if determined to affirm their will to live, work with the utterly appalling indefatigability of a machine. The timetable of the enterprise, proceeding now at half steam, now at full, is held to with a precision already bordering on the uncanny. For superstitious music critics ominous Friday has lost its terrors, since now on Wednesday, if not on Saturday, the inevitable takes place in the Bösendorfersaal. This awful punctuality disturbs us. There is something inhuman about it. As with many a *jour fixe*, it is unshakable; it allows of no flexibility, and Wednesday, of all days, fits the bill best. Herr Kretschmann should have thought of this in good time. But to the point —

Of the five concerts given thus far, the third was outstanding as concerns both the program and the artistic performance. A Haydn Symphony in E minor,[1] sounding very like a symphony by Mozart, was splendidly played, as were two symphonic poems, "Vyšehrad" and "Vltava," | Moldau|[2] by Smetana. Since the composer uses Slavic airs in both works, we cannot speak of his powers of invention. But the treatment of the themes discloses so much intelligence and musico-poetic sensibility that we were sheerly astonished to be meeting so extraordinarily gifted a composer in the concert hall for the first time. His command of form, moreover, is amazing, and his instrumentation on the order of Berlioz. In short, we have here two masterpieces. That is enough to restrain the Philharmonic from concerning itself with works of such a kind, and since Dvořák and Brahms are most generous in the provision of fuel, many another burnt offering will have to be sacrificed to the Philharmonic audience before the sickly vapors will have evaporated that, under the prevailing circumstances, threaten to stifle every deeper artistic breath.

Wagner's "Siegfried-Idyll" suffered not a little under the brutality of the woodwinds. The conductor, too, in the matter of tempo, had much to answer for. The beginning, for example, was conspicuously dragged, the ending rushed. Herr Kretschmann overestimated the ability of his orchestra in reckoning it ready for so delicate a task. There are few pieces so challenging to an orchestra as the "Siegfried-Idyll." The colors are applied so tenderly, light and shadow so finely judged, the ornamentation so extraordinarily multifarious, the entire structure so artful and yet so harmonious that for all the luxuriance of detail the contours of the picture in their totality emerge ever more plastically. To achieve this overall impression without denying the listener his pleasure in the charmingly episodic is just what the Kretschmann orchestra failed to do.

The fourth concert brought an Overture to *Macbeth* by Brüll and a Serenade for String Orchestra by a Herr Mannheimer. In refraining from any criticism whatsoever we are satisfied that we have demonstrated a sufficient degree of benevolence toward both composers. A Mozart concerto was played by Herr Labor[3] fluently but to our ears in rather too dry a manner. The uncommonly watery music to *Melusine* by Herr Julius Zellner[4] was not without some essential characteristic coloration.

We were unable to hear the fifth Kretschmann concert, preferring the recital by the cellist Herr Robert Hausmann,[5] a bit of carelessness on our part that we were able to regret only when it was too late. Herr Hausmann really needed Herr Dr. Johannes Brahms as a drawing card, thus assuring himself a "receptive" audience. And, indeed, his "accomplishments" were greeted with enthusiasm, although we can attest to having seldom heard so mediocre a cellist. Herr Hausmann's playing was as cold and contrived as the compositions he played, and as boring, too. May the cello sonata of Corelli, with piano, please him who thinks he understands it; may a Bach sarabande and bourrée excite visions and the sound of angel voices; may one be a lunatic and find a redeeming world-riddle behind every note from the pen of the great Bach — good, we will try to find some sympathy for such absurdities. But to write down, print and have performed something such as the new Sonata for Violoncello and Piano (in F major, Opus 99) by Herr Dr. Johannes Brahms, actually to have a hand in it, moreover, to demand that it please, to see that it pleases, and to take the assurance of such pleasure not as diabolical irony, but as sincere applause, to offer this new work as heaven knows what — to observe all this, and not to be infected by such madness, that is beyond joking, and, so help me, I begin to gain some measure of self-respect. What is music, today, what is harmony, what is melody, what is rhythm, what is form — if this tohuwabohu is seriously accepted as music? If, however, Herr Dr. Johannes Brahms is set on mystifying his worshippers with this newest work, if he is out to have some fun with their brainless veneration, then that is something else again, and we admire in Herr Brahms the greatest charlatan of this century and of all centuries to come.

The first Quartet Evening of the Rosés began well enough. But then from excellent performers one could reasonably expect excellence. We were especially and agreeably surprised by Herr Rosé's energetic, forceful playing, which stood the Mendelssohn Quartet, [in E flat], Opus 44, in good stead. The discipline of the players enjoyed a triumph in the fast, headlong course of the

Scherzo. All honor and respect before such accomplishment. To add to the evening's delights, Frau W. de Serres, better known under her former name of Montigny-Remaury,[6] distinguished herself in the second movement of Schumann's Trio in D minor, Opus 63. This composition, with the exception of the Scherzo, bears strong traces of the later period of the ill-fated master. Nor was the first movement played with anything like the "energy and passion" called for by the composer. The more effective, then, the rhythmic power of the Scherzo. Frau des Serres played the piano part with great delicacy and insight, and harvested the most enthusiastic applause. In Beethoven's Quartet in E minor, Opus 59, there were many shortcomings, especially on the part of the violist, whose playing, now too forward, now too restrained, inhibited a uniform ensemble in the first and second movements. The last two movements, on the other hand, were highly satisfactory.

That the recital by Signorina Teresina Tua, who has so quickly become a favorite in Vienna, would draw a packed house was a foregone conclusion. The Viennese will have his fun, whether in the theater or in concert, in public or within the four walls of his home, and thus, too, he listens to Tua for the fun of the thing. And truly, there was fun to be had, and aplenty. It began rather seriously. Mendelssohn's Violin Concerto is cheerful, but by no means a laughing matter. But after Zarczycki,[7] followed by the familiar [Sarasate] "Zapateado" and other nonsense as encores with which the amiable and conquettish signorina sought to satisfy the appetite of an audience howling "da capo!" it was all pretty merry. At the end we heard nothing but flageolets, pizzicatos, whirring double trills and arpeggios. It was all dancing and flickering and frills, and through it all the delicate sugar fairy with the astonished eyes and the childlike smile and the impatient mincing steps. Ah, who would not be driven mad?

We spent an agreeable evening with Fräulein Hermine Spiess.[8] The young lady rejoices in a sympathetic organ, darkly colored, and knows well how to express the most varied moods in a highly dramatic manner.

1. The so-called "Mourning" Symphony.

2. The first two of the six symphonic poems comprising Smetana's "My Country."

3. Josef Labor (1842-1924), a blind Bohemian pianist who toured widely, settled in Vienna, took up the organ, and was soon reckoned the finest organist in Austria.

4. Julius Zellner (1832-1900), a Viennese composer but primarily an educator. The piece referred to here was actually a symphonic poem, "Die schöne Melusine."

5. Robert Hausmann (1852-1909), German cellist, a pupil of Piatti, from 1879 to 1907 cellist of the Joachim Quartet in Berlin.

6. Fanny Montigny-Remaury (1843-1913), a niece of Ambroise Thomas, and an internationally celebrated French pianist.

7. Alexander Zarzycki (1834-1895), Polish composer of salon music and, for a time, director of the Conservatory in Warsaw.

8. Hermine Spies (1857-1893), contralto pupil of Julius Stockhausen, especially noted for her singing of Brahms.

94. Serenades and Boredom

December 5, 1886

In order, by way of a change, to draw a new and unfamiliar subject into the realm of our critique, let us turn once again to Theobald Kretschmann's thirty orchestra concerts. A fifth of this onerous passage has already been covered — and with some success. The orchestra is still at full strength, the conductor resolute and utterly determined to see it through. There will be no capitulation [if only] for the simple reason that the hoped-for siege will not take place. If it were to do so, Herr Kretschmann and a mere half of his cohorts would be able to throw the besiegers back before the very portals of the concert hall — or there are no more serenades for strings.

The successes enjoyed by Robert Fuchs's [serenades] leave our "favorites" not an hour's repose, and terrible must be the symptoms when the brains of serenade composers begin to experience labor pains. What pitiable objects are they then! How they groan and croak and whine and weep and yawn like post boxes, all expectency for things that should come but do not. To rid oneself of such afflictions, really nothing but pure boredom, there are means enough, at once pleasurable and innocent. But serenade composers, who live not for themselves, but for the general public, can do nothing with innocence and pleasure. And so, instead of uniting to attack boredom, or to sleep it off, drink it off, loaf it off or gamble it off (a sure-fire device), they write it off in serenades, and render publishers, conductors, musicians, critics and all that have ears (and critics do have ears, don't they?) miserable.

Herr Dr. Johannes Brahms, who also deals in serenades, but who, as Ludwig II (as Bülow jokingly called him), happily distinguishes himself from serenade specialists by his universality, can hardly confine himself to this one grateful genre as a means of coping with his own portion of boredom. He reckons that he owes it to his fame to impregnate every form of instrumental and vocal music with that precious sensation, on which account he has recently taken to composing symphonies — to the great satisfaction of our worthy Hofkapellmeister, Dr. Hans Richter.

But getting back to Kretschmann's orchestra concert, to deny that Herr Kretschmann and his cohorts still dominate the battlefield long after the audience has begun a disciplined retreat would be a falsehood, and we shall leave to one side the question as to whether or not this premature longing for movement and fresh air may be attributed to a mysterious interreaction of the audience's ears and certain instruments of torture in the orchestra. It is regrettable in any case that so able a general as Herr Kretschmann has mostly recruits to command, cannon fodder who perform admirably in the powder and smoke of a tumultuous fortissimo, but lose their heads when exposed as outposts on halfway difficult terrain where presence of mind is essential. The woodwinds, particularly, distinguish themselves as despisers of all tonal beauty. They may be good enough to train cobras, or to give the necessary musical profile to a Brahms piano concerto, but they are hardly up to anything better than that. Rehearsals are no help, although better instruments might be. Our criticism concerns not the more or less competent playing of the blowers, but solely the tonal ugliness, the vulgar sound, of the instruments themselves.

Herr Hermann Grädener, who conducted the concert, allowing Herr Kretschmann to function as cellist, spared no efforts to carry through the program as perfectly as possible, to adjust the highly unequal relationship of winds to strings, and thus to achieve the desired homogeneity among the diverse masses. If he was only slightly successful, it was less his fault than that of the orchestra, still insufficiently schooled and disciplined. Best played, relatively speaking, was the Trumpet Overture of Mendelssohn [in C major, Opus 101] (an effective piece with, as the title suggests, plenty of brass), since it offered the orchestra ample opportunity to blow away to its heart's concent. A Sinfonietta, Opus 14, by Herr Grädener was enthusiastically received. In respect of form, length, richness of detail and careful structure it might even have been a symphony. The composer may have dubbed it a sinfonietta because of its cheerful character. But whether symphony or sinfonietta, the composition pleased us, if less for its musical than its moral quality.

I say moral because the piece makes no pretense of being more than it is: a nice, amiable, unassuming thing, dealing with no wondrous matters, but chattering away pleasantly, sometimes even farcically, verging on the bizarre *à la* Berlioz, at least to the extent compatible with the position of a conservatory professor. The scoring is clean, and piquant, too. There is, of course, a lot of triviality, but this also pleased us because of its naturalness. Any musical journeyman can be profound and unintelligible like Dr. Johannes Brahms if it suits him to deceive both himself and his audience — assuming that the latter extends the requisite faith.

95. Weber and Der Freischütz D'Albert and Rosenthal

December 12, 1886

All musical Germany is celebrating the centenary of the birth of its most national composer, the inspired founder of German opera, the glorious singer of freedom and fatherland, the man who honored Germany's rebirth with the most precious gift, the composer of *Der Freischütz:* Carl Maria von Weber.

To what German has *Der Freischütz* not become a treasure? What expatriate has not dreamt himself back to childhood in the rustling of its forests, in the dawns and twilights of its ghostly shadows, and found asylum? And what of the great historical importance of *Der Freischütz,* whose victory over the effeminate Italian operatic idiom also dealt a fatal blow to its toughest opponent, the spectacle opera of Spontini? German national consciousness, newly awakened and strengthened under Napoleonic oppression, literally thirsted for its cultural manifestation, and it was reserved to Carl Maria von Weber to sound the strings vibrating in the souls of his countrymen in one mighty chord.

It is only from this point of view that one can explain the fascination of *Der Freischütz* for its own time, still far from ripe enough to appreciate the full significance of its novelty and daring. Did not Tieck,[1] a friend of Weber, and fine connoisseur of music, call *Der Freischütz* the most unmusical din that ever roared from any stage? And Spohr, a year later, could write:[2] "Since until that time I had not rated Weber's talent as a composer very highly, I was eager to make the acquaintance of this opera, hoping to find out why it had been so enthusiastically received in Germany's two capital cities [Berlin and Vienna]. A closer acquaintance did not solve, for me, the riddle of its enormous success, unless it was simply Weber's gift of writing for the masses." And then, finally, E.T.A. Hoffmann, the brilliant interpreter of *Don Giovanni* and the Beethoven symphonies and the works of Gluck, who felt that for the Wolf Glen scene, the "high point" of the work, the designer and the engineer deserved the "heartfelt thanks of all tender souls."[3] Weber had to hear from every side that the opera owed its success solely to deviltry and fireworks. This is reflected in a letter he wrote to Lichtenstein:[4] "You may well believe that there are adversaries. It is only natural, also, that all the deviltry often confuses me, too, and were it not for honorable souls who pressed my hand in satisfaction, I might well think, 'All right, M'sieur Samiel did it all alone.'" What charming skepticism!

Now it was Weber himself, of course, who most emphatically insisted upon a realistic evocation of the nocturnal-ghostly upon the stage. When the imaginative designer of the Berlin opera, Gropius,[5] proposed to represent the horrors of the Wolf Glen as proceeding from the battle of elemental forces, and the ghostly apparitions as figments of Kaspar's and Max's imagination, bringing them to the spectator as suggestions rather than realities, Weber countered: "Your ideas are too subtle for opera. They are all right for *Hamlet* and *Macbeth*. But who will appreciate my music in the hellish spectacle from your crags and cloud formations? Make the owl's eyes really glow, have proper bats flying around, don't hesitate to introduce a couple of ghosts and skeletons, and see to a fine crescendo with the casting of the bullets."

These words speak for the practical stage wise conductor who always knows exactly what can be done with the resources at hand, and who knows, too, when those resources, assisted by the engineer and the designer, are capable of achieving the intended effect. Very advantageous for an understanding of the opera was the production of *Preciosa*[6] that had taken place a short time before. Weber himself acknowledges this. In a letter to Lichtenstein the master says: "I can well believe there is much in *Der Freischütz* that may puzzle you. There are things in it never before seen on the stage in this form, things which I drew from my own fantasy without the slightest reference to precedent. I hope to God that I have hit the mark. I am very happy to hear from you, too, that *Preciosa* had a solid success. It is a good preparation for *Der Freischütz,* for it contained, from the ordinary journeyman point of view, many daring things." In terms of our own concepts of "daring," the journeyman would find the score of *Preciosa* pretty tame, but then what revolutions have not taken place in the world of music in the last sixty-six years!

In our opera house, too, which seems to be inaugurating a Weber festival, *Preciosa* introduced *Der Freischütz* and, at the same time, a so-called "Weber Cycle" mixed with compositions by Ingaz Brüll, a charming idea that fits perfectly within the frame of our Weber festival, and that cannot be credited too highly in a certain sense to the ingenious head that thought it up.

As exciting as was the performance of *Preciosa,* thanks to the assistance of actors from the Court Theater, just as depressing was the impression left by the production of *Der Freischütz.* Only the chorus and orchestra under Direktor Jahn's exemplary direction measured up to the requirements. The principals gave little or no satisfaction. That our opera house, despite a milky way of stars, could not properly cast the role of Agathe is sad but true. That one found it necessary to engage Frau Sucher from Hamburg in order to make a production of *Der Freischütz* possible is no less sad. That, despite all this, Agathe cut a sorry figure is, unfortunately, only all too true. We have never been blind to Frau Sucher's estimable capacities, and have sung her praises in no hoarse falsetto. Indeed, we have rather pitched our praise a couple of tones too high. But her work on this occasion pleased us not at all. During the entire scene and aria it was as if a cold draft were blowing through Agathe's cosy room. How peevish and frosty was the sweetest prayer that any innocent ever addressed to heaven! Truly, it can hardly have risen above the flies. In movement and gesture, too, Frau Sucher was a very model of ennui. Heaven knows whether others felt the same way. If so, I am sorry for Frau Sucher. If not, well, we won't quarrel about it.

Some years ago, our opera house possessed in Fräulein Pirk an uncommonly gifted soubrette. The engagement was soon terminated, probably because of too much ability on the part of the artist. The management of our opera house cannot abide having truly important artists as resident members of the company. In Fräulein Pirk's place we had Frau von Naday. Splendid! But if one were to have restricted Frau von Naday's area of activity to the role of Coppelia — I mean the creature of Coppelius — it would be the same as if she had sung Ännchen. Herr Schrödter's Max was more a sleeper than a dreamer. One had the impression that Herr Schrödter had concerned himself only superficially with the role, as reflected, too, in frequent collisions with the orchestra. Herr von Reichenberg [Kasper] promises to be a treasureable demon, but he must learn to control himself. Self-control is possibly the only virtue that becomes a proper demon. Herr von Reichenberg was all depravity and vileness. The Wolf Glen was brilliantly set and highly atmospheric, but seemed to make little impression upon the audience. Probably it was too "riveted" to move its hands to the applause the spectacle truly deserved.

Two pianists of the very first rank, Moriz Rosenthal and Eugène d'Albert, played one after the other in the Bösendorfersaal. The playing of the two virtuosos, in the relationship of one to the other, was rather like a brillant rocket and a glowing coal fire. Rosenthal's playing ignites, d'Albert's warms. The one inspires to deeds, the other to contemplation. Rosenthal plays more brilliantly, more exuberantly, more confident of victory. He plays the man of the world at the piano, and astonishes with his knowledge. D'Albert, on the other hand, plays more conscientiously, and more to satisfy himself than to delight the audience. When Rosenthal is already thundering, d'Albert is just beginning to rumble. But after the storm when the moon breaks through the clouds, d'Albert dreams and muses while his rival is still battling with the clouds. In short, d'Albert strikes us as the more maidenly, more sensitive of the two, Rosenthal as the more energetic, the more virile. Both artists had plenty of applause to bear.

Nota bene: That Fräulein Dürrnberger assisted *gratis* at d'Albert's concert may have passed unnoticed by many in the audience, for her contributions were of a silent sort, and came from her seat in the audience, whence she accompanied the virtuoso's playing with truly inspired facial expression and gesture, and with astonishing ostentation. If Fräulein Dürrnberger could play as expressively on the piano as she does on the air — hats off!

1.   Ludwig Tieck (1773-1853), German poet, critic and dramaturg, leader of a school of "romantic" poets. He was the German translator of "Don Quixote."

2.   Not a year later, but in his autobiography *(Selbstbiographie)*, recalling impressions gained while attending piano rehearsals for the first Dresden production (January 26, 1822).

3.   The reference is to unsigned articles that appeared in the *Vossische Zeitung* on June 26 and

28, 1821, generally assumed, until recently, to be by E.T.A. Hoffmann. Wolfgang Krons, in a detailed study titled "Die angeblichen *Freischütz*-Kritiken E.T.A. Hoffmanns" (The Supposed E.T.A. Hoffman *Freischütz* Critiques), published in Munich in 1957, challenged persuasively the accuracy of the attribution. Hoffman's writings on Beethoven, *Don Giovanni* and Gluck were the product of a long and important association with the *Allgemeine Musikalische Zeitung.*

4. Heinrich Lichtenstein (1780-1857), professor of zoology at the New University of Berlin and co-director of the Berlin Singakademie, a lifelong friend and correspondent of Weber.

5. Carl Wilhelm Gropius (1793-1870), stage designer at the Royal Theater in Berlin, a pioneer of modern theater decoration. The twentieth century painter, Walter Gropius, was the grandnephew of Martin Gropius (1824-1880), Carl Wilhelm's cousin.

6. A dramatization by Pius Alexander Wolff (1782-1828) of "La Gitanillo," the first of Cervantes' *Novelas Exemplares,* for which Weber had written incidental music.

96. *Weber and* Oberon

December 19, 1886

Carl Maria von Weber was already a doomed man when he created his last great work, *Oberon.* That this creation, a luxuriant flower garden of life, should be the work of one thus condemned, a man whose life hung from the minute hand of time, whose every painful breath had to be wrung from lowering death, to whom a mere handful of hours was conceded for the completion and production of his last work and then, far from his own people, to lay his weary head for ever in alien earth? Frightful, capricious, horrible fate! To dash the fragile vessel, and with it to destroy the fragrant, blossoming contents as they wafted aloft once more as enchanting incense! Seldom has an artist's genius been so sovereign over earthly affliction. Thoroughly aware that he had only a short time to live, he set to work on *Oberon.*

"Dear friend," he said to Gubitz[1] when the latter, concerned for Weber's health, pointed out to him the dangers of a journey to England, "I shall earn in England a substantial sum of money. That much I owe my family. But I know perfectly well that I go to England, there to die. No, don't contradict me. I know it."

On another occasion he said to Böttiger,[2] who also tried to dissuade him from crossing the channel:

"Böttiger, it's all the same. Whether I travel or whether I don't. I shall be dead in a year. But if I travel my children shall eat, even though their father is dead, while if I remain they will starve. What would you do in my place? But I would like to return to see Lina, Max and Lexel once again. Then let God's will be done in God's name. But to die there — that would be hard."

This last bitter cup too, he had to drain. The unhealthful climate, disillusionments, hard work, the excitement and the worries consumed his fragile body faster than the master had anticipated. He wanted to set June 6 [1826] as the day of his departure, but during the night from the 4th to the 5th he was already embarked on his last journey. The immortal expired in the home of his friend, the musician Smart.[3]

Oberon enjoyed a most enthusiastic reception at a first and twelve [eleven] subsequent performances, all conducted by Weber himself. The critic of *The Hamonicon* reported [No. XLI, May 1826, here given in the original English]: "M. von Weber himself conducted the orchestra; he was received with a warmth that has rarely, perhaps never, been exceeded in a theatre: many rounds of applause, hats and handkerchiefs waving, with every other demonstration of approval that could be devised, testified how strongly the public opinion was in his favor. All this was repeated at the end of the opera when, — by a vulgar and odious custom creeping into this country, but now prohibited in France, where it had its birth, — he was called on the stage; a call which, much to his credit, he complied with in a manner that showed his reluctance to be brought forward."

For the rest, the critic deplored the shortcomings and planlessness of the libretto, but praised the precison of the stage machinery and the sumptuous sets, which earned the applause of Weber, too: "The splendor and perfection of the sets is beyond description [in a letter to his wife following the premiere], and I shall probably never see such a thing again. I am told that the opera cost 7,000 pounds sterling, or about 49,000 talers." The *Harmonicon* critic added that Weber's music was not without melody, as many claimed, but that its melodies, for the unpracticed ear, were mostly covered by an almost overpowering fullness of instrumental accompaniment. What would this honorable gentleman have said had he also heard Wüllner's recitatives? He would, in all probability, have simply run away. If only Direktor Jahn had chosen to give *Oberon* in its original form! To make the best of Wüllner's bad bargain shows little respect for the genius of a German master.

Herr Jahn would really be of some use to the work if he would give some attention to a gentler singing of the choruses, to more sensible scenic arrangements, and to a more purposeful casting of the roles, notably that of Oberon. Herr Schittenhelm is an industrious singer, but the title role is not and never will be for him. Oberon would be a part for Herr Schrödter, but then what would become of Scherasmin, performed by Herr Schrödter with all his characteristic warmth, and in a manner that gives the role a dramatic significance surpassed only by Weber's musical characterization? For an infatuated knight with a sense of honor, redoubtable in combat when duty calls, and at ease in the higher as well as the lower extremes of his range, Herr Müller [Huon] is ideal. A bit more fire and tenderness would become him well, and render him more attractive in Rezia's eyes. Huon, as played by Herr Müller, lacks the inner spark. Frau Sucher was no lovable Rezia, to be sure, but she sang with warmth and dedication, and had a great success with the ocean aria.

Fräulein Braga was not bad in the grateful role of Fatima. Fräulein Kaulich was a suitable Puck. Others sang Wüllner, or silently filled out the necessary tableaux.

To complete the Weber cycle, *Abu Hassan,* too, was staged. The farcical material dramatized by the playwright-actor Hiemer,[4] contains distinct reminiscences of the dark side of Weber's *Sturm und Drang* period at the court of the Duke of Württemberg, whom the twenty-one year-old artist served as secretary. A high point of the opera which, with much that is good, has its share of the old-fashioned and the trivial, is the very dramatically worked out chorus of the creditors: "Money, money, money!" It is composed from the heart, so to speak, and owes its eloquence to the fact that Weber had not neglected the most conscientious "preparatory studies." Herr Müller was an astonishingly gay Hassan, a *filou par excellence!* Who would have expected this mobility, this roguishness, from Herr Müller's sober character? Fräulein Lehmann's star, too, shone more brightly than ever, and Fatima was the sweetest of vixens. And Herr Mayerhofer's Omar! A masterpiece, as is always the case when this wonderful artist sings comic opera, which reminds us how regrettable, how sinful even, it is to entrust roles such as Figaro, Leporello, Papageno, etc., to other singers when Herr Mayerhofer alone is the man for the job.

Abu Hassan made practically no impression upon an audience whose principal concern was the new ballet by Wüllner and Brüll.[5] That's an odd combination: Weber and Brüll! And this as part of a Weber festival? An obvious alternative would have been a production of the ballet *Rococo,* in which Weber's "Invitation to the Dance" is dominant. Dances to Weber's Polonaise, Rondo and Polacca Brillante would not have been a bad idea, and certainly more appropriate than a ballet by Brüll. But "appropriate" and "lucrative" loom in the eyes of our opera adminstration as two mutually incompatible concepts, wholly unsusceptible of any honorable accommodation.

The memorial for Franz Liszt went off well, even peaceably, without the originally threatened execution of "Les Préludes." And yet it would have been better if our jovial Hans Richter had stuck to "his" "Les Préludes," on which there is nothing left to destroy, rather than murder "our" "Ideale." We will gladly do without any Liszt if he is to be played with so little spirit and feeling as was the case with "Ideale." We assume that Herr Richter first learned this piece at the dress rehearsal, in other words, at the last critical moment, and promptly took this lovely and suitable moment to rehearse strings and brass separately, a wise procedure in preparatory rehearsals, but not for a dress rehearsal. We had, thus, a highly inaccurate and dispirited performance of this eminently poetic composition, which suffered more under the ruthless hand of the conductor than from the brutality of the orchestra. Herr Richter would do well to memorize thoroughly the Preface to Liszt's symphonic poems, but he should do it before the dress rehearsal. He might then note that such things are spoken of as "recurring utterance," the "prominence of special accents the rounding off of melodic and rhythmic nuances" and similar relevant matters, of all of which, in his performance of "Ideale," there was precious little to be discerned, not to mention the wrong tempi.

The following Piano Concerto in A major found in Herr Reisenauer[6] an intelligent and technically adept interpreter. The 13th Psalm for Chorus, Solo and Orchestra may well be the most fervent prayer that ever burst forth in harmony. It is the quiet turning in upon itself of a profound and truly religious nature. The music breathes a saint's joy in the faith, the transfigured devotion of a martyr. It is the most glorious apotheosis of Christianity. After this composition, in which the Choral Society distinguished itself, and with Herr Winkelmann singing the solos beautifully and movingly, after these consecrational sounds, the memorial should have come to a close. To follow it with the Hungarian Rhapsody No.4 was simply tasteless, not to say tactless.

1. Friedrich Wilhelm Gubitz (1786-1870), writer, publisher and woodcarver, professor of wood carving at the Berlin Academy of Art, also a dramatic critic.

2. Karl August Böttiger (1760-1835), writer, philologist and archaeologist, one of Weber's intellectual circle in Dresden where he was director of the Museum of Antiquity.

3. Sir George Smart (1776-1867), one of the original members of the London Philharmonic Society and frequently its conductor. Weber was a guest in his home during his stay in London.

4. Franz Karl Hiemer (1768-1822), German painter, actor and playwright.

5. *A Tale from Champagne,* a three-act ballet.

6. Alfred Reisenauer (1863-1907), a pupil of Liszt, pianist of international repute and, from 1900 to 1906, director of a master class at the Leipzig Conservatory.

97. Euryanthe

December 25, 1886

Euryanthe was performed on December 18, the master's birthday, bringing the Weber Cycle to an end. To have this work produced here must be counted among the rarest of artistic pleasures, something to be greeted with wholehearted joy by everyone sincerely concerned with our cultural prosperity. We are speaking, however, of anticipation, for we doubt that the opera can bring full artistic satisfaction to the truly sensitive, and many who will have entered the opera house with high hopes on the day of a *Euryanthe* performance will have left it crushed and disappointed.

It was Weber's fate to be able merely to suggest his high-flown plans, not to realize them. *Euryanthe,* this master's child of sorrow, is actually nothing other than a practical handbook for opera composers, showing them precisely what to do and what not to do. It is an experiment with which Weber had the most painful experiences, but from which his great heir, Richard Wagner, profited enormously. With *Euryanthe* Weber set forth on his great journey of exploration toward the envisioned music-drama. He chose the right route, but he was badly equipped, having to set his heavenly music to a miserable wreck of a text. In vain he hoped with the rudder of music to find the way to Utopia. The faltering vessel came to grief in the towering waves of grand opera, and the bold seafarer with broken rudder saved himself only by fetching up on a lonely enchanted island where, shattered in body and spirit, he breathed his last song through Oberon's magic horn — and expired.

The full greatness and significance of *Euryanthe* lies not, as in *Der Frei-schütz* and *Oberon,* in its absolute, but in its relative artistic worth. In his conception of *Euryanthe,* in what he had in mind in projecting it, he took a big step ahead of the other two operas. Thus, it is not so much the work itself that excites our admiration as the artistic and philosophical principles underlying it. If Weber, in the composition of *Euryanthe,* was nevertheless untrue to his principle of the union and equality of all sister arts in an indivisible artwork of musical drama, the blame must certainly fall primarily upon the poetess,[1] and only then back upon the composer, who felt obliged to fill the gaps with "melodic" music. He did this without the slightest inner compulsion, and thus the "union of the sister arts" was rendered precarious, the work's essential vacuity the more glaringly obvious.

To regard and assess *Euryanthe* from the purely musical standpoint, how-ever, is inadvisable. Weber rejected a proposed concert performance of *Eur-yanthe* in Breslau with the words: "Euryanthe is a purely dramatic experi-ment, seeking effectiveness solely in the cooperation of all sister arts, and certainly hopeless if deprived of their assistance."[2] Whoever has been en-chanted simply by this or that melody, or been moved by this or that scene simply because of its uncommonly dramatic music, or who remains undis-turbed by certain brutal aspects of the plot because it is ennobled by the music, or who is not outraged by the accused Euryanthe's stupid obstinacy at the close of the second act, which has no other purpose than to extend the story by another act, excusing it because the music speaks the more eloquently — such a one has certainly not grasped the true worth of *Euryanthe.*

Yes, I even believe that it is precisely these "musical" individuals who deplore — and not without reason — the lack of melodies, the kind of melody that can be sung independently of the dramatic situation to which they apply without losing their significance and immediacy. Such melodies do, indeed, often blossom magically, and exhale their enchanting fragrance in this curious score. But the melody hunter will be only half satisfied. One who understands what Weber was about will wish for less melody and more dramatic expres-sion. Here, too, we encounter incongruities. It is, then, these contradictions that rule out the totally satisfying overall effect essential to a work of art. The sensitive listener will alternately be delighted and affronted according to whether the composer is being borne along by the dramatic situation or simply bearing the weight of poetic nonsense.

The performance was zestful and lively. the choruses, which take up the greater part of the score, and participate actively in the sorry story, were well prepared. The dew-fresh and melodically noble hunting chorus was fascinating. There was a storm of applause following the overture. This was directed, one hopes, at the incomparably poetic and grandly conceived composition, and not at the performance itself, which was distinguished only by the manner in which the brass once again, shamelessly, made a lot of noise. It's odd that so sensitive a conductor as Direktor Jahn should tolerate such mischief! Frau Sucher, as Euryanthe, was a touching figure, to which her shrill voice produced a curious contrast. She may have been especially indisposed on this occasion. She managed, nevertheless, through the warmth of her singing to bring poetic excitement to the cavatina, "Hier dicht am Quell," [Here hard upon the fountain], while her performance of the cavatina in the first act ["Glocklein im Thale" — Little Bells in the Valley] was rather designed to excite impatience. Frau Sucher made up for missing aural delights by her highly expressive acting, so that in the end we could congratulate ourselves on such a Euryanthe.

It was predictable that an artist whose Ortrud is accepted as definitive could not paint Eglantine, this sisterly peer of Ortrud, in other than colors characteristic of the darkest corners of iniquity. The horrible, uncanny shadow of Eglantine appeared before our astonished eyes as if sprung from the soul of Weber's music. And this shadow was no mere airy image of fantasy. On the contrary, it took thoroughly concrete form in the physical embodiment of Frau Materna. With this role she added a new garland to the freshly blooming laurel wreath of a career rich in such honors. Herr Winkelmann was a splendid Adolar, although lacking the soft tones required to do justice to the lyrical passages. Herr Sommer has not the asperity of expression to make such a role as that of Lysiart adequately effective. Herr von Reichenberg was every inch the "love-rich king."

Frau Sucher's engagement, fortunately, has not been confined to the Weber Cycle. To this we owe a rewarding performance of *Lohengrin*. Her Elsa was winning not only in appearance and bearing, but also as a vocal achievement. Indeed, the whole performance proceeded under a lucky star. If Herr Horwitz would not force his voice so horribly, and if he would just sing a bit more correctly, there would be nothing wrong with his Telramund. The participation of Frau Materna and Herr Winkelmann made a successful performance a foregone conclusion.

Another visitor, Herr Bulss,[3] from Dresden, has made himself conspicuous upon our stage in the most advantageous manner. A seasoned actor and well-schooled singer, he made the most of Petrucchio in *The Taming of the Shrew*. The incomparable achievement of Frau Lucca as Katharina borders on the wondrous. I would never have thought it possible that even the most gifted singer could bring halfway to life so weak a score. And see! The opera pleases. What do you know? One is delighted, and loves the piece. For my part, I hate this garrulous, anemic music, but I love Frau Lucca.

1. Wilhelmine (Helmina) von Chezy (1783-1856), a minor Berlin-born poetess who had lived in Paris, Heidelberg and Cologne before crossing Weber's path in Dresden and Vienna.
2. Letter to the Breslauer Akademischer Musikverein, December, 1824.
3. Paul Bulss (1847-1902), a German baritone whose career covered engagements in Lübeck, Cologne, Kassel and Berlin as well as his long association with the Dresden Opera (1876-1889).

98. *Saint-Saëns and — Herbeck*

January 1, 1887

The Camille Saint-Saëns soirée given by Frau Caroline W. de Serres for the benefit of the Fund to Aid Disabled Railwaymen Unqualified for Pension and Their Widows and Orphans can properly be termed a social affair. The brilliantly decorated facade of the hall — two giant candelabra, brightly illuminated by candles, at each side of a stage forested with exotic plants provided a festively gay setting whose radiance was somewhat dimmed only by the dull reflection of Saint-Saëns' sometimes melancholy music — an audience glorying in its wealth, and, finally, a rather odd program set the occasion off — and not exactly advantageously — from the conventional physiognomy of most concerts.

Aside from the tasteful decoration of the stage, the brilliant illumination, Frau de Serres' admirable playing and its certainly even more admirable purpose, there was little about this concert that pleased me. What I liked most was the Septet for Piano, Strings and Trumpet [Opus 65], and what was most engaging about this piece, distinguished by its skillful exploitation of the trumpet, was its brevity. A bit longer, and it would be a bore. This shrewd moderation and pithiness is admirable, and absolutely not to be underestimated. How many a German composer might envy Saint-Saëns this virtue! It is common to all French composers, and to none more becoming, perhaps, than to Saint-Saëns, who composes more "wittily" than his fellow countrymen [I am not familiar with Massenet and Massé][1], and who, well aware that brevity is the soul of wit, carefully avoids all sentimental chatter, and only once or twice touches a sensitive nerve. Even then, he is quick to return to his curiously iridescent manner of speech, a superficial mode of address, but not without spirit.

Saint-Saëns is reckoned by the French, oddly enough, a classicist, as hard to digest, as a learned composer, and heaven knows what else. Saint-Saëns' classicism is rather like Brahms's, with the distinction that with Saint-Saëns it is a natural outgrowth of his musical development (he was for some time an organist) while with Brahms it serves simply to disguise his creative impotence. I refer here to the Handelian mask. But how harmless is Saint-Saëns in his Handelian mummery, and how pretentious is our own essentially merely harmless Brahms. If only the critics would spare us their hysterical seizures every time Herr Brahms gives birth, then one could speak amiably of a Brahms composition as of any other basically insignificant matter. But all this heroic critical crowing about a Brahms chick after every hatched cuckoo's egg gets on one's nerve after a while, like any fun that gets out of hand. But I have lost the thread of my discourse, and, taking it up again, I would still wish to pay my respects to the gracious artist whose lovely talent not only stood Saint-Saëns in good stead and delighted the audience, but also wafted its magic wand over the impoverished and the suffering.

In the stress of the Weber Cycle, we have, for the time being, rather lost sight of Kretschmann's Orchestra Concerts. What happened in the meantime has been absolutely inascertainable, as even on Wednesdays and Saturdays no programs were to be discovered. All I have been able to establish is that on those days music was made according to schedule. For Herr Kretschmann that is the main thing, for us certainly not. The eleventh concert was designed to be especially attractive for the public, and it was Herbeck's "Künstlerfahrt" [Artist's Journey] that was intended as the irresistible bait. Herr Kretschmann, however, either overestimated Herbeck's composition or underestimated his putative audience's taste. The hall was almost empty, and I awaited only the humorous remarks of the conductor appropriate to such occasions, the ironic obeisances of the orchestra, and the latter's disciplined goosestep to the left toward the door. There was, curiously, nothing of the sort. For suddenly we heard a consumptive whining in F minor, half Schumann, half Schubert and, in any case, all Herbeck. The "artist's journey" had begun. Whither? To the forest, of course, for a German artist must dream, and that he can do only in the woods. But this Herbeckian artist has pulled his nightcap too deeply over his ears, and he will not awake, despite desperate horn calls, despite anxious listening in the many pauses, despite the many raps on the nose in the too frequent pizzicatos and despite the rude pokes in the ribs from the fat double bass figures. And always along the way the sickly sweet tooting, the affected Austrian amiability, that nauseating flirtation with Viennese localisms, sometimes blossoming so enchantingly in Schubert's compositions, so repulsively in Herbeck's imitations. And in this key it continues through five full movements.

Now I ask you if it is an act of piety, again and again to evoke Herbeck's pale shade from the tomb? Is his memory honored thereby? I think not. Herbeck's image as conductor will forever remain as a reminder of times when the desert of our popular culture, fructified by his warm breath, turned green. It was a short spring. The venomous fang of influential criticism, following Herbeck's death, went to work on the tender roots. Servility and the majesty of our "splendid" Hans Richter did the rest, and so we have landed happily in the swamp whose foul odors our most recent "jubilarean elder"[2] inhales with such reverence and pleasure as a youth-bringing elixir of life.

1. Felix Marie Massé (1822-1884), who wrote a long series of operas for the Opéra-Comique — all now forgotten — became a professor of composition at the Conservatoire, and was elected to succeed Auber at the Académie.
2. "Jubelgreis," presumably Hanslick, whose sixtieth birthday had been celebrated in September of 1885.

99. *Brahms Lays an Egg*

January 9, 1887

Something took place at the most recent Philharmonic concert for which no one immediately concerned with our cultural life was prepared. Our public, on that day, came of age. It shed the critical diapers in which Herr Hanslick had wrapped it, and stood on its own feet. Tired of Hanslick's chaperonage, the audience sought finally to see the mysterious X Brahms with its own eyes. Now see what happened! This X Brahms looked like any other X. Indeed, the audience saw clearly and distinctly only a little insignificant x, far different from the immoderately blown up X drawn by Hanslick and his consorts, and saw it, moreover, become an uncommonly gross and horribly inflated U. The prestidigitator's trick was discovered, the deception failed.[1]

Brahms Symphony No. 4, given a second performance at this last Philharmonic concert, experienced a failure [*Durchfall*, which also means diarrhea] (a notable characteristic of Brahmsian music) as quiet as can hardly ever have been suffered by any other work. Softly, silently, as if nothing had happened — and, indeed, nothing did happen except the playing of the Symphony in E minor — the audience left its cherished seats. Its bearing during this general retreat was in no way cowed, nor was it provocative or convulsive. One could see in the facial expressions neither mortal fear nor anger nor resignation. The corners of its mouths disclosed nothing of that impertinent, supercilious grin that always greets the misfortunes of extraordinary creations such as, for example, the symphonies of Bruckner, and which so becomes all blockheads. No! Its bearing and demeanor expressed cheerful repose, with a slight suggestion of irony. It seemed impelled in its astonishment at the symphony, so blown up by the critics, to cry out with wry amusement like Faust at the spirit, first bloated to hippopotamus and elephant, then reduced to an itinerent scholar: "So that's what's at the bottom of it all!"[2] And with that it hit the nail on the head.

Herr Alfred Reisenauer, at the moment one of the most gifted pianists, who has appeared here twice with much artistic, if little financial, success, will be giving his third concert on the 14th of this month. Because of his substantial and original programs, uncontaminated by the name of Brahms, his exceptional accomplishments have been treated wryly by certain critics. Herr Reisenauer, fortunately, is no Hans Richter, permitting himself to be intimidated by a couple of snarling scribblers. The program of his coming concert will be, like his previous programs, well chosen. Whoever would like to pass an agreeable evening away from home should not miss it. To hear such an extraordinary artist and no Brahms — who except my friend Eduard Hanslick could still hesitate?

Finally, we cannot fail to recommend most warmly to our readers the lively song, "Rezensent"[critic], published by Spina, and dedicated by the composer to "his dear Eduard."[3]

1.   A play on the German saying: "Ein X für ein U vormachen," in plain English, "to deceive."

2.   "Das also war des Pudels Kern" — see footnote No. 3 to the notice of May 11, 1884.

3.   This paragraph is a puzzler. An immediate assumption would be that the composer was Brahms, but I have been able to find no record of his having written any such song, nor was he published by Spina. That firm had, in any case, been taken over by F. Schreiber in 1872, after which the Spina name was discontinued. One is reminded, of course, of Wolf's own "Abschied," the last of his settings of Mörike, which deals with a visit by a critic to the narrator, and ends with the critic being kicked down the stairs (see footnote No. 3 to the notice of April 18, 1886). But "Abschied" was not set until a year later, in 1888. H. P.

100. "The Flight into Egypt"— and A Dirty Trick

January 16, 1887

After an interval of twenty-eight years, Berlioz's "The Flight Into Egypt" has been exhumed from the archives. Who knows whether this fragment, last heard in Vienna in 1859, would have emerged from its moldering vault had not Richter's easygoing nature fortunately come to its assistance? There exists, indeed, in the entire literature of music hardly another piece that presents the conductor and the performer so few difficulties, and this compelling circumstance must surely have acted as an incentive to Richter's enormous enterprise. It is just as probable, on the other hand, that we would have heard the entire work, "The Childhood of Christ," of which "The Flight into Egypt" is only the second part, had not our splendid Hans Richter again, and unfortunately, stood in its way.

The origin of this work, which, by the way, offers no pretensions of reforming the traditional oratorio form, is rather amusing, and I am confident that the reader will thank me if I offer herewith the letter which Berlioz attached in dedicating the French score to Ella,[1] director of the Musical Union in London. It bears the following motto [in English]:

"Some judge of author's name, not works, and then
Nor praise nor blame the writings, but the men."

"My dear Ella:

"You asked me why the legend, 'Attributed to Pierre Ducré, alleged Master of Music' appears on the score of 'The Flight Into Egypt.' It all began with a mistake I once made, a serious blunder that I learned greatly to regret, and for which I have never forgiven myself. Here is what happened:

"One evening I found myself in the company of a former fellow scholar at the Academy in Rome, the architect Duc, at the home of Baron de M..., an intelligent and sincere friend of art. Everyone was playing cards, some écarté, some whist, some brelan, everyone, that is, except me. I loathe cards. By dint of patience and thirty years of effort I have achieved the distinction of knowing not one single game of that kind, and of being exempt from recruitment by those in need of a partner. I was visibly bored when Duc turned to me and said, 'Since you have nothing to do, you might at least write a piece of music for my album.' I replied, 'Gladly.'

"I take some sheets of paper, draw some horizontal lines, and there soon appears a four-voiced Andantino for Organ. It strikes me as having a certain character of rustic and naive mysteriousness, and it occurs to me to set to it words of a similar nature. The organ piece disappears, and in its place we have a chorus of Bethlehem shepherds addressing their farewells to the infant Jesus at the moment of the Holy Family's departure for Egypt. The card games are interrupted to hear my biblical tale. The medieval flavor both of my words and of my music is found amusing.

"'Now,' I say to Duc, 'I'll put your name to it. I'll compromise you.'

"'What a thought,' he replies. 'My friends know full well that I know nothing of composition.'

"'That, come to think of it,' I say, 'is an excellent reason for not composing. But wait. Since your vanity prevents your accepting my piece, I'll invent a name of which your name is a part. It will be that of Pierre Ducré, and I'll make him Master of Music at the Sainte-Chapelle de Paris in the seventeenth century. That will lend to my manuscript the value of an antique rarity.'

"And so I did. But I was on my way to committing a Chatterton.[2] At home, a few days later, I wrote my piece, 'Repose of the Holy Family,' beginning this time with the words, and adding a little fugued overture for small orchestra, in a slight, innocent style, in F sharp minor without the leading tone. This is a device no longer in use, resembling plainsong, and thought by scholars to derive from some Phrygian, Lydian or Dorian mode of ancient Greece, which has nothing to do with the case, but which obviously accounts for the melancholy and rather artless style of old folksongs of lamentation.

"A month later, having thought no more about my antiquarian score, I was preparing a concert when it turned out that a choral number was missing. I thought it might be amusing to substitute the shepherds of my oratorio, retaining the name of Pierre Ducré, Master of Music at the Sainte-Chapelle de Paris (1679). The choristers, at the rehearsals, were immediately taken with this music of their forefathers.

" 'Where in the devil did you excavate that?' they asked me.

" 'Excavate is just about the right word,' I replied without hesitation. 'It was found in a walled-up closet, not long ago, during the restoration of the Sainte-Chapelle. It was written on parchment in old notation, which I had some difficulty in deciphering.'

"The concert takes place, the piece of Pierre Ducré is very well performed and even better received. The critics, two days later, sing its praises, and congratulate me on my discovery. Only one expresses any doubt as to its authenticity and antiquity. Let that stand as proof that, whatever you Gallophobes may say, there are men of intelligence everywhere. Another critic expressed pity for the poor old master whose musical genius is revealed to Parisians only after 173 years of obscurity. For, he said, none of us has ever heard of him, and Fétis' *Biographie Universelle des Musiciens*, which contains many extraordinary entries, says nothing about him.

"The following Sunday, when Duc found himself in the company of a lovely young lady who greatly loves old music and shows only contempt for modern music when she knows its date, he addressed this salon queen as follows:

" 'Now, Madame, how did you like our last concert?'

" 'O, yes and no as usual.'

" 'And the piece by Pierre Ducré?'

" 'Perfect, delightful. Now that's music! Time has destroyed nothing of its freshness. That is real melody, whose rarity is brought home to us by the composers of today. Least of all will your M. Berlioz ever produce anything like that.'

"Duc, at these words, could not restrain a fit of laughter, and was indiscreet enough to reply:

" 'Unfortunately, Madame, it was precisely our Berlioz who wrote 'The Departure of the Shepherds,' and he did it one evening before my own eyes at the end of a card party.'

"The lovely lady bit her lips, her pale cheeks reddened in anger, and, turning her back peevishly on Duc, she hurled at him the following awesome pronounement:

" 'Monsieur Berlioz is a rascal!'

"You can imagine, my dear Ella, my embarrassment when Duc informed me of this rebuke. I hastened to make amends by publishing the work under my own name, although inscribing on the title page: 'Attributed to Pierre Ducré, alleged master of music,' in order that it might constantly remind me of my deception.

"And now, say what you will, my conscience is clear. I no longer run the risk of being the cause of injury to the sensibility of good and decent people, of making pale ladies blush, and of shaking the credulity of certain critics accustomed to believing anything they are told. I shall sin no more. Farewell, my dear Ella, and let my sad example be a lesson to you. Never trifle with the faith of your subscribers. Fear the epithet hurled at me. You have no idea what it means to be treated as a rascal, especially by a lovely, pale lady.

Your contrite friend,
HECTOR BERLIOZ"

To close the concert we had Brahms' "Triumphlied." A Handelian *bal masqué*, and unfortunately rather boring, as are all Brahms masquerades. A bibliographic note in the program of the Society of Friends of Music speaks of the "Triumphlied" as a "powerful" work. So, propaganda, already! Why was Bruckner's "Te Deum" not heralded as a powerful work by the generous writer of such notes? What is the meaning of those "fine" distinctions? Or does the epithet "powerful" apply to the size of the work? Was it hoped thereby to prepare the audience for a lengthy torture? Hints of that kind might be recommended to accompany the production of Brahms's compositions were there not a more grateful means of dealing with all discomfort. The reader already knows what I mean.

Hurrying to a conclusion, we shall touch only briefly on the concert given by Signora Marcella Sembrich.[3] A wonderfully cultivated throat. As coloratura singer phenomenal. These nightingales, unfortunately, sing only inane stuff. It kills the nerves and cripples the imagination. On the other hand, to judge by the immoderate applause, it has an animating effect on the hands.

1. John Ella (1802-1888), English violinist, impresario and music critic, who founded the Musical Union, a series of morning concerts, and directed them for thirty-five years. This letter can be read in Berlioz's *Les Grotesques de la Musique*, and the text as given here is translated from the French original rather than from Wolf's German.

2. Thomas Chatterton (1752-1770), an English eighteenth century poet who published his own works as those of earlier poets.

3. Marcella Sembrich (1858-1935), one of the greatest coloratura sopranos of her generation. She began her vocal studies with Rokitansky before going on to Milan to study first with Giovanni Battista Lamperti, then with his more celebrated father, Francesco.

101. Dvořák — and Hanslick!

January 23, 1887

Dvořák's symphony [No. 2, in D minor, Opus 70], whose performance by the Philharmonic was thanks solely and exclusively to Herr Hanslick, was amiably but decisively rejected by the audience. The latter's attitude toward this work was that of a great personage who condescends with the requisite indifference to hear some poor devil of a petitioner's tale of woe, favors him with a few friendly words, and most courteously turns his back on him. With Job-like patience it heard the piece through right to the fervently awaited end, rubbed its hands a couple of times, and then departed, sufficiently edified by the infamous manner of this Bohemian Marsyas.

We would not have paid the slightest attention to the fiasco of the Dvořák symphony were it not that a defeat for Dvořák (and Brahms) represents also a considerable comedown for the critical prestige of Herr Hanslick. It was the third time in two weeks that Hanslick's protégés encountered a reluctant audience, the third time in two weeks that the most resounding trumpet fanfares of Hanslickian propaganda found no echo among the public. Indeed, things have come to such a pass that my colleague does not hesitate to confess "how little effect the two works (symphony and 'Triumphlied') had this time upon the audience." How must it stand with Herr Brahms's "popularity" when a friendly tongue broadcasts such intelligence.

Even if one sees in these concessions to veracity no more than a political maneuver on the part of my illustrious colleague, he will now have to shuffle his cards more carefully if he wants us to believe his politically motivated show of "objectivity." Even then, it is doubtful, with a public now grown skeptical, that he can bring it off. The famous critic's feuilletonistic siren trills may sound ever so insinuating on paper, but there, where they should echo most loudly in an audience's ears, namely in the concert hall, they are lost in the desert of Brahmsian chaos. However stoutly a public conditioned by Hanslick's Brahmsiades could persevere against its own convictions, against the evidence of its own ears, against its own horse sense, against deadly boredom, there had to come a time when, at last, its patience ran out. Fed up with the eternal assurances of the heavenly joys in store for those who, through the requisite sensual and spiritual asceticism, could achieve an understanding of Brahms (which, however, would not materialize despite even the most arduous penance), it opted for the only exit that might still lead to the promised delights of heaven, the exit from the concert hall prior to every Brahms composition. The public has already trod this path, and is now again enthusiastic about music.

It is a path, however, that goes against the grain of my enthusiastic colleague, and he is thinking now about treating the public with the barbaric precept: "And if you are not willing, I shall have to use force."[1] To this end it is planned to inhibit flight by wedging a piece by Brahms between two very attractive pieces, much as one gives a patient a bitter pill enclosed in wafers in order to diminish his distaste. What sort of insipid fellow, in the opinion of my shrewd colleague, must Beethoven have been, whose symphonies can excite ecstasy in an ever so bored and indifferent audience at the close of a concert? Herr Hanslick says: "One thing, and one thing only, is always and everywhere certain, namely, that the most difficult, the most important, the most exacting piece should not be imposed on an audience already tired and distracted." So, are Beethoven's symphonies, which usually come at the end of a concert (presumably without Herr Hanslick's approval), light and insignificant? Granting that, one still asks why my unbiased colleague, when works less popular than Beethoven's — the Berlioz and Bruckner symphonies, for example, which also normally come at the end of a concert — are not granted any allowance for certain "sickly tendencies" in the audience. We fear that these works, quite aside from their "insignificance," are not "exacting" enough to share a prerogative that Herr Hanslick, with astonishing generosity, accords to Brahms.

In the most recent Kretschmann concert we heard, besides Schumann's Overture to *Hermann and Dorothea* and Schubert's "Tragic" Symphony — two works that the composers might have dedicated to the goddess of oblivion — a suite in canon form by Julius Grimm? The form of the canon, when not treated with genius, tempts a composer to the most vacuous doodling. To indulge in this tomfoolery through four full movements, however, and to expect of the listener that he follow, for better or worse, this parrot-like imitation by the second voice, which always has the last word, is utter madness. How could the composer commit such an absurdity? Not even a Herr Johannes Brahms would do that!

1.   "Und bist du nicht willig, so brauch' ich Gewalt." Wolf is quoting from Goethe's "Erlkönig."
2.   Julius Otto Grimm (1827-1903), German pianist, composer and pedagogue. This was one of two suites he wrote in canon form for string orchestra.

102. Bülow — as Autopsist

February 6, 1887

Heiss' mich nicht reden, heiss' mich schweigen,
Denn mein Geheimnis ist mir Pflicht;
Ich möchte dir mein ganzes Inn're zeigen,
Allein das Schicksal will es nicht.[1]

The famous concert orator, Hans von Bülow, in the course of his Beethoven recitals, made himself conspicuous only at the piano. An "acute hoarseness" is alleged to have restrained him from doing in Vienna, too, as he recently did in Prague and some other German cities. How sad it must be to live under the constraint of public order.[2] Poor Bülow has thus become a victim of his calling. Poor Papageno!
    Where, then are the apostles with courage to carry on the master's delightful

innovation of spicing scholarly musical productions with witty asides to the audience between numbers, now that the master is denied recourse to oral elaboration, and must bow silently to higher authority? Fateful question!

But however much Herr von Bülow suffers under the bann of the holy Hermandad,[3] he cannot resist the temptation to establish rapport from time to time between the audience and his own uncommonly important self. Since purely artistic means alone are not enough, and since his larynx is condemned to inactivity, he substitutes for his remarkable oratorical and rhetorical talents a highly expressive, if not always lovely, play of gesture and facial expression. Whenever he turned his little bald Medusa head in a swinging curve toward his listeners, convulsive grimaces betraying the agony of a tongue condemned to silence, it struck me as though he were parodying the final lovely concluding lines of the strophe quoted above:

Allein ein Schwur drückt mir die Lippen zu,
Und nur ein Gott vermag sie aufschliessen.[4]

This dainty Mephistopheles seems, in any case, not to "hit it off well with the police." Unfortunately, he is on a rather strained footing with Beethoven, too. Above all, he stands in awe of the living Beethoven. And so to get at him, he simply strikes him dead. And now begins his real work as a Beethoven player. The corpse is carefully dissected, the organisms traced in their subtlest ramifications, the intestines examined with the zeal of a haruspex — the course in anatomy is under way. This dissected and sawn-up Beethoven belongs, however, in the conservatory, not in the concert hall, just as at an art exhibition we expect pictures, and not jointed dolls and skeletons. In fact, Bülow gives the impression of one who would like to be a painter but can't get beyond anatomy. Forever showing us only the notational skeleton, and concerning himself primarily with the ingeniously arranged interrelationship of the big and little bones of the musical organism, he makes of every art work a dance of death, surpassing in cutting irony anything ever achieved in this popular genre.

How greatly Herr von Bülow errs in thinking to emphasize the educational faculty of his playing by the suggestive term, *Beethovenvorträge* [literally, interpretations]! Is his playing truly instructive? As horrible example, certainly. Does the term *Beethovenvorträge* properly characterize his playing? Yes, insofar as instruction can also be termed "decomposition" and lecture "assassination." The concert bill, accordingly, should announce not *Beethovenvorträge*, but "Beethoven Vivisections,"[5] were the public to be properly apprised of the true character of this ghastly Beethoven massacre.

The only gratifying (!) thing about this Beethoven operation was the skill with which it was performed. Bülow's technical equipment is, indeed, astounding, his infallible knack of wounding or killing at the very first incision absolutely hair-raising. But to breathe life and soul into the dead body he is utterly wanting in the requisite vaccine. He is merely a skilled surgeon. When Rubinstein and others deal roughly with the living Beethoven from time to time, and, carried away by their enthusiasm, give the mighty man a bloody nose, or do him some other injury, then Bülow is the man to mend the damage. None knows better than he how to patch and glue. This autopsist is forever directing his listeners' attention to liver and kidneys rather than to the pulsating heart.

A Saxon, explaining the tortures of Prometheus to his little son in a picture gallery, excited the youngster's deepest compassion.

"Poor eagle," said the little Saxon.

"Why poor eagle, and not poor Prometheus?"

"Liver every day," was the little boy's heartfelt response.

Thus our Hanus[6] strikes me as an aged raven, who, throughout his entire life, has been picking at the liver of good taste and artistic dedication to nourish his personal renown.

Poor eagle! Poor Bülow!

Liver every day!!!

1. "Bid me not speak, bid me be silent, for my secret is my bond; to you I'd gladly bare my soul, but fate will not allow it." From the verse that concludes Book V of Goethe's *Wilhelm Meister*, subsequently set by Wolf himself in his Goethe Lieder.

2. In October of the preceding year, Bülow had given two concerts for the benefit of the Czech Artists' Cooperative in Prague. At a banquet in his honor between the two concerts he had made a speech extolling the musicality of the Czechs. German nationalist opinion was outraged (note that Wolf refers to Prague as a German city). There were riotous scenes in Dresden and Breslau when Bülow played in those cities, each requiring police intervention. A number of concerts had to be cancelled, including one in Graz just prior to Bülow's four Beethoven programs in Vienna. The latter were permitted, but Bülow was required to assure the police that he would remain silent. "I shall not speak," he had assured them. "I'm hoarse anyway."

3. In Spanish, "brotherhood," used in the Vienna of Wolf's time as a humorous term for the police.

4. "'Tis an oath alone that seals my lips, and only a god can break the seal."

5. Wolf's word, although hardly appropriate to a subject just struck dead!

6. The Czech form of Hans. German nationalists had held it against Bülow that in his Prague concerts his name had appeared thus on the program.

103. César Thomson[1]— A Latter-Day Paganini

February 13, 1887

The horrible war of extermination Hans von Bülow, that teeth-chattering autopsist, has been waging against the mighty shade of Beethoven with varying degrees of success has ended happily, to the satisfaction of all critics. The little storm cloud looming.in the musical heaven of our city has finally vanished without depositing a torrent of invective upon its citizens. Everyone breathes more easily, and rejoices in a good musical digestion. The enthusiastic audience at the concert given for the benefit of the German Aid Society was a gratifying confirmation. Since the program promised mostly dainty and light pleasures, this circumstance, shrewdly seen to by the impresario, may well have whetted the public's appetite, it not being given to everyone to possess the stomach of an ostrich, nor to those so endowed, to expose it to unnecessary danger.

The concert began with the Overture to *Oberon*, conducted by Hofkapell-meister Hellmesberger and played by the orchestra of the Conservatory with fire and pace. It was now the turn of the violin virtuoso César Thomson to come on, and on he came, although I could not believe that this could be Herr Thomson. I thought I espied a vampire risen from the grave and, I involuntarily hummed the refrain from the Marschner ballad: "Bewahr' uns Gott auf Erden, ihm jemals gleich zu werden" [Preserve us, God on earth, that we should ever be his like — from *Der Vampyr*]. Yes, as my pretty neighbor, a very young lady, fixed her opera glass on this fiddling corpse, I was struck dumb with horror. I could restrain myself no more, and, *con sordino*, whispered in her ear the admonitory verse:

Kind, sieh den bleichen Mann nicht an,
Sonst ist es bald um dich getan.
Weich schnell von ihm zurück!
Schon manches Mägdlein jung und schön,
Tät ihn zu tief ins Auge sehen,
Musst es mit bittern Qualen
Und seinem Blut bezahlen,
Denn still und heimlich sag' ichs dir,
Der bleiche Mann ist ein Vampyr!

(Child, look not at that pale face,
You'll perish soon in his embrace.
Draw quickly away.
Many a maiden, young and spry,
Who looked too deep into that eye
In bloody torture had to pay,
An object of his foul, foul play.
For I tell you softly, dear,
A vampire 'tis, don't get too near.)

The effect was extraordinary. Whether the lovely and curious young lady dropped her opera glass from horror at the ghoulish whispering of a stranger, or at the death mask of the virtuoso, I could not determine from the angry look that rewarded the sympathetic voice. Perhaps the young lady is a medium, and susceptible to magnetic insinuations. Perhaps this doll of a Senta saw in Herr Thomson the Flying Dutchman of her melancholy dreams, as, indeed, certain saga initiates have thought to recognize in the pale artist the living Dutchman. There are others versed in history and witchcraft who claim to have found in Herr Thomson a conspicuous resemblance to the soul of the murdered Julius Caesar, although nothing definite has been said about the ominous number of stigmata on Thomson's immortal body. Yes, the imagination of some fantasists has gone so far as to deny him every spark of anthropomorphism and to declare without further ado that he is neither human nor the ghost of a human, but the embodiment of Satan. This view, offensive as it may be in respect of the artist's personal appearance, is, nevertheless, in respect of the virtuoso, the most pertinent of any of those mentioned thus far.

Yes, it is true! Herr Thomson plays Satan upon his instrument, and his violin sounds as if an invisible hellish chorus accompanied the infernally mournful tones that stream from it. And how he masters the instrument, how the bow dances gracefully and gaily over the strings! How easily he conquers the most iniquitous difficulties — octave passages from the highest conceivable, or inconceivable, positions to the lowest, covered with the speed of lightning, with pizzicati, trills, cantilena and scratching along the way, and all this at almost the same time! Is that the playing of a mortal? Are those not diabolical delusions? And all the while this impassive bodily repose!

Hardly does the hand that guides the magic bow betray that what is here afoot is not enchantment and Satanic trickery, but the art of a man of flesh and blood like any other. This diabolical pied piper was rewarded by applause of dimensions we have seldom experienced. Following the Paganini Variations [on Rossini's "Non più mesta"] there was an outburst of roaring and raging and shouting such as to suggest the dawning of Judgment Day. The artist was recalled five times to acknowledge the audience's gratitude. Five times this tombstone reappeared. His mournful countenance remained fixed and cold, his lifeless eye peered vacantly into space, and no outward sign betrayed his satisfaction or jubilant pride in such an enormous success. "Now that it's all over, is he still a vampire?" asked my little neighbor as she prepared to leave. And a heavy sigh from her young breast repeated the delicate question: Is he really a vampire??

Following this, Frau Lucca sang Schubert's "Erlkönig," too melodramatically in my opinion. This rough theatricality does not work to best advantage in the concert hall. Nor was her declamation as correct as one would have wished. She did not come off much better with one of her showpieces, Mozart's "Das Veilchen." Her pretentious interpretation made a very "long-stemmed violet" out of this obscure little flower. (This "abortive compliment" is turned by a young dandy of the *Fliegende Blätter* upon his flame of the moment when she calls attention to the limping of his verses. He, feeling called upon to be witty, replies subtly: "There are also long-stemmed violets." Only in the big aria from Massenet's *Le Cid* did we recognize the dramatic artist whom we treasure and admire.

Some Lieder sung by Herr Reichmann were well received, although the utterly undramatic rendition of Loewe's[2] ballad, "Edward," left the audience cold. How is it possible to sing a song that places us immediately in the center of a dramatic situation with the amiability of a night-watchman? Why this ambling tempo? Why this passion in a high collar? From so splendid a dramatic singer as Herr Reichmann one is entitled to expect better.

All praise to Herr Winkelmann for his warm singing of Pylades's aria from Gluck's *Iphigenie en Tauride.* The singer had to repeat the aria, so great was the impression made alike by the wonderful piece and the manner in which it was sung.

Richard Wagner's "Kaisermarsch," which closed the concert, would certainly have had an incendiary effect had the conductor troubled to get a couple of better cymbals and a competent cymbal hitter. Such miserable, common, toneless instruments may add a lot to carnival performances, but they had no place here. Such cymbal crashes are traitorous stabs in the back for a work of art, and such cymbal players nothing more than hired assassins. A proper musical performance should have no truck either with daggers or murderers.

Liszt's marvelous tone poem, "Orpheus," had to be repeated at the last Kretschmann concert by unanimous popular demand, and at the end of the concert, too. There is, I think, nothing to be added to the reporting of the fact. The audience handed down a verdict.

The second Lieder recital of Herr Walter drew a large audience to the Bösendorfersaal despite an uninviting program. The retired opera singer warbled more sweetly than a dying swan, and the applause of the deeply affected listeners fluttered about his Jupiter head like angels' pinions. May his tenor be a long time dying![3]

1. César Thomson (1857-1931), Belgian violinist, a pupil at one time or another of Vieuxtemps, Wieniawski and Massart and successor to Ysaÿe as professor of violin at the Conservatoire in Brussels. He was later professor of violin at the Conservatoire in Paris, and taught at the Juilliard in New York. A spectacular technician, he was largely responsible for a revival of interest in the compositions of Paganini.
2. Johann Carl Gottfried Loewe (1796-1869), creator of the German ballad as an art form.
3. It was. See footnote No. 9 to the notice of February 2, 1884.

104. For Cat Lovers

February 20, 1887

The new ballet, *Die verwandelte Katze* [The Transmuted Cat], adapted by F. Zell[1] and K. Telle[2] from a French subject, and with music by [Joseph]

Hellmesberger, Jr., was enthusiastically received. The happenings in this piece, complex as they may be, require no special scenic assistance to be rendered intelligible. But don't be frightened by so awesome a title as "specialist in the metempsychosis of souls"; otherwise, all is lost. Whoever has chosen to read the mysterious smuggler paths of such metempsychosis of souls under the guidance of Koeppen[3] (whose famous treatises on esoteric and exoteric Buddhism prompted the first fruitful initiatives for the founding of a Buddhist club in Unter St. Veit[4]) will hardly have grasped in sufficient depth the sublime lunacy of the plot. Leave all profundity aside, therefore, and put yourself calmly in the agreeable situation of one who has fallen in love with his cat.

Nothing so extraordinary in that. One becomes infatuated with turkeys, baboons and young downy goslings — and old geese, too! Why not, then, a beautiful, white Angora cat? I grant that such tender, platonic attachments are unsatisfactory in the long run, but that can be true of less platonic Toggenburgiades,[5] too. Our young hero, however, the impressionable painter, Wilm van Campen (the setting is a Dutch seaport), is still at the height of his infatuation, and couldn't care a cat about what others think of his curious propensity. It is quite otherwise with the awesome "specialist in the metempsychosis of souls," Houtman by name. The eccentric absurdities of the odd painter make Houtman sick — if I interpreted correctly the effective nuances in Herr Frappert's[6] acting — and he resolves to put an end to the nonsense. Playing on the demented lover's gullibility, he spins a tall tale, and declares his readiness to transform the cat into a lovely young maiden.

The worthy van Campen can wish for nothing better. The transmutation takes place without further ado behind the bed curtains in the painter's house, and the delighted fantasist, initially enchanted at the successful experiment, and the feline character of his transmuted sweetheart — who is none other than Mina, the daughter of a herringmonger — looks forward impatiently to the wedding day. Fortunately, however, that day is still some way off, giving the poor young fellow time to learn that even the loveliest little cat can misbehave, and that the loveliest paws, too, cannot refrain from administering a box on the ears, nor conceal their treacherous claws.

Now, when the whole cat court appears before the wedding guests, and does its worst in the most uninhibited manner, with even the bride being more catlike than ever, chasing mice, threatening bystanders with her claws, and boxing the bridegroom's ears from time to time, the latter's patience is at an end. He pleads with the great Houtman to restore the troublesome cat-virgin to her original shape, a request that the uncanny specialist, with a delightful show of charlatanism, readily satisfies. But the poor young fellow is already so much a slave of his love addiction that he thinks himself unable to live without the maiden. When the latter is now introduced, shorn of her feline attributes, he has already recovered from his *idée fixe*, and nothing further stands in the way of their union.

For this difficult subject, Herr Hellmesberger has written an attractive and effective, if hardly original score. The composer, while at work on it, may well have bethought himself of the apostle's [St. Paul] saying: "Prove all things;

hold fast that which is good"[I Th 5:21]. And his work does, indeed, represent a charming bouquet of the best thoughts of Delibes, Doppler,[7] Strauss, etc. The sensitive and thoroughly skillful exploitation is unquestionably to Hellmesberger's credit, and certainly not the least of his accomplishments. As for originality, however, that is a ticklish matter —

As a very young man, I was innocent enough to show the great Wagner some of my piano pieces, in order to hear from the master's mouth whether or not I had musical talent. As he was amiably leafing through the manuscript, I could not refrain from observing that they were all pretty much in a Mozartean style. He replied, to my great relief, half seriously, half jokingly: "Yes, yes. . . . One can't be original right from the start! I wasn't, either."[8]

Herr Hellmesberger, Jr., is, to be sure, quite a grown-up young fellow [he was thirty-two], and it would seem to be almost time for him to be thinking seriously about his originality. In the meantime, he will lose nothing while waiting, nor, I think, will we.

And therewith we close the chapter.

1.   Pseudonym for Camillo Walzel (1829-1895), who at one time combined the offices of a captain for the Austrian Danube Shipping Company and director of the Theater an der Wien. He was the librettist of *Eine Nacht in Venedig, Boccaccio* and *Der Bettelstudent.*

2.   Karl Telle (1826-1889), a choreographer at the Court Opera.

3.   Carl Friedrich Koeppen. The reference is to his *Die Religion des Buddha*, published in two volumes in 1847 and 1859.

4.   A suburb of Vienna.

5.   Ritter Toggenburg, hero of a poem by Schiller, who, when his lady love enters a convent, sits in front of her window until he pines away.

6.   Louis Frappert (Ruault) (1832-?), French-born dancer, mime and choreographer, came to the Court Opera from the Théâtre-Lyrique in Paris in 1854, and remained until 1895.

7.   Albert Franz Doppler (1821-1883), Polish flute virtuoso, was for many years conductor of ballet at the Court Opera and the composer of many ballets.

8.   See footnote No. 1 to the notice of November 1, 1885.

105. *Farewell to Kretschmann*

February 27, 1887

Just as everything in this world must come to an end, so too, and very soon, will the bitter cup of the Kretschmann Orchestra Concerts have been drained. Let us rejoice, and be not ungrateful to merciful Father Time, that great sponge soaked in the tears of mankind which cheerfully wipes away the hours and years of our life, and which will surely erase the memory of Kretschmann evenings as it does that of so many painful experiences. For the time being, to be sure, or at least until my report is finished, I would prefer not to be surprised by that kindly old gentlemen, but I would not wish, on the other hand, to rage for too long against my own flesh. I shall this time, accordingly, be brief.

The program was more varied than ever, including three novelties and an Overture to *Iphigénie en Tauride* by Bernard Scholz — this a novelty for me, and probably for most of the audience, too. The *Kleine musikalische Lexikon* of Julius Schuberth[1] says of the composer: "Born 1835 in Mainz, pupil of Dehn, and an excellent Lieder composer."[2] It may well be that Scholz is an "excellent" Lieder composer, but several thousand musicians, of whose existence perhaps only Julius Schuberth knows, are also "excellent" Lieder composers according to this amusing little booklet, swarming with creative artists who have produced nothing but important, exemplary, great, brilliant, etc., works. Among these "geniuses," Herr David Popper constitutes an agreeable exception. Of him we read simply: "As composer he has yet to make his mark." Somewhat more pretentiously, to be sure, and far more presciently, resounds the anticipatory praise expended in this optimistic booklet upon an utterly obscure genius whose name unfortunately escapes me. He is praised to the skies for his accomplishments as a virtuoso, and then at the end we are told in a tone brooking no contradiction: "He will yet make his mark as a composer." Well, let's hope for the best.

But let's see what this remarkable Schuberthian oracle has to pronounce about Scholz: "The opera *Carlo Rosa* is a highly melodious work. More important (!) is the opera *Die Ziethenschen Husaren*, a string quartet, etc., beautifully scored." (Which, the opera or the string quartet?) "His Requiem is significant (!). Kapellmeister in Hanover until 1865, when he moved to Berlin, etc." That his Overture to *Iphigénie en Tauride* could have been written only by a theater Kapellmeister was obvious to me at a first hearing. A certain theatrical pathos without deeper agitation, a gasping enthusiasm, a melodically lukewarm richness of figuration, sentimental and loquacious secondary themes, a lot of hot air and, fortunately, little inflammable matter — these are the ingredients making up that curious brew we call Kapellmeister music. Scholz's overture offers no crude example of the species I have just described. The composer's talent aspires to purer regions without, however, being able satisfactorily to deny important traces of "terrestrial remains."[3]

Fräulein Marie Pohl, who now abused Beethoven's Piano Concerto in C minor, was ill-advised to poke her nose into matters becoming solely and exclusively to that musical avenging angel, Hans von Bülow. He, at least, kills Beethoven with respect and good manners, rather systematically, and that, too, is an art. But to fall blindly upon the Titan as upon a finger exercise by Czerny is going too far. Respect for genius! Beethoven is no children's playground, his spirit no proper nourishment for the immature impulses of adolescent females. He is not the composer for kindergartens and nurseries, for salons and marionette shows, nor, when Fräulein Pohl plays, for Kretschmann's Orchestra Concerts.

Herr Otto Roth was more discreet. He played Bruch's Violin Concerto No. 2 [in D minor, Opus 44], and bored the audience most amiably with his unending flow of tone. Herr Roth has reasons to present himself as an "expressive" player, since he cannot allow himself the luxury of an ever so modest technical display. Two days later, when I made the acquaintance of the sympathetic physiognomy of the "sentimental coachman" in the last number of the *Fliegende Blätter*, I thought immediately of the heartbreaking violinist of the most recent Kretschmann concert, which is not to say that Herr Roth played like a sentimental coachman.

Authors of the novelties mentioned earlier were the Messrs Blasser[4] and Louis Rée.[5] Had I to draw a parallel between the two composers, I would come to a quick decision and say: The one composes gaily, the other sadly, and both as trivially as can well be imagined. Herr Blasser made his debut with a small Serenade for String Orchestra, adding most respectfully a few thoughts of his own. Herr Rée made his with a Funeral March and a Gavotte. We were left with eerie and certainly very funereal apprehensions about the fate of the two composers.

As my neighbor said, Herr Rée is reputed to be a charming, delightful fellow. I was glad to hear it. To be a bad composer and an unlikable fellow, too — indeed, that would be too much!

1. Julius Ferdinand Georg Schuberth (1804-1875), publisher of a number of musical periodicals in Hamburg, Leipzig and New York, notably the *Kleine Hamburger Musik Zeitung*, the *Musik Zeitung* (New York), and *Schuberths Kleine Musik Zeitung*. Wolf refers here to his *Musikalisches Conversationslexicon*, which went through ten editions, the last of them published in 1877.

2. He died in 1916.

3. "Uns bleibt ein Erdenrest zu tragen peinlich" [There's still an earthly remainder painfully to bear], sung by the angels as they carry Faust's immortal soul to higher regions at the close of *Faust* II.

4. Gustav Blasser (1857-?), a prolific Viennese composer.

5. Louis Rée (1861-?), a pupil of Leschetitzky in Vienna, better known for his playing as duo-pianist with his wife, Suzanne Pilz.

106. *Suppé's* Bellman

March 6, 1887

Meister Suppé has this time put the patience of his numerous admirers to an unreasonably severe test. More than two years have passed since his *Die Afrikareise* [The Journey to Africa], and only the opening of a new libretto firm, undertaking to provide usable new texts — a great rarity, as we all know — persuaded him to break his silence. This libretto firm, Ludwig Held[1] and M. West,[2] had a genuine success with *Der Vagabund*[The Vagabond],[3] and so Suppé did not hesitate, despite a subject rather foreign to his nature, to provide a musical setting for the firm's latest product. The action of the new operetta, *Bellman*, given its premiere last Saturday in the Theater an der Wien, takes place, as this name suggests, in the north of Europe, in Sweden.

Bellman[4] is the northern Bocaccio, the pride of Sweden. He was an amiable poet who idled away his life, conceiving his poems while drinking wine in the company of congenial companions. Sweden, to this day, honors him in the spring with the so-called Bellman Festival. On this day, everyone tries to be carefree and imaginative. Masquerades and bubbling champagne assist the festive mood appropriate to the occasion. The librettists of this new operetta, however, have forgotten all about Bellman the inspired idler. They have presented him as a great patriot and a no less accomplished lover. The poet has successfully wooed for himself and his songs the richest and most beautiful maiden in all Stockholm, the daughter of a millionaire of the herring trade. Just before the wedding, with the bridal procession already under way, disaster looms. The Countess Ulla, mistress of the King, has been taken prisoner by the opposition party, but has fortunately escaped. She finds Bellman, whose "first love" she once was, and persuades him, appealing to his patriotism, to remain at her side and conduct her safely to the King. Bellman's old sentiments are awakened. He deserts the wedding and his "last love," and makes off forthwith with the first. In the face of all kinds of danger, and not without the traditional episodes of disguise and distress, the flight succeeds. The Countess is restored to her King. Bellman becomes the King's private secretary, and as such rediscovers the way to the heart of the herringmonger's daughter.

The play abounds in references to current events and the present political situation. Although it is centered on the war between Sweden and Denmark, and although the politically colorless herringmonger assures us that in Sweden one dare say nothing, one senses instinctively where the axe is supposed to fall. The audience, too, at the premiere, went along sympathetically with the bias in the handling of the subject, and thus the piece's success was uncommonly lively. Certain characters are very well drawn, especially the two plotters, a pair of schemers who seek to lure the millionaire's daughter away from the fickle poet. Thus, on the whole, this essentially serious libretto stands well above the usual confections of the genre, and one can only hope that the firm of Held and West is hard at work creating other viable texts for our talented composers. The old operetta nonsense has outlived its time. One demands nowadays from an operetta, too, a sensible plot and nicely shaded local color.

Meister Suppé's music had a lot to do with the great success. Right up to the finale of the second act, which is too operatically developed, and too pretentious, the entire score is an uninterrupted succession of descriptive and melodious numbers. Most successful were the droll duet of the two plotters, "Ach, lieber Bruder, treu vereint" [Ah, dear brother, loyally hand in hand], and a quartet in the second act, in which a Swedish folk tune is cleverly employed. The love songs of the poet, too, of incomparable ardor, were enthusiastically applauded, as was the excellent couplet: "Aber — in Schweden darf man nichts reden" [But in Sweden one may say nothing].

The casting of the novelty was admirable. The Theater an der Wien is now probably the best German operetta stage. Although the first buffo, the first tenor and the prima donna are all on leave and now — at the height of the season — delighting provincial cities with their art, it was still possible to provide Suppé's work with performers of the first class. Herr Joseffy (Bellman sang languishingly and fervently, as demanded by his role. Fräulein Stein's (Countess Ulla) accomplished acting and splendid voice were effective. The Messrs. Lindau and Eppich were admirable plotters. Fräulein Zimmermann was a lovely millionaire's daughter, and Herr Lunzer the true Lapp slob. The greatest success of all was Herr Stelzer's with his straightforward and, precisely on that account, very effective delivery of the couplet mentioned above.

The staging of the operetta betrayed the master hand of the invisible director of the Wieden[5] stage. The bridal procession in the first scene, the camp and storm scenes in the second act, and the audience scene in the third were masterfully arranged. One congratulates the enterprising management without further ado. Its repertoire problems are surely resolved for a long time to come.

1.   Ludwig Held (1837-1900), Viennese theater critic, administrator and librettist.

2.   Moritz West (Nitzelberger) (1840-?), Viennese librettist.

3.   Music by Karl Zeller (1842-1898), first produced at the Carltheater on October 30, 1886.

4.   Carl Michael Bellman (1740-1795), wrote popular drinking songs and biblical parodies, the most famous being "Fredman's Epistlar," parodying the Pauline epistles.

5.   The district of Vienna where the Theater an der Wien is situated.

107. Liszt's Faust Symphony

March 13, 1887

One of the most grandiose creations in the entire literature of music, Liszt's *Faust* Symphony, was introduced at the last Philharmonic concert, for the first time, to an audience long accustomed to perceive in Franz Liszt's works only the composer's musical inadequacies instead of acknowledging its own inability to follow the eagle's flight. But to demand an admission of such inadequacy from our Philharmonic audience would be like looking for modesty in arrogance, universality in limitation, objectivity in prejudice.

These people will never learn that it is for the audience to raise itself to the work of art, not for the art work to lower itself to the audience. They want, at any price, to play off their one day in the sun against the immortality of genius, and they pursue this worthy enterprise with an earnestness nicely calculated to render the ridiculousness of such aspiration immortal. Instead of taking to heart their own intellectual poverty, and remembering that the utterance of the great spirit is not necessarily confused simply because a number of idiots find it confusing, they nevertheless make snap judgments, hiss, or loftily leave the hall. "A knavish speech sleeps in a foolish ear," says Hamlet, and Lichtenberg sums it up neatly when he declares that a hollow sound issuing from the collision of a head with a book is usually attributable to the head.

To what extent this quotation is applicable to the attitude of the Philharmonic audience toward the *Faust* Symphony would seem, after all that has been said, to require no further discussion. And it is all the same whether or not this work, representing the culminating point of modern instrumental music, is now appreciated and understood (despite the fact that it was composed thirty years ago). Of the utmost indifference to the admirers of Liszt is acceptance or rejection on the part of the Philharmonic audience. That this work, unique in the depth of its thought, would not enthuse this audience, after all the fine examples of poor judgment it has offered in its reception of every important work at a first hearing, was easily predictable. The stamp of immortality is so distinctly impressed upon this symphony that no critical twaddle, however wittily formulated, can besmirch the halo, nor popular opposition stem for long the inner power of this tremendous tone poem. It will be left to future generations to mine the rich treasure that Liszt's genius piled up with prodigal generosity in this miraculous work.

Yes, I name the *Faust* Symphony a miraculous work, for the miracle of the human incarnation of the art of music has been completed in it. One may confidently apply to Liszt's daring deed the final verse of the Chorus Mysticus [*Faust* II Act 5]: "Das Unbeschreibliche, hier wird's [*recte:* ist es] getan"[The indescribable, here is it done]! The plastic representation in concise strokes of three fundamentally different but mutually fulfilling characters speaks for Liszt's enormous powers of description. We stand here utterly as before a miracle, contemplating a thematic texture whose threads, interweaving characteristically and artfully through all three movements, disclose the most profound relationships in the transformations taking place in the emotional world of Faust and Gretchen and — with Mephistopheles' critical intelligence seeking in vain to entangle them in a confused skein — constitute a musico-poetic masterpiece of the weaver's art unexampled in the entire literature of music.

An exhaustive analysis of the *Faust* Symphony from the critical-esthetic point of view would require a whole book. I can attempt nothing of the sort in the space at my disposal. I refer the amiable reader, therefore, to *Franz Liszt,*

Studien und Erinnerungen [Franz Liszt, Studies and Reminiscences] by Richard Pohl,[1] in which the author exposes Liszt's *Faust* Symphony to a critique as intelligent as it is pertinent and poetically written.

A gala concert was given in the Grosser Musikvereinssaal to raise funds for the monument to be erected in Bozen [Bolzano] to Walter von der Vogelweide. There were outstanding artists, an enthusiastic audience and a program that had, at least in part, the famous Minnesänger as its subject. Nothing could have been better calculated to emphasize the festive character of the concert than the imposing inaugural chorus [from *Die Meistersinger*], "Wach auf, es naht gagen den Tag" [Awake for day is near], well performed by the chorus of the Wagner Society, augmented by members of the Choral Society and the Conservatory Orchestra. A prologue, fashioned in warm and cordial words by Direktor Wilbrandt,[2] and vibrantly declaimed by Herr Emmerich Robert,[3] led intelligently to the next number, "Am stillen Herd" [By the quiet fireside, from *Die Meistersinger*]. For this splendid accomplishment Herr Winkelmann earned such applause that he had to repeat the verses. The second number, from Liszt's "Die Legende von der heiligen Elisabeth" [The Legend of Saint Elisabeth], on the other hand, thanks to the insecure and utterly uncomprehending direction of Herr Schütt,[4] fell flat. Two old German a capella choruses by S. Senft[5] and Hans Leo Hassler[6] were well received, and the second, a dance song, even had to be repeated — to my not inconsiderable astonishment. The public, for whom no piece can be sufficiently decked out and prettified, has grown so corrupt in its judgment and taste that it can no longer appreciate idiomatic simplicity. A set of poems by Walter von der Vogelweide, some humorous, some serious, brought much honor to their interpreter, Herr Robert. In the following ballad, "Heinrich der Vogler" [Henry the Fowler], Herr Reichmann demonstrated once again that he lacks the slightest understanding of this genre. A ballad by Loewe needs to be interpreted as well as sung. Herr Reichmann, however, appears to be of the opinion that all one has to do is sing, and everything will come out all right. Such was not the case, and I can assure him that he sang pretty badly, that he made a mess of the ballad, and that he was most ably assisted in so doing by his accompanist.

An event of far greater interest than the gala concert just discussed was the concert by Wilhelmj,[7] often scheduled, just as often postponed, now finally given. After an absence of twelve years, during which he has grown decidedly older in appearance [he was forty-two], he appeared, laden with decorations, before the Viennese public, and was immediately given the warmest welcome. Then, as his virile powerful tone gathered the listeners ever more closely into its magical embrace, the audience's enchantment and insatiability increased to the point where, at the end, a full fifteen minutes of applause was expended in an attempt to wring from the artist a second encore. He, unfortunately, was no longer in a generous mood.

Wilhelmj belongs among those rare artists who, following their own star, go their own way securely and serenely, unmoved by the always volatile moods of audiences and critics. What is it to him whether he pleases or not? He simply doesn't play for the public. He seeks to satisfy only himself and his art. Hence the unembellished truth of his conceptions, the quiet immersion in the spirit of the composition, the dignified, manly bearing in performance, that especially qualify him as an evangelist of Beethoven's gospel.

1. Richard Pohl (1826-1896), prolific writer of books and articles in behalf of Liszt, Wagner and Berlioz.

2. Adolf Wilbrandt (1837-1911), poet, playwright and director of the Court Theater from 1881-1887.

3. Emmerich Robert (1847-1899), actor and regisseur at the Court Theater.

4. Eduard Schütt (1856-1933), pianist, composer and conductor who, in 1881, had succeeded Felix Mottl as conductor of the Academic Wagner Society.

5. Presumably Ludwig Senffl, one of the outstanding German musicians of the sixteenth century and, although a Catholic, reputed to have been Martin Luther's favorite composer.

6. Hans Leo Hassler (1564-1612), one of the first great German composers, and the first to have gone to Italy for schooling (with Andrea Gabrieli). The propriety of his music for this occasion was enhanced by the fact that he was born in Nuremberg.

7. August Wilhelmj (1845-1908), one of the greatest of all German violinists and, as itinerant virtuoso, better known abroad even than Spohr, David and Joachim. He was a pupil of David in Leipzig, and his first wife was David's niece. It will not have been unknown to, or lost upon, Wolf that Wilhelmj had been concertmaster of the orchestra at Bayreuth in 1876.

108. *Lortzing's* Der Waffenschmied

March 20, 1887

We are in a bad way when it comes to the cultivation of comic opera. The place accorded this treasurable genre in the wide spaces of the opera house provides it a roof, but not a home. Comic opera is tolerated as a gay parasite of grand opera and ballet. It is not accepted as an equal of either. Indeed, how could it be otherwise when this stepchild of the operatic theater has always been fitted out in the hand-me-downs from the wardrobe of the serious opera, or, to put it plainly, has had to make do with "coryphaei" about whose eligibility for pension not even the most benevolent criticism could entertain a moment's doubt.

There has been, I grant, a change for the better in the past few years. The engagement of the Messrs. Schrödter and von Reichenberg brings a flow of new blood into the senility of our performances. The latter, especially, has gradually revealed his affectionate, fatherly heart, and dedicated it to the management for use as convenient in the service of the comic muse. But that is by no means enough. The real problem is the big opera house. It's as if one were to hang a miniature in an enormous ceremonial hall. And this ludicrous spectacle is repeated every time a comic opera is produced, although very few among the public seem to sense the grotesqueness, even unpleasantness, of such incongruities.

That Lortzing's cheerful muse, given such circumstances, comes off worst of all is not to be denied, and one truly does not know whether it might have been better for *Der Waffenschmied* [The Armorer] to rest another fourteen years in the archives, by which time the Comic Opera may, perhaps, have been built, than to ruin its small voice in the big house. Still, the opera enjoyed the friendliest reception. It was greeted as an old and treasured friend, although, as previously stated, the terrain was not congenial to the renewal or consolidation of an old friendship. When I prepared this opera at Salzburg six years ago, it pleased me a lot more, despite an inadequate cast and an abominable orchestra, than now in our famous Court Opera with its famous orchestra, its famous singers, its famous box office attendants and its no less famous stalls, and for the simple reason that the small stage provided the right sounding board for this little work, and reflected faithfully all the tones and nuances given it by the composer. The musical flow from orchestra to stage was just sufficient to project its magnetic force in the small area in such a way that the singer, wherever he might be on the stage, was always in touch with the orchestra. It was possible, under these circumstances, even with inferior performers, to achieve a homogeneity attainable in a big house only with a big opera.

The casting of this *Der Waffenschmied*, moreover, granting exceptions for the Messrs. Schrödter, von Reichenberg and Stoll and Fräulein Baier, was by no means satisfactory. Frau von Naday, if only because of her pronounced Hungarian accent, is very ill-suited to the role of a bourgeois German maiden. And the sounds she makes are suitable for anything but naiveté. She sang the middle section of the aria, "Wir armen, armen Mädchen" [We poor, poor girls] with the testiness of an old spinster, not at all like a pretty, amiable goldsmith's daughter. The latter would never get so worked up over a couple of scandalmongering cousins. And how she distorted the arioso, "Reichtum allein tut's nicht auf Erden, das ist nun einmal weltbekannt" [Wealth alone is not enough on this earth, as every one now knows]! A ruined speculator, for all I know, might address his empty pants pocket with such fatalistic scorn, but from our adorable Marie one is entitled to expect more simplicity and faith in God. A few lovely pianissimi were all that Frau von Naday had to offer as Marie. The audience appeared to be thoroughly satisfied.

Herr Bötel, from the Hamburg Municipal Theater, made a guest appearance as Arnold in *William Tell.* The singer is well and most favorably remembered from last year. His voice is as melting as ever, the high notes the same. Nor has he grown any taller, and I hardly know what further to say in his favor.

I arrived at Fräulein Hermine Spies's concert just in time to hear Rosenthal. Stepanov had been announced, to be sure, but it was, in fact, Rosenthal who played. Unprepared as he was (he didn't even have time to don evening dress), this little pianistic devil stormed over the keys like a roaring flood. He played godlessly (godlike sounds too commonplace), and demonstrated beyond the shadow of a doubt that the devil is the supreme authority in art. I don't remember exactly what he played. I think it was the Hungarian Rhapsody No. 12, a Waltz in A flat by Chopin, etc. When he finished I had the feeling of having escaped from a frightful deadly peril. As long as this exorcist cast his spell at the piano, I seemed to feel the glowing claws of Beelzebub at my neck, or I feared to be swept away in a heavy surf, or to be swallowed up in the fiery crater of a volcano. But I still live, thank God, to the delight of my fellow creatures and to the consolation of my unforgettable friend, Johannes Brahms.

109. *Richter and the "Siegfried Idyll"*

March 27, 1887

At the last Philharmonic concert we heard among other things Richard Wagner's "Siegfried Idyll." It is to be hoped, in the interest of this composition, that the Philharmonic will not make it a part of their repertoire, at least as long as Herr Richter remains the conductor. Is it, indeed, necessary that our worthy Kapellmeister demonstrate his friendly disposition toward anything related to Wagner's concepts by laying his hands on Wagner's works and mutilating them when even our revered Herr Hanslick is content with the sacrifices laid out on the altar of the goddess of impotence in honor of her chosen favorite, Johannes Brahms?

Why all this useless eagerness, all this importunate fawning? We are thoroughly convinced of the sincerity of his laudable conduct. Herr Richter is a clever practitioner, and practical people are held, as a rule, to be ultimately decent folk. They achieve respect and renown easily, and soon have "hay in their boots." There may well be times with people of this kind when their principles collide, and they find themselves compelled to a sort of double-entry bookkeeping, the honest entry for moral reasons, in order to despise themselves, the fraudulent for ordinary money-making, for their honorable position in society, a kind of self-rehabilitation. That happens from time to time, as I have just said, but our worthy Kapellmeister is free of such pressures, and for the simple reason that he is not concerned with such childish matters as principles, views, confessions of faith, etc. That kind of trivia is not for him, and whenever he senses the stirring of something like scruple or doubt, he takes his baton and smashes the offender to bits and pieces.

Unfortunately, this impenitent time-beater[1] remains untouched by scruple even when confronted with a musical work for which mere time-beating is not enough, such a work, for example, as the *Faust* Symphony, whose second movement Herr Richter simply chopped into mincemeat, or the "Siegfried Idyll," which, under Richter's "winged" baton took on the form of a gallopade. Whoever in the audience was hearing this heavenly work for the first time could not possibly have had any proper impression of the lovely magical mood that pervades this fragrant tone painting like May sunshine. Under such circumstances it would be better to play nothing but Brahms symphonies. In them, at least, there is nothing to be spoiled.

Fräulein Spies's second Lieder recital was followed promptly by a third. We may even be threatened with a fourth if Herr Hanslick continues to snore away his touching solo on the big tenor drum. This incessant sounding of reveille by that worthy old gentleman [he was sixty-one] is certainly depriving a good portion of our public, duped as it is by critics, of their delicious early morning slumber. Concern for the fashionable stall gnaws at its heart night and day. Every unused fleeting minute can be critical for its happiness. For everyone "runs, scrambles, flees"[2] to Fräulein Spies's recitals.

And why? Well that's the funny thing about this stupid business. It's because a critic declares, black on white, that Fräulein Spies is the first female Orpheus to make a truly profound impression on him — a declaration the more characteristic of the writer in that Orpheus, as we all know, appealed to many a hefty quadruped. I have no wish to play the furious bacchante tearing this piping Orpheus to pieces. God forbid! Fräulein Spies is a much too modest, normal person to merit being struck down by thyrsus blows[3] — or showered with panegyrics. It would seem appropriate to observe, however, that Fräulein Spies's accomplishments do not surpass the level of good, modest mediocrity, and that every unbiased listener must confess that the paeans in her behalf sound far better than her singing.[4]

1.　"und wenn sich je etwas wie Skrupel und Zweifel in ihm regt, schlägt er mit seinem Taktstock doch alles wieder zu Boden. Leider kommen diesem verstockten Taktschläger auch dann keine Skrupel," etc. Wolf is having fun here with a play on the words *verstockt* [impenitent] and *Taktstock* [baton].

2. "Alles rennet, rettet, fluchtet," from a poem, "Die Glocke" [The Bell], by Schiller, describing a conflagration that turns night into day.

3. A staff surmounted by a pine cone, employed in Bacchic rites.

4. Hanslick's summation: "In Fräulein Spies are united artistic cultivation and the freshest naturalness. The blend is as irresistible as it is rare." It seems pertinent to note that Hanslick was especially pleased with her singing of several songs by Brahms, whose friend she was, and who, at his funeral, was the first to throw a handful of dirt into the grave.

110. *Lieder Recitals*

April 3, 1887

Lieder recitals are slowly becoming epidemic. Everything that sings and sounds, and doesn't sound, wants to warble and crow from the platform. (We shall soon be having a Lieder recital from our admirable Mime, Herr Schmitt.) — And yet, it was not so long ago that our excellent Walter, whose mysterious voice is slowly but surely degenerating into a croak, bore alone the burden of delighting a receptive public.[1]

Only in the past few years has Walter's profitable notion of giving Lieder recitals found intelligent imitators. Frau Papier, who combines great artistic talent with a sense of the practical, was not only one of the first to follow her predecessor's altogether admirable example. She was also one of the few who could compete successfully with a solidly established rival. Her significant triumphs in the recital hall could not escape the watchful eye of others. Suddenly our resident singers were seized with the most profound compulsion to distinguish themselves, too, in Lieder recitals. The epidemic has even spread abroad, so that our local competitors are now threatened. This concert season has been visited by a bad [*liederlich*] patch.

Now, with this surplus of Lieder recitals, one might presuppose a greater variety in the building of programs. One would assume that from 600 songs by Schubert, and the 300[2] that flowed from Schumann's pen, one or another "viable" song might find its way into a program in addition to the traditional dozen that have had to sustain the popularity of the two composers. But how would compositions of the famous "springtime" variety, served up to the public as stimulants for heart and stomach, properly be honored if one were to make the public taste susceptible to nobler pleasures. The singers' preference, however, for the utterly trivial, if "grateful," is traceable to their personal vanity. They want to play the leading role, and would gladly content themselves with merely yodeling in order to claim the slightest applause for themselves alone. But when compositions as boring for the audience as they are ungrateful for the singer are offered only because of some tedious harp accompaniment — that is cause for concern.

How could Herr Reichmann be so tasteless as to include three songs of so futile a kind as those by Riedel[3] in the program of his second Lieder and ballad recital? Does Herr Reichmann think he is helping the composer by exposing his deficiencies to public scrutiny, or does he think that he concealed them adequately by the beauty of his voice? It cannot be denied that he had to repeat Riedel's "Biterolf." But the applause was directed at the harp accompaniment as much as at the singer. We are utterly convinced that the introduction of a triangle or a trombone or a Jew's harp would have prompted countless repetitions of that song. (Herr Riedel will not, I hope, ignore this tip, even if it gets to him only indirectly.)

Since we are tarrying at this lamentable "Biterolf," I would like to advise Herr Reichmann that his unsolicited alterations of the text could hardly count on the applause of the ravished poet. In "Biterolf" Herr Reichmann finds no pleasure in sylvan-green Thüringland [Thuringia], so he undertakes to improve it by making it Thüringsland. In the next strophe, similarly, he sins against both poetic expression and grammar by adding a fatal consonant to the verse, "Ich grüss die Heimat mein, weit über Meer" [I greet my homeland, far overseas], making it "übers" [over *the*] instead of "über," etc. etc. Such improvisations are disturbing, and can easily be avoided.[4]

Herr Reichmann sang Brahms' deeply felt and deeply expressive "Von ewiger Liebe" [Of Everlasting Love] with warmth and immediacy. This song is regarded correctly as the best thing Brahms has accomplished in this genre. It is hard to believe that the same composer who wrote this splendid song could also write four symphonies whose ludicrous solemnity, a model of involuntary humor, deserves preservation as a droll souvenir of the promised messiah. The performance of Schumann's "Flutenreicher Ebro" [Torrential Ebro] was less satisfactory. Reichmann sang rather coldly, listlessly and glibly. And what a melodic Eldorado this composition is! What warm, blossoming life pulses therein! One would think it impossible to miss its tone and message had not Herr Reichmann proved the contrary.

That Herr Reichmann does not meet the requirements of ballad singing we have often noted in this space. Once again he sang the ballad, "Heinrich der Vogler," and once again with the same indifference toward the now epic, now dramatic character of the poem. Whether it is the narrator or the hero who speaks, it's all the same to him. With Herr Reichmann one dares not expect to hear the various groupings plastically illustrated by modulation of voice and mode of delivery. All that he has to offer are lovely, sweet, mellow sounds. Simply to hear him is an aural delight. Whoever expects from art, however, no more than the satisfaction of sensuous titillation will recognize in Herr Reichmann the ideal artist. Our man he is not.

A group of songs sung by Frau Marie Wilt put us in a very reflective mood. *Vanitas! vanitatum vanitas!*

1. Gustav Walter, probably more decisively even than Julius Stockhausen (Hermine Spies's teacher) would seem to have established the precedent and the format for the Lieder recital as we know it today. Stockhausen, in Vienna in 1856, had been the first to offer a Schubert song cycle ("Die schöne Müllerin") complete in public. He repeated the gesture for Schumann in Hamburg in 1861 with "Dichterliebe" (with Brahms at the piano). But he seems always to have had the assisting artist still considered essential if an evening were to have what was still reckoned the requisite variety. "Dichterliebe," for example, was sung in two parts, with Brahms contributing episodes from Schumann's "Kreisleriana" between them. Bülow and Rubinstein, at about the same time, were pioneering with the sole piano recital, but the solo recital without assisting artists did not become commonplace until well into the twentieth century. Note that Rosa Papier in her recital, reviewed in the notice of April 17, had an assisting artist.

2. Recent research, notably by Eric Sams, puts the number at something closer to 260.

3. Hermann Riedel (1847-1913) was born in Vienna and served for some years as coach at the Court Opera.

4. A subject close to Wolf's heart, as he himself had set the same Scheffel text just two months earlier, on December 26, 1886.

111. *Murdering Harold*

April 10, 1887

It takes no special gift of divination to pronounce with the utmost precision, even before the premiere, the fate of a new German opera. One need know neither the title nor even the subject matter. The composer's nationality alone suffices. Is there any need to spell out the fate of Wagner's numerous successors in the field of opera, the still white-hot *Armins, Kunihilds Sakuntalas, Urvasis* and however — God knows — they are all called?[1]

Poor Harold! A splendid title, to be sure, for a grand historic-romantic opera, compared to which *Der Ring des Nibelungen* must appear almost puny. One can understand a young conservatory student on the battlefield of his bloodthirsty fantasy, and with all the enthusiasm of which such dangerous people are capable, doing Harold in once again, and all for the sake of so imposing a title.[2] Only the motley mob excites the bloodlust of these mass murderers, for they are nulls, aroused to aggression at best by some superficial bauble, among which the nomenclature of their operas plays a far from insignificant role.

But now what in heaven's name could have prompted our excellent chorus director, Herr Pfeffer,[3] to the composition of so absurd and silly a libretto as that here under discussion, a libretto in which there is absolutely nothing that could awake a musical echo in the breast of even the most highly gifted, a libretto in which a truly Egyptian darkness envelopes the motives of the proceedings and in which the drawing of the characters is as vague as the dialogue is flat to the point of being ludicrous? It is, in brief, a libretto that exposes as glaringly as possible all the inadequacies and sins of the usual opera libretto.

What, then, could have moved Herr Pfeffer to find the composition of this libretto attractive? As silly as the answer may seem, it still goes right to the heart of the matter. Just remember that Herr Pfeffer has occupied the position of a chorus director at our Court Opera for a number of years, and you will understand that a chorus director, wrestling with opera composition in his spare hours, found himself exposed to great temptation when confronted with *Harold.* In fact, under the guiding hand of Herr Paul Krone,[4] the plot is broken up into a succession of episodes which, as chorus of hunters, chorus of women, chorus of knights, chorus of monks, chorus of — settlers, etc., set off in Herr Pfeffer such a spasm of ecstasy that he forgot all else, even the awaiting of musical ideas.

Herr Pfeffer set to work accordingly "in his way," and has now provided new proof that one can compose four acts absolutely self-sufficiently, without the slightest dependence on other composers, and this thanks solely to an inspired kind of vacuity. Not even our great symphonist, Brahms, has been able to bring off such feats. Brahms, every once in a while, steps out of his comfortable role, and on such occasions is not loath to deck himself out in others' feathers [*Federn*, meaning both pens and feathers]. Herr Pfeffer, however, sits firm in the saddle on the lean nag of his muse. He deviates neither to left nor right, but slogs along imperturbably on his own path. I salute his probity and singleness of purpose. I salute his intrepidity. I like his "policy." Like Caesar, he will be all or nothing, and he has elected to be nothing. This voluntary resignation suggests antique grandeur of sensibility, an overripe philosophy. Herr Pfeffer is not only a dangerous nihilist in respect of musical invention. He is also a great philosopher. May he be satisfied with this praise, even if he comes off in it as an utterly miserable opera composer.

As far as production and cast were concerned, nothing was left undone to make this unpleasant evening as agreeable as possible. Herr Winkelmann, in the title role, laid the entire weight of his imposing personality on the scales of success. But such was the leaden weight of the music that, despite the efforts of all concerned, the sum of their contributions proved too light to achieve even a tolerable balance between the two factors. That the chorus, loyal to its worthy leader, would discharge its assignments admirably was predictable. An effective picture at the rear of the stage was the Battle of Hastings. This carnage provided the high point of the evening. *Harold* would be ideal as a benefit for the poor supers who, come to think of it, play a leading role in this fatal opera. They went through their paces stoutly, and emerged from the affair with much dignity, which can be said neither of the poet nor the composer, who, in insignificance and irrelevance to the success or failure of the opera, were hardly in a class with the least significant piece of moveable scenery.

The Lieder recital of Herr Paul Bulss and Frau Schuch-Proska[5] aroused understandable public interest. The former has already proved himself, in the Bösendorfersaal, a Lied and ballad singer of the very first rank. The latter we know and treasure as one of the most delightful and charming soubrettes in the field of opera. The unaffected, tasteful vocalism, the articulate phrasing, and the refinements of inflection gave to Frau Schuch's singing, especially in humorous songs such as Loewe's "Lullaby," an indescribable fascination. Herr Bulss, on the other hand, and in contrast to the pert disposition of his lovely partner, languished in bonds of profoundest melancholy, and found the most moving tone for two, or at least one, of Schumann's finest melodies: "Wer machte dich so krank?" [Who made you so sick?] and "Alte Laute" [Old Sounds].[6] But he soon pulled himself together, and in "The Two Grenadiers," which he sang surpassingly well, the conquering power of his virile baritone rang out so splendidly that Herr Bulss, in order to still the thundering applause, had to sing the song again. But on one account we must take Herr Bulss emphatically to task, namely, that on this occasion he sang no Loewe ballads, a sin of omission admitting of no pardon.

1. *Kunihild*, by Cyrill Kistler (1848-1907), first produced in Sonderhausen, where Kistler was active most of his life, primarily as pedagogue and theoretician, encouraged Kistler's adherents to hail him as Wagner's legitimate successor. *Sakuntala* was the first opera of Felix Weingartner (1863-1942), produced under the egis of Liszt in Weimar in 1884. Weingartner, of course, went on to a career as conductor that greatly overshadowed his considerable output as composer and author of books and treatises on musical subjects. I have been unable to identify *Armin* and *Urvasi*, although the latter subject was set by a Polish composer, Erasmus Dluski (1857-?), a student of Rimsky-Korsakoff, and produced in Lemberg in 1902. H.P.

2. The reference is to an opera, *Harold der Viking,* by Andreas Hallén (1846-1925), a Swedish composer and conductor, a pupil of Reinecke in Leipzig, where this opera was produced in 1881.

3. Karl Pfeffer (1833-1897), a Viennese, chorus master at the Court Opera from 1859 to 1883. His opera, *Harold,*, was produced at the Court Opera on April 3.

4. Dates unascertainable. He was the librettist, between 1860 and 1887, of a number of long forgotten operas by long forgotten composers, including another opera, *Nordlicht* [Northern Lights], by Pfeffer.

5. Clementine Proska (Prochazka) (1853-1932), a pupil of Mathilde Marchesi in Vienna, wife of Ernst Schuch (1847-1914), conductor and subsequently general musical director of the Royal Opera in Dresden, where she was for many years the leading coloratura soprano.

6. The point being that both songs have the same melody.

112. Rosa Papier's Lieder Recital

April 17, 1887

With the ever growing popularity of Frau Rosa Papier as Lieder singer, it already appears that the Bösendorfersaal is hardly adequate to accommodate this singer's countless admirers — entrance being paid not only in money, but in words, very good words — and there is reason to fear that Frau Papier, tempted by the successful procedure of her rival, Herr Reichmann, may move the scene of her carefree [*liederlich* — the pun again] endeavors to the Musikvereinssaal, an obvious disadvantage for the attentive listener and the no less inquisitive spectator. As long as our fears remain unsubstantiated, however, we shall burden ourself with no superfluous anxieties and, instead, simply thank heaven for continuing to guide its blessed daughter in the right path — in the choice of a hall, if not, unfortunately, in the selection of the program.

This was a very mixed bag, if shrewdly assembled. Let's examine it song by song. Anton Rubinstein's "Es blinkt der Tau [Sparkling Dew] has already won an enduring little spot in the hearts of the public and in the programs of those who sing. Frau Papier sang it tenderly and fervently, just as the song itself sings. "Es war'ne Maid" ("There was a Bonie Lass") by Ignaz Brüll. The charming poem of Robert Burns, folk-like in character, requires an appropriate musical setting. The composer has conformed sensitively to the peremptory demands of the poem, and has made the edifying salon Tirolese popular in the world of music, too. In Frau Papier's singing of it the words were more decisive than the tune, the latter breathing something of the tart spiciness of folk utterance that floods forth so movingly in the poetic blossoms of this wonderful poet.

We already knew Eduard Schütt's "Im Grase taut's" (Dew Falls in the Grass). Unfortunately, dew fell not only in the grass, but all over the song. This composition is more boring even than a thaw (*"Tauwetter,"* a pun derived from the dual meaning of *"tauen"* as *"thaw"* and *"dew)",* and just amusing enough to permit the listener to suppress a dangerous yawn with dignity.

"Die Quelle" [The Fountain] of Goldmark owes its popularity to Franz Schubert, its source to be found in the picturesque piano accompaniment to "Gretchen am Spinrade" [Gretchen at the Spinning Wheel], whence, with the aid of a prodigal pump, it was channeled into Goldmark's melodic watershed

— a thankless task, and one that has brought the composer scant credit. In the ensuing interval Fräulein Susanna Pilz attracted favorable attention through her playing of a Raff Gigue and Variations.

Nothing could characterize the next four songs, "Mein zitterned Herz" [My Trembling Heart] by Albert Amadei; "Trennung" [Separation], by Johannes Hager; "Blühender Schleh" [Blossoming Sloe], by Karl Schön,[1] and "Willkomm" [Welcome], by Rudolf Weinwurm[2] better than Probstein's words: "Although the song had little to say, the air was still most unmelodious." Sheerly absurd, however, and utterly contrary to the sense of the poem, was Amedei's composition, which set to the suppressed fire and suffocatingly hot sultriness of the text a music calculated in its now psalmodizing, now arpeggiating way to persuade the listener that what was afoot was a parody of Gregorian chant, or of a "De Profundis," or some other sacred matter infiltrated into this genre.

Separation | *'Trennung'* | from Hager's song exacted as much general rejoicing as Weinwurm's perfidious welcome | *'Willkomm'* | excite great indignation. Herr Schön's "Blühender Schleh" came closest to truth. The mood is not badly struck. The harmony moves in respectable circles, but the melody might have been picked up out of the street, and so the whole effect was nil. An "Irish Folksong" by Hans von Zois[3] was unassuming and cheerful. The effect of Heuberger's "Herzenbeklemmung" [Anxiety] upon the listeners justified its title. Another of those perfumed things flirting coquettishly with the naive simplicity of folk music, and in a Brahmsian mask at that! Oh, the hypocrites! Of all the novelties, Goldschmidt's[4] "Sommertag" [A Summer's Day] came off by far the best. Frau Papier sang this charming song very prettily, to be sure, but, it seemed to me, not so tenderly as the fragrant character of this little piece demands. That the artist was rewarded for her distinguished accomplishment with every conceivable demonstration of the audience's most flattering sympathies goes without saying.

The Rosé Quartet concluded its concerts for this season with its fifth chamber music evening. We have repeatedly been prevented from enjoying the truly artistic offerings of this ensemble. What was provided on this occasion, however, was not to our taste. But the manner in which Herr Rosé served up the musical sleep and forgetfulness potions that made up the program, his eagerness to lull his reverent listeners in gentle dreams, is admirable, if hardly worth imitation. Pfeffer, Rubinstein and Brahms! Now, that's no small dose of sleeping powder for weak nerves. Such a program reeks of lethal intent, and should really be forbidden by the police. But when I remind myself that it lay entirely in Herr Rosé's province to enlarge this pretty trifolium by a Brüll or a Dvořák, then I am astonished again at our worthy concertmaster's wise moderation, and am delighted at the unexpected opportunity to close not with disparagement, but with the heartiest good wishes for the well-being of the Rosé Quartet.

1.   Karl Schön (1885- ?), director of the Vienna Singakademie, vocal coach, composer of masses, choruses, songs, etc.

2.   Rudolf Weinwurm (1835-1911), founder of the Academic Choral Society of the University of Vienna, subsequently conductor of the Singakademie and musical director of the University of Vienna.

3.   Hans Freiherr von Zois-Edelstein (1861-?), Styrian composer of operas and songs.

4.   Adelbert von Goldschmidt (1851-1906), at that time a young man of means, an early sponsor and intimate of Wolf, and a prolific minor composer of operas, songs, etc.

113. *What an Opera House Owes Its Stars*

April 24, 1889[1]

With the departure of Frau Kupfer we have a gap in a category of role for which our local "forces" have proven so highly qualified that a box office attraction such as, for example, *Lohengrin* would have to molder in the archives, did not the lovely custom of guest engagements — conferring honorary citizenship or even honorary membership on both foreign and indigenous artists — prevent such a disaster.

Instead of seeking a unified ensemble and an intelligent grasp of a given work, in order thus to salvage even for the less successful individual performance the semblance of totality, and aiming for a conception as nearly ideal as possible with the artists at hand, we get precisely the opposite. With stamina and dedication worthy of the noblest objective, one concerns oneself not only with the engagement of mediocre singers or with their retention; one is at pains to diffuse even this slender endowment of artistic resources — which, properly conserved, might yield substantial dividends — to cater to egotism, and to stifle any sense of common purpose and enterprise. To raise the dignity and artistic stature of our opera will require drastic reforms if its stage is not soon to resemble a gypsy camp where everyone does as he pleases, and if art is to mean more to its servants than merely a bubbling kettle of soup satisfying the meanest appetite.

One speaks in glowing terms of our company's stars, and of how they bring it honor and glory. It seems to me rather that such praise is hardly flattering to the institution itself. One would have to assume that it implies reciprocity, which is by no means the case. Frau Materna, for example, is considered a precious jewel of our opera house, but what has the opera house to offer Frau Materna? Expectancy of an eventual honorary membership? Assuming such expectancy to be well founded, the relationship remains one-sided because —

as imposing and consequential as such a distinction may be, it is purely a formality.

It can matter little to Frau Materna which theater enjoys the benefit of her art. She will feel herself a stranger or at home according to the character of her surroundings, whether in New York or Vienna. Whether the members of our Court Theater are at home on any stage, or whether they flourish only in an atmosphere, nourished by the cultural blessing of the holy sweat of many excellent artists expended over many years, an atmosphere that has proven fruitful to this day — that is another question.

For the moment, I know only that Frau Herbert-Förster[2] will hardly take root on our stage as Elsa in *Lohengrin*, however forcefully a notice in the *Neue Freie Presse* may have given voice to an opposite opinion. Frau Herbert-Förster, from the German [sic] Theater in New York, is a substantial lady, too substantial, unfortunately, to keep a tenderly radiant apparition such as Elsa within the bounds of the beautiful. As to her performance, the singer calls upon the dependable resources of routine, and gives us a conventional Elsa. Voice — pretty good. Performance — reasonably correct. Special distinctions — none.

Herr Winkelmann is held to be an excellent Lohengrin. We shall not go into that now, but simply call to his attention that his high notes excited the claque beyond all measure, and that their noisy demonstrations while the performance was still in progress cannot possibly have been as agreeable to his ears as they were offensive to ours. Herr Reichmann sang and acted exceptionally beautifully. We make this happy observation the more emphatically as only too often has it been our sad duty to mercilessly expose this worthy singer's shortcomings. But what is one to say of Herr Rokitansky's King? To say what should be said would be indelicate; but one can think it.

1. This last notice was not included in the published edition of Wolf's Criticism.

2. Theresa Herbert-Förster, a Viennese soprano who occupies a more consequential place in musical history as the lady who brought Victor Herbert (whom she had married in 1886 when he was a cellist in the Court Orchestra at Stuttgart) to New York. She had been engaged for the Metropolitan Opera season of 1886-87, and had secured for Herbert a chair in the cello section of the Metropolitan orchestra. The Metropolitan, after its inaugural season in 1883-84, became a German house in the following season, and remained so through the season of 1890-91, with all operas sung by German singers in German, hence Wolf's reference to the German Theater in New York. Frau Herbert Förster's roles during her two seasons at the Metropolitan included the Queen of Sheba, Aida, Elsa, Elisabeth and Irene (in *Rienzi*).

Index